ALSO BY JAN ASSMANN

Moses the Egyptian

The Search for God in Ancient Egypt

THE MIND OF EGYPT

JAN ASSMANN

THE MIND OF
EGYPT

History and Meaning in the Time of the Pharaohs

TRANSLATED BY
ANDREW JENKINS

METROPOLITAN BOOKS
HENRY HOLT AND COMPANY
NEW YORK

Metropolitan Books
Henry Holt and Company, LLC
Publishers since 1866
115 West 18th Street
New York, New York 10011

Metropolitan Books™ is a registered
trademark of Henry Holt and Company, LLC.

Originally published in Germany in 1996 under the title *Ägypten. Eine Sinngeschichte* by
Carl Hanser Verlag, Munich.

The translation of this book has been subsidized by Inter Nationes, Bonn.

Library of Congress Cataloging-in-Publication Data

Assmann, Jan.
　[Ägypten. English]
　The mind of Egypt : history and meaning in the time of the Pharaohs / Jan
Assmann.
　　p.　cm.
　Includes bibliographical references.
　ISBN 0-8050-5462-6 (hc.)
　1. Egypt—History—To 640 A.D.　2. Historiography—Egypt.　I. Title.

DT83 .A8813 2002
932'.01—dc21

2001044504

Henry Holt books are available for special promotions and
premiums. For details contact Director, Special Markets.

First American Edition 2002

Designed by Cathryn S. Aison

Printed in the United States of America

1　3　5　7　9　10　8　6　4　2

CONTENTS

PREFACE

"THE IMPOSSIBILITY OF WRITING a history of the development of the ancient Egyptian mind . . . a pity"—this note is to be found among Jakob Burckhardt's jottings in 1868 for a lecture, "On the Study of History." In parentheses he adds: "At best in hypothetical form, say, as a novel."[1] In a sense, then, this book sets out to do something that the great Swiss historian consigned to the realm of impossibility and would have countenanced, if at all, only in parentheses and "in a hypothetical form."

The terms used by Burckhardt—Geist (which means "spirit" as much as "mind") and "development"—are part of a paradigm of the philosophy of history that has become alien to us. "Spirit" conjures up an idea of something that infuses cultures, nations, and epochs from within and expresses itself *in* the testimonies they bring forth. By contrast, the word "meaning," which I propose to put in place of "spirit," refers to something that is an integral part *of* those testimonies themselves, something that cultures construct and produce. Unlike the singular Geist, "meaning" as used in this book exists only in the plural, as the kaleidoscopic range of "semiologies" or "semantic paradigms" that mark and define cultural difference, competing with, influencing, replacing, and inheriting from one another. This book describes certain preeminent semantic paradigms identifiable in ancient Egypt, how they originated, and what became of them. Though I recast them in the intellectual and conceptual mold of our own century, I am still addressing issues that Jakob Burckhardt saw as belonging to the "study of history." And though I replace his conjunction of "history and spirit" with that of "history and meaning,"

I am still inquiring, as he was, into the intellectual, religious, cultural, and political parameters of human action and the traces, messages, and memories of that action that make up the subject matter of historiography. Where I examine ideas articulated and reflected upon in texts and images, I move in the realm of what Burckhardt meant by "spirit." But my approach also extends to the fundamental attitudes generally referred to as "mentality," attitudes that are implicit in texts, images, and the events of history without being explicitly expounded or commented upon.

Accordingly, events and "major" historical data and dates recede into the background. Only the most significant of them figure prominently. History is seen here above all in terms of the way changes, crises, and new departures reflect shifts in existing structures of meaning. Their sequence may indeed be understood as a "development," but only as long as we resist seeing it simply as progress and decline—that is, as a one-way process heading straight for some ineluctable destination. If we discern coherence in this process, it is a coherence we owe to cultural memory and the way it contrives to take past meaning preserved in the written word and the pictorial image, reactivate it, and incorporate it into the semantic paradigms of the present.

Meaning and history belong together. We see this most clearly when dramatic upheavals occur, as, for example, at such major turning points as 1789 and 1989. In both the French Revolution and the collapse of the socialist empire, history stands revealed as a cultural form. As Reinhart Koselleck has shown, the concept of "history" as a collective singular emerged in the years of the French Revolution; the semantic paradigm that originated then is that of historicism, the total historification of reality. In the years after 1945, and especially before and after 1989, we find precisely the opposite taking shape; the relativization of the historical. The late eighteenth century taught us to think in the categories of "history" rather than in terms of individual (hi)stories. The post-1945 period generated various attempts to develop concepts of nonhistory and posthistory and to relativize the inherited idea of history.

History appears to us today not as an abstract, immutable category but as a cultural form that changes in accordance with the semantic framework society places it in. History is a profoundly human affair: we produce it by producing meaning. A "history of meaning" discusses history as a cultural form in which the course of events forms the backdrop and the discourses generating and reflecting meaning occupy the front of the stage.

The idea of writing a history of meaning with reference to Egypt was born to some extent of the experience of witnessing a historical turning point of the kind described in this book. In a narrower sense, however, it owes its existence to two external impulses. In 1992, Jörn Rüsen invited me to take part in a project on "historical meaning formation." While practical reasons prevented me from participating, the idea of approaching the history of Egypt from the point of view of "meaning formation" captured my imagination so completely that I was unable to get away from it. In the same year, Christian Meier developed a plan for a "World History in Essays," and the Carl Hanser publishing house approached me for an essay on Egypt. While the size of the present book drastically exceeds what they proposed, its "tentative" approach remains that of an essay. Ancient Egypt is still too alien and remote to justify a study that merely sets out to shed new light on things we otherwise take for granted.

The most difficult thing about such a work is not starting but finishing. Where and when does one call it a day and declare the enterprise over and done with? Here my thanks go to Eginhard Hora, whose critical and encouraging reading left its decisive imprint on the final version. His perspicacious editing rid the text of many superfluous digressions, and his was the deciding vote when the time came to draw the line.

Much of the book was written at the J. Paul Getty Center in Santa Monica, and such qualities as it may have owe a great deal to discussion with and suggestions from Salvatore Settis, Carlo Ginzburg, Jacques Revel, Krzysztof Pomian, and Louise A. Hitchcock, who also assisted me in obtaining the books I needed. My heartfelt thanks to all of them.

For the American edition, my gratitude goes to Andrew Jenkins, Bruce King, and especially Sara Bershtel, whose careful reading saved me from so many imprecisions. Shara Kay was ever helpful in preparing this manuscript for publication.

THE MIND OF EGYPT

INTRODUCTION

The Meaningful Form of History

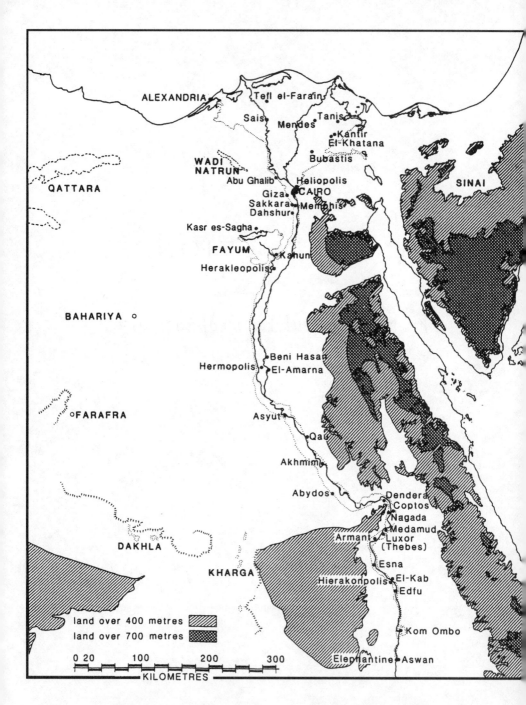

(from J. B. Kemp, Ancient Egypt: Anatomy of a Civilization, *Cambridge, 1989, fig. 1)*

SPIDERS AND WEBS

History Overt and Covert

HISTORY HAS TWO FACES, one turned toward us, the other averted. The face turned toward us is the sum total of event and remembrance. It is history recalled by those involved in it, as shapers or witnesses, doers or sufferers. The hidden face of history is not what we have forgotten, but what we have never remembered, those products of imperceptible change, extended duration, and infinitesimal progression that go unnoticed by living contemporaries and only reveal themselves to the analytic gaze of the historian. Overt and covert history relate to each other as case history to diagnosis.

Until well into the eighteenth century, historiography was thought to be synonymous with the recording of remembered events from the past. History books would not have concerned themselves with subjects like the evolution of grain prices in Ramesside Egypt or Imperial Rome, for such topics would not have qualified as historical phenomena. History was res gestae: the deeds of men as planned, perceived, and recalled; events with clearly defined temporal contours, inscribed into the collective memory. In the early modern age, the res gestae of antiquity (including ancient Egypt) was thought to be a closed chapter, set down once and for all by classical authors such as Herodotus, Thucydides, Polybius, Livy, Diodorus Siculus, and Tacitus. This kind of history defied rewriting. But gradually historians realized how biased and tendentious such a history had been, and two new approaches superseded the old, each claiming to provide a corrective to the questionable objectivity of classical historiography. The one collected traces, the other sparks.

The search for traces was the preserve of the "antiquarian," whose guiding principle was collection as opposed to interpretation. Collection involved loving concern for the unremembered and for the reconstruction of forgotten connections. In this sense, "collecting" is the opposite of "recollecting." As the antiquarian believed it impossible to rewrite history, he set out to do no more than complete the one-sided, tendentious picture that had been handed down, and to illustrate it by amassing concrete testimonials, objects like coins, vases, ruins, and inscriptions. What these mute witnesses from the past lacked in eloquence they more than made up for in authenticity.

Collecting sparks was the concern of historians who, like Lessing, Herder, and Wieland, were interested in the history of the mind and deplored the classical historians' silence on this aspect of the ancient civilizations. Fundamental for these historians was the philosophy of history propounded by Adam Weishaupt, a founder of the Order of Illuminati, a secret society of radical Enlightenment thinkers, to which Herder also belonged. Weishaupt saw the history of ideas as a history of loss. The knowledge acquired in the beginnings of civilization had been forfeited in the subsequent succession of wars and conquests, conflagrations and floods. Ancient Egypt had unhindered access to this knowledge, which Moses, Orpheus, and other intermediaries brought to Israel and Greece. But while "sparks" of this most ancient knowledge had indeed been handed down to the Western world, its primal unadulterated abundance remained shrouded in impenetrable darkness.

The work from which these images are taken—the prevailing darkness, the scattered sparks—was written by Ignaz von Born, an Illuminist and Freemason. He was Grand Master of the lodge Zur wahren Eintracht ("True Concord") in Vienna, an intellectually pre-eminent European masonic brotherhood that under his aegis developed into a veritable academy of sciences. All that was left of the wisdom of the Egyptians, he wrote, were "some scattered fragments gathered by those fortunate sages who, although foreign, were granted access to the mysteries, received instruction from the guardians of the sanctuary, lit their torch from the bright blazing flame, and brought it back to their fatherland. From that torch the attentive scholar will still detect some living sparks here and there in the writings they have left us."[1]

Drawing on Marcus Aurelius' comparison of his role as emperor to a spider lurking in its web waiting for prey, von Born came up with a particularly graphic image to illustrate the limited purview of traditional historiography: "It recorded—if I may avail myself of a figurative comparison—the native cunning of the swallow lying in wait for the industrious bee and finally snapping it up; but it forgot to tell us that the bee makes honey and wax in the service of gods and men. It retailed the internecine wars of the spiders, their stratagems to prevent surprise attack, their cunning attempts to outwit each other; but it said nothing of the artful webs they weave in silence."[2]

Von Born called for a history of webs to stand alongside the history of the spiders, a history of culture, knowledge, and intellectual progress. But in his time, the collective knowledge that formed the foundation and framework for the activities of the ancient peoples had to be given up for lost, even if some last remnants might still be glimpsed in the light of the "sparks" glowing in scattered testimonies from the past.

For a history such as I am essaying here, no better image could be found than von Born's webs. Humans are like spiders in that they act within the framework of the—admittedly invisible—webs they have woven. Of course, human webs are the product of interaction, not of solitary weaving; they are worlds of meaning, whose horizons delimit human action, experience, and remembrance. Without these horizons organized human activity would be unthinkable.[3] "Meaning" here is more or less coterminous with context or coherence, the connection between means and ends, causes and effects, cost and benefit, parts and wholes. When we say something is meaningless, we are saying that we cannot "make sense" of it, that it has no connection with anything else we know. As a synonym for "meaning," "sense" also connotes the idea of direction; cognate with "sense" is the French *sens* (*sens unique* is a one-way street) or the German *Sinn* (*im Uhrzeigersinn* means "clockwise"). In fact, "direction" transcends "connection." We may easily imagine phenomena that display connections but lack any perceivable direction; we describe such phenomena as meaningless. "Connection" and "direction" also have something to do with space and time. The essential point here is that meaning is produced by societies living within particular contexts of space and time. For space and time are not abstract categories within which all civilizations evolve in the same way. Rather, they are fictions of coherence produced by specific human societies at specific junctures. And history, the spatio-temporal evolution of civilizations, cannot be regarded independently of the particular fictions of coherence produced by those civilizations.

Unlike the antiquarian collection of traces from the past, the history of webs does not belong entirely to the province of covert history. It is, of course, true that we are not normally conscious of our fictions of coherence, the semantic structures within which we act, experience, or remember. But periods of crisis, junctures where a civilization breaks with its own traditions, regularly engender discourses that illuminate the terms of reference within which that civilization has been operating. Sometimes this illumination may result in profound changes to the prevailing semantic paradigms; sometimes those paradigms advance from more or less unconscious collective "mentalities" to the status of conscious "ideologies." This discontinuous, stepwise transformation of mentality into ideology through anthropological self-scrutiny is a, if not *the*, central function of literature, in Egypt as elsewhere. Since such changes in the semantic structure of societies largely coincide with historical turning points, the history of webs is anything but incidental to the political history of remembered facts and events. On the contrary, it is precisely memory—through retrospective narratives—that provides us with access to the semantics of a civilization or epoch. Thus, I would distinguish three components for analysis: the collection of traces from the past, the remembrance of events, and von Born's "collection of sparks."

Traces, Messages, Memories

ESTABLISHING TRACES OR CLUES is the job of the antiquarian, and it is from this tradition that modern archaeology has evolved. Archaeology is the model for a form of historical research that brings to light unremembered facts from the past. It alone has the capacity to correct the existing record of remembered events. Further, archaeological research is the only tool that effectively contests the claims of memory, which, as we know, is both fallible and biased. Archaeology has the same *primum gradum certitudinis*—"first rank of certainty"—that Jacob Burckhardt postulated for *Kulturgeschichte*, the history of culture:

What we usually call historical facts, those events passed down to us in the form of narration . . . are in many ways uncertain, controversial, colored, or else (given what we know of the Greek talent for fabrication) fictions entirely dictated by imagination or bias. Cultural history, by contrast, possesses *primum gradum certitudinis,* for it revolves largely around that which sources and monuments tell us unintentionally and impartially, involuntarily, unconsciously, indeed even by means of inventions, over and above those things that they may intentionally set out to record, advocate, and glorify, and which also make them instructive.[4]

With acute perspicacity, Burckhardt points out the link between remembered history and narrative form. The record of historical events will invariably be narrative in structure, and—"given what we know of the Greek talent for fabrication"—narration is tantamount to fiction. The archaeological and culture-historical turn ushered in by Burckhardt and others in the eighteenth and nineteenth centuries was fundamental to the reorientation of historical research in the twentieth century, which regularly focused upon gradual, imperceptible processes, phenomena manifesting themselves across long expanses of time. The history of culture now takes many forms, with many different methods, directions, and disciplines—social history, micro-history, psychohistory, historical anthropology. Amidst this profusion of histories, the historiography of events has withdrawn to an aesthetic position, where, having accepted its inevitable narrativity (Burckhardt's "fiction"), it has proceeded to make a methodological virtue out of this apparent impasse, defining itself as a specific rhetorical form, a methodologically rigorous, if necessarily narrative, reconstruction of the past.[5]

Enlarging on Burckhardt's idea that historiography is shaped by narrative form and thus partakes of fiction, we might indeed suggest that the spirit of narration not only shapes history as it is handed down to us but also crucially informs the very "making" and experience of ongoing history. Thus, the meaning that makes events memorable is not just retrospectively imposed, not merely the interpretative work of historians, who give history a structure and hence, according to Burckhardt, falsify it. No, such memorable meaning—and it does not have to be the same meaning—is already inherent in the course of historical events as experienced by contemporary witnesses. To put it more technically, those experiences are themselves semantically organized. The world in which we live, act, and feel is a meaningful structure, and its meaning is made up of collective projections and fictions. Hence narration and the construction of fictions of coherence is not simply and solely the work of historians, but rather a necessary condition for any kind of historical awareness, any experience of history.

The study I am attempting proposes an approach that is distinct from both cultural history and the historiography of events. It sets out to explore a third dimension: the history of Egypt as a chapter in the history of meaning. To draw on Burckhardt's terminology, it is precisely the "fabrications" that are of interest, the fictions of coherence with which the Egyptians organized their memories and experiences. I make no attempt to dismantle these fictions, to get at the "real" facts behind them. My focus is not on "actual history," but rather on the meaning that the Egyptians gained from their construction of history. This study proceeds on the assumption that every instance of the "present"—in this case, the ancient Egyptian "present"—leaves both unconscious "traces" and conscious, semantically charged, meaningfully structured "messages" and "memories"; accordingly, any approach to history as present-in-the-past can take the form either of an examination of the "semantically charged" and constructed forms of expression or of a more purely "scientific" and analytic species of research. We can see the forms in which Egyptian history has been transmitted to us as traces, left by a largely irretrievable past, which are worth protecting, collecting, and ordering; or we can look at the Egyptian past as a set of messages that demand to be read and understood. But my intention is not merely to inquire into those forms and how we should see them. Nor do I ask whether, and in what sense, ancient Egypt belongs to "our" past, and is therefore something we must account for and, for that reason, recall. Much more and primarily, I am interested in the way the Egyptians themselves related to their own past, the constructions of meaning and the fictions of coherence by which the Egyptians incorporated the legacy of the past into an ongoing present. The last thing such a history of meaning will do, of course, is to play off the "traces" as *primi gradus certitudinis* against the "messages" and "memories." It is precisely the fabrications, constructions, and projections—the fashioning of meaning—that are my concern. On the other hand, it is only possible to discern these constructions by viewing them against the background of the nonconstructed, the traces. But in so doing I shall constantly be asking in what sense and to what extent we can really claim to know anything about Egypt as past history.

Traces, messages, and memories correspond to three alternative

scholarly approaches: the archaeological, the epigraphic or iconographic, and the mythological. The first of these studies archaeological
formations, their temporal sequence, their spatial extension, and the
way they overlap. Archaeological study directs its attention to the past
as a sequence of everyday events—which, precisely because of their
everyday character, were left uninvested with meaning by the people
living at the time. Archaeology examines excavated remnants—pottery, lithic testimonies, skeletal remains—as "indexical signs," to use
the terminology of semiotics. Typical indexical signs are, for example,
the symptoms of a disease; footprints; cloud formations. They are
reliable pointers to a superordinate whole that expresses itself in them,
causes them, and is bound up with them in a natural way (like "high
temperature" and inflammation, or "footprint" and foot).

In contrast, the epigraphic or iconographic approach concentrates on the meanings invested in ongoing events by their contemporaries, notably the representation of politically significant
happenings in images and inscriptions, which are—to use the language of semiotics again—"symbolic signs." Unlike indexical signs,
symbolic signs "stand for" what they signify within the framework of
a semiotic system; hence, the relation between symbolic signs and the
things they signify is not natural or "God-given" (as with "high temperature" and "footprint"); rather, it stems from a cultural semiotic
system. Writing is a typical instance of symbolic significance. The
characters stand for sounds or words or concepts, all within an
agreed, conventionalized code. But there are many other signs totally
unrelated to writing, such as traffic signals or (to cite systems less
familiar to us but of major relevance in earlier civilizations) emblems
of rule, marks of origin, potter's marks, etc. Thus symbolic signs,
unlike their indexical counterparts, function only within the confines
of a particular cultural code; they are not "natural." Where inscriptions are concerned, the deciphering of this semantic code is known
as epigraphy. I intend to use this term in a rather broader sense. As
symbolic signs presuppose the existence of conventionalized codes
and notation systems, the way that these signs develop allows conclu-
sions about the social groups that use them. The use of conventionalized signs requires knowledge that must first be disseminated for
those signs to be read (in the broadest sense) and "decoded" by their
intended audiences.

A subset of symbolic signs is specifically iconic. These signs also
"stand for" something, but the relation between them and what they

designate—their semantics—does not rest on a code, or a conventionalized consensus, but on similarity. Hence, unlike symbolic signs, iconic signs can be created ad hoc. Thus they allow much greater scope for imagination, creativity, and innovation than symbolic signs. The study of the semantics of such signs is known as iconography. To use the example of the evolution of the Egyptian state, the epigraphic or iconographic approach inquires into the forms or "messages" in which this process was semantically encoded by its contemporaries. Luckily we have an abundance of such messages, and it is of especial interest to observe the extent to which their meaning diverges from the testimonies left by the archaeological "traces."

The third approach, the mythological variety, inquires into the forms in which a particular epoch is modeled and recalled in its transmission over time. I call this process mythological because I am of the decided opinion that the formation of significant events into tradition is a basic function of myth. Myth is not to be understood as being "in opposition to" history. On the contrary. All history that finds its way into collective memory as normative tradition becomes myth. Myths are the fundamental figures of memory. Their constant repetition and actualization is one of the ways in which a society or culture affirms its identity. Turning again to our example of the evolution of the Egyptian state, we would then ask how these processes of evolution inscribed themselves into the collective memory of the Egyptians. We might call this approach mnemohistorical, for the issue is not merely the remembering of history but equally the history of memory; accordingly, I do not set out to examine (collective) memories as a way of achieving a purchase on the past, but rather to look at those memories for their own sake. How is the past remembered? And what elements of the past actually get remembered?

But when we speak of the remembrance of the past, we must keep in mind that such remembrance invariably plays a sustaining role (in the truest sense) for the present. Narratives look to the past in order to shed light on the present; memories are the fictions of coherence out of which we organize our experience. We are what we remember, which is another way of saying that we are nothing other than the stories we can tell about ourselves and our past.

A further aspect of these fictions of coherence that link the past with the present is that they are not merely links, but also obligations: they are "binding" in character. Not only is the present invariably bound up with histories of and from the past, but also the present, any present, will always feel obligated to the past. The links preventing today from severing its relations with yesterday are those of duty and responsibility. This is not merely a conservative interest in staying the same today as we were yesterday, but rather a moral and social obligation. The coherence that gives our lives structure and identity is to some extent imposed on us from outside, or at the very least has its roots outside ourselves. Historical awareness, historical experience, and historical representation are all situated to a very high degree in such external relations of obligation, responsibility, and commitment. To quote Johan Huizinga's famous definition, we can say that "history is the intellectual form in which a culture accounts for its own past."[6] We are responsible for "our" past and we have a responsibility to "the" past. The links that keep our yesterdays present in our todays are manifold; the fact that such links are all cultural constructions does not make them any less binding.

THE CULTURAL
CONSTRUCTION OF TIME

The Egyptian Chronotope

EVERY TRAVELER WHO ENCOUNTERS a foreign culture is familiar with the feeling of entering a different time frame, where time has either stood still or run ahead, either stagnates or goes around and around in a circle. A West German traveling to, say, Halle in East Germany just after the fall of the Wall might have felt spirited back to his childhood during the war and postwar years, while a foreign visitor arriving in San Francisco today may have the impression that he has been catapulted into the future. Egypt is the classical locus for such an experience of time. The ancient Greeks had an image of Egypt as a land where time stood still. For them a journey to Egypt was a journey back in time, a journey into the distant past.

A place where time seems to pass according to laws very different from those prevailing elsewhere is also described in Thomas Mann's *The Magic Mountain*. In Mann's sanatorium, where a treatment organized around the repetition of the same routines must end in either death or cure, time is experienced differently and takes on a different form from that of normal life. The same difference in the experience of time is manifest in the encounter with other cultures. Hence the idea of a "chronotope"—Mikhail Bakhtin's term for the literary treatment of areas with a time scale of their own—can legitimately be applied in the domain of cultural studies.[7]

Of all the constructions of meaning that my history must trace, the cultural construction of time is the most fundamental and all-encompassing. It provides the basic framework for any account of history and for any understanding of the shape and course taken by history; only within that framework can we clearly recognize that cultural configurations have histories of their own and that history itself is cast in a mold that is culturally specific. These matters are of particular urgency for Egyptologists because, as we shall see, the history of the pharaohs displays highly conspicuous formal peculiarities. The temporal bounds of that history—ca. 3200 B.C.E. to ca. 300 C.E.— are defined by the initial appearance and the eventual disappearance of hieroglyphic writing, phenomena that coincide with the rise and fall of the specifically pharaonic form of government in a way that is anything but coincidental. While the conventional historian will set out to describe the history of this form of rule, the historian of meaning will be concerned with the particular cultural form of this history. Other cultures have other histories. Consequently, history of meaning is always relativist in its approach, conceiving of history not as a universal, uniform frame within which each culture develops in its own different way, but rather as a product of culture, a cultural form.

Linear and Cyclical Time

Cultural time is constructed differently in different societies and different epochs. Cultures unfold not in physical or global time but in local time—that is, in time as the natives construct and interpret it. Like all other dimensions of a cultural semantics, cultural time is organized around certain fundamental guiding distinctions. Among these I would highlight the distinction between memory and renewal or, more abstractly, between linear and cyclical time.[8]

I use this distinction, however, in an entirely different sense from the way it has been used since Augustine, for whom Christ's death on the cross was the irreducibly unique and irreversible event that, for the believer, creates a newly linear time. While the heathens wander around in circles, Christians move toward the consummation represented by redemption.[9] With this distinction between cyclical (profane) and linear (sacred) time and history, Augustine laid the foundations of the medieval understanding of time and history.[10] "In the Christian chronosophy of the High Middle Ages," writes Krzysztof Pomian,

the notion of linear, irreversible time is exclusively restricted to sacred history, in which God is the sole protagonist. In its permanence, the history of the Church as an institution both visible and supernatural shows that it is impervious to the destructive influence of profane time. Regarding profane time as cyclical meant regarding it as time not in the sense of chronology but in that of the calendar, punctuated by the rhythms of mornings, noons, and evenings, births and deaths, repeating themselves over and over again indefinitely.[11]

In this formulation, the Christian church, like ancient Egypt, figures as a chronotope set apart from its changeable environment, a locus of permanence created by the cultural achievement of its construction of time.

An "either-or" is essential to this Augustinian conception of cyclical and linear time. For Augustine, cultural or religious semantics form time into either a circle or an arrow. But the two forms are mutually exclusive. A people lives either in the linear time of the *historia sacra* or the cyclical time of the *historia profana,* never in both. This formal distinction between linear and cyclical time has entered into modern cultural theory, principally through the work of the religious studies scholar Mircea Eliade. In his book *Le Mythe de l'éternel retour* (1949), Eliade advances the theory that mythical thinking constructs time as circular, and experiences all events as the recurrence of primordial patterns, whereas historical thinking constructs time as a line or the path of an arrow, along which events are experienced as breach, innovation, and change. The structuralist cultural anthropologist Claude Lévi-Strauss made of this contrast a criterion for distinguishing between "hot" and "cold" societies. "Hot societies," according to Lévi-Strauss, are "characterized by a voracious need for change and have internalized their history in order to make of it a motor for development." Cold societies, by contrast, not only live outside history, they continuously keep history away, lock it out, avoid "having" such a thing. "By means of the institutions they give themselves," cold societies seek "to more or less automatically expunge the effects that historical factors might have on their equilibrium and continuity"; they appear "to have acquired or preserved a special wisdom that causes them to put up embittered resistance to any change in their structure that would permit the incursion of history."[12] Thus, what Lévi-Strauss designates as "cold" is not the absence or lack of something but a positive achievement ascribed to a special "wisdom" and to specific "institutions." "Cold" is not the zero state of culture, but has itself to be generated. This insight represents an epoch-making breakthrough for the study of cultural time and the reconstruction of cultural chronotopes.

Ancient cultures typically generated cold and "froze out" change through the ritual cyclicalization of time. Rites cyclicalize time by observing regulations to the letter and by ensuring that each ritual celebration corresponds exactly with the preceding ones. The model for such cyclical congruence is the cosmos, with its orbital recurrence of astronomical, meteorological, and seasonal cycles. Hence the generation of cyclical time within a "cold" society serves to harmonize the human order of things with the cosmic. According to Lévi-Strauss, cultures typically generate heat through the linearization of time by historiography, by remembrance of historical development, and by planning for the future. The generation of linear time serves to consolidate power and sociopolitical identity; it goes hand in hand with statehood and a written culture.

We must not misunderstand the opposition between cyclical and linear time as meaning that a culture lives in either one or the other. Rather, cultural time is everywhere organized in terms of the distinction between reversibility and irreversibility, circle and arrow, in the same way that law is organized in terms of "right" and "wrong," morality in terms of "good" and "bad," aesthetics in terms of "beautiful" and "ugly," or politics in terms of "friend" and "foe."[13]

So instead of asking whether a culture has a cyclical or a linear concept of time, we should rather inquire into the sites of the linear and of the cyclical within a culture and the relations between the two. Cultures are normally complex and encompass within themselves "sites of memory" and "sites of renewal," of cold and of heat. My inquiry is directed at the role these sites play in a given culture's structures of meaning—the forms in which they are institutionalized, and the tensions that ensue between institutions of cold and heat, linearity and cyclicality. It is the specific interplay of heat and cold and/or linearity and cyclicality that determines the form and content of a cultural chronotope.

If we regard cultures not as homogeneous wholes but rather as both "hot" and "cold" and marked by both linear and cyclical time forms, and if we further assume that every culture is inherently diverse and consequently marked by tension, then we can refute the objections repeatedly leveled at the relativist stance in cultural theory. The relativist approach to culture, with its working assumption that every culture lives in a reality of its own and that knowledge is culturally determined, is confronted by two problems. First, if all concepts, knowledge, and experience are culturally determined and preordained, what explains the fact that societies can change, criticize, modify, and expand their image of the world?[14] Second, how can there be interchange, translation, and understanding between cultures if each is encapsulated in its own semantic systems and conceptual worlds?[15]

These objections stand disarmed if we grant an inherent plurality of forms within each culture. Cultures are organized by multiple systems and with differing degrees of diversity. The potential for both internal change and intercultural understanding is determined by the degree of this internal diversity. The more compact and undiversified a culture is, the less able it is to engage in self-criticism and change. Pharaonic culture, for example, was unable to conceive of any form of legitimate political order other than the monarchic system. The cultural and social organization of pharaonic monarchy was such that no counterposition could materialize from which alternative options for political order could be discussed. The problem of legitimacy only ever posed itself in terms of the *person* of the ruler (usurpers, for example, or women), never in terms of the actual system of pharaonic monarchy. In Israel the possibilities were different; the prophets represented a position from which the issue of political order could be addressed as such. So, too, in Greece there was the oracle at Delphi, as well as the Seven Sages, institutions that over the centuries developed into the independent position of philosophy. In Egypt there were also alternative forms and agencies—the priesthood, the officials, the military, the scribes, the farmers, as well as numerous traditions generating old and new texts, old and new concepts, experiences, and insights—but these were only operative below the supreme level, which itself remained impervious to critical reflection.

For all the importance placed on the capacity for internal change and intercultural understanding, these are not invariable and axiomatic preconditions for the existence of culture; nor should we assess theories of culture in terms of whether they take adequate account of those preconditions. A theory of culture not only explains how change and translation are possible but also why they are not always equally possible in all cultures at all times, and what conditions govern their relative presence or absence.

One of the main principles that emerges from the discussion so far is that meaning is not a question of a specific time form, say the linear as opposed to the cyclical, but rather that both linear and cyclical time forms represent cultural constructions of meaning. Meaning is something like a pointer, a direction. Time and history are meaningful to the extent that they have a predictable direction. While "line" and "cycle" are convenient abbreviations for this kind of directional meaning, both forms have to be culturally developed and interpreted. All our discussions converge in the assumption that history, time, and reality are social constructions and symbolic forms that undergo specific shapings and weightings in every culture and every age. Accordingly, societies dominated by the institutions of "cold" not only experience history differently from "hot" cultures but *have* a different kind of history. For history is not only what "happens" to groups, nations, or cultures, but also—in the framework of their own objectives and constructions of meaning—what they aspire to in their actions and enshrine in their collective memories.

Thus a history of meaning centering on Egypt must inquire into the specifically Egyptian constructions of time, history, and reality. And since meaning becomes visible only through the window of specific cultural parameters, it is those parameters—the history, conceptual world, and symbolic representations of Egyptian civilization—that we must examine.

DYNASTIC STRUCTURE
AS THE CONSTRUCTION
OF PERMANENCE

The Notion of the Two Eternities

GENERALLY SPEAKING, the distinction between circle and arrow, cyclical and linear time, renewal and memory may be regarded as a central element in the construction of cultural time. In the form of the "notion of the two eternities," Egyptian thinking displayed an equally fundamental duality. The Egyptians distinguished between cyclical and noncyclical time, calling the former *neheh* and the latter *djet*.[16] *Neheh,* or cyclical time, is the never-ending recurrence of the same; it is generated by the movement of the heavenly bodies and hence determined by the sun. This kind of time is associated with the concept of "becoming," represented in the Egyptian script by the image of the scarab, the central symbol of salvation in Egyptian thought, which itself pivoted not on the idea of Being but on that of Becoming. Cycles come and go, and what takes shape in the individual cycles disappears again in the hope of renewed becoming. The other kind of time, *djet,* is associated with the concept of stability, of remaining, lasting, being permanent; its sign is that of the earth, its symbols are stone and mummy, its god Osiris, who guards the realm of the dead. *Djet* is a sacred dimension of everness, where that which has become—which has ripened to its final form and is to that extent perfect—is preserved in immutable permanence. This is precisely the meaning of the name borne by Osiris as lord of *djet:* "Wennefer" means "he who lasts in perfection." Hence *djet* is not a linear concept of time, but rather the suspension of time. In Egyptian thinking, the opposite of the line was represented not by the circle but by the idea of a space.[17] *Djet* is not linear and diachronic, nor does it consist of an ongoing succession of time points, nor is it organized into future and past. In short, it is not the locus of history. *Djet* is time at a standstill. Only in *neheh* does time move.

Dynastic Structure as Symbolic Form

THERE IS NO PLACE for history in the system of *neheh* and *djet*. Each in its way denies the very idea of history: *neheh* by emphasizing reversibility, *djet* by emphasizing immutability. Hence history takes place in a dimension that is negated by these two concepts: the dimension of irreversibility and change. The concepts the Egyptians used to refer to this dimension are first of all words for limited time units, most notably a word that basically means "lifetime" and extends from there to take on a more general meaning of time as something limited and transient; also, Egyptians used the word *kheper* ("become, originate, change"), whose hieroglyphic rendering, the scarab, is, as noted, one of the primordial symbols of the Egyptian world. The actual dimension of history is the "pre-history" of *djet* time: the phase concluded by the perfection of becoming, an attainment that enters the sacred dimension of permanence. It is in this dimension that the events take place whose concatenation yields the form of history peculiar to Egypt.

The form of pharaonic history in Egypt is indeed most remarkable. Two features of it are immediately obvious and may indeed be unique to Egyptian civilization. One is its immense duration. The unchanging fundamentals of its symbolic meaning-world extend across a period of three and a half thousand years, from 3200 B.C.E. to 300 C.E. This unbroken unity and sense of unchanging collective identity is surely without parallel. The second remarkable feature of Egyptian history is the rhythmic succession of ups and downs throughout its immense duration, a pattern of apogees and interims reminiscent of a work of art:

3100–2670 B.C.E.	Archaic Period (Dynasties I–II)
2670–2150 B.C.E.	Old Kingdom (Dynasties III–VI)
2150–2040 B.C.E.	First Intermediate Period (Dynasties VII–XI)
2040–1650 B.C.E.	Middle Kingdom (Dynasties XI–XIII)

1650–1550 B.C.E.   Second Intermediate Period (Dynasties XIV–XVII)
1550–1070 B.C.E.   New Kingdom (Dynasties XVIII–XX)
1070–664 B.C.E.   Third Intermediate Period (Dynasties XXI–XXV)
664–330 B.C.E.   Late Period (Dynasties XXVI–XXXI)
330 B.C.E.–350 C.E.   Greco-Roman Period

What is striking about the form of this history—what makes it special
and hence requires explanation—is its remarkable pattern of disruption and continuity, departure and return. My interest is not in the
purely formal succession of cycles of flourishing and decline, but in
a corresponding cyclicality of substance and content. The so-called
kingdoms not only succeed each other after interim periods of
decline, they make connections to each other. The Middle Kingdom
connected itself explicitly to the Old as did the New Kingdom to the
Middle. The Late Period undertook even greater efforts in this direction and asserted its connection to all three preceding periods at once
in a highly complex and eclectic way. This epoch carries the largest
quantum of past in itself and is thus central to my investigation of
Egypt's meaning-world. But even under the foreign rule of the Persians, Greeks, and Romans, the commemorative contact with the past
never broke off.

Through the ongoing efforts of cultural memory, essential elements of the formal language and conceptual world of the Old Kingdom maintained their presence right through to the Greco-Roman
Period. Let us imagine for a moment the case of an educated Egyptian
living in the period of the Roman Empire—under Hadrian, say—and
visiting the remains of the mortuary cult of Djoser from the Third
Dynasty. This man would be able to read not only the inscriptions
left during an epoch dating back over two thousand eight hundred
years (that he would probably completely misinterpret their import
is beside the point) but also the hieratic graffiti of other visitors before
him—fifteen hundred years before! He would contemplate the monument with the awareness of belonging to the same culture; his cultural identification thus would extend back over thousands of years,
and would result not from an exceptional personal education or
"sense of history" but from his present cultural parameters, which
ensure that the old is so well preserved in the new as to make identification with it possible. In Egypt, the old remained present; it never
became alien in the sense of representing something left definitively
behind, something unrecoverable or irretrievable. The old was always
available for present reference. Kings could copy the monuments of

the past or simply appropriate them by the inscription of their own names. The past was a model that could be replicated, adopted, and prolonged. In a sense it was never past. Earlier views of Egypt tended to regard the constant presence of the past in Egyptian civilization as a weakness, indicating cultural inertia, a debilitating reluctance to change and develop. But in our perspective this phenomenon appears rather as a special cultural achievement—indeed, one perhaps unique.

The division of Egyptian history into the Old, Middle, and New Kingdoms rests on a modern Egyptological convention dating back no further than the nineteenth century. By contrast, the division into dynasties goes back to antiquity. Here Egyptology adopts the chronology advanced by an Egyptian priest by the name of Manetho, who under Ptolemy II in the first half of the third century B.C.E. wrote a history of Egypt in Greek. Manetho counts thirty-one dynasties. The series begins (after the rule of "gods" and "demigods") with Menes, the unifier of the kingdom, as the first king of the First Dynasty, and ends with Nectanebo II. Manetho draws on older sources that he certainly listed in his work's introduction, which is no longer extant. Two such sources are, however, still accessible today: the annals and the king-lists derived from them.[18] The annals (described in greater detail below) started with annual entries identifying the years by means of names, such as "Smiting the Nubians" or "Opening the Temple." After the introduction of a counting system, the annals continued and became rather more detailed. All the extant fragments are from the Archaic Period and the Old Kingdom, but we know from later sources that annals must have been kept until the end of pharaonic history. This genre is, therefore, as old as the political state itself and shows how closely state and time belong together.

The king-lists (lists of pharaohs' names inscribed on a temple wall or on papyrus) confirm this connection between state and time. Years of interregnum, when the pharaonic throne was vacant, are labeled "idle" or "empty." The extant king-lists all stem from the New Kingdom. These include the fragmentary Royal Canon of Turin, which apparently contained all the king names recognized by official tradition, as well as a number of inscriptional lists containing excerpts from that tradition. The best-known and most extensive of these fragments is the king-list in the Temple of Abydos. This list has a liturgical function, as part of a scene that represents Sethos I of the Nineteenth Dynasty performing mortuary offerings before an assemblage of his predecessor kings. Normally, commemorative rites revolved around a cyclicalization of time. But in the Temple of Abydos, at this supremely political level, the linear element dominates. True, the rite as such is repeated over and over again and is hence an instance of recurrence and cyclical renewal. But the repeated acts of Sethos I commemorate a linear series and stress an awareness of time as a linear succession of kings. There was a similar rite of linearity in ancient Rome. Every year on September 15, the *dies natalis* of the Temple of Jupiter Capitolinus, an official of the Roman republic drove a nail, the *clavis annalis*, into the wall of the temple.[19] This ritual act was designed to celebrate and symbolize the linear, irreversible aspect of time. The number of nails in the wall showed how many years had passed since the building of the temple, just as the king-list showed how many kings had reigned since Menes. In both cases, the visible marking of linear time was a ceremonial act of major political significance, by which the state affirmed itself as the guarantor and generator of permanence.

State and Time

The notion of continuous duration implies the absence of breaches, profound changes, and dark ages. Accordingly, Egyptians of later epochs regarded the pyramids not as testimonies of a "heroic age" and the work of giants, Titans, or Cyclopes, but as belonging to their own age, an age admittedly extending far back, but far back into *their* past.

The state rules over and guarantees this continuity of time, and the invention of the calendar and of counting in terms of years rank among the very first achievements of human civilization.* Time thus codified has no special significance, however, which is precisely why it needs to be recorded. Otherwise it would remain in the memory like the myths that tell of genuinely significant time, the time of upheavals and foundations. The continuity and permanence constructed by the annals and by the king-lists based on them have no significant relation to the myths, and no narrative qualities. In Egypt (with the exception of relatively late and rudimentary attempts) there are no known instances of retrospective historical narrative.[20] Only a very few turning points were ever as such made the subject of cultural memory. Among them are the change to statehood, the change to

---

*Each time a new king ascended to the Egyptian throne, a new year began and was counted as "Year 1, under the reign of (that specific king)."

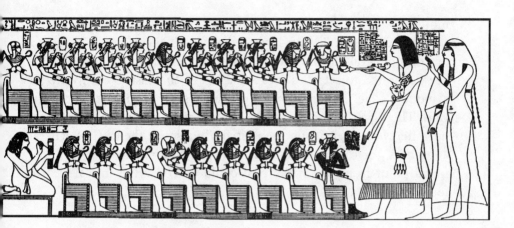

The Tomb Owner Bringing Offerings to the Kings of the Past
Thebes, Tomb 359 (ca. 1200 B.C.E.)
(from H. Bonnet, Bilderatlas zur ägyptischen Religionsgeschichte,
Leipzig, 1924, fig. 66)

building in stone, the change that came with the Fifth Dynasty (which represented a turning point in the understanding of the institution of kingship and a change in its structure of legitimacy), the transition to the Middle Kingdom after a preceding period of "chaos," the return to tradition after the Amarna Period, and the change from the Nineteenth Dynasty to the Twentieth. But there are no chronicles reaching back into the past such as we have, say, in Mesopotamia.[21] The Egyptians had relatively little engagement with their own past, despite the fact that it was visibly present everywhere in the form of monuments and was also chronologically accessible via annals and king-lists.

This is a typical characteristic of continuity and permanence as constituted by the state. Historical awareness in the genuine sense, and a corresponding interest in the past, only manifest themselves when continuity is disrupted and cracks and fissures become apparent. Examples of such "cracks" are the significance for Mesopotamia of the conquest of the Sumerian realm by the dynasty of Akkad and its ultimate demise or, much later and much more radically, the significance of Babylonian exile for Israel or the Persian Wars for Greece. Egyptian history is full of disruptions of this kind: the collapse of the Old Kingdom and the First Intermediate Period, the Second Intermediate Period and the reign of the Hyksos interlopers, the monotheistic revolution of the Amarna Period, the establishment of a theocracy in the Twenty-first Dynasty—all these were severe and drastic upheavals of the traditional order, which might indeed have been expected to set off a recapitulation of the past, even if only on a modest scale. But in Egypt one searches for such a retrospect in vain. The Egyptian state and the culture as a whole were manifestly not interested in elevating such discontinuities to the level of general awareness, for to do so would have been to admit the idea of a terminal point from which the past could be conceived in a narrative form.

PART ONE

The Predynastic Period and the Old Kingdom

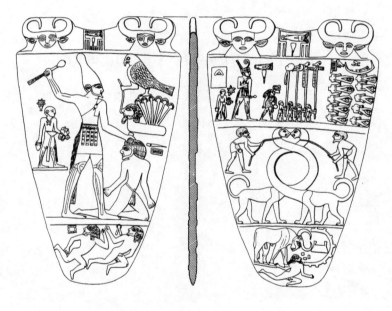

The Narmer Palette
(from J. B. Kemp, Ancient Egypt: Anatomy of a Civilization, *Cambridge, 1989, fig. 12)*

1

THE BEGINNINGS

"DEEP IS THE WELL of the past. Should one not call it unfathomable?" Thus begins the Prelude to Thomas Mann's *Joseph* tetralogy. In an incomparable way, Mann's novel shows that an inquiry into beginnings can easily lead to a complete loss of bearings. On closer inspection, all beginnings tend to reveal themselves as mere "fronts" behind which an infinite series of precursors and incipient beginnings await discovery. Indeed, the question of beginnings might seem idle; and so, we might just start somewhere. But in Egypt the inquiry into beginnings comes up with a clear answer, if we pose the question properly: not, What are the first traces of human settlement in the Nile Valley? but What are the beginnings of *pharaonic culture* and the *ancient Egyptian state*?

Traces

TO OUR INQUIRY INTO BEGINNINGS, the answer offered by the traces is unequivocal: Naqada. Naqada is one of the cultures in the Nile valley in the fourth millennium B.C.E.—the Late Predynastic or Chalcolithic Period. It owes its name to an archaeological site in Upper Egypt. This culture is clearly distinguished from the other cultures of the Nile valley, and in the course of centuries it either ousted, engulfed, or incorporated them. Ultimately, this process of cultural encroachment culminated in political unification and incipient statehood.

The following examination of the "Naqadization" of Egypt is

geared to two concerns. First, how are we to envisage the specific kind of diversity preceding the process of assimilation and unification? How different and/or autonomous were the cultures encroached upon and gradually ousted by the Naqada I culture? What archaeological testimonies do we have of this multiplicity and diversity? Second, how is the "Naqadization" of the Nile valley and the Delta to be interpreted in ethnic, political, and cultural terms?

To understand the multiplicity of the cultures present prior to the unification process, it is best to begin with an overview of these cultures and their most important sites.[1]

	5500	5000	4500	4000	3500	3300
North						
Delta			Merimda (5200–4700 B.C.E.)		Buto from 3500	Minshat from 3300
Northern Middle Egypt					Maadi from 3500	
		Faiyum (5300–4700)		el-Omari A (4200–3900)	el-Omari B from 3500	
						Abusir el Melek from 3300
Middle Egypt	Tasa Badari A (6100–4500)		Badari B (4500–4000)			
Northern Upper Egypt			Naqada I (4500–3900)	Naqada II (3900–3300)		Naqada II (3300–310(
Southern Upper Egypt					Hierakonpolis from 3500	
Dates	5500	5000	4500	4000	3500	3300

While a legitimate answer to the question of where it all started is Naqada, there is no denying that Naqada had its own prehistory. There are a whole series of sites from other cultures in the Nile valley coeval with or prior to the earliest traceable emergence of the Naqada culture in Upper Egypt. Hence the question arises whether the Naqada culture might have developed from one of these or whether it originated elsewhere. Looking back from the Naqada culture to further predecessors and origins, we ultimately find ourselves in Lower Egypt. The nearest relative of the Naqada culture is the older Tasian culture, which in its turn displays much greater similarities to sites in Lower Egypt than the contemporaneous Badarian culture, which has links with Nubia.

The specific interest of these archaeological data is the light they shed on the origin and significance of the marked north-south dualism identifiable in the self-image of pharaonic civilization. This dualism goes so far that, to the very last, reference to Egypt is invariably to the "Two Lands" and every new accession to the throne was celebrated as a unification of those two lands. Even the Hebrew name for Egypt, Mizraim, is a dual form. To ask after the origins of the pharaonic state is necessarily to ask after the origin and significance of this north-south dualism. Mesopotamian civilization is also marked by a north-south dualism, but there is no doubt as to its early ethnic origins: Sumerians in the south, Semitic Akkadians in the north. Later, once the Sumerians had disappeared as an ethnically identifiable group and the Semites dominated the area, the north-south opposition took on a political complexion through the Assyrians in the north and the Babylonians in the south.

In Egypt, nothing comparable can be observed in historical time. With the exception of the intermediate periods, there were neither ethnic nor political boundaries between Upper and Lower Egypt. Isolated references in texts indicate that people from the north could not make themselves understood to people in the south (and vice versa), but this can only be a reference to different dialects, not to different languages.[2] Thus, in the absence of any foundation for a north-south opposition in the historical epochs, it is tempting to conclude—and, indeed, it used to be assumed—that this dualism in the political symbolism of Egypt was a direct legacy of prehistory. The cultures of the north (Merimda, Buto, Maadi, Omari, Wadi Digla, Faiyum A) and those of the south (Tasa, Badari, Naqada I) were grouped together into two major blocs representing two cultures, a southern and a northern, separated by siteless middle Egypt, the northern with links extending to the Near East,

Painted Vessels from the Naqada I Period
(from H. Müller-Karpe, Handbuch der Vorgeschichte II, *Munich,*
1968, pl. 18)

and the southern with links in the direction of Africa. These two cultures were once thought to display major anthropological differences: the Delta peoples were sturdy, the Naqadas slight of build; the Delta peoples were Europeanoid, the Naqadas Hamitic; the Lower Egyptians were sedentary tillers of the soil, the Upper Egyptians hunters and nomads. Even ethnopsychological distinctions were proposed. The Delta peoples were phobic, warding off their fears by means of cults of divine adoration designed to tame and propitiate "their primal prehistoric fears embodied in numinous figures."[3] By projecting a whole series of dualisms and dichotomies into this period, scholars explained the establishment of the kingdom as the unification of two different political entities via the conquest of one by the other, while the idea of the dual kingdom was interpreted as a memory, persistently revitalized, of this original condition.

Much new evidence, however, calls into question the simplistic picture of a north-south dichotomy. Current archaeological research has shown that cultural union took place long before political unification. This means that the unification of the kingdom occurred in an area that was already culturally homogeneous; the incursion of the Naqada culture was fundamentally peaceful.[4] If there was cultural dualism at any point, it must have been well before the time of the political unification. And if unification was preceded by conflicts, they took place not between representatives of the Naqada culture and other groups, but between Naqada groups themselves.

As early as stage I, the Naqada culture displays evidence of expansionism, and at the end of this stage (3900 B.C.E.) begins to extend to Badarian sites in the north and south, finally encompassing the entire area from the First Cataract to Assiut and perhaps beyond; this grouping is the first unified culture of Upper Egypt.[5]

Prehistorians tend to correlate archaeological and ethnic formations. Archaeological formations ("cultures") are ensembles of distinctive features of artifacts read as indications of ethnic identity. Thus, "Badari" and "Naqada I" not only designate styles in ceramics, stone tools, and other archaeological remains, but also different groups of people. For a prehistorian, an interpenetration of styles points to trade relations, while the eclipsing of one style by another points to conquest. From this perspective, the expansion of the Naqada culture can be read as a gradual conquest and subjection of more and more extensive areas of the Nile Valley, until the whole of Upper Egypt was under Naqada control by 3900 B.C.E. By the end of the middle stage of Naqada II this expansion would have reached the southernmost tip of the Delta, while the late Naqada II epoch marks the Naqada culture's arrival at the Mediterranean and the eastern limit of the Delta. The question remains, however, whether this equation of archaeological and ethnic formations is acceptable. A very different view is possible. The archaeological evidence might indicate not so much an ongoing process of migration and conquest as a constantly growing sales market for pottery and other cultural commodities from the Naqada region—that is, a Naqada economic network and eventual monopoly. Instead of cultural proliferation we might then argue for a process of specialization, professionalization, and industrialization of pottery production, beginning in Upper Egypt and gradually imposing itself elsewhere. In support of this position, we should note that the region around Abydos and Naqada had one decisive advantage: a more highly developed social structure.[6]

Previous scholars regarded the difference between Upper and

Lower Egypt to be one of lifeways: hunting and nomadism in the south, settled farming and cattle husbandry in the north. Today we know that the representatives of the Naqada culture were also sedentary agriculturalists and livestock farmers. But among them a leisured class gradually emerged, a master stratum that went hunting because of the prestige involved in the activity. Moreover, the people of the Naqada culture lived in a stratified society with an elite that had others to work for it and that built up long-distance trade networks in response to its own demand for luxury goods. A society with an elite structure has a need not only for luxury goods but also for a semantics of its own: that is, for signs and symbols that assert and represent membership in the elite, for images expressive of elite power, and for myths that legitimize the elite's political aims and ideas.

Initially, these images were conveyed by the typical utensils of everyday life: ceramics, palettes, knife handles, mace heads, combs. Not surprisingly, these objects soon begin to display an increasing stylistic differentiation from similar artifacts developed by other cultures in the north.

Messages: The Semantics of Unification

THE GRADUAL EMERGENCE of history in word and image within the Naqada culture is a fascinating process. We may legitimately speak of a historical awakening, an incipient awareness of history, relating, however, not to the past but to the present. The images suggest a growing desire to keep a lasting record of historical events. This development culminates in a form of pictorial annals that later disappears with the culture that brought it forth. It is then a long time before Egyptian art gets so close to history again.

In its very earliest stage (Naqada I), the Naqada culture is already remarkable for a richness of pictorial imagery that sets it apart from the other cultures of the Nile valley. The white-painted vases of Naqada I develop a system of imagery that goes far beyond purely decorative concerns to the embodiment of central features of cultural semantics; this tradition of commemoration via illustration later found its continuation in graffiti and petroglyphs. Subject matter relating to history first appears late in the middle Naqada II epoch, in the decorated tomb of a chief of Hierakonpolis.[7] This is the first extant instance of the motif of "smiting the enemies," which recurs throughout pharaonic history.

The decorated tomb of Hierakonpolis shows no traces of writing. Thus it is impossible to say with certainty whether its memorialized chieftain already bore the title "Horus," which is the oldest known form of royal title in Egyptian history: its emergence may be said to mark the beginning of the Egyptian state. That the chieftain held the title does, however, seem likely. Hierakonpolis means "City of the Falcon"; it was the name given by the Greeks to the city of the falcon god Horus, who was reincarnated, so the Egyptians believed, in each ruling king. Recent excavations suggest that the emergence of this title is very near in time to the decorated tomb of Hierakonpolis; in elite Naqada tombs, potmarks have been found with names of chiefs preceded by the sign of the falcon designating them as rulers.

Hierakonpolis is also the site of the most important monument containing a "message" about a—if not *the*—decisive event of the unification period. The ceremonial slate that a king by the name of Narmer had set up in the Horus temple of Hierakonpolis is one of the large group of objects that carried the new messages of this early period of Naqada culture. Soon afterward, the state developed monumental genres specifically designed to represent political power and eternalize historical events. Before this, however, the messages of the nascent state appear on traditional media, such as ceramics and rock carvings, and on objects belonging to the royal sphere, such as palettes used for preparing cosmetics, weapons, and, most notably, mace heads. The function of these illustrations obviously goes far beyond mere decoration; they strive to record and interpret the revolutionary deeds and events of the unification period and to immortalize their significance. This work of immortalization could not be done without writing: only by adding signs referring to specific places and protagonists could the uniqueness of these events be adequately rendered. The prime concern, however, was certainly not to save central events from oblivion but rather to publicize them, that is, to make them visible. Although the Narmer Palette was set up in a sanctuary accessible only to the few, it remains a work of "publication," for the world of the gods also represented a "public"; indeed, it was for the gods in the first instance that these great deeds had to be preserved.

The developing system of political meaning required visual symbolization. In this connection, it is worth taking a closer look at the Narmer Palette as an early example of a historical record. The name of the king, Narmer, is found on both sides of the palette, at the top between two bull's heads and inscribed within the hieroglyph for "palace," as a symbol of rule. The obverse is divided into three sections, of which the central and largest is dominated by two "snake-neck panthers" whose intertwined necks symbolize the unification of Upper and Lower Egypt. In the bottom section, a bull tramples an enemy with its hooves and destroys a city with its horns. Like the falcon and the lion, the bull is one of the main images of pharaonic royal power; bull's heads occur on both sides of the palette and flank the name of the king. The events depicted in the lower section of the obverse side are not individualized by hieroglyphs; whether these images refer to unique historical events or to constantly recurring aspects of reality is thus unclear. By contrast, the upper section is rich in hieroglyphs. The king Narmer, his name inscribed to the right of his head, marches ceremoniously toward the right, wearing the red crown of Lower Egypt, followed by a sandal bearer whose title is written with a rosette of the goddess of writing, Seshat, and which therefore presumably stands for "scribe."[8] The king is preceded by a man with long hair; his hieroglyph probably indicates that he is a vizier. At the head of the procession are four small figures, each carrying a standard. These four standards are part of the classical repertoire of symbols for pharaonic rule; in a later form they came to be known as Followers of Horus. The king's destination is represented by ten decapitated figures laid out with their heads placed between their feet. Above these are a ship and a number of identifying hieroglyphs. The signs in front of the ship can be read as "great gate" and may well refer to the scene of the event. Above the ship we see a falcon with a harpoon ("Horus has conquered the harpoon nome"?). The scene is evidently a depiction of the king viewing the corpses of executed enemies rather than those of enemies fallen in battle.

The main section of the reverse side shows the figure of the king, who wears the white crown of Upper Egypt and grasps a kneeling foe by the hair with the left hand while smiting him with the right. Subsequently this scene was stylized into a pictogram of triumphant kingship often found upon the outer walls of temple pylons. The foe is characterized by two hieroglyphs that can be interpreted either ideographically as "harpoon lake" or "harpoon nome," or phonetically as "Wash"—the name of the conquered foe. In the upper right-hand corner, before the king and above the foe, is a complex figure midway between image and script. A falcon, perched on a papyrus thicket with six blossoms, holds in one claw a rope attached to a head that protrudes from the soil on which the papyrus thicket grows and thus "personifies" it. The scene may be interpreted as follows: The falcon (the king or the god) has conquered the land of the papyrus (the Delta or Lower Egypt). Six, the number of blossoms, may also have a symbolic significance, such as "and he took six thousand prisoners," or something similar.

However we interpret the details of these scenes, the references to history are apparent. Four of the five sections represent the death-dealing power of the king; the message centers on war, violence, death, and subjection. This is a depiction not of peaceful expansion but of lethal conflict, no process of long duration but an event unique in time and place: a victory of the south over the north. The king already wears the two crowns of the unified dual realm. He is no longer the Horus chief of a Naqada state but the ruler of the forcibly unified kingdom.

On both sides of the Narmer Palette, the sign for a fortified city appears in connection with overthrown enemies, on the recto as an image, on the verso as a hieroglyph. Narmer is shown fighting not against tribes but against settled, civilized opponents who inhabit fortified towns or citadels. It is entirely conceivable that at this early stage of cultural and political development Egypt might equally well have developed in an alternative fashion, namely, toward a confederation of city-states like the one in Mesopotamia. For Mesopotamia and Egypt, the earliest states in human history whose structure and functioning is known from written sources, also represent the two forms that the state formation process usually takes: the federation of city-states, and the territorial state. Clearly, the choice between these two forms will not only have political and economic consequences but will also generate different semantic systems.

Federations of city-states tend to generate highly competitive semantic systems, as in the Greek *poleis* of the archaic and classical eras and the city-states of the Italian Renaissance. By contrast, territorial states develop an integrative and cooperative semantics; a notable example alongside Egypt itself is Confucian China. In both those instances, a highly inclusive semantic structure forms against the background of a precedent phase of rivalry between small states—in China the Warring States Period, in Egypt the phase of rival chiefdoms.

The rival chiefdoms of the Naqada III phase (3500–3300 B.C.E.)

resided in fortified towns. In the system of imagery prevalent in this period, warfare was associated with the destruction of a fortress. Stout circular walls of mud brick with bastions and gates have been archaeologically documented; these are the remnants of forts or citadels to which the inhabitants could retire in the case of conflict. Settlement policy in Egypt's Third Intermediate Period, some two thousand years later, presents the same picture: the cities were fortified; armed conflict took the form of siege and conquest; and the protagonists were princes and kings with territories comparable to the rival chiefdoms of the Naqada period.

Egypt's territorial state, the first in human history, did not develop from smaller units of political and social order; it was established against resistance from the polycentric system of city-states. The territorial state of unified Egypt imposed one kind of order by smashing another. This, at any rate, is the "message" left us by the relics. The celebration of force in these testimonies also finds expression in the names adopted by the early kings, such as "Scorpion" and "Cobra." Narmer means "Fearsome Sheathfish," Hor-Aha "Horus the Warrior," Den "Cutter," Djer "Catcher" or "Snare Layer," Ka'a "He with the Arm Raised [to Strike]."[9] This warlike, not to say bloodthirsty and violent, form of self-representation takes on its fullest implications when viewed in the context of the ideology of solidarity and cooperation that later characterizes the Egyptian state. The turn to the state is represented as a move away from force and toward law, from competition and to cooperation. The ethic of integration developed in the later texts only gains its full significance against this backdrop.

Memory: The Mythodynamics of the Egyptian State

Annals and King-Lists

In the codification of collective memory accomplished by the annals and king-lists, all recollection of a stage of rival kingdoms has been expunged. This systematic amnesia is, however, a product of a future epoch, later than the decline of the Old Kingdom, possibly later even than the Middle Kingdom, an epoch that compiled definitive king-lists as constructions of permanence and continuity. There is, however, one document from the Old Kingdom that surprisingly corroborates the implication of both traces and messages that the history of pharaonic rule began long before the First Dynasty. This document is the so-called Palermo Stone, a fragmentary tablet of black basalt on which the annals of the kings of the early period and the Old Kingdom are recorded.[10] The list goes back far beyond Manetho's First Dynasty and begins with a series of kings wearing only the red crown, which in the later tradition signifies rule over Lower Egypt. Though we cannot know whether the first part of this list also contained kings with the white crown of Upper Egypt, the monument must have listed at least twenty-five rulers who preceded the First Dynasty. This testimony of "official" memory thus extends well back into the Late Predynastic Period. Excavations in recent decades have adduced corroborative evidence in the form of "traces" and "messages," including the names of some of the kings in question. These kings are collectively allocated to "Dynasty O" (=late-middle Naqada II–Naqada III, ca. 3300–3100 B.C.E.).

The Egyptian hieroglyph for "year" suggests that, in the early period, years were recorded by means of notches in a palm branch, a practice that corresponds precisely to the *claves annales* in the Temple of Jupiter Capitolinus. But the years were not only recorded, they were also given names corresponding to the most important events taking place in them, which were invariably state actions—never, for instance, natural events. One year was called Triumph over the East, another Birthing of Anubis (referring to the completion of a statue of Anubis). Some years are identified by a whole series of events. The primary purpose in recording such events was to serve the running of the state economy—as a reminder of when taxes were due, of how much revenue the state had received in a year, of the storage life of warehoused goods—and to provide a basis for future economic planning, not (as was Herotodus' project) to rescue the great deeds of humanity from oblivion. Indeed, the events recorded on the Egyptian tablets are largely ritual in nature; most of them are festivals. Our normal understanding of an "event" is something out of the ordinary, outside the normal scheme of things. In Egypt, by contrast, the only events recorded are those that actually constitute the "scheme of things."

The annal tablets on which events were recorded had a dual purpose. On the one hand, they served as "labels" for wine and oil bottles, thus putting a date to the production of these goods. On the other, they provided a rudimentary chronicle of important festivals, occasions, and

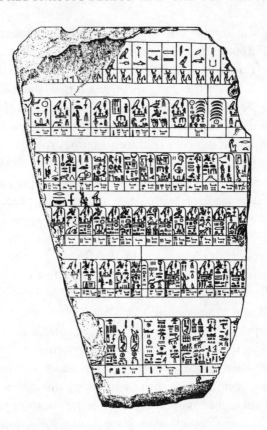

The Palermo Stone
(from H. Müller-Karpe, Handbuch der Vorgeschichte II, *Munich,*
1968, pl. 54, L)

Nile risings, to facilitate the organization of state control and supply a record of developments taking place over extended periods. It is this second function that led to such data being recorded and hence to the beginnings of a kind of annalistic memory. The events encoded in the names of the years are largely identical to the messages found on the cosmetic palettes. Thus the annals that recorded the events of a given year also served to transform "messages" into "memories."

Unlike the Palermo Stone, the later king-lists show the history of rule beginning with gods and "transfigured spirits" (comparable to the Greek demigods). Nevertheless, they clearly distinguish the figure of the state founder, heading the list of kings who are pharaonic in the genuine sense of the word. The king-lists are paradoxical: while they show the rule of kings to be a divine institution, as old as the world itself, they also use royal rule to mark the end of mythic time and the beginning of history. So history, as seen by the Egyptians, is the period of time in which the office of kingship lies with pharaonic rulers as opposed to gods or demigods. Modern Egyptological practice conforms to this notion of where history begins. The name given to the founder of the state in the king-lists is Meni, transformed by Manetho into the Greek Menes and misunderstood by Diodorus as Mnevis (Mnevis is the name of the sacred bull of Heliopolis). As yet, no reference has been found to the name in contemporary traces and messages; indeed, the name Menes may be peculiar to codified memory. In Diodorus' history, Mnevis/Menes figures not only as the founder of the realm but also as a lawgiver and the bringer of civilization. The memorial figure of a founder of the realm and a great "civilizer" appears to originate and gain resonance as the Middle and New Kingdoms give way to the Late Period. Or to put it differently, the boundary thus drawn between history and prehistory becomes more clear-cut as time goes on. The significance of this figure is that of a touchstone, an ideal point of reference. Menes' great achievement was susceptible of repetition. For a community, to remember its beginnings is to reascertain and reassert its foundations. In the form of "Menes," the semantic world of Egypt takes on something of the time-resistant structure of a religion with a single founder.

If Menes is a purely memorial figure, there is no point in seeking correspondences in the traces and messages. It is equally idle to inquire whether he is identical with Narmer, Scorpion, Horus-Aha, or any other king of the Early Period; rather, the figure of Menes is likely to be a conflation of a number of these historical kings.

The Myth of Horus and Seth

WE HAVE NO MYTH of the birth of the Egyptian state. What we do have is the myth of Horus and Seth, which presupposes the existence of the state while narrating a reorganization and reformation of decisive significance. The myth of Horus and Seth relates the foundation of the state in terms of the overcoming of aggression. The essential text is an excerpt from the *Memphite Theology*, a large basalt slab from the Twenty-fifth Dynasty (760–656 B.C.E.) which, like the Palermo Stone, reproduces a papyrus original. The text contains something in the nature of a "myth of unification."

[Geb commanded] that the Ennead assemble before him,
and he separated Horus and Seth,

Horus and Seth "Unifying the Two Lands"
Throne pedestal from Lisht, Sesostris I (ca. 1950 B.C.E.)
(from B. J. Kemp, Ancient Egypt: Anatomy of a Civilization, *Cambridge, 1989, fig. 6)*

he prevented them from carrying on their conflict.
He set up Seth as *nswt** king in Upper Egypt
even to the place where he was born in *Sw.*
And thus Geb set up Horus as *bit* king in Lower Egypt
even to the place where his father had drowned.
Thus Horus stood in the one place,
and Seth stood in the other place,
they "agreed" on the two countries in Ayan.
That is the boundary between the two lands.

Bad it was in the opinion of Geb [or: Geb regretted]
that the share of Horus was equal to the share of Seth.

*"*Nswt*" means both "south" and "political"; "*bit*" means "north" and "religious."

Then Geb gave Horus the heritage of his father,
for he is the son of his son, his first-born.
Geb speaks to the Ennead: I have declared | Horus | you to be
 successor to the throne
Geb speaks to the Ennead: you alone | Horus | the heritage
Geb speaks to the Ennead: belongs to that inheritor | Horus | My
 heritage
Geb speaks to the Ennead: belongs to the son of my son | Horus |
 to the Upper Egyptian jackal
Geb speaks to the Ennead: To an opener of the body | Horus |
 Wepwawet
Geb speaks to the Ennead: That is a son who was born | Horus |
 on the birth-day of Wepwawet

Horus stood up over the land
he it is who united this land.
Called by the great name Tatenen
South of his wall, lord of *djet* [eternity]
The two magic realms grew on his head
There appeared [or: has appeared] Horus as as *nswt* and as *bit*
 king
who united the Two Lands in *Inb-hd* [Memphis]
at the place at which the Two Lands were united

It came about that reed and papyrus were attached to the double
 gate of the house of Ptah
That is to say: Horus and Seth, who made peace and united
by pledging brotherhood so that they ceased their conflict
at any place to which they came—
united in the house of Ptah, the scale of the Two Lands,
in which the Upper Egyptian and the Lower Egyptian lands had
 been weighed.[11]

Of primary importance within the myth is that the conflict between
Horus and Seth takes the form of a legal dispute, which will be
decided by Geb. The conflict between the brothers is resolved not by
a test of strength but by law.

 After the first adjudication, however, the judgment is revoked
and a new verdict passed. The myth suggests two alternative meanings: a division of history into a phase of dual rule by Horus and Seth
and a phase with Horus reigning alone, or an emphasis upon the

motif of sole reign by Horus via express negation of dual rule by the two brothers, which is mentioned only to be immediately canceled.

The story's central motifs of division and unification are manifest in its organization into three sections. The first is the dispute, then comes arbitration via division, and then the final third phase, peace through unification. The concepts "boundary" (between the Two Lands) and "unification" (of the Two Lands) appear at exactly the same place in the final lines of the stanzas. The unification of the lands takes place on the basis of a peace already concluded. The motif of unification implies the idea of reconciliation. Though Seth is overcome, he is integrated, not ejected.

In ascending the throne, every king repeats the unification of the Two Lands. On the king's throne, the unification of Horus and Seth is depicted graphically. According to early royal theology, every king is an incarnation of both gods, Horus and Seth; thus the king bears two titles, "*nswt*" and "*bit*," referring to the dual character of the Egyptian state, and the title of the queen is: "She who sees Horus and Seth."

The extant version of this text stems from the Twenty-fifth Dynasty (760–656 B.C.E.) and contains many passages that can hardly be very much older. The god-name Tatenen, for instance, makes its first appearance in the Middle Kingdom.[12] But it remains highly likely that the original text was a great deal older and had been reworked numerous times. Various parallels in the Pyramid Texts (the texts inscribed in the burial chambers of the pyramids beginning with King Unas) indicate that the account of Horus and Seth has its roots in the Old Kingdom.

For the Twenty-fifth Dynasty, the text was of interest for its links with Memphis. In the Late Period, Memphis embodied Egypt's traditional political and cultural identity. But the myth, which tells of the changeover not to the state but to political unity, is undoubtedly much older. The existence of the state is already taken for granted, and is referred to as "heritage." On the other hand, it is apparent that the turn to political unity is identical with the historical events we interpret as the turn to the state, the process of state formation. The text mythically represents the supersession of a historical period of two rival partial realms by an all-encompassing unity; supreme importance is now attached by the victorious side to integrating the

defeated party. Horus stands for the Horus kingdom of Hierakonpolis, and Seth for the kingdom of Naqada; Naqada/Ombos had been
the home of this god since time immemorial. Originally, the myth
centered on a local conflict between Hierakonpolis and Naqada. Later
this conflict was generalized to refer to Upper and Lower Egypt. In
the *Memphite Theology,* however, the protagonists change sides, with
Horus standing for Lower Egypt (north) and Seth standing for Upper
Egypt (south).

The antagonism between Horus and Seth draws a dividing line
that is not merely geographical. The essential meaning of this conflict
is the opposition between civilization and barbarism or between law
and brute force. The symbol for Horus is the eye, for Seth the testicles.
Aggressive force is thus associated with procreative energy. Another
typically Sethian notion is "strength," which—like force—has positive
connotations. Seth is not a Satan; rather, he embodies an indispensable feature of life—one that would be literally castrated in his
absence, just as life would be blind without the Horus power of the
eye. The contrast between eye and testicles represents an opposition
between light (reason) and sexuality, a familiar contrast in the history
of religion.[13]

A text from the reign of Queen Hatshepsut further develops this
contrast:

> I united the two lords, that is, their parts,
> by ruling like the son of Isis [= Horus]
> and being strong like the son of Nut [= Seth].[14]

Here Horus symbolizes rule, and Seth force. In the mythological calendar (a calendar of "lucky and unlucky days," in which each day of
the year is associated with a specific mythical episode determining
whether it is lucky or unlucky) Horus and Seth are attributed to
arable land and desert respectively:

> 3rd month of the flood season, day 27.
> Good! Good! Good!
> Separation of Horus and Seth. Seizure of the warring ones.
>   Hunting of the rebels.
> Settlement of the tumult. Pacification of the two lords. Causing
>   the land to live in peace

by giving all of Kemet to Horus and all the desert to Seth. Arrival of Thoth, who resolves the legal dispute before Re.[15]

The contrast between Horus and Seth also appears to symbolize the change from old disorder to new order. Seth is the god of Naqada, and he also stands for the Naqada period superseded by the establishment of the state. In the mythic version of this change, order triumphs over chaos, rule over anarchy, law over force. But the myth of Horus and Seth lends itself equally well to an interpretation as a myth of unification through integration: the state appears as a lawful order to which brute force must submit. The state integrates aggression and transforms it from a natural to a cultural force. The opposite of state order and culture is not cast into outer darkness; it is neither demonized nor vilified.

Seth personifies the opposite of the pharaonic, highly civilized rule of law. Ancient Egypt's integration of the opposite of itself has frequently and rightly been seen as an indication of that civilization's unusual wisdom. Seth is a major god in the Egyptian pantheon, not a devil. He is called "son of Nut," the goddess of the firmament. The legal dispute between Horus and Seth is resolved with a contract, fully in line with the Egyptian legal principle that the best judgment is the one that both parties are satisfied with. The award of Upper Egypt to Seth is not of any major duration. The judgment is revoked. The new award enthrones Seth as ruler over the desert and over the foreign lands. But in a tradition widely disseminated (especially in the New Kingdom), Seth has a much more important role. Re takes him into the sun bark and entrusts him with the task of warding off the dragon Apopis, who menaces the course of the sun with standstill. A theory of force underlies this tradition: as force cannot be legalized, the law must be equipped with force—force must be placed in the service of the law.

As we have seen, traces, messages, and memories all tell different stories. The traces indicate a slow process of cultural interpenetration, the messages are replete with violent conflicts between rival chiefdoms, and the memories reduce those conflicts to a dualism between north and south, Horus and Seth. A history of meaning will refrain from any attempt to reconcile the contradictions between the sources or to construct a coherent model of "what really happened" out of the disparate information provided by traces, messages, and memories. It is, of course, true that the traces can claim *primum gradum certitudinis;* they reveal that there is no proof for the theory of violent conquest that the messages suggest. But the reality of history lies not only in what really happened. Equally important is the way that reality was remembered and what it meant to later epochs.

2

THE OLD KINGDOM

Historical Outline: The Course of the Old Kingdom in Colonization, Bureaucratization, Demotization

THE OLD KINGDOM can be described in terms of three processes: internal colonization, administrative bureaucratization, and cultural demotization.

The process of internal colonization brought the organization of the kingdom up to the level of what had already been achieved in material culture at the beginning of the Naqada III Period and in political culture with the unification. At the outset of this process, the king and his court, the "Followers of Horus," traveled from one place to another within the realm to collect taxes, to redistribute economic goods, and to ensure the visibility of political rule. This "king's journey" was the basis of an elaborate symbolic system that informed Egyptian culture throughout its duration. The course of the sun across the sky by day and through the underworld by night was interpreted as just such a king's journey, with the sun god engaging in his travels in order to keep the world in motion. In Egyptian thought, rule and motion were closely connected concepts. The texts describing the rule of the dead king in the afterlife are especially notable for their emphasis on physical motion as an essential element in the exercise of royal power. The dead king voyages through the realms of Horus, passing by the realms of Seth; he sails upstream in the morning bark, and downstream in the night bark. These images present remnants of the semantic system of the Archaic Period, when the boat was the most important instrument of rule.

46

This "patrimonial" form of rule—one that administers the state like a family business and that lacks any system of popular representation—is central to the exercise of government in the first two dynasties, the Archaic or Thinite Period (3100–2670), associated by Manetho with the nome of This (Abydos). Later, the king delegated these administrative functions—collecting taxes, storing harvests, redistribution—to officials and institutions. The king's residence became increasingly important, while the significance of the provinces diminished. In the provinces, royal estates were established and placed in the charge of an overseer, who—like other officials—was recompensed via the estates and whose mortuary cult was sustained by those estates.[16] Local administrative action was entrusted to officials dispatched from the royal residence to the provinces. Members of the administrative elite were not recruited from the provinces; rather, they were initially residence officials before being appointed to posts in the provinces. A two-tier structure thus emerged, within which a narrow, gradually expanding residence elite administered a broad provincial stratum about which the sources tell us nothing, for the symbolic forms of the residential culture contain no references to family clans or village communities. Such groupings are passed over in silence and were presumably actively clamped down on.

The process of internal colonization led to the division of the overall territory into nomes. Formerly, scholars assumed that these nomes were continuations of prehistoric forms of territorial organization. The nautical standards on the Naqada II vases and the standards of the king's entourage on the palettes of the unification period were thought to be predecessors of the later nome ensigns. But more recent studies have shown beyond doubt that there is no continuity between the standards of prehistory and early history and the nome ensigns; rather, the division into nomes represented a thoroughgoing reorganization of the territory, undertaken probably as late as the reign of Djoser (2687–2667 B.C.E.).[17] There is thus no continuity between the rival chiefdoms of the Naqada Period and the nomes of the Old Kingdom. Indeed, the structures that had evolved before the advent of the state were ruthlessly suppressed by the symbolism of pharaonic residential culture.

Generally speaking, the administration of the provinces assured supplies to the residence, while the residence assured supplies to the provinces. Administration was thus in the first instance administration of agricultural produce. Taxation, though important, was not as important as storage. The prime official concern was to ensure against the unpredictability of the Nile floods and against fluctuations in local harvest yields, and to keep the standard of living as consistently high as possible.[18] This administrative interest effected a change in the supply structure across the whole of the land. The individual regions were no longer self-sufficient, but were dependent on a centralized supply system. If this system broke down, major supply crises and famines would result.

The interventionist reorganization of the provinces brought with it the creation of various institutions. There were nomarchs, overseers of the temples, overseers of the estates, and "overseers of the new cities," apparently directly answerable to the central administration. As bureaucratization increased, the recruitment criterion for the administrative elite changed from kinship to competence. This conversion was a function of the increasing intricacy of the system and the attendant need for expertise. Specialists were needed, and these were recruited from the ranks of trained scribes. Learning to write was synonymous with training for an administrative post. Administrative know-how was imparted along with the ability to write and was later deepened in the individual sectors of administration by a system of secretarial training. In short, the ruling families were gradually ousted by a "literocracy."[19]

The process of cultural demotization was a covariant of internal colonization and bureaucratization. It involved not everyday culture but high culture, especially written culture. During the Naqada II period (ca. 3300 B.C.E.), the use of writing developed into an attribute of rulership limited to the immediate circle of the chief. After unification, monumental architecture and the pictorial arts developed parallel to writing. In the course of centralization, a residential culture took shape, encompassing not only writing, art, and architecture but also a corpus of knowledge, a semantic system, a standard language, and a code of ethics.[20] Residential culture became the form of self-expression of the literocracy, which was sharply divided from the lower orders in its language, behavior, clothing, and knowledge. The "demotization"—or spread—of this written culture meant not that broader sectors of society learned to read and write but that writing as a tool for implementing administrative agendas had an impact on more and more areas of life. Even those unable to write were affected by and made to recognize the importance of writing. The murals in the tombs with their scenes of "everyday life," and the three-dimensional models of such scenes in the tombs of the First Intermediate Period, show the extent to which scribes were involved in almost all processes connected with food production, artisanship, and administration.

Crisis and Collapse

THE UNEXPECTED and intriguing culmination of these processes was not the establishment of a functional, well-organized state but chaos. Today there is general agreement that this chaos was not the product of conquest, infiltration, natural disasters, climatic change, or other external factors; rather, the causes of chaos were internal. Indeed, the crisis of the Old Kingdom was the logical, endogenous result of the very same processes that led to the emergence of the state. This is a point of cardinal importance: the crisis, the decline, and the collapse of the Old Kingdom are implicit in the specific logic of its evolution.

The causes of this internally generated crisis were various, though presumably rooted in the discrepancies between elite and lower orders, residential culture and provincial culture.[21] In a sense it is misleading to speak of a provincial culture at all, as developments in the provinces were a complete reversal of the expansion of the Naqada culture in the fourth millennium B.C.E. A process of cultural desiccation is evident, an insidious impoverishment as a result of depopulation. The small villages covering the territory in prehistoric times were replaced by urban administrative centers, such as estates and storage depots; in short, institutions of residential culture, manned exclusively by the administrative elite, ousted the provincial culture. The country broke down into rulers and ruled, with the ruling stratum and its residential culture as a thin veneer superimposed on the provincial mass. The resulting structure of participation was extremely artificial and unstable. The Old Kingdom was in fact a highly artificial construction through and through. The people were almost entirely uninvolved in government or culture.

This kind of "participation crisis" will invariably change into a "penetration crisis" when a government can no longer impose its will, when the chains of interaction that pass on directives from the center to the periphery snap. Government then withers into an almost nominal institution practically devoid of influence. Its outlying representatives represent in name only and start taking things into their own hands. The action radius of the central government shrinks, being finally limited to the residence itself and completely losing touch with the periphery. This is precisely what happened in the period from the Eighth to the Tenth Dynasty.

Traditional analysis distinguishes two forms of organized economic activity: market economy and supply or redistribution economy. While market economies rest on the principles of exchange, competition, and the balancing of supply and demand, supply economies rest on the principles of storage and distribution, cooperation and price stability. Market economies can function in restricted areas; supply economies are dependent on the infrastructure of a wide-ranging distribution system. Ancient Egypt had very little indeed in the way of markets; the dominant principle was that of a supply economy with its patriarchal semantic systems and a value structure based on cooperation and distribution.[22] Goods circulated along the same paths as the political and administrative directives. Political activity was restricted largely to the organization of the economy, the storage and redistribution of yield, and the guarantee of supplies through the establishment of a storage system designed to offset fluctuations in yield. In a social and economic system of this kind, "penetration" and "distribution" are two sides of the same coin. A "penetration crisis" will inevitably—and very quickly—turn into a "distribution and supply crisis," and ultimately famines will be the result.

From Official to Patron

THE SUPPLY CRISIS did not lead to social revolutions but to a change in social structure that concords with a change in cultural semantics of paramount importance for a history of meaning. Central to this transformation was the emergence of a new social type: the patron.[23] A patron headed a supply community encompassing the extended family plus lesser wives and their children, concubines, slaves, and a more or less large number of "dependents" or clients. Whereas the officials, the leading social class in the Old Kingdom, were largely responsible to the king, and acted only on his instructions, the responsibility of the patron was largely to his inferiors and dependents. A patron's legitimacy was linked to his supply performance. Accordingly, the social structure now accommodated intermediate strata between the individual family and the state.

Such intermediate forms had certainly existed in prehistory in the shape of clans, for, before the development of the stratified society in late prehistory, Egyptian society was undoubtedly "segmental"—organized horizontally into clans, not vertically into rulers and subjects. These prehistoric clan structures were, however, systematically dismantled in the Old Kingdom. The king ruled, with the help of his officials, over an undifferentiated mass. The (extremely fragmentary) sources for the Old Kingdom of the Fourth and Fifth Dynasties contain no reference whatever to estates or classes, tribes, clans and families, local princes, or magnates, or to centers or concentrations of power. The king and his clique exercised absolute rule over an inchoate mass of subjects.

The first stage of transformation is reflected in the tombs that administrative officials newly began to erect for themselves—tombs not in the residence but in the province to which they had been sent. The precondition for this local tomb building was heredity of office. Tombs were best set up where the prospects of a well-regulated mortuary cult were most promising. As the inheriting son was the one responsible for the maintenance of this cult, it was clearly wisest for a father to have his tomb where his son would discharge his administrative service. At the beginning of this period of transformation, an official proceeded on the assumption that his son would serve the residence. But even if his son inherited his appointment, there was no certainty that he would be assigned to the same administrative district; hence, a tomb in the residence was the safest bet. In the course of time, offices became increasingly permanent in terms of location, thus increasing the likelihood that the son would reside where his father had resided. Fathers were now motivated to establish their tombs not in the residence but in the province, where the family would take care of his mortuary cult. From the son's point of view, the motive for being buried in the province was different: he wanted to be buried where he had been born. For most fathers the traditional desire to be buried in their birthplace—the residence—was overridden by the need for a favorable location for the mortuary cult. As the son, however, had been born at this new (provincial) location, his place of birth and the location of his mortuary cult were one and the same. And so for the son the birthplace motif moves into the foreground, as an inscription from the Sixth Dynasty testifies:

I have set up this [tomb] in Abydos for myself
as one cared for in the afterlife under the majesty of Kings
   Pepy II, Merenre, and Pepy I

out of love for the nome where I was born
by the lady of the royal harem Nebet
and for my father, the Prince and Noble . . . Khui.[24]

A permanent local upper stratum of society thus developed in the provinces. The officials gradually turned into feudal lords. This new stratum gained ever greater power, as the central authority delegated to provincial authorities an increasing number of state monopolies, notably those of force (recruiting militia), taxation, and supply.

Khui, incidentally, was not only the father of Djau, from whom this inscription stems, but also the father-in-law of Pepy I, who married two of his daughters. Khui was probably governor of Upper Egypt and as such resided in Abydos, the traditional location of that office. Earlier, this matrimonial union was frequently interpreted as a political marriage by which Pepy I could assure the loyalty of a powerful provincial family. However, right to the end of the Old Kingdom such powerful provincial families do not in fact appear to have existed; rather, they were only gradually emerging, slowly transforming themselves from representatives of the central government into feudal lords who were well able to compete with the central government and whose loyalty would therefore have to be assured by means of marriage. Khui belongs to the early stages of this process; he is a representative of the central government and nothing more. Might it indeed be possible that the nomarchical families had completely disappeared by the end of the Old Kingdom, yielding their position to entirely different social strata?[25]

The Age of the Pyramids:
The "Stone Age" in the Egyptian History of Meaning

Language and Architecture

One seminal story brings together language and architecture: the myth of Babel. There was a time, so this story goes, when all people spoke the same language. They resolved to set up a mighty structure reaching as far as the heavens "so that we can make a name for ourselves and are not scattered over the face of the Earth." The plan for this great tower was thus an attempt at unification as one single people (to "make a name for ourselves") and at one single place (as opposed to being "scattered over the face of the Earth"). The means to this "ethnogenetic" end was to be the collective construction of a gigantic structure—an enterprise that would be possible only if all spoke the same language, thus ensuring communication and coordination. Building work in particular depends on verbal communication, on explicit planning and agreement. Language is the medium that coordinates the various specialist elements and the manual work involved. Thus all God had to do to put an end to this enterprise once and for all was to wreak linguistic confusion. Now instead of the people claiming authority for themselves and attempting to create a unified nation based on common speech and architectural prowess, there were seventy-two different nations, and God designated Abraham as the father of one chosen people.

This story is not Egyptian nor does it make any reference to Egypt. The tower of Babel resembles not the pyramids but the Babylonian Ziggurat. And yet, the story fits Egypt much better than Babylonia. Egypt is the classic case of ethnogenesis by means of building. The Old Kingdom has been called the Age of the Pyramids, as justly as the Gothic period in Europe is referred to as the Age of the Cathedrals. The Old Kingdom is not only the period in which the pyramids were built, but also the time that was defined and indeed "created" by the pyramids—as planning time, building time, cult time, and eternal time. The Old Kingdom saw the beginning of the pyramid form, its development and culmination in the Fourth Dynasty, its drastic diminution and combination with other building forms, such as pyramid temples and sun temples, and its disappearance (to be revived at a later date). The history of the pyramids is thus the history of the Old Kingdom.

Naturally, the pyramids did not represent a concerted effort on the part of the *entire* Egyptian people. Such a gigantic building site could never have worked, and the Egyptians would have starved in the process. But if we extend our purview to the material and administrative infrastructure required for the construction of such huge edifices, then the proposition that the entire Egyptian people was involved no longer looks quite so exaggerated. The laborers themselves were recruited from all over the country and lived in villages specially constructed for them. Although they certainly did not speak "with one tongue" when they arrived at these settlements, they learned to do so in the course of decades of joint effort and cohabitation.

Amongst these laborers, a common language was not the prerequisite for a joint building enterprise, but vice versa: the common enterprise was the school in which the participants learned to communicate with one another. Yet in this inverse form, the connection between language, building, and belonging remains evident.

It is difficult to write about the pyramids without at least mentioning the problems of both social and technological organization that such gigantic projects involved. A history of meaning may safely forgo the purely constructional problems, but the question of the social status of the laborers could hardly be more pertinent. For if there were any truth in the customary idea, nurtured by the biblical image of Egypt, that the pyramids were built by "slaves," then I could hardly speak of ethnogenetic symbolism. Slave labor has no potential for creating identification. However, in the case of the pyramids, it is completely erroneous to speak of slave labor in the true sense of that term. The pyramids were built by laborers who, while they had no choice in the matter, were at least paid for their work. Egypt was a leiturgical state, one that had the right to demand certain services of its subjects.[26] The best parallel that we have to this system is universal conscription, notably in times of war, which also represents a combination of compulsory service and a high degree of identification. In wartime, even those sections of the population not actively involved are affected to such a degree that they will think back to the period in question as the "war years." In the Age of the Pyramids, the construction of these massive monuments not only demanded a veritable army of artisans actually working on the job but also drew in the entire population, with the significant difference that the building work went on throughout the Old Kingdom so that the "standing army" of artisans never experienced the respites that soldiers enjoy in times of peace. The army of artisans was constantly mobilized. When the pyramid was completed, the workforce turned to the tombs for the princes and officials. Huge necropolises took shape around the pyramids themselves.

The "Opening of the Stone" and Lithic Semantics

The invention of monumental stone building under King Djoser represents a turning point of supreme cultural significance. In recognition of this achievement, Djoser was commemorated until well into the Late Period. In Saqqara he was venerated as a god, visitors covered

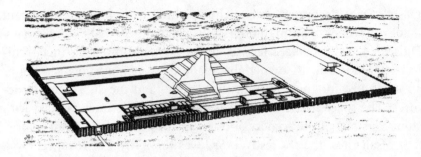

Djoser's Step Pyramid
(from R. Stadelmann, Die großen Pyramiden von Giza, *Graz,*
1990, fig. 34)

his monuments with graffiti, and he was given the epithet "Opener
of the Stone." His vizier and architect, Imhotep, was even deified and
cultically venerated as the son of Ptah.[27] The fact that a technical feat
could be attributed such outstanding prominence in cultural memory
has to do with the unique significance accorded in Egypt to stone as
a medium of immortality. Djoser marks the beginning of what might
be termed a megalithic age in Egypt, which reached its absolute zenith
soon after him with Snofru, Cheops, and Chephren, and was subsequently never equaled.

   Djoser's step pyramid in Saqqara is the symbol of this cultural
turning point. The various stages of its construction both reflect the
process leading up to it and suggest the developments that followed.
The apogee of an evolution that began with Naqada, this pyramid
also signaled the start of something new that would culminate in Giza
and would stand as an exemplar to the end of pharaonic history.
Djoser's tomb at Saqqara is, on the one hand, the culmination of the
traditional idea of the tomb as a monumentalized palace, complete
with the symbolism of the niche-filled façade and the elongated rectangular shape. At the same time, it is the first instance of the conception of the tomb as a place of ascent to heaven, represented by
the geometrical symbolism of the pyramid. Djoser's construction
combines both ideas; he retains the niche-filled façade and the elongated rectangle in the enclosing outer wall, and initiates the new
design with the step pyramid inside it. The enclosing wall is nothing
other than the façade of the archaic brick mastaba. The mastaba was
a tomb that consisted of a rectangular massive block of mud brick
(later stone masonry). In the first two dynasties the outside of the

mastaba was decorated with niches painted to imitate a palace-tent made of wooden beams and richly ornamented mats. At Saqqara, Djoser takes this "palace façade" and elevates it into a distinct architectural feature in its own right, made of stone and now serving as an enclosure for the pyramid, the temple, and the subsidiary structures. The space it encloses, the rectangular inner court, is filled with stone versions of the scenery and ritual structures of the most important of all rites, the *sed* festival. *Sed* was the festival of royal renewal, which was celebrated after a generation (thirty years) of a king's rule had elapsed, to revive the aging ruler's powers; the rite was then repeated every three years. Djoser's casting of the ritual structures in stone rather than the transient materials previously employed served the purpose of enabling the king to continue the *sed* festival into all eternity or to perpetuate the ritual's salvation effect so that the king could carry it with him into the afterlife.

It is likely that Djoser's *sed* festival model and the enclosing wall are throwbacks to the "valley enclosures" of Abydos. Abydos was not only the location where the kings of the first two dynasties had their tombs erected; independently of these, they also had rectangular courts built surrounded by stout, niche-filled walls in which, alongside smaller brick constructions, scenery-like structures of perishable material were set up for ritual purposes. The rites performed may have been either connected with the *sed* festival or part of the funeral ritual. At all events, the connections between these structures and Djoser's stone architecture are very striking. The essentially new idea introduced by Djoser was that of eternalizing a ritual and its salvational effects by using stone.

Signs and Gods

Djoser's monumentalization of the *sed* festival is nothing less than a semiotic revolution. Iconic symbolism, hieroglyphic script, and massive stone are recognized as more adequate to the mode of existence and the needs of the dead than the transitory material things they stand for. The model is not a "substitute," but an eternalized form of reality. The scene of the offering tablet with its list of meats is nothing other than the eternalized form of the cult of the dead.

Eternalized forms as such belong to the province of the gods, as a tomb inscription of the Snofru period makes clear: "He made his gods in a form that cannot be wiped out."[28] This statement refers to the inscriptions and decorations in the cult chamber of the tomb, which are indeed executed in the novel mode of a sunken relief encrusted with colored paste. Script and images are here designated as "gods," an association explained by the intrinsically sacred character of stone and symbolism in this period. The symbols are gods because they are visible, durable, eternalized forms, and at the same time refer to something invisible. They bridge the gap between here and not-here, now and not-now.

The use of stone ushers in a change in the formal idiom of tomb architecture and, by extension, of funerary art. The first indication of this was that funerary art was largely banished from the new stone contexts and became almost a royal privilege. In the late Third and early Fourth Dynasties mastabas featured inner rooms, rich decorations, and tomb sculpture. Under Snofru, entirely new restrictions were introduced: tomb sculpture was replaced by "reserve heads" (limestone portraits of the deceased) in the burial chamber; wall reliefs gave way to the offering table attached to the sloping wall of the mastaba; inner rooms in the mastaba block were replaced by a small brick porch before the offering site. These radical restrictions and regulations imposed on funerary art and architecture were designed to keep close control over the new "avenue to salvation" cast in stone and to assure the special status of the king in the sphere of symbolic forms. Stone tomb sculpture existed before Snofru, but only now came the full realization of its significance as an eternalized form of the body, or rather, of the person.

Pyramid Symbolism

The pyramids take this symbolism of eternalization a stage further. They cannot be regarded as the eternalized form of a transitory entity. Nor are they "models" in the sense that the *sed* festival site of Djoser is a replica of a real cult site. They are not iconic signs; they are not an image of anything. Yet the pyramids are certainly symbols, and as such represent a bridge between the visible and the invisible, the here and not-here, the now and not-now. The construction stages of the Djoser pyramid clearly show that the realization of this symbolic purpose was intimately connected with its elevation, its vertical axis. To achieve height, Imhotep stacked a number of mastabas, changing the ground plan from rectangle to square in the process. The rectangular form was transferred to the enclosing wall.

The rectangular form as an element of iconic symbolism converting palace and cult site into the eternalized stone form ends with Djoser. The pyramid form, however, and its aniconic symbolism begins with Djoser. The pyramid does not *stand for* anything visible, it *makes* something visible. Its elevation makes it a pointer to the heavens. This element of the pyramid's symbolism can be substantiated with three different arguments. The first argument concerns the linguistic form in which the Egyptians referred to the pyramids. What I have in mind here is not the Egyptian word for pyramid, *mr*, which is etymologically uncertain, but metaphorical designations. The central concept here is *akhet*, a word we traditionally translate as "horizon" but that in Egyptian refers to a region of the heavens where the sky nears the earth and the sun god ascends from the underworld in the morning and returns in the evening. In Egyptian the pyramid of Cheops (whose Egyptian name was Khufu) is called *akhet* of Khufu. *Akhet* is the threshold region between the sky, the earth, and the underworld; in particular, *akhet* is the place where the sun rises. The etymological root of the word has the meaning of "blaze, be radiant"; likewise, the hieroglyph for *akhet* has nothing in common with the pyramid, but is a pictogram of the sun rising or setting between two mountains. The pyramid does not represent such an *akhet*, but symbolizes it in an aniconic way. The term of comparison between *akhet* and pyramid is the idea of "ascent to heaven." As the sun god ascends from the underworld to the *akhet* and appears in the sky, so the king interred in the pyramid ascends to heaven by way of his *akhet*, his threshold of light.

The justification for interpreting the *akhet* symbolism of the pyramid in this way derives from a second argument resting on the testimony of the Pyramid Texts, which are the inscriptional, eternalized form of the transient cult recitations that were put into the tomb with the dead king, starting at the end of the Fifth Dynasty. The central topic of these texts is the idea of ascent to heaven. Their recitation and the accompanying rites aided the king in his ascent to heaven and incorporation into the circuit of the sun. The Egyptian word for this ritual function, like the word "*akhet*," derives from the root meaning "blaze, be radiant"; it is the causative form that signifies "to make into a spirit of light." This function of the Pyramid Texts replicates the architectural form of the pyramids, which are themselves the symbolic realization of the king's ascent to heaven and inclusion within the circuit of the sun.

This interpretation is confirmed by a third argument concerning "pyramidia," which relates to the reception history of the pyramid form. Such an argument must be handled with care, since the reception of a form can be bound up with all kinds of reinterpretations. Nothing compels us to assume that the meaning given to the pyramid form in the Middle and New Kingdoms is identical to that given it in the Old Kingdom. My argument can only claim validity in connection with the preceding arguments. Pyramidia have come down to us from the Middle and New Kingdoms: small pyramids of hard stone set on top of the brick pyramids of the period. These pyramidia have inscriptions, which leave no doubt about the belief that the dead joined in the circuit of the sun. They speak of the eyes of the dead person being opened so that he can behold the sun god on his travels and accompany him in his bark. In the New Kingdom the four sides of these structures show the four phases of the arc described by the sun: morning, noon, evening, night, corresponding to east, south, west, and north.

The extraordinary accuracy of Old Kingdom pyramids with regard to the cardinal points expresses a relationship between these structures and the heavens that can justly be termed iconic. The cardinal points of the pyramids represent an image of the heavens in directional terms, for the Egyptians connected south, east, north, and west with the sky, the course of the sun, and the constellations. The earth also had its direction, which was determined by the course of the Nile; tombs were normally aligned with the direction of the Nile. The pyramids, however, are oriented not to the Nile but in strict accordance with the points of the compass. In this way, they represent the heavens on earth. For the duration of pharaonic civilization, the sacred space of the pyramids was understood as an enclave in which the earth and its directions mirror the topography of the heavens.

Sacred Space and Chronotope

With its orientation to the heavens, sacred space in Egyptian architecture also represents a chronotope, a dimension where heavenly time reigns. To build a sacred space was to establish not only a spatial but also a temporal link with the heavens; it was a realization of eternity. And for that reason, the construction of sacred precincts in Egypt is closely bound up with kingship. During the ritual of the foundation of the temple, the gods say to the king:

> As truly as your monument stands on its foundations
> like heaven on its pillars
> your work will endure with its lord
> like the earth with the Ennead.
> Its years are those of *akhet*,
> its months are those of the decan stars.
> It knows no destruction on earth for all eternity.[29]

Monumental time is heavenly time. In the Old Kingdom, the king not only figured as the sole owner of sacred space but was also its inhabitant. In this period, all the construction work done by the state concentrated on the pyramid as the epitome of sacred space. In contrast, the small brick chapels erected as temples of the gods were completely devoid of heavenly symbolism. Places of sacrifice to the gods did not need to represent a threshold area between heaven and earth.

This situation changed drastically in the Middle Kingdom. From this period we have one very extensive inscription that exemplifies the obligation of the king to construct a sacred space.[30] Its subject is the erection of a temple to Atum in Heliopolis. Mutatis mutandis, certain elements of the inscription can be applied to the building of the pyramids in the Old Kingdom. Here are some excerpts:

> [The king speaks to his counselors:]
> See, My Majesty resolves [to put up] an edifice,
> and commemorates a deed
> as something salvational for the future.
> I will erect monuments and establish stelae for Horakhty.
> [There follows a lengthy description of the prenatal designation
> of the king by the god, establishing the building project as an
> act of gratitude.]
> I have come as Horus after I have counted my body [acquired
> self-control = come of age as a man],
> to establish the offering cakes of the gods,

to accomplish the building works in the temple of my father
  Atum,
to make him rich even to the degree that he had me take rule,
to provide his altars with food on earth.

I will put up my house on his ground,
so that my perfection be remembered in his house.
The pyramid is my name,
the sacred lake is my monument.
Neheh-eternity it means, to create the salvational.
A king who is named for his works does not die,
a monument that he has planned cannot disappear,
and so his name is named on it.
The things of *djet*-eternity do not die.

The works that were done are what [truly] exists.
[Doing such works] means striving for the salvational.
An excellent food is the name.
It is acquired by being vigilant about the concerns of *neheh-*
  eternity.

[The counselors answer the king:]
. . . Noble and sublime it is to look to the morrow
as something that is [already] salvational for the time of life.
The crowd can do nothing without you.
Your Majesty is [= has] the eyes of all.

In this text a central recurring concept is *akh,* which I have rendered
as "salvational." *Akh* derives from the same root meaning "blaze, be
radiant" from which the words for "horizon" and "transfigured spirit
of the dead" also stem. In applying a concept like "salvation" or "path
of salvation" to Egypt, we must orient ourselves primarily to this
idea of heavenly radiance. *Akh* designates the usefulness and efficacy
of those human actions that are able to reach out into the sphere of
heavenly eternity. Building for god—creating and extending sacred
space—is the supreme form of salvational action. As the text clearly
shows, the "salutariness" of this action lies in the realization of eternity. Action on such a grand scale can be undertaken only by one
who envisages eternity.
    The text stems from Sesostris I of the Middle Kingdom, but it

can legitimately be transposed to the Age of the Pyramids. Though the kings of the Old Kingdom built pyramids not for the sun god but for the gods they themselves incarnated, they nonetheless strove to create a sacred space partaking of the eternity of the heavens.

In a sense the great pyramids of Giza represent the culmination of a process that began in Naqada. The tombs become increasingly monumental and the power of the chief (later the pharaoh) becomes greater and greater, taking on divine dimensions until the pharaoh becomes akin to the Supreme God. This increasing divinization of the ruler finds visual expression in the development of the royal tombs—a process that reaches its logical conclusion at Giza. The pyramids of Giza convey the impression that not only the invention of building in stone but the very foundation of the state itself is associated with the divinization of the king. The state provides the immense forces and organizational resources without which this architecture would be impossible. Thus the pyramids also symbolize and visualize the organizational prowess of the state, as embodied in the king, whose will is strong enough to move mountains.

After Giza, monumental architecture never reached the same level again: the pyramids of Cheops and Chephren are by far the tallest and most scrupulously aligned.[31] But the near miraculous features of the two great pyramids in Giza were not part of the standard program that Egyptian architects associated with the idea of a pyramid. Indeed, it is not at all clear that the Egyptians regarded the pyramids at Giza to be representative of traditional pyramid design. In any event, when the kings of the Middle Kingdom built pyramids for themselves, they did not look back to Fourth Dynasty examples like Giza but to the much smaller pyramids of Unas and Pepy II. These pyramids seem to us much less impressive. Yet in one aspect they represent the consummation of an architectural form that was still in a transitional state at Giza: the temples on the eastern side of the pyramids. These temples gained their definitive form only in the Fifth Dynasty, when the kings suddenly broke with the Giza tradition and started to erect, in addition to smaller pyramids, cult sites for the sun god, with an obelisk taking the place of the pyramid. These sun temples, which were closely connected with the royal cult of the dead, newly embody an attempt to realize the eternity of the king by combining the cult of the dead with the cult of the gods. Mentuhotep

II was later to revert to this tradition in the Eleventh Dynasty, and in the New Kingdom it became canonical. But in the Old Kingdom it disappeared with Unas, the last king of the Fifth Dynasty.

But with that same king Unas, a tradition began that once again illustrates the close relationship between language and building reflected in the myth of the Tower of Babel. Under Unas' rule the sealed burial chambers of the pyramid were for the first time provided with written texts evidently transferred from the papyrus scrolls of the funerary rituals to the walls of the tomb; by this means, the dead king was assured of the salvational effect of these rituals for all eternity. This custom was carried on by Unas' successors, and the resulting corpus of "Pyramid Texts" represents the beginnings of Egyptian funerary and mortuary literature, as well as the earliest corpus of religious texts in the known history of mankind. The idea of inscribing texts onto walls and other parts of buildings suggests itself more obviously in Egypt than elsewhere. The stone of which these buildings for eternity were constructed was also the writing surface for the hieroglyphs. Unlike hieratic cursive, hieroglyphic writing is writing on stone. It was designed for the inscription of monuments, just as monuments were designed to be inscribed with hieroglyphs. In Egypt, stone structures and inscription—building and language—achieve a unique connection, constituting a "monumental discourse" that reflects an unprecedented attempt to construct sacred time.

The Message of the Tombs

From Style to Canon

It is not idle speculation to imagine what picture of ancient Egyptian civilization we would have if it had ended with the Old Kingdom. Egyptian history would then not have its characteristic cyclical form but the linear profile of an irreversible rise and decline. It would be free of canonizing, archaizing recourses to the past and hence free of internal self-illumination. For in these recourses to memory a culture reflects on itself and develops its implicit semantics. If Egyptian history had come to a halt in 2150 B.C.E., we would still have the great pyramids, thousands of monumental inscribed tomb complexes, tens of thousands of statues and statuettes of kings and high officials; we would have some official documents and letters, and the Pyramid

Texts. We would have hundreds of biographical tomb inscriptions in which officials list their offices and honors, their services to the state, and their attitudes to the basic ethical norms of their society. So we could not say that the mute traces of this civilization would be more enigmatic than revealing, facing us with all but inscrutable mysteries. If there were no Middle or New Kingdom, we would not know significantly less about the Old Kingdom than we do now.

But what we would not have is the self-reflective dimension of Egyptian civilization. We would not know how this civilization saw itself, how it set itself off from its neighbors, what central values it cherished, what social and religious norms it developed; nor would we know in what ways Egypt related to its own past and developed a historical awareness, how it saw the relation between gods and humans, what role it attributed to the gods in the history and destiny of humans, or what responsibility it felt humans had to the gods. The fact that we can pose such questions with some hope of finding fairly well-substantiated answers is due to sources that we customarily group under the heading of "literature"—all of which are later than the Old Kingdom. With this literature, Egyptian civilization in its later stages created a locus and institution of self-illumination that has no parallel in the Old Kingdom. If we did not have these sources, Egypt would be a closed book from the point of view of a history of meaning. It is necessary to recognize the particularities of these sources in order to grasp the precise nature of the way in which Egypt is accessible to us. Ancient Egypt, and, of course, Mesopotamia are accessible to us in the same way as Israel and Greece, China and India. We are not in the presence of exotic curiosities dragged to light by archaeology—sunken, forgotten civilizations dug up in shards and brooded over by experts. Nor are we in the presence of a primeval entity completely beyond any attempt to make sense of it. Rather, ancient Egypt is an intellectual and spiritual world that is linked to our own by numerous strands of tradition.

But another thought seems to me even more important. If only the Old Kingdom had been preserved, we would have no way of understanding the canonical normativity of this monumental building style. The formal language of the monuments, from pyramid to statuette, from the temples to the false doors, stelae, and offering tables, would display the typical features of a common cultural style. It is only the remarkable persistence of this formal idiom over later centuries and millennia that makes clear its extraordinary binding force. Only when we look back to the Old Kingdom from the vantage of later history do we recognize that the Egyptians not only established a style strong enough to integrate each individual artifact into a broader context, but that they also developed a second-order style—a macro-style—designed to preclude stylistic change.

Now, no style is entirely free of an element of change; style assures datability. To do something "in style," whether an action or the manufacture of an object, means more than mere routine or imitation, more than the reproduction of an existing mold or pattern; rather, it means fulfilling the pattern in an outstanding and striking way. Implicit in the idea of style is not merely the impulse to conform to a standard but also the impulse to set oneself apart.[32] Egypt confronts us with a principle that endeavors to preclude datability. But this principle can never succeed entirely. Thus, we are rarely at a loss to assign a reasonably accurate date to Egyptian objects. On the other hand, there is no gainsaying the presence of a counteractive principle dictating a formal similarity that transcends the passage of time. This principle is known as canonization; it is a ban on variation. In music, a canon is a form of polyphony in which the parts are identical but make their entries at different times. "Canon" here means the principle underlying an aesthetic of identity, a principle assured by an extreme form of regulation. In a different sense we also speak of the Holy Scriptures as a canon, meaning a set of texts that must not be changed. Here again, there is a ban on variation. My theory is that to a significant degree the form peculiar to Egyptian history is a product of the effectiveness of such canonizing principles, which we need to understand (in their collectivity) as forms of a specific kind of memorial culture. The Old Kingdom is the epoch that developed the style and repertoire of Egyptian formal idioms. By reverting to these forms, the later epochs canonized them, elevating style to the status of canon.

Canonization, then, is the institutionalization of permanence, a strategy for foiling time, and hence one of the most favored cultural techniques for constructing a specific chronotope.[33] In Israel and Alexandria, the canonization of the central inherited traditions served to perpetuate a time-resistant cultural identity. The canonization of the formal artistic idiom in Egypt had the same effect, but it was inspired by the desire to overcome individual mortality. In Egypt, this desire was expressed by the construction of monuments, and the canonization of the formal idiom was designed to establish those monuments as realizations of eternity, of the sacred time called *djet*. This "monumental discourse" gave an elite group of individuals the chance to place their own historical identities into the "sacred space of permanence," the monumental tomb.

Tomb, Writing, Immortality

There is surely no other funerary tradition in the world comparable to the Egyptian tomb in its representation of the entire culture: the here-and-now and the beyond, professional life and mortuary cult, individual and social existence. The unparalleled, unique cultural significance of the tomb in Egypt is something that had already struck travelers in antiquity. The remarks devoted to this phenomenon by Hecataeus of Abdera, who lived in Alexandria from 320 to 305 B.C.E. and journeyed through Egypt, remain pertinent from the point of view of modern Egyptology:

> The natives attribute very little value to the time spent in this life. But they attach the greatest possible significance to the time after death in which one is preserved in the memory through recollections of virtue. They call the dwellings of the living "temporary abodes" because we only spend a short time in them. The tombs of the dead they call "eternal houses" because the dead spend infinite time in Hades. Accordingly they give very little thought to the equipment of their houses, whereas the effort they put into the tombs can never be high enough.[34]

A corresponding Egyptian testimony has been preserved in a tomb inscription from the New Kingdom:[35]

> I erected for myself a magnificent tomb
> in my city of eternity.
> I equipped most lavishly the site of my rock tomb
> in the desert of eternity.[36]
>
> May my name endure on it
> in the mouths of the living,
> while the memory of me is good among men
> after the years that are to come.
>
> A trifle only of life is this world,
> [but] eternity is in the realm of the dead.

Praised by god is the noble
who acts for himself with a view to the future
and seeks with his heart to find salvation for himself,
the burial of his corpse, and the revival of his name,
and who is mindful of eternity.[37]

Here too the extraordinary sumptuousness of the tomb is justified by
the belief that the time spent "on earth" is only "a trifle" in comparison to the "eternity" spent in the "realm of the dead"; the all-
important thing is to be remembered by the living. We can only
understand the Egyptian tomb if, like Hecataeus, we look beyond the
architectural, iconographic, and epigraphic givens and inquire into
the underlying value systems, the cultural construction of time and
eternity, of memory and immortality, of social "virtue" and biographical significance. The overwhelming presence of eternity in the form
of monuments and inscriptions meant that, in comparison, life on
earth appeared not only as a "trifle" but as something more akin to
a dream than to reality. Thus, in the famous *"Harper's Song,"* handed
down in a tomb inscription and also contrasting the here-and-now
with the afterlife, we hear the following:

I have heard these songs that are in the tombs of the forefathers
and what they tell to glorify the here-and-now and to belittle the
    afterlife.
Why is suchlike done to the land of eternity?
[...] Our people rest in it since earliest primordial time,
and those who will be in infinite years,
they all come to that place. There is no remaining in Egypt. [...]
The time that one spends on earth is only a dream. But
    "Welcome, safe and sound!"
one says to him who has reached the West.[38]

The monumental tombs of Egypt are not graves in any contemporary
sense. Their significance in Egyptian civilization is comparable to that
which we attach to art and literature. This comparison may seem far-
fetched, but it is found, as we know, in Horace, who compared his
odes with the pyramids. In doing so, Horace himself stands in a
literary tradition that ultimately dates back to ancient Egypt. A
famous passage in the wisdom text preserved on the verso of the
Papyrus Chester Beatty IV and stemming from the Ramesside Period

(thirteenth century B.C.E.) says the following about the great classical authors of the past:

> They have not created for themselves pyramids of ore
> nor stelae of iron;
> they have not contrived to leave heirs in the form of children,
> to keep their names alive.
> But they created themselves books as heirs
> and teachings that they have written.
> They employed the scroll as "lector priest"
> and the slate as "loving son."
> Teachings are their pyramids,
> the reed their son,
> the polished stone surface their wife.
> Great and Small
> were given them as children;
> the scribe, he is the supreme one of all.
> Gates and chapels were made for them—they have crumbled.
> Their mortuary priests have gone hence,
> their altars are besmirched with dirt,
> their tomb chapels forgotten.
> But their names are recalled on their writings, that they have
>   created,
> as they endure by virtue of their perfection.
> Their creators are remembered in eternity.[39]

This comparison of books with tombs and with the cult of the dead not only stresses the memorial aspect of literature, with books as the truer and better pyramids; it also plays upon the bookishness, the literary nature, of the tomb. One aspect shared by book and pyramid is the survival of the name: immortality in the memory of posterity. Like books, the Egyptian tombs address a posterity of readers. Indeed, most of what we know about the professional groups who specialized in reading and writing, and who were therefore the vehicles of literary tradition, comes from tomb inscriptions, more specifically from the "appeals to the visitors to the tombs."[40] But the most important common denominator of tomb and book is authorship—a denominator without parallel in other cultures. Where else does the owner of a tomb figure as the "author" of his burial place and the life recorded within? Elsewhere, tombs are generally erected by surviving relatives or friends, sometimes admittedly on the basis of long-term preparation and detailed instructions from the deceased person. But normally those tombs can hardly be regarded as vehicles of an all-encompassing literary and graphic self-thematization. This "literary" element is unique to the monumental Egyptian tomb. For the Egyptian, the tomb was the most important thing in the world, the "work" for which he lived and in which he invested both his financial resources and his intellectual powers; his tomb recorded in a visible and preeminently durable form his acts and designs, his exits and entrances, his value and significance, his virtue and his standing. The noble Egyptian planned his tomb during his lifetime and left a record of that activity in his biographical inscription:

> I am he who prepared this place,
> that it may serve me as necropolis and to fulfill my wish.
> I devoted my attention to it in every respect, when I was among
>   the living;
> I come to it now, after having reached an excellent age,
> after I had spent my time among the living
> protected by the king in the status of a tomb owner.[41]

In his burial inscription, Megegi of Thebes describes himself as one who has made the most conscientious use possible of his lifetime. An essential feature in this self-assessment is the care expended on his own tomb:

> I was one who loves the beautiful and hates the bad,
> who spends the day in accordance with what it requires.
> I have not taken time away from the day,
> I have done no damage to a beautiful hour.
> I have spent my years on earth
> and have trod the paths of the necropolis,
> after I have prepared for myself every accoutrement of the tomb
> that is made for a well-provided tomb owner.
> I was one who spent his day and followed his hour
> in the course of every day.[42]

A chief priest from Assiut emphasizes his own part in the inscription on his tomb:

I have moreover completed this tomb and given order for its
   inscription,
and this in person, while I still lived.[43]

With his tomb the Egyptian created a place whence he could look
back on his life from the perspective of its consummation, a locus of
self-observation and self-thematization. He looked at his tomb as at
a mirror holding up the ideal form and final shape he wanted to give
to his life, the form in which he wished to be remembered forever.
In its abundance of images and inscriptions, the tomb symbolized the
sum of his life and achievements.

The multiplicity of allusions from one tomb to another forms a
network of intertextual references that justify the term "monumental
discourse" and represent the most important medium of cultural
memory; by means of this monumental discourse, Egyptian society
could reach beyond the everyday and gain for itself a form of collective identity that transcended mundane concerns. The tombs belong
to the constellation of pyramids, temples, obelisks, statues, stelae, and
sphinxes with which the Egyptians attempted to create a sacred
dimension of permanence, a place that was an assurance both of
immortality for themselves and of visibility for what they held sacred.
The Egyptians assured their entry into this dimension of permanence
by means of the monumental form they gave their tombs and com-
memorations; and, above all, they wrote themselves into permanence
through the medium of their inscriptions. The tomb inscribed its
owner into a network of social memory: a network of verbal intercourse, mutual regard, and reciprocal action that in the eyes of the
Egyptians constituted the essence of human society.[44]

Writing and Rites

The Liturgical Construction of Permanence

Another aspect of this same aspiration to permanence is the astounding tenacity with which the Egyptians clung to the graphic realism of
hieroglyphic writing. In all other walks of life, hieratic script imposed
itself; like all originally pictographic writing systems, it rapidly grew
simpler and more abstract. Only for the inscriptions on the monumental tombs did the graphic representations of the hieroglyphs

remain unchallenged. The principle that informs hieroglyphic writing is maximum iconicity: the written signs remain interpretable as images. Thus hieroglyphs, like all other written signs, are related to language; but unlike other written signs they also relate visibly to things, in a realistic way that puts them in the same category as pictorial representations. The Egyptians made no strict distinction between writing—hieroglyphic writing—and pictorial art, so the intentional suspension in the development of writing arrested the progress of art in general. Hieroglyphic writing was considered an artistic genre, a special kind of script learned only by artists. The Egyptians called the hieroglyphs "words of god" or divine speech. For the Egyptians, the idea of an immutable "divine language" centered most particularly on the graphic nature of hieroglyphic script and, by extension, on monumental art in general. By fixing the expression of divine speech in monuments and hieroglyphics, they sought to give tangible form to the sacred and ensure unbroken communication with it.

The suspension of forms and the construction of an immutably permanent chronotope had repercussions in two closely related areas: rites and monuments. Where ritual was concerned, the proscription of change and innovation took the form of repetition. Everything hinged on precise reiteration. Maximum care was taken to prevent deviation and improvisation. This negative cultural imperative makes a very early appearance in the shape of the "lector priest," the "bearer of the scroll," whose task was the recitation of the sacred texts. The lector priest was not a shaman, not a charismatic or an ecstatic. His contact with the supernal powers rested entirely on his knowledge of the script and his ability to recite accurately. His task was to ensure that precisely the same text was repeated at precisely the same time in the context of the same ritual event, thus bringing meaning, duration, and action into precise alignment. The lector priest with his scroll appears in the pyramid temples and officials' tombs of the Old Kingdom, as well as—unchanged—in the temples of the Greco-Roman Period; and among the texts recited in that period the Pyramid Texts again appear, preserved in largely the same form for the same cultic purpose over a period of two and a half thousand years.

The cultural imperative observed in these practices was formulated by the Neoplatonic philosopher Iamblichus in his book on the mysteries of the Egyptians. He notes that the Egyptians regarded their ancient and venerable prayer texts as "sacred asylums" and brooked no change to them. The magic power of the texts to conjure the sacred through the act of recitation takes precedence over their meaning or normative authority. Every performance of the sacred text had to be an exact repetition of the preceding one. According to Iamblichus, this imperative to repetition is due to the immutability of the gods. The sacred does not change, so the symbolic forms that make present the sacred must not change either. The response that contemporary anthropologists obtain when they ask why certain patterns and models are meticulously copied offers an instructive parallel: "We do things the way we do because these are signs [images] of our ancestors."[45] Ritual repetition—the long-term memory of a culture—serves to safeguard the links with another world. Ritual regulations are precisely observed to ensure that the connections with that other world remain unbroken. In Egypt, the rites emulated not only the ancestors but also the gods. Rites and recitations were an exact mimesis of cosmic life and the cyclical recurrence of its natural phenomena: day and night, summer and winter, the motions of the stars, the inundations of the Nile, sowing and reaping, decay and regeneration. The purpose of this ritual mimesis was dual: first, it was designed to incorporate the human world and its routines into the sacred circularity of cosmic life, thus countering decline and decay with a chance of regeneration (which in Egypt meant in the first place ensuring the prospect of new life after death); second, it served to sustain cosmic life itself in its circularity, not merely to "keep" time by observing its calendrical progress but actually to generate it. The ritual calendar was not just a representation of the cosmos, but a cultural form that stabilized the cosmos it represented. The motive for repetition was not, as Iamblichus supposed, that the gods are conservative and only want to hear the same sacred formulas repeated in perpetuity, but the conviction that the cyclical stability of the cosmos is constantly in jeopardy and has to be sustained by ritual repetition. The ritual institutionalization of permanence thus has a cosmic significance: it generates *cultural* order with a view to sustaining *cosmic* order; *memoria* is raised to the rank of cosmogony. The world is commemorated in order to counterbalance the perpetual drift toward decline, inertia, entropy, and chaos.

Rituals and monumental art are thus the two areas of Egyptian life where the principle of the canon imposed itself. The written record of the sacred rites assured perfect reiterability, while the immobilization of the formal idiom of monumental art, including hieroglyphic script, assured maximum intelligibility for divine speech. Both spheres had their official location in a single cultural institution, known in Egyptian as the "house of life," where language and writing were learned, texts copied, and theological and philosophical works compiled and collected; the house of life was the center of the cultural endeavor to preserve and ensure the ongoing progress of cosmic, political, and social life.

This sustenance and renewal of time through ritual complements the construction of sacred permanence through monumental discourse. In this conjunction, we discern the two aspects of Egyptian thinking in connection with time, *neheh* and *djet*. *Neheh,* the generic term for all regularly recurring units of time, is cyclical; it is formed and kept in motion by the rites. *Djet,* the unchanging permanence of that which has achieved perfection, is mirrored in the sacred spatial dimension of permanence constructed through the medium of monumental discourse.

State and Immortality

A history of meaning studies the semantic systems that underlie historical processes and that achieve tangible form in traces, messages, and memories; such constellations of meaning are themselves the definitive markers of epochs. Looking back on the Archaic Period and the Old Kingdom, I discern two such configurations, both of which remained operative beyond the Old Kingdom and thus became an integral part of the fundamental semantics of Egyptian civilization. Both are responses to the question of the meaning of the state. It is perhaps worth reiterating that the emergence of this state was anything but inevitable; as far as we know, Egypt is the earliest territorial state in the history of humanity. The earlier and contemporaneous forms of political order in the Near East, Elam, and the Indus valley were rival groups of city-states, the same form of political organization that was smashed by the chiefs who unified the Egyptian realm. The "messages" of this period stress that, far from being a "natural" process, the unification drive was forcible, not to say violent. Moreover, unification was consciously instituted and implemented with the rhetoric of "new versus old." In Egyptian recollection the birth of the state is connected with an act of foundation, ascribed to King Menes.

Menes is the Egyptian "Moses," in the sense of an initiator of political order and also in the sense of a religious founder, for the Egyptian state was the institutionalized form of a religion, and its primate was first the incarnation and later the son, the representative, and the image of the supreme god.

A state imposed by force and coercing its subjects to pay taxes and perform civil and military service could hardly have maintained itself if it had not rested on a core semiology that was as persuasive as the state itself was demanding. What was it that prompted the people from Elephantine to the Delta to subjugate themselves to the lords of Naqada? Earlier, the answer to this question was sought by a process of analogy. The common denominator of most early civilizations—Egypt, Mesopotamia, Indus, China—is their geographical situation in a river valley. It was on the basis of this commonality that the theory of "hydraulic societies" developed, especially as propounded by Karl August Wittfogel. His conviction was that states evolved from these water-based cultures in order to raise the huge workforce necessary to erect colossal irrigation and drainage systems, dikes, and other water-connected engineering projects. With regard to Egypt, the trouble with this theory is that there is no confirmation to be found for it, neither archaeologically nor in the messages and memories. Of course, Egypt is, by nature, a river oasis, and there is no question that the fertility of the soil is a product of manipulation of the aquatic environment without which the Nile valley would be an uninhabitable swamp. But the annual inundation by the Nile, with its fertilizing effect upon the soil, meant that the interventions required for cultivation were not all that extreme. The problems involved could be solved locally and had indeed been solved long before the realm was unified. To organize the labor force as agriculture required was not a task of such magnitude as to necessitate centralized state measures. But while the Nile floodings relieved the Egyptians of the necessity for civil engineering projects of colossal dimensions, the river did present them with a different problem that could not be resolved by civil engineering: the fluctuations in the height of the Nile when it overflowed its banks made it impossible to forecast reliably how high the harvest yield would be. Thus, a model that looks to economic reasons as the main factor in the emergence of the state would have to replace the hydraulic theory with the demands made by a centralized supply economy. It could then be argued that the vagaries of the Nile risings prompted the Egyptians to establish large central granaries to store surplus production to fall back on in emergencies; this surplus was declared to be "tax," which the state was entitled to collect, store, and redistribute as necessary.

This theory has the advantage of being demonstrably substantiated in traces, messages, and memories. However, by far the most unequivocal memory stems not from an Egyptian but from a Hebrew text, the biblical story of Joseph. Joseph interprets the two dreams of the Pharaoh as a prophecy of seven fat years and seven lean years and counsels the king to store the surplus gained in the bountiful years to provide against shortages in the lean years (Genesis 41). During the lean years, the king would not only keep the starving Egyptians alive by selling the stored grain but could also contrive to gain control of all privately owned land in the country. In this interpretation, the biblical story of Joseph is an etiological myth that accounts not only for the idiosyncratic property system in Egypt but also for the origins of the state. True, we have no Egyptian narrative of comparable persuasiveness. But the royal inscriptions of later periods give central prominence to the king as provider and to the image of the overflowing granaries of the state. Further, the office of Overseer of the Granaries ranked very high in the Egyptian hierarchy and the remnants of huge storage barns lend additional credence to what the messages tell us.

The fundamental trouble with this interpretation is that the storage problem could have been just as easily—in fact more easily— dealt with locally or polycentrically; it cannot have been the decisive motive for the foundation of the state, and thus it has no part in Egyptian memory. The story of Joseph represents an outsider's view of the economic and administrative practices in Egypt and records his astonishment at how very alien they are; it has no bearing on the semantic system fundamental to Egyptian civilization.

If we limit ourselves to the Egyptian sources, a very different picture emerges. To elicit the semantics that underlie the establishment of the state, we have to combine the statements in the contemporary "messages" and the memory represented by the myths, notably the Horus-Seth myth. The messages tell of the violent destruction of a polycentric system of city-states; the unity of the state is established by means of the warlike subjection of rival princes. The myths, on the other hand, can be read as a depiction of the triumph of Horus' law over Seth's force. This opposition is made additionally pointed by the traditional characterization of Horus as a "weakly child" and of Seth as "lord of strength." Together these sources constitute an ideology of pacification by force. The state legitimizes itself by transforming the external political concatenation of warring princedoms or city-states, which it presents as a condition of lawlessness and discord, into a peaceful political sphere where the rule of law holds sway. The central symbol for this idea of a peaceful sphere ruled over by law is the image of unification. The Egyptian state never forgot that it was not the result of the natural organization of an ethnic and geographic unity but the artificial unification of a multiplicity (which the myth stylizes as a duality). Unification is the central memorial figure that informs pharaonic Egypt's image of itself, a figure that finally coalesced into a symbol. Just as Moses founded the people of Israel by the Exodus, an act of scission, so Menes established the Egyptian state by an act of fusion. Unification means not only political unity, but includes consensus, harmony, solidarity, a shared commitment to a superordinate system; in short, a complex of political, social, moral, and religious ideas able to capture the imagination of the masses and thus press them into service.

The second operative semiology originated with the "opening of the stone" and the onset of a megalithic phase. During the Third Dynasty, building with stone became the leading principle in the system of cultural values. The state employed whole battalions of quarrying parties, artisans, and forced laborers, and invested at least as much energy in architectural, sculptural, and epigraphic constructions of eternity as others did in conquest and defense. In the Fourth Dynasty building activity took on such epic forms as almost to convey the impression that the whole state had been created for the purpose of erecting these monumental edifices. As this semiology developed, a marked dichotomy took shape between mud and stone.[46] While stone was used exclusively for sacred edifices and the representation of eternity, mud brick was the material of all utilitarian structures, such as dwellings, administration buildings, and storage facilities. The rigorous consistency of this symbolism is also evocative of a strong allegiance to rule-governed form. The collective longing expressed in these mammoth cultural efforts is for redemption from the transience of the world of mud and participation in the cosmic eternity promised by the durability of stone.

The conjunction of state and immortality is one of the most remarkable aspects of the Egyptian state. The king was the "lord of burial" and presided over the means to salvation—the magic of stone, on which the Egyptians of the governing elite pinned their hopes of immortality. In the Old Kingdom this semantic formation is only identifiable in the traces. The vast number and the immense size of the monuments bespeak the will and the purpose behind them. In the Middle Kingdom, that conjunction becomes the explicit subject of the messages.

PART TWO

The First Intermediate Period

Stela from Naga-ed-Der
(First Intermediate Period)
(from Boston Museum of Fine Arts)

3

HISTORICAL OUTLINE

"FIRST INTERMEDIATE PERIOD" is the name given to the state in which Egypt found itself at the end of the Sixth Dynasty (ca. 2150 B.C.E.), after the collapse of the Old Kingdom. The intermediate period lasted some hundred and twenty years and ended with the reunification of the realm around 2040. The expression has no equivalent in ancient Egyptian terminology (but neither do the terms "Old/ Middle/New Kingdom" and "Late Period"). In fact, this periodization actively contradicts the king-lists, as they have been transmitted on the Turin papyrus and in Manetho's history. The king-lists do not testify to any interruption in the line of kings after the Sixth Dynasty. The Seventh, Eighth, Ninth, Tenth, and Eleventh Dynasties follow without a break and are presented as having ruled over all Egypt. But if we look at these "dynasties" somewhat more closely, we find that they translate a state of factual disintegration into a form that preserves the outward appearance of continuity. The Seventh Dynasty consists of "seventy kings" ruling for "seventy days." This play on the figure seven is a symbolic expression for the condition of relative anarchy that supervened at the end of the Sixth Dynasty. In the case of the subsequent dynasties, the lists transform historical contemporaneity into chronological succession. Whereas the Ninth Dynasty of Herakleopolis really did follow the Eighth Dynasty of Memphis, the Eleventh Dynasty of Thebes was coeval with the Tenth Dynasty of Herakleopolis. The king-lists were not a medium of historiography but an instrument for measuring time and providing chronological orientation—linearity. Charting parallel developments was felt to be unnecessary; all that mattered was that the line be perpetuated without any caesura, that there be no "dark ages" or "intermediate periods" resisting inclusion in the grand chronological scheme. Accordingly, intermediate periods are absent from the king-lists. This must not be taken to mean, however, that the continuity the king-lists are at such pains to suggest actually existed in historical reality. In fact, it is patently obvious that the stages of consolidated pharaonic rule we refer to as the "Old" and "Middle" Kingdoms were separated by a fairly long period of crisis in which centralized rule broke down altogether.

It is customary to refer to this interval with the term "Intermediate Period" in order to set it off from the "Kingdoms," in which central rule functioned as it was designed to. The significance that this short period has gained in Egyptological studies, and also, as I intend to show, in Egyptian cultural memory, is out of all proportion to its relatively short duration, as well as to its relative paucity of notable events.

Events or facts take shape as such only within the framework and on the basis of a particular semantic system. If the semantic system is that of the epoch itself, then the events in question will be referred to in contemporary messages. If it is the semantic system of a later epoch, then the events will only be learned of from sources of a retrospective and commemorative nature. But in neither case do such references necessitate that anything we historians would acknowledge as an "event" actually took place. Messages and memories may give prominence to events that we would hardly classify as such; or they may relate to events that we know cannot have actually happened as they are presented, either because they are contradictory in themselves or because they contradict the testimony of the traces. The testimony of the traces, on the other hand, acquires its status as a readable reference to events retrospectively, from the semantic system operative in our own time. Thus there are three different semantic systems—messages, memories, and traces—to be taken into account when we draw on "events" as the basis for a description of the First Intermediate Period as a historical epoch.

These three semantic systems are of course operative in any historical epoch; interpretative problems arise only when the three systems prove highly divergent. Such is the case with the beginnings of the Egyptian state, for which two entirely different models were developed retrospectively by the Egyptians themselves: the model of petty kingdoms, dating back to well before the unification of the Two

Lands and symbolized by kings wearing either one of the two crowns or the double crown; and the foundation model, symbolized by the figure of a founder-king who inaugurates human rule after the reign of gods and demigods. With the Old Kingdom, however, there are no such divergences: traces, messages, and memories cohere into a unified picture.

With the end of the Old Kingdom this unified picture breaks apart again. Even more clearly than in the predynastic and early dynastic era, the traces, messages, and memories are split up across very different and distinct forms and genres. The traces are archaeological: pottery, architecture, art. The messages are associated with monumental epigraphy: inscriptions on stelae, tomb walls, and statues. Entirely new is the medium of memory, which puts us in the presence of texts of a kind without precedent in the Old Kingdom.

For the first time in history, and immediately in a highly eloquent form, we witness the alliance between memory and literature. These texts are poetically crafted, subjectively expressed, highly stylized productions that address issues of a fundamental nature. They were not found on tomb walls or stelae, but on papyri and ostraca (fragments of pottery or chips of limestone bearing a drawing or text)—media designed for dissemination, not fixed to one spot. The content of these texts suggests that they were not limited in their circulation to the two realms of literate culture established in the Old Kingdom, administration and cult. Rather, they belong to a different and new sphere of written culture, which did not fully develop before the Middle Kingdom and which we shall be looking at in more detail in part three. Of interest at this juncture is the fact that the memory of what we now call the First Intermediate Period is a central topic.

The alliance between memory and literature typically expresses itself in forms of glorification like myths and epics that declare the past to be heroic or elevate it to the status of a Golden Age. Yet in Egypt such mythologizing is not found: the First Intermediate Period did not look back to the Old Kingdom as a Golden Age; and when the Middle Kingdom did come to look back to the First Intermediate Period, the image was not heroic but one of catastrophic mayhem. Thus the Middle Kingdom, by means of its retrospective view of the First Intermediate Period, asserted its own claims as a period of restored peace and its own qualification as a Golden Age. The retrospective view of the First Intermediate Period was not nostalgic but self-congratulatory. In the alliance between literature and memory, the third confederate is the political state of the Middle Kingdom.

We can divide the First Intermediate Period into three phases:

1. From the end of the Sixth Dynasty to the end of the Eighth Dynasty (2170–2140 B.C.E.). Toward the end of the extremely long reign of Pepy II (2250–2155), central government was no longer able to assert itself against the officials and the nomarchs in their bids for independence both from one another and from the ruling monarch. Under the nominal government of Memphis, real power fell to the rival magnates, a chaotic situation reflected in the king-list as a disproportionate number of kings' names in a small number of years.

2. The "Herakleopolitan Period" (the Ninth and Tenth Dynasties of Herakleopolis, 2140–2060 B.C.E.). This phase was marked by the simultaneous coexistence of a large number of princelings who subjugated their neighbors and assumed the title of king but who did not attain any supraregional influence, let alone central power. During this period, frontiers dating back to the time of the rival chiefs of the predynastic age reemerge: northern Middle Egypt (formerly el-Omari, Maadi, and Abusir el-Melek) is now represented by Herakleopolis; the northern Upper Egyptian area (formerly This) by Abydos (including Assiut and Koptos); and the southern Upper Egyptian region (formerly Hierakonpolis) by Thebes and Edfu. At the same time, polycentric structures started developing that were to resurface twelve hundred years later in the Third Intermediate Period. For from beneath the monocentric surface of the territorial state dominant in the "Kingdom" phases of Egyptian history, a polycentric deep structure repeatedly broke through whenever the surface crumbled. This alternation between surface and deep structure is mirrored in the change between cooperative and competitive semantic paradigms. In the phases where central rule relaxed its grip, competitive values gained the upper hand over the values favoring integration. In the First Intermediate Period we see this most clearly in the messages in which, as in the period of the unification, the "violent-hearted" asserted themselves.

One king of the Herakleopolitan dynasty, Nebkaure Achthoes (Khety), who reigned around 2100 B.C.E., stands out from the long list of otherwise obscure rulers because two of the most celebrated of ancient Egypt's literary works—the *Tale of the Eloquent Peasant* and the *Instruction for King Merikare*—are associated with his name. In the *Eloquent Peasant*, Khety makes an appearance as a connoisseur of fine oratory, so taken with the Peasant's rhetoric that he commands that the lawsuit in which the Peasant is involved be artificially prolonged so that he can hear as many of his formal addresses as possible and make a written record of them. The *Instruction for King Merikare* even purports to have actually been written by Khety. The king's involvement, though surely fictional, nonetheless associates the Herakleopolitan period and its court with literature in a remarkable way.

3. The Eleventh Dynasty of Thebes. Parallel with developments at Herakleopolis, the Theban nomarchs succeeded in asserting themselves over their neighbors, placing the south under their control, and assuming the title of king. Thus at the end of the Herakleopolitan Period (2120–2060 B.C.E.), the overall situation seemed about to revert to a renewed north-south dualism. Mentuhotep II of Thebes (2060–2010), however, engineered the second unification of the realm in 2040. With this ruler, Egypt returned to the grand style of monumental state architecture. His mortuary temple in the valley of Deir el-Bahri harks back to the grand tradition of the Old Kingdom; its architectural, ideological, and cultic forms remained a model for a long time to come. In Egyptian self-commemoration, Mentuhotep II was revered as a founder king and a unifier of the realm. But central rule had not come back to stay. After the premature death of his successor Mentuhotep III (2010–1998), unrest flared up again. After seven years, the dynamic vizier Amenemhet succeeded in ascending the throne as first king of the Twelfth Dynasty, and peace once again returned.

4

TRACES

IN CONSIDERING THE ARCHAEOLOGICAL EVIDENCE, an approach that focuses exclusively on pottery is much too reductionist. Even if there were no other remnants surviving from the Intermediate Period, such a lack could hardly be more eloquent. The absence of monuments would be a far more decisive "trace" than continuity in ceramics. The concept of "trace" relates, after all, not to a class of objects but to a methodological perspective. Everything, including the pyramids, can be considered a trace. And indeed, the trace of the pyramids breaks off here. In itself this break would not be sufficient indication of an "intermediate period," but would at most signify the demise of a semantic paradigm. But the Middle Kingdom did not develop a new paradigm for its royal tombs; it reverted to the pyramids of the Old Kingdom. In other words, in the tradition of pyramid construction there is a definite caesura corresponding exactly to the expanse of time known as the First Intermediate Period. The last pyramid—it was never actually built—belonged to a king of the Eighth Dynasty called Qakare Iby. The burial chamber and its pyramid texts have come down to us. The superstructure, planned for erection on a thirty-meter-square base, was never completed.

But there was no corresponding interruption in "monumental discourse." The planning and building of monumental tombs went on. At Herakleopolis a necropolis has been found with miniature mastabas displaying the most exquisite bas-reliefs and decorated in the finest Memphite tradition. Decorated rock tombs, stelae, and other elements of monumental discourse have been excavated at Kom el-Koffar, Mo'alla, Gebelein, Thebes, Assiut, Naga-ed-Der, and other sites. Considered as traces, these monuments present as clear a testimony of change as does the negative trace of the absent pyramids. North and south diverged stylistically. In the north, the refined tradition of Memphite residential culture continued, albeit on a smaller scale. The south, by contrast, adopted innovative stylistic features that ignored (intentionally or unintentionally) the canon of residential culture and conveyed a clumsy, barbaric, but very vigorous impression, offering the starkest imaginable contrast to the "academic" reliefs of Herakleopolis. The sense of these traces could hardly be more unequivocal: the expressive forms of monumental discourse in north and south had lost their binding, normative character. The subsequent conclusion is that the state-controlled organization of the workshops and construction sites, which worked on the basis of the traditional canon, had completely broken down. Now local workforces, not artisans imported from Memphis, built monuments. Thus the disruption of residential culture also engendered new, local traditions of commemoration, no longer under the sway of the residential canon and its strict laws.

This pattern of discontinuity and new growth is also evident in the traces left by the great residential necropolises of the Old Kingdom, in Giza and Saqqara. Here at the end of the Sixth Dynasty a period of intensive building rapidly changed the "urban" layout of the cemetery complex with its streets and lateral connections into a warren that was much more confusing, inaccessible, and to that extent chaotic. All open spaces were mercilessly crammed with buildings, an indication that the cult of the dead in the great mastabas had faded away and there was no one to assure their accessibility. In fact, accessibility no longer played any role whatever. The cultic "interconnection" of the tombs had broken down. In the Old Kingdom, the "reversion of offerings" (the circulation of offerings, first presented to a deity, among various recipients) had united the individual tombs and linked them to a central cult. The tomb owners partook of the offerings of the central cult and thus, in the hereafter, supped at the table of the "great god," just as they had supped at the table of the king in this world. Lord over this central cult was the king himself, whose pyramid formed the center of the residential cemetery. Free access to the tombs was thus a major priority because it was the medium through which the unifying interconnection of the tombs took place. The access granted to those making offerings not only bound the individual tomb into the symbolic system of provision built up around the central cult, but also served to include that tomb in the communication with posterity. The tombs were designed to be visited by the living, as attested to both by their accessibility and, more especially, by the inscriptions addressed to those visitors. For the Egyptians, the monumental tomb and the offerings it elicited were the means by which the dead remained incorporated in the society of the living—a function that fell into desuetude once the accessibility of the tomb complex ceased to matter.

We must, of course, distinguish between the secondary inaccessibility of tomb complexes crammed with additional constructions at a later date and the primary inaccessibility of tomb complexes simply designed to be inaccessible. The criterion of primary inaccessibility certainly cannot be said to apply generally to the tombs of the First Intermediate Period. But there is a trend in that direction. We note it, above all, in the fact that certain features of the formal organization and the content of monumental discourse and the mortuary cult were transposed from "outside" to "inside," thus forfeiting their monumental and cultic character. This shift from outside to inside led to the emergence of two new genres: "models" and mortuary literature.

"Models" are three-dimensional installations about the size of a doll's house that reproduce with astonishing vividness scenes depicted outside on the tomb reliefs—for example, work in the fields, navigation, household chores, exercise of official duties. These models, made of painted wood, were part of the mortuary equipment for the use of the dead only; they were not meant for the eyes of visitors. Thus the *communicative* link with the world of the living was replaced by a *magical* link—by the symbolic representation of things absent. This shift to symbolic representation holds a number of possible meanings. The "interconnection" between the worlds of the living and the dead was not only a matter of facilitating access to the tombs, say by means of paths, doors, and "walk-in" chambers, but extended equally to institutions such as the cult of the dead and the reversion of offerings, as well as to cultural mores and practices: visiting the tombs, for instance, or reciting prayers. Such customs required that an organization stand guard over the tombs to prevent their being damaged, defiled, plundered, or broken up for building material. The fact that the tombs were no longer designed to accommodate these links with the outside world suggests that the cult of the dead was no longer practiced, or at least that confidence in its practice had been terminally undermined. The same applies to the custom of visiting the tombs. Tomb owners no longer put much stock in the solidarity or piety of later generations. Or else they lacked confidence in the security system's ability to protect the necropolis. Probably all these factors played a role.

Just as the models transpose forms of monumental discourse from the external and accessible parts of the tomb into the internal and inaccessible area of the burial chamber, so the mortuary literature of the "Coffin Texts" transfers religious ritual (notably recitation) from the external dimension of the temple and tomb cult to the closed-off area of the burial chamber. Here again we may speak of a move from the communicative to the magical. Because the Coffin Texts stand in the tradition of the Pyramid Texts of the Old Kingdom, one might argue that they do not represent anything fundamentally new. The only difference between Pyramid Texts and Coffin Texts, one might further contend, is that what was once a prerogative of kings was now practiced by a much broader section of society.

Though such demotization of the Pyramid Texts is indeed a highly eloquent "trace" (which I shall be looking at in more detail), it does not do full justice to the difference between Pyramid Texts and Coffin Texts. It would be erroneous to regard the Pyramid Texts as a substitute for the cult via the medium of magical conjuration. Rather, we must assume that the Pyramid Texts are an exact replica, on the subterranean walls of the tomb, of the texts recited during the mummification and burial rituals, and later in the offering and veneration cult. The cult is not replaced, nor is it supplemented by other texts. The cult is simply performed in two distinct media: ritual recitation and inscriptional record. By contrast, the Coffin Texts include, over and above the cult recitations, an abundance of other texts designed to equip the deceased with essential knowledge (for example, the *Book of the Two Ways*). Only where this function is found in addition to the record of the rituals can we speak of mortuary literature in the true sense of the word. Mortuary literature served a dual purpose: on the one hand, it was a magical repository for the immortalizing force (*akh*) of the rituals (a function taken over from the Pyramid Texts); on the other, it supplied the dead with knowledge they would require in the hereafter.

This second function is expressed notably in a particular category of language for which scrupulous scribes used red rather than black ink. It includes titles of spells, annotations, and instructions for use: in short, texts not designed for recitation but themselves containing information about the texts to be recited. This metatextual dimension was absent from the Pyramid Texts, where it would have been superfluous since the dead king did not himself have to make use of the texts. They were written into the burial chambers only as a supplement to and confirmation—or rather perpetualization—of the cult conducted "up above." Mortuary literature in the proper sense of the term no longer displayed this correspondence between above and below, inside and outside.

The metatextual dimension is the hallmark of magic. In Egypt, magic was religion for "domestic" use. Although entrusted to professionals, notably physicians, magic spells had to make explicit a great deal of information that, in the case of temple and tomb cult, was intrinsic to the context of the rite. At the cultic level, the purpose and location of the recitations and actions were defined by the ritual itself. Magical recitations and actions, on the other hand, were by their very nature extraneous to established ritual; they had to be conducted ad hoc in a given situation and create a context for their purpose. Hence, the spell, the "recipe," the exact prescription, is an indispensable feature of magic.

Thus the Coffin Texts, with their metatextual, magical elements, were mortuary literature in a new and more specific sense. But the Coffin Texts also continued the tradition and function of the Pyramid Texts, as they still consisted to a very large degree of cultic recitation texts placed with the dead for the purpose of perpetualization. They recorded the recitations that formed part of the cult (notably in connection with mummification and burial) and as such placed the corpse under the enduring protection and salvational power of those rituals. Many of these liturgies were taken over from the Pyramid Texts. In other words, it was largely the mortuary liturgies of the Pyramid Texts that were incorporated into the Coffin Texts. Mortuary liturgies were recitation rituals that accompanied the dead person on his passage into the hereafter and confirmed his new status in the world of the gods as one of the "transfigured dead." They were recited at the end of the mummification process, during the burial, and at festivals of the dead.

Since we are regarding the Coffin Texts as traces, we must for the moment desist from examining their content and ask first what their existence as such has to tell us. As we have seen, the emergence of mortuary literature is a pointer to the new dominance of magic over cult, a development also reflected in the "models." But the incorporation of the Pyramid Texts further testifies that the protective walls previously put up around the privileges and knowledge reserved for the king had fallen. The tomb owners of the First Intermediate Period had clearly gained access to the scrolls kept in the royal archives—in itself an obvious indication of discontinuity. True, there is no caesura in the king-lists at this point, but the kings of this period did not hold the same office as before. And this change related not only to the access to immortality formerly exclusive to that office—an access that the corresponding rites and texts had now made available to a broader literate elite—but also to the divine character of the office as a whole.

A recent systematic study by Stephan Seidlmayer of the "cemeteries between the Old and the Middle Kingdom" centers on the emergence of a new kind of tomb. "In the sphere of the great tombs," Seidlmayer writes, "the social framework changes radically in the late Old Kingdom. The Egyptians started building tombs catering for the burial of a greatly extended group of persons."[1] This change in tomb architecture may be interpreted as a reflection of the emergence of a new social type we have already encountered: the patron.

In comparative sociology, a patron is one who exercises power not by virtue of any office in an established, superordinate hierarchy, but on the grounds of his own ability to provide for a number of other persons and hence assure their dependence. The institutions of patronage require a certain structure, which we might term "vertical solidarity." We find ample evidence of this in the messages of the First Intermediate Period. Of immediate interest here is the formal side, as reflected in the archaeological traces. The new type of collective tombs had what Seidlmayer calls a "hierarchic structure." There was a main burial and a number of subsidiary burials; thus the structure of the burials mirrors the system of patronage within which they took place. Here again we see how the tombs of the First Intermediate Period turn external relations inward. The individual tombs in the elite cemeteries of the Old Kingdom also displayed a hierarchic structure reflecting the prevailing system of social relations. There were clear distinctions between center and periphery, privileged and less privileged locations. These social relations determined the position of the tombs, probably also their size and the lavishness of their equipment, but not their internal form.

But the tombs not only reflect a change in social structures, they also reflect a new sense of identity at the level of message, as Seidlmayer stresses. The emergence of local traditions suggests both the disappearance of a superordinate canon and the emergence of a local aristocracy that actively endeavored to present itself in formal idioms of its own.

Summarizing what these traces have to tell us, we can say that they point to a fundamental cultural and political change. The decline of the center had its counterpart in the upswing of the periphery; the demise of a universal canon went hand in hand with the rise of local traditions. Memphite traditions endured in Lower Egypt until well into the Ninth Dynasty; they then yielded to new forms developing simultaneously in Upper Egypt.

5

MESSAGES

T HE TRADITION OF BIOGRAPHICAL INSCRIPTIONS consti-
tutes the "messages" of the First Intermediate Period that most
bespeak the objectives and motives of the age's protagonists, their
idea of what is meaningful, and the prospects they envisage. Already
during the Old Kingdom, the ancient Egyptian literocracy had developed this type of "monumental discourse" into a unique instrument
of self-representation. In the Middle Kingdom, biographical inscription became the starting point for a literature that went beyond
self-representation to become a medium of self-reflection, self-
illumination, and also self-enhancement. The First Intermediate
Period was not a caesura in this tradition, but rather an unequaled
flowering. Here is an epoch of Egyptian history that remains a dark
age to the historian of events, but whose conceptions of meaning and
view of itself are vividly illuminated by its biographical inscriptions.
These messages communicate a collective semantics quite distinct
from the paradigms of meaning prevalent in the Old Kingdom.

In their autobiographical inscriptions, the protagonists of the
First Intermediate Period draw a very gloomy picture of their times,
not least in order to present their own salutary actions in a period of
general hardship in an all the more radiant light. Regardless of the
historical accuracy of this picture, it is an indispensable part of the
new semantic configuration of the age. The basic problem implicit in
all these inscriptions is the sudden disappearance of the kingship,
which traditionally motivated and recompensed the achievements
vaunted by tomb owners. In the inscriptions of the First Intermediate

Period, this void is now filled by other means. Frequently, appointment by the king is replaced by a new motif of "appointment" by a god. The absence of a "commission" from higher places is filled by strong claims to personal initiative. The first person singular is foregrounded as the source of forward-looking design and implementation, an emphasis completely alien to the inscriptions of the Old Kingdom and much less prominent in the Middle Kingdom. The absence of the motivating authority of the king sparked off a whole new philosophy of human agency, featuring a self-image that derived meaning from within rather than without. My theory is that the semantic paradigms and the image of kingship encountered in the Middle Kingdom go back not to the Old Kingdom but to the semiologies of the First Intermediate Period and the symbolism and subject of its messages.

Instead of a compendium culled from the hundreds of inscriptions preserved from the period,[2] I propose looking at an extensive excerpt from one of the tomb inscriptions of Ankhtifi of Mo'alla, governor of the third nome of Upper Egypt, who lived during the Ninth Dynasty.[3] Ankhtifi recounts how he was summoned to the nome of Edfu by the god Horus to establish a new order; he describes the conditions he found there:

> I came upon the house of Khuy,[4] flooded like a new land [?],
> neglected by the one responsible for it,
> in the grip of an insurgent and under the planning of a good-for-
> nothing.

The description of the havoc reigning in the area provides a suitably dismal backdrop against which the author's achievements in restoring order can shine all the more brightly. This motif typical of later royal inscriptions apparently originated with the nomarchs and magnates and was then adopted as part of the self-representation of the kings of the Middle Period.[5] The ruler figures as a restorer of order, as a rescuer in times of need; his assumption of power is equated with a turn toward salvation. But even a king never called an unworthy predecessor by name.

> I caused a man to embrace the murderer of his father or of his
> brother,
> in order to give new order to the nome of Edfu.

How beautiful was the day I found salvation in this nome.
I shall not permit the heat [of anger] to gain sway over it
after the abolition of all bad deeds, which people hate to
    commit.

Ankhtifi presents the restoration of order against a background of internecine strife reminiscent of civil war, as the phrase "murderer of his father or of his brother" suggests. Such violent strife corresponds closely to the image of the period that the kings of the Middle Kingdom took over and to which their court poets gave full literary treatment. Just as Ankhtifi describes the conditions in Edfu, so the poets depict conditions in the First Intermediate Period—though so bold an image as the embrace between murderers and victims is nowhere to be found in their writing. The following section exemplifies the new heights of self-glorification achieved in the medium of monumental discourse:

I am the beginning and the end of the people,
who found a saying where there was none,
at the head of the land, due to my wise planning;
with skillful mouth and stout heart
on the day of the unification of the three nomes.
I am a hero without peer,
who speaks according to his voice [who speaks frankly and
    freely] when the Pat [the dignitaries] keep quiet,
on the day when fear is instilled
and Upper Egypt lapses into silence.

The phrases "I am the beginning and the end of the people" and "I am a hero without peer" recur like a refrain throughout the text. Such repetitions are a typical feature of Egyptian poetry. We must therefore assume that the text intends to convey an impression of ambitious literary organization, perhaps in the style of a heroic lay.

As for each of those over whom I held my hand,
over none of them ever came misfortune
because of the secrecy of my heart and the excellence of my
    planning.
But as for every ignoramus and every wretch
who rises up against me,

he will receive in accordance with what he has given.
Woe! they say about him whom I have set up [brought before
    the court and proved to be a rebel];
his board takes water like a boat.
I am a hero without peer.

This section celebrates loyalty as a central element in the new ideology
of patronage. The commitment of the client to his patron originated
in his own free will. He was not born into this relationship or otherwise obliged to enter into it. He chose to cast his lot with a patron
because he was convinced of that patron's superior abilities. Thus,
from the point of view of the patron, mankind was divided into the
faithful, the dissidents, and the ignoramuses. Allegiance to the patron
meant security: "over him comes no misfortune," as the text repeatedly intones. History and the future were realms of menace from
which the only safeguard was refuge with the patron, whose circum-
spect and wise planning provided protection.[6] Again, the inscriptions
of the Old Kingdom are completely devoid of this kind of pessimism.
The phrase "never came misfortune over me" is extremely frequent
in inscriptions of the First Intermediate Period and is symptomatic
of the temper of the age.[7]
    The following section reaches new heights of self-glorification,
unparalleled not only in this particular text but, as far as I can judge,
in the entire history of biographical inscriptions.

I am the beginning and the end of the people,
for one equal to me has not appeared and will not appear,
one equal to me has not been born and will not be born,
I have outdone what the forefathers did,
and [my successors?] will not rival me in anything I have done,
in millions of years.

Though such a paean to the peerlessness, uniqueness, and unrepeat-
ability of the author's own achievements is never again to be encountered, the inscription's general tenor is typical of the magnates and
patrons of the First Intermediate Period, who owed their advancement not to the favor of kings but to their own energy and accom-
plishments. This sense of personal uniqueness also finds its way into
the royal imagery of the Middle Kingdom, but there the individualism

and self-magnification exemplified by this inscription is counter-
poised by the ethic of self-effacement typical of the later period. Here
we are still in the presence of a "violent-hearted one" of the kind that
was later to become anathema to the ideal of self-deprecation prevalent in the Middle Kingdom.

> For if this troop of Hefat is content,
> then this land too is quiet.
> But if anyone treads on my tail as on a crocodile,
> then the north and the south of this whole land will tremble.
> When I reach for my oars [= sail downstream]
> I find the herds of cattle penned in and the bolt closed.
> When I set sail [= sail upstream] in the direction of the Thinite
>   nome
> against one who has forgotten himself,
> then I find him, the watchers on the walls.
> When I surge into battle, "Woe!" is what he cries, the wretch.
> I am the hero without peer.

Nowhere in his inscriptions does Ankhtifi speak of his military
exploits, only of the fear that his very arrival strikes into the hearts
of his foes. The forays in question were punitive expeditions carried
out against those who had "forgotten themselves," that is, who were
not mindful of their duties to their superiors.

> I bade the *qenbet* of the Overseer of Upper Egypt come,
> which resides in Ta-wer,
> to confer
> with the count and chief priest,
> nomarch of Hierakonpolis, Hetep.
> This was not found done by other nomarchs
> who had been in this nome.
> Because of my excellent planning and my lasting speech,
> my concern by day and by night,
> I am the hero without peer.

To understand why Ankhtifi is so emphatic about the extraordinary
nature of what might appear to us a rather insignificant measure, it
is necessary to know that Abydos was the seat of government of the
Ninth Dynasty. The *qenbet* of This was a kind of regional court, here

described as coming all the way from Abydos to Mo'alla to confer
with Hetep, Ankhtifi's father. Ankhtifi's ability to command such
attention is reported as a feat worthy of being recorded for all time
and an event unprecedented in the annals of the nome.

> The prince and count, the commander of the troops
> Ankhtifi the Strong says:
> But then came the general of the troops of Armant and spoke:
> Come then, you hero, [free] the fortresses [. . .]
> thereupon I journeyed northward through the western territories
>   of Armant.
> There I found the whole Theban nome and the nome of Koptos
> as they [took] the fortresses of Armant on the heights of
>   Sekhemsen.
> When I arrived there,
> I tensed my arms like a harpoon
> in the snout of a fleeing hippopotamus.
> Then I journeyed upstream to destroy their fortresses
> with the troops of Mo'alla.
> I am the hero without peer.

The "poetic" quality of the images in this account of the war against
Thebes is noteworthy: the harpoon in the snout of a fleeing hippopotamus, the crocodile whose tail gets trod on. Crocodile and hippopotamus are animals symbolizing aggressiveness and wildness; as
such they belong to the sphere of Seth, not of Horus.

> I journeyed downstream with my trusty young squad
> and landed in the west of Thebes.
> The head of the fleet was at the hill of Sekhemsen
> the end of the fleet was at the estate of Tjemii.
> The trusty young squad sought battle
> in the whole Theban nome,
> but no one came out for fear of it.
> Then I journeyed downstream and landed in the east of Thebes,
> the end of the fleet was at the tomb of Imbi,
> the head of the fleet was at the Wiese Sega,
> whose walls were besieged,
> as "he" upon sighting it had closed the bolts out of fear.
> Thereupon this strong and trusty young squad became a search
>   commando

scouring the west and the east of Thebes
in quest of battle, but no one came out for fear of it.
I am a hero without peer.

The description of the enemy's fear and the transformation of Ankhtifi's crack military unit into a "search commando" combing the fields for someone to fight is clearly ironical and not without an element of comedy.

As for every ruler who will rule in Mo'alla
and who will perform an evil bad action against this tomb,
and against any monuments of this house,
his arm shall be cut off for Hemen when he sets out
any stela—his arm shall be cut off for Hemen when he sets out
any east side—his arm shall be cut off for Hemen when he sets
    out
any meal—his arm shall be cut off for Hemen when he sets out
any sacrifice [?]—his arm shall be cut off for Hemen when he
    sets out
any great thing [?],
may Hemen not accept his sacrifice
on the day of every slaughter.
May Hemen accept nothing of his property,
his heir shall not inherit from him.

This inscription belongs to the genre of curses on tomb robbers, which plays only a marginal role in the Old Kingdom and the later periods but a very significant one in the First Intermediate Period and the early Middle Kingdom.[8] It bespeaks the insecurity of a period in which trust in the state's ability to guard over the tombs had been severely undermined; in response, the role of the gods as both owners of the land and legal authorities had grown proportionately. What is highly unusual about this text, however, is that instead of the customary maledictions aiming at the total destruction of the interloper it opts for a form of punishment that although cruel is limited in scope. The inscription is not, then, a curse in the normal sense but the announcement of laws; malediction and jurisdiction intermingle in a curious way.

For I have set up this tomb
and all monuments of this house

with my own arms,[9]
for there is no one else's door and no one else's pillar in this
    tomb.
For I have taught Upper Egypt to fight
and this land to seal its heart.
I have given reason to be praised for my strong doors,
my doors and coffins,
for I had made this coffin of wood
from the forest of the Nome of Two Lords [Koptos].
None shall say the same of themselves!
I am indeed the hero without peer.

The inviolability of the tomb precinct was traditionally justified by
reference to the rightfulness of its erection, which in turn rested on
strict respect for others' property.[10] There was a ban on the reuse of
any parts of older tombs; hence the emphasis on everything having
been done by the tomb owner.

I gave the hungry bread
and clothing to the naked,
I anointed the unanointed,
I shod the barefoot,
I gave him a wife who had no wife.

Up to this point, Ankhtifi has remained more or less within the confines of traditional idealized autobiography. But now he moves on to
his achievements as a beneficent provider, achievements that transcend the norms of customary generosity associated with "vertical
solidarity" and form a significant part of the new image of the patron
and magnate:

I kept Mo'alla and [Hor-mer] alive,
when the heavens were clouded and the land in storm;
[everyone died] of hunger
on this sandbank of Apopis.
[The south arrived where I was] with its people,
the north came with its children.
It brought this fine oil to barter [?] for my Upper Egyptian
    barley,
which was given to it.

My Upper Egyptian barley it was that traveled upstream and
    reached Wawat,
that traveled downstream and reached This.
All Upper Egypt died of hunger.
Everyone ate their children.
But never did I permit it to happen that anyone died of hunger
    in this nome.
I have given Upper Egypt a loan of seed
and lent Upper Egyptian barley to Lower Egypt.
One can find nothing like this [done] by earlier rulers.
Never has any other commander of troops of this nome done
    the like.
But I have kept the house of Elephantine alive,
I have kept Iat-Negen alive in these years,
after Mo'alla and Hor-mer were content.
One can find nothing like this [done] by my fathers and
    forefathers.
I was a mountain for Mo'alla
and a cool shade for Hor-mer.

This whole land has become a locust in the wind.
The one journeys downstream,
the other upstream,
but I never permitted that one full of sorrow from this nome
    should end up in another nome.
I am [a hero without peer].

Famine and provision were typical subjects of the inscriptions of the
First Intermediate Period. Provision for one's nome in times of hardship was the prime source of legitimacy for the rule exercised by these
magnates. While "sandbank" was a traditional metaphor for famine,
"sandbank of Apopis" is notably unconventional. Apopis is the enemy
of the sun who—in the form of a huge water snake—threatens to
drink the sea of heaven dry, producing shallows and sandbanks that
hinder the progress of the sun bark and bring it to a standstill. The
metaphor projects local disaster onto a cosmic plane.

    The "sandbank" metaphor has normally been taken to mean that
the famines were due to insufficient Nile risings—that is, to natural
causes. The noteworthy achievement of the nomarchs would then be
to have stored enough grain in good years to survive the lean years—

the motif of the legend of Joseph. But one of the nomarchs, Khety of Assiut (Tomb V), boasts of a different feat: the introduction of artificial irrigation. He had a canal ten cubits wide dug so that certain fields could be irrigated—estates on which agricultural workers did forced labor. With this innovation he was able to ensure the provision of his nome:

> I am one with abundant northern barley—[but now] there is a [general] rise in price—one who provides the city with food [. . .]. I let northern barley be carried away for themselves by the citizen and his wife, by the widow and her son. . . ."

With these (and numerous similar) texts as sources, as clues and traces of real events, we can only conclude that there must have been famines and food shortages in Egypt at that time. And yet we must insist that the fact of famine is not the primary message of these texts; they are not concerned to provide an accurate record of shortages but to document the personal achievements of the tomb owner. The deprivation motif is merely the background for the speaker's recitation of achievement.

Ankhtifi's inscription continues with a form of self-praise that takes us away from the historical level to the plane of more general self-characterization:

> I am a noble and lord of riches,
> I am an Apis and lord of cattle,
> a Sekhat-Hor and lord of goats,
> a Nepri and lord of Upper Egyptian grain,
> a Tayt [weaving goddess] and lord of garments.

The comparison of the self with the deities is a further innovative aspect of these texts. A close parallel to Ankhtifi's text is found on the stela of Mentuhotep in London:

> I am a son of Nepri, a spouse of Tayt,
> one who has bred cattle for Sekhat-Hor.
> A lord of riches in all precious stones,
> a Mekhenet and a Khnum, who creates men."

Ankhtifi appears to have been aware of the audacity of his comparison with the gods, for he carries on with the following protestation:

> I say all this as truth;
> it is not as with the offices of the necropolis.

"Offices of the necropolis" is a frequent expression in the inscriptions of this period.[13] It refers to titles, functions, and services appropriated in the inscriptions but never actually borne or performed in the tomb owner's lifetime. Here "offices of the necropolis" is unmasked as a kind of fiction. The tomb owner—a member of a new class of power holders—explicitly pillories the self-representation of those officials who claimed for themselves countless functions of a more and more fictional nature; his disapproval is characteristic of the later stages of the Old Kingdom.

In the following sentences we encounter the motif of "saving justice":

> I rescued the weak from the strong,
> I gave ear to the matter of the widow.

This leitmotif of vertical solidarity had already appeared in the biographical inscriptions of the Sixth Dynasty.[14] The subject is therefore not an expression of a new awareness peculiar to the First Intermediate Period. But it does play a major role in the autobiographies of the time.[15]

> I was the mouth of the army for these
> to the frontier of Elephantine and to the frontier of Armant and
>   Iusut.
> Never came misfortune over me.
> I was the mouth of the army of recruits in Mo'alla
> and in every region to which it was dangerous to descend.
> Never came misfortune over me
> because of my strong bow and my excellent planning.
> But who listened to my counsel,
> over him came no misfortune.
> Who heeded me, praised god.
> But who heeded me not said: "Woe!" . . .

... is what he did.
For I am the protection of the timorous
and the fortress of him who had fled far.
I am a hero [without peer].

Here the loyalty commandment is reiterated with the utmost clarity. Individual fortune or misfortune is dictated by the decision for or against the patron, for or against obedience. Those who cast their lot with the patron and maintain allegiance to him have nothing more to fear: over them will come no misfortune. Those who ignore his counsel will live to regret it. The polarization of society into friend and foe reflects the contingency of the patron-client relationship: it was possible to plump for a different patron or to attempt to get by without a patron. Subjection to one particular patron was not an inevitable form of social obligation, but a decision. The patron had rivals vying with him; hence the demand for loyalty. He was a "jealous" lord, in the biblical sense of the term. Indeed, it was this jealousy that motivated the grandiose autobiographies of the nomarchs, which contrast so strikingly with the wordless architectural memorials of the kings of the Old Kingdom.

Seldom does the interaction between social and semantic change appear so distinctly as in the messages of the First Intermediate Period. With his constant concern to assure the allegiance of his clientele, the new social type, the patron, develops a correspondingly new rhetoric—a rhetoric characterized by the terms "crisis," "salvation," and "decision." True, Ankhtifi was more than just a patron: he was a nomarch. But in his attempts to extend his sphere of influence to other nomes and to incorporate them into his clientele, he made use of the new rhetoric.

The rhetoric of crisis and salvation foregrounds the patron as a savior whose achievements have preserved the nome from the certain disaster seen everywhere else. This rhetoric is by its very nature a rhetoric of stark simplification: the greater the crisis, the greater the savior. It is the intention behind these texts that is at issue here, not the degree to which they represent reality. Our concern is not just with the historical facts that might have produced the rhetoric of crisis, but also with the reason why this subject was given such prominence and to what end. The explanation resides in the new socio-semantic paradigm of the patron and the rhetoric of salvation.

Naturally, these texts were not completely without foundation in reality; otherwise they could not have achieved their purpose. It is indeed a supremely plausible assumption that the Egyptian economic system was dependent on a "strong man." The self-regulatory mechanisms of a market economy operating on a small geographical scale had been systematically dismantled in the Old Kingdom and transformed into the wide-ranging structures of a centralist planned economy that could not possibly function without some kind of organization. The collapse of economic organization by the state created a planning and supply vacuum in which the magnates of the First Intermediate Period could establish themselves. They represented this vacuum as a state of chaos.

The same stark simplification is found in the rhetoric of decision that sets off the well-being of the loyals against the dreadful fate of the ignoramuses and renegades. The contrast between chaos and order is "anthropologized," as a judgment upon individuals and their fates; it is represented as an expression of the resolutions and attitudes of the people. Again, it is not the real hardship prevailing in the land that is at issue but the "biographical" hardship that will strike the individual if he makes the wrong decision. The rhetoric of decision represents the anthropologization of the idea of salvation. The patron becomes the beneficent lord over individual destinies.

This anthropologizing strategy hinges on the construction of a connection between action and personal destiny, doing and faring, which in fact represents the most important aspect of this new semiology. If personal welfare is a matter of making the right decision, then the responsibility for happiness or misfortune rests entirely with the individual. Hence the insistence with which the voices of this period protest that "never misfortune came over them." Misfortune and happiness are both just deserts. Good fortune is the unmistakable attribute of one who has chosen the right patron and served him loyally. In the rhetoric of decision the patron presents himself as the biographical savior able to protect his dependents from disaster and assure their good future.

6

MEMORIES

THE RULERS OF THE MIDDLE KINGDOM adopted the "patronal" semiology of the First Intermediate Period, with its rhetoric of crisis, salvation, and decision. Just as the magnates and nomarchs of the First Intermediate Period vaingloriously legitimized their actions as the aversion of present and ubiquitous disaster, so the state of the Middle Kingdom legitimized itself with reference to the aversion of past disaster—disaster now portrayed in the form of a memory of the First Intermediate Period. The Middle Kingdom needed the First Intermediate Period as a locus of chaos from which it could set itself off as savior by adopting the semiologies of that same First Intermediate Period; it had to memorialize the idea of chaos. But whereas the nomarchs, magnates, condottieri, and patrons of the First Intermediate Period made reference to this disaster as a reality prevailing everywhere except where they themselves held sway, the rulers of the Middle Kingdom had only the memory of the past. They held sway everywhere, so there were no contemporaneous conditions of chaos against which they could set themselves off. In a united kingdom there are no "others" dogged by ill-fortune; foreign countries were beyond the pale for comparative purposes. Thus "otherness," in the form of hardship averted by the king, was stylized into a fiction anchored in the past.

This extension of crisis from the immediate environment and its provision of problems to the whole "world" is mirrored by the expansion of the description of chaos from a subsidiary motif within a larger argumentative context to a literary form in its own right.

Such an expansion could only take place at the level of pharaonic responsibility for the world, for only the pharaoh could avert global disaster, only the pharaoh could restore order and balance in a world out of joint and threatening to fly apart. At the pharaonic level, the rhetoric of salvation developed into the messianic form of political self-representation central to the semiologies of the Middle Kingdom. The acute sense of mission we find in the Twelfth Dynasty is nothing other than the intensified and generalized form of the patronal ideology of the First Intermediate Period.

The messianic political temper of the Twelfth Dynasty is exemplified by a text known as the *Prophecies of Neferti,* which gives fullest expression to the role of the new state as a savior institution. In this text, welfare is no longer a matter of supply and protection, of economic and political order. The salvation theme is elevated to an all-embracing cosmic dimension.

The fictional framework is the story of King Snofru, who is seeking entertainment from a "wise man." Neferti, a typical representative of the new educated intelligentsia of the Middle Kingdom, is summoned and prophesies the future of the land, the ultimate test of wisdom. The future is set out in the form of a description of chaos, a world turned on its head. In the descriptions of chaos, three dimensions of order and coherence—three forms of "connectivity"—are portrayed as being in a state of dissolution or inversion: the cosmic order; social justice; and brotherly love.

The natural system of the elements has gone awry:

Light:
The sun is hidden and shines not so that people could see,
one cannot live when clouds shroud [it] ...
Water:
The river of Egypt is dried up, one crosses the water on foot.
The flood tuns into shore, the shore into flood.
Air:
The south wind will quarrel with the north wind
and the heavens will be one single windstorm.

The links between creator and creation break:

Re will set himself apart from the people.
Though the hour of his rising is still there,

no one knows any longer when it is noon,
for no shadow can be distinguished anymore.
No face will be blinded that looks upon him.
. . .

What is created has been destroyed.
Re can start all over again with the creation.
The land has been quite destroyed without a remnant,
not even the dirt under one's fingernails has remained
of that which Re has ordained.

The social order has been upended:

I show you the land in severe illness.
The weak is now strong,
one greets him who formerly greeted.
I show you the lowest on top, what lay on its back now has its
   belly downward.
One will live in the cemetery.
The beggar will amass treasure.
The lowly will eat bread,
the servants will be elevated.

The closest human bonds break asunder:

I show you the son as adversary, the brother as enemy,
a man who kills his father. . . .

But at last the advent of a salvation-bringer, a king, is prophesied,

who shall come from the south, Ameni by name,
the son of a woman from Ta-Seti, a child of Upper Egypt.
. . .
Then Ma'at will return to her place,
while Isfet is banished.

Controversy still rages as to how this text is to be properly understood. Some consider it the more or less historically accurate description of conditions during the First Intermediate Period.[16] Others see
it as a ritual fiction: because from the Old Kingdom onward every

king in Egypt set himself up as a guarantor of *ma'at* (truth, justice, divine order), every king had the job of establishing *ma'at* in the place of *isfet* (untruth, injustice, chaos). Hence every king enhanced his own significance with drastic fictional depictions of *isfet* remedied by his presence. An appreciation of kingship required constant confrontation with what things would be like without kingship. The "world of lamentations" is a fictional counterworld to the security and order of the Middle Kingdom. What we have here, in short, are tendentious political pamphlets without any grounding in historical fact.[17]

This theory has much in its favor and has served as a necessary corrective to the naive readings of earlier Egyptological literature; it opens our eyes to the literary character of this discourse. But this theory signally fails to explain why the lamentation genre and the motif of political chaos should have peaked in the Middle Kingdom rather than any other. If the *Prophecies of Neferti* really were nothing other than a ritualized fiction of the chaos every king had to combat, one would expect similar examples from other epochs as well. But this is not the case. The only later descriptions of political chaos that might compare come from the Third Intermediate Period (see the Papyrus Pushkin 127) and from times of Persian and Greek rule—in other words, from times of crisis when such chaos was part and parcel of daily life.

But the *Prophecies of Neferti* is neither a historical description nor a ritual ideological fiction; it is codified memory. It takes the memory by which the Middle Kingdom retrospectively transformed the First Intermediate Period and molded it into a symbol, a commemorative figure. All memory, as Maurice Halbwachs was the first to show, reconstructs the past in the parameters of the present.[18] But that does not mean that memory is a matter of pure invention. Just as no image of the past is free of reconstructive intervention, so no memory is purely phantasmagoric, devoid of any experiential ties. The past does not exist "as such," but only to the extent that it is remembered; and it is remembered—both by individuals and by cultures—to the extent that it is needed. The Twelfth Dynasty needed the First Intermediate Period as the epoch of hardships now overcome and developed the medium of literature to symbolize and hence stabilize this required memory. The literary description of chaos in the *Prophecies of Neferti* presents exactly the same picture of fear and anguish, violence and disarray, hardship and hunger that forms the backdrop for Ankhtifi's self-representation. The literary text intensifies the

image of hardship into that of a world turned on its head, a condition of complete chaos that even disrupts the natural order. The
depiction of chaos no longer forms the background for a magnate's
glorification of his merits as a provider, but now occupies the front
of the stage. In the account given by Neferti there are no savior figures; rather, the position of the magnates in the inscriptions is
taken by the future king. The relation established by the inscriptions between the general state of emergency and the refuge offered
by the patron is here placed on a temporal plane, as the relation
between an irremediable present and a redeemed future. The king—
or the institution of kingship as conceived by the Middle Period—
succeeds the nomarchs of the First Intermediate Period; he requires
the legitimization born of disastrous hardship.

Thus there is a very simple explanation for the difficulty of eval-
uating these texts as historical sources. The texts do indeed refer to
the First Intermediate Period, but from the vantage of the Middle
Kingdom. The First Intermediate Period is constructed as a period of
apocalyptic catastrophe against which the Middle Kingdom signifies
the advent of salvation. But the medium of retrospection is not historiography but lamentation or chaos description.[19] These apocalyptic
visions evoke a climate of peril and a need for protection in which
the pharaohs of the Middle Period shine out as bringers of salvation.

But the significance of the literary lamentation for a world gone
awry is not wholly encompassed by its political function within a
rhetoric of crisis. It is true that descriptions of chaos perform precisely
this function in the messages of the First Intermediate Period; and it
is also true that there are links between the messages that highlight
the salutary agency of the magnates and the *Prophecies of Neferti*, with
its announcement of the advent of the savior king. But there are also
texts that bewail a world out of joint without celebrating or proph-
esying the advent of a savior king. These texts likely reflect the experiences undergone by at least some members of the upper stratum of
society during the period of decline and form part of a "therapeutic"
literary tradition that reaches back to the Sixth and Eighth Dynasties.

Every major experience of loss precipitates heightened memory,
and this memorializing perspective on what has been forfeited gives
rise to a construction of the past. Only loss or the prospect of loss
makes us aware of the precarious nature of a world that we otherwise
take for granted as timeless. Only loss compels us to recognize our
world's historical nature. The more intensively the past is regarded as
a cherished order of things, the more the present will seem alien and

chaotic. Thus the experience of loss in relation to the past will automatically involve an experience of estrangement in relation to the
present. This experience of estrangement also finds expression in
the literary lamentation.

Take the *Admonitions of Ipuwer*, part of a manuscript from the
Ramesside Period (thirteenth century B.C.E). No parallel texts have
come down to us, but in a Ramesside tomb in Saqqara this same
Ipuwer is portrayed along with other major officials and authors of
the past, so he must have been part of the canon of Egyptian classics.[20]

Here I quote the text in the version by Bertolt Brecht, who
worked part of it into the "Song of Chaos" in his play *The Caucasian
Chalk Circle.*

> Sister, cover your face; brother, fetch your knife,
> the time is out of joint.
> The nobles are full of lament and the lowly full of joy.
> The city says: Let us drive the strong from our midst.
> The offices have been burgled, the lists of the vassals destroyed.
> The lords have been bound to the millstones.
> They who never saw day have gone out.
> The offering chests of ebony are smashed,
> the magnificent *sesnem* wood is hacked up to make beds.
> Those who had no bread now have granaries,
> those who begged alms of grain now distribute to others.
> The son of the respected is changed beyond all recognition;
> the child of the lady has become the son of her slave girl.
> The officials seek shelter in the granaries;
> those who were hardly allowed to sleep on the walls now wallow
>   in beds.
> Those who plied the oars now own boats;
> if their owner looks for them, they are no longer his.[21]

To be sure, some slight modifications were necessary before Brecht
could change the Egyptian lamentation into a triumphal paean to the
Revolution. Brecht found this source in Adolf Erman's *Literature of
the Egyptians.* Here is a literal version of Erman's translation of the
verses selected by Brecht:

> It is surely thus: the nobles are full of lament and the lowly full
>   of joy;
> every city says: let us drive the strong from our midst.

> It is surely thus: the burghers have been bound to the millstones.
> They who never saw day have come out.
> It is surely thus: the chests of ebony are smashed; the
>   magnificent *sesnem* wood is hacked up to make beds [?]
> It is surely thus: the office rooms are opened and their lists taken
>   away; the vassals have become the lords of . . .
> Behold, who had no grain now possesses granaries; who begged
>   alms of grain now distributes it himself.
> Who was not able to sleep on [?] walls now owns a bed.
> Behold, who earlier did not make himself a boat now owns ships;
>   if their owner looks for them, they are no longer his.[22]

My motive in choosing Brecht's adaptation is to show how little effort the playwright needed to redeploy his source text. Apparently the Egyptian lament at the collapse of established political order and a modern revolutionary composition are not worlds apart. An element of timelessness and universality links the two, as the Russian historian S. Luria pointed out in an article querying the assumption that the Egyptian laments were descriptions of an actual social revolution. Luria places them in an entirely different context. With reference to Sir James Frazer, he writes:

> Very many peoples on this planet annually enjoy a period of license where all social boundaries are overthrown. Not only do the slaves sit at the same table as their masters, sup with them, and behave like freeborn men and women; frequently enough things are turned topsy-turvy, with the slaves sitting at table, waited on by their masters. An even more frequent custom is to express this inversion of social relations by exchanging clothes. In such periods, the laws are out of force; criminals are amnestied. . . . Very often this upheaval is performed onstage like a sacred play.[23]

For Luria these lamentations are not historical descriptions but mythic performances. In his view, they conjure the "time of Seth" in conjunction with an annual performance of the myth of the battle between Seth and Horus. Moreover, Luria argues that even if these texts did relate to historical experiences, they avail themselves of a schematic form, a "template" that is ritually established in everyday life after the manner of annual chaos festivals like the Sumerian *akitu* or the Roman Saturnalia. Luria adduces the most astounding evidence for the timelessness and universal dissemination of this template. Among the Annamites there are songs in response to the French conquest of Indochina that closely resemble the Egyptian chaos descriptions:

> Le ciel est bas, la terre est haute,
> Ceux qui n'avaient pas de culotte ont aujourd'hui des souliers . . .
> les filles publiques sont devenues des grandes dames . . .
> les vauriens sont tout-puissants. . . .

> (The sky is low, the earth is high,
> Those who had no trousers now have shoes . . .
> the prostitutes have become fine ladies . . .
> the good-for-nothings have become all-powerful. . . .)

Of course, the allusion to chaotic revels establishes a frame of reference to which the ancient Egyptian lamentation texts may not have originally belonged. But it is remarkably well suited to the Egyptian texts and underlines their astounding universality and resonance. Today it is largely acknowledged that Saturnalian festivals did not exist in ancient Egypt, so we cannot very well speak of this literature as a proper reflection of Saturnalian ritual. The formal schema of inversion, however, has been shown to be bound up with another ritual that apparently had very little to do with anything Saturnalian; rather, it was a lament for the dead, which in Egypt frequently took the form of a confrontation between "Then" and "Now."[24] In adopting the style of a ritual dirge, the literary lamentations portray the land as dead or death-stricken, bereft of its normal order, and turned upside down.

In summary, these chaos descriptions intone a threnody on a world out of joint. They turn their gaze away from the disarray of the present; some look to the past, as in Ipuwer's admonitions:

> Remember . . . how incense was shaken,
> how water was offered in the libation vase in the morning;
> remember how *Ra* geese, *Trp* geese, and *Set* geese were brought,
> and offerings offered up to the gods.

Remember how natron was chewed and white bread prepared
by someone on the day of the anointing of the head.
Remember how flagstaffs were raised and stelae inscribed,
how the priest purified the temples and the gods' houses were
    whitewashed with white milk,
the fragrance of the "horizon" [king's tomb] was made lovely
    and the offering loaves were endowed. . . .[25]

Other chaos descriptions look to the future, as in the *Prophecies of Neferti:*

A king will come from the south,
Ameni, justified, by name,
the son of a woman from Ta-Seti,
a child of Hierakonpolis.
He will seize the white crown and put the red crown on his
    head,
he will unite the two "powerful ones" and satisfy the two lords
    with what they want.
The "field-circler" is in his fist and the oar in motion.
Rejoice, you people of his time!
The son of a man will make his name
for ever and anon.
Who plan evil and plot revolt,
their sayings shall be undone for fear of him.
The Asiatics will fall by his massacre,
and the Libyans by his flame,
the enemies by his wrath and the rebels by his force.
The uraeus* on his forehead pacifies the insurgents for him.

In the literary form of the lamentation, the experience of the First
Intermediate Period remained alive and memorially operative in the
culture of Egypt until late antiquity.

    To experience the collapse of established order is to be aware of
order's fragility. Because in Egypt this knowledge was cast into the
mold of literary works of classic status, it lived on as an intrinsic
element in the Egyptian understanding of the world.

*The royal cobra worn as part of the pharaoh's crown or headdress.

PART THREE

The Middle Kingdom

Sesostris III
Fragment (ca. 1850 B.C.E.)
(New York, Metropolitan Museum of Art)

7
HISTORICAL OUTLINE

T HE EMERGENCE OF THE MIDDLE KINGDOM mirrors that of the Old, albeit under changed circumstances. The initial foundation of the state as a unified realm, embodied in later cultural memory as the work of Menes, had been preceded by a phase of rival chiefdoms that culminated in a clear-cut dualism between north and south. One thousand years later, after the decline of the Sixth Dynasty, the kingdom once again disintegrated into regional forms of rule only nominally under the aegis of the central administration, first in Memphis, later in This. As before, rivalries led to changing arenas of conflict and changing coalitions. In terms of power and influence, the major economic providers and procurers now found themselves jockeying for position with military leaders and strategists. Again, the conflict culminated in a confrontation between north and south, centering this time on the Herakleopolitans (the Ninth and Tenth Dynasties) and the Theban nomarchs (the Eleventh Dynasty), who eventually prevailed and engineered a reunification of the land under Mentuhotep II. But this consolidation was not long-lived. After the death of the last of the Mentuhotep line, unrest flared up again and erupted in civil war. Only with the accession of Amenemhet (Ammenemes), the vizier of the last Mentuhotep, in 1991 B.C.E. and the founding of the Twelfth Dynasty did the pharaonic state regain its stability. The success of the Twelfth Dynasty rests upon a conscious and explicit revival of certain traditions of the Old Kingdom. Especially noteworthy in this respect was the fact that these kings made no attempt to rule the land from their native Thebes, but instead set up their residence further north and established a new capital and necropolis in Lisht, to the south of Memphis.

The Twelfth Dynasty represents a cultural apogee in the history of Egyptian civilization. In the New Kingdom, the literature of this period was elevated to the canonic status of classics; the language of the Middle Kingdom remained in use for sacred purposes until the end of pharaonic history; and in art the archaizing style of the Late Period largely took its bearings from the mature style of the Twelfth Dynasty. Later epochs considered the cultural achievements of the Middle Kingdom the timeless and definitive expression of Egyptian civilization.

The kings of the Twelfth Dynasty succeeded in restoring the sacral dimension of pharaonic rule in all its "terrible glory" of divine kingship. But in order to reassert the divine kingship, the rulers of the Twelfth Dynasty could not simply hark back to the disrupted traditions of the Old Kingdom, whose monarchs had reigned as gods on earth. The basis of their authority and legitimacy had required no explicit articulation or discursive justification; instead, it found overwhelming expression in the huge edifices of the pyramids and officials' tombs. The kings of the Twelfth Dynasty were in a fundamentally different position. They did not rule with a "literocracy" of educated officials over an illiterate mass, but had to assert themselves against a largely literate and economically and militarily powerful aristocracy of nomarchs, magnates, and patrons with all their wide-ranging clans and adherents. The resultant degree of social tension was unprecedented up to that point, and only rarely reached a similar pitch afterward. The political leadership now had to assert and substantiate its claims to supremacy vis-à-vis the aristocracy and win over the lower strata; it had to expound the rationale behind its aims, legitimize its own position, and provide tangible services in return for the obedience it demanded. These objectives could not be achieved by force alone, nor by the impressiveness of monumental architecture, but only by the power of eloquence and explanation. The assertion of political power was no longer a matter of apodictic self-glorification, but was accomplished via a "rhetoric of motives" that justified political measures in terms of an underlying structure of responsibility.[1] This rhetoric was by no means purely formulaic or symbolic. The ruler was aware of his "downward" responsibility and accountability; he reigned not by force but by the power of the word. "Be an artist in speech," recommends one text, "then you will be victorious. For behold: the sword-arm of a king is his tongue. Stronger is the word than all fighting."[2] The kings of the Twelfth Dynasty understood the close links between politics and the instantiation of meaning. As Carl Schmitt, a leading authority on authoritarian government, puts it: "No political system can last even as long as one generation on technical grounds or by the assertion of power alone. Central to politics is the idea, for there can be no politics without authority, and no authority without an ethos of persuasion."[3]

The kings of the Twelfth Dynasty reverted to the explicit link between rule and divinity. But they did not simply reanimate the ideas of the Old Kingdom; rather, they took up the symbolic forms of the First Intermediate Period and deployed them to express three new ideas: the status of the king as a son of god, the importance of loyalism, and the value of achievement. The idea of the ruler as son of the deity (representative theocracy) was based on the new form of legitimization employed by the nomarchs in which they represented their power as deriving explicitly from the local deities of their respective cities. The kings of the Twelfth Dynasty took this up and magnified it into the idea of prenatal ordination by the god of the state: while still in his mother's womb ("in the egg"), the king is divinely appointed son of the god and ruler over the state. The idea of loyalism goes back to the institution of patronage and the principle of vertical solidarity, or protection in return for obedience, that had developed in the First Intermediate Period. The Twelfth Dynasty elevated this ideology to the status of a religious form, a path to salvation promising faithful adherents not only success in this world but also eternal life after death. The idea of merit, finally, placed kingship in the Middle Kingdom on an entirely new plane of legitimacy, supplementing but not replacing the traditional religious foundations of sacral kingship. This notion of merit also derives from the nomarchs of the First Intermediate Period, who represented themselves as providers for the hungry, shelterers of the persecuted, fathers of orphans, husbands of widows, champions of the weak, saviors of the oppressed, and guides of those gone astray. The rulers of the Middle Period likewise portrayed themselves as saviors in times of hardship. But as there was no hardship to save anyone from at the time, they preserved the memory of the First Intermediate Period and stylized it into the chaos that their newly restored order would prevent from recurring. In their quest for achievements to legitimize them, the kings of the Middle

Kingdom went beyond safeguarding internal peace to engage in large-scale colonization projects. Nubia was brought into the sphere of pharaonic rule as far as the Second Cataract and kept in check with a system of fortresses; the Faiyum was colonized by means of a sophisticated system of sluice gates.

The reasons for the decline and fall of the Middle Kingdom are unclear. Initially, the process appears to have resembled the one leading to the demise of the Old Kingdom. The authority of central rule declined, and the king-list is full of numerous ephemeral names, an indication that there were a multitude of kings reigning at the same time.[4] The decisive event of this epoch was the seizure of power by the Hyksos, chiefs of Semitic tribes, who settled in the Delta and subjected the rest of Egypt to their rule during the seventeenth century and part of the sixteenth. Their accession spelled the end of the Middle Kingdom and ushered in the prehistory of the New.

8

STATE, SCRIPT, EDUCATION: DESPOTISM ILLUMINATED FROM WITHIN

The Birth of the Schools

THE SPIRITUAL CLIMATE of the Old Kingdom can only be guessed at. The abundance of surviving textual sources from the Middle Kingdom, on the other hand, allows us to reconstruct that particular era in greater detail than any subsequent pharaonic age; in fact, very few epochs of the ancient world have left such extensive documentation. The Middle Kingdom, or more precisely the Twelfth Dynasty, not only restored the order of sacral kingship, but also reflected upon that kingship. The Middle Kingdom redefined the position of kingship between cosmos and society, gods and humans, and also, crucially, attached the utmost importance to publicizing its qualities. To this end, the Middle Kingdom created a new genre of royal inscription that went beyond eternalizing the king's deeds and decisions to justify and laud them in a propagandistic way. In addition, the kings of the Middle Kingdom drew on another genre—literature—and developed it for their purposes. While literary texts have, of course, survived from later epochs as well, they rarely if ever display the political, propagandistic dimension peculiar to works from the Middle Period. The close association between literature and politics is exclusive to the Middle Kingdom; politics, rhetoric, and literature combine in a way that is unique in the entire history of Egyptian civilization.[5] Accordingly, the Egyptian state of the Middle Kingdom was a political organism displaying a very high degree of self-awareness and self-reflection.

At this point it is necessary to enlarge on two concepts that may initially appear anachronistic and incongruous: "politics" and "propaganda." In the context of ancient Egypt, "politics" means a cohesive structure that incorporates the individual into society and relates society to the authority of the pharaoh. In the Middle Kingdom this cohesive structure had a different complexion from that of the Old Kingdom. It adopted the loyalty principle introduced by the patrons of the First Intermediate Period, and extended that principle into a full-fledged ideology of royal service or loyalism. Instead of "ideology" we could with equal justice use the term "religion." For after the secularization of royal rule in the First Intermediate Period, the king now figured once again as the incarnation and the son of god on earth.[6] Now, however, there was a new emphasis on the status of the king as one "chosen" by the gods. Further, not only was the ideology of the patrons from the First Intermediate Period magnified to a scale commensurate with the entirety of the Egyptian state, it was also explicitly formulated, set down in writing, and disseminated. This form of "annunciation to the heathens" can with some justification be termed "propaganda" in the sense in which that term is used in Catholic missionary theology.[7] Its aim was the normative and formative dissemination of the loyalist religion. The medium of this dissemination was literature in a new and specific sense of the word, a combination of "messages" and "memories" with which the Middle Kingdom fashioned for itself, for later epochs, and hence for us today, a much more detailed and differentiated image of itself than anything we have for other epochs of Egyptian history.

The texts that constitute this genre of literature have come down to us not as inscriptions but in manuscript form, on papyri, tablets, and ostraca. None of these manuscripts dates back earlier than the Middle Kingdom, and much evidence indicates that literature as a division of written Egyptian culture originated in this period.

A wider perspective can illuminate this phenomenon. In Egypt, writing initially developed, broadly speaking, in two areas: administration and temple cult. Official records and rituals were the genres in which the scribes refined the mastery of their trade to the level of virtuosity. Red and black script, vertical and horizontal lines, split columns, rubrics, tables, and much else that had developed in the bureaucracy and in the temples was taken over from there into other areas of written culture—for example, the extensive field of "mortuary literature."[8] Originally, the "art" of literature had no place in all this; it remained the specialized preserve of the myth narrators and storytellers, the singers and musicians, the purveyors of the sagas, legends, and anecdotes that exist in all mnemonic cultures.[9] In its early stages, Egypt too was a mnemonic culture, which transmitted its cultural knowledge through the channels of oral traditions. Only certain areas were entrusted to written culture: bureaucracy, with its plethora of contingent data beyond the powers of memory; religious rites, where the smallest error could have fateful consequences; and finally mortuary literature, where writing functioned as a substitute for memory and speech.

Around the turn from the third to the second millennium, when bureaucracy and priesthood were restored and reorganized following the collapse of the Old Kingdom, a third subdivision of written culture appeared, consisting of texts that we normally group under the heading of "literature": narratives, wisdom literature, lamentations, dialogues, hymns, and panegyrics.[10] As these texts had no bearing on the concerns of officialdom or the temples, it is tempting to interpret the domain they developed in as a "sphere of license" that transcended functional expediency and was located at a higher level—a praxis-reflexive or "meta-practical" form of discourse not restricted to pragmatic contexts or strictly bound up with specific functions.[11] This is not entirely erroneous; however, the texts in question were *not* produced within a sphere of license, but within the domain of the schools, which were no less purpose-oriented and rule-governed than the temples or officialdom.

"School" in the ancient Egyptian sense was something very different from what comes to mind when we use the term today. There were no professional teachers; literacy and numeracy were acquired by apprenticeship at the centers of written culture, the major administrative offices and the temple scriptoria. Beginners received instruction in small groups; more advanced learners became assistants to high-ranking officials or priests.[12] There were no teaching manuals. The ability to write was acquired through learning texts by rote and rewriting them from memory, pericope by pericope. Thus learning to write automatically meant acquiring a fund of established knowledge. But that knowledge—and this is a point of cardinal importance— was not a form of specialized expertise that ensured the correct performance of administrative or religious duties. Rather, it was knowledge of the fundamental normative and formative attitudes of Egyptian culture, the acquisition of which made an apprentice scribe into an educated, well-brought-up, right-thinking Egyptian. To know these texts by heart (the Egyptian expression means literally "giving them into one's heart") was to be in possession of the basic cultural attitudes, interpretative patterns, and value systems that constitute an "invisible religion."[13] The literary knowledge gained in an Egyptian school was akin to our notion of literature not by virtue of its "poetic license"—its "aesthetic" or "fictional" character—but by virtue of a high degree of universal reference that transcended mere functional expertise. Literature fulfilled a dual role. On the one hand, it disseminated a cultural program that made students not only into scribes but also into cultivated Egyptians and committed servants of the state. On the other, it served the society of the Middle Kingdom as a medium of self-illumination. The term "propaganda" would indeed be too restrictive if we were to use it in the sense of "political indoctrination from above," for these texts were addressed not only to court officials and royal subjects but also to the kings themselves. They conveyed a comprehensive educational program for the king and his subjects alike and encouraged profound reflection on the fundamental structure of society, extending even to the position and role of the king within the larger community.

Wisdom and Education

WISDOM LITERATURE CONCERNED ITSELF with social norms in the broadest sense. The codification of these norms in the medium of the new literature ushered in a far-reaching shift in the communicative economics of Egyptian culture. The ideal scribe was no longer merely a competent administrator, bureaucrat, or ritualist; rather, he was educated, scholarly, wise.[14] Cultural knowledge, in its central sense as binding norms of behavior, was encoded in written form. Learning to write meant more than learning to plan, organize, and administer; it meant—in a very broad sense—learning to live. The changes this occasioned can hardly be overestimated. What was hitherto intangible was now rendered visible—and in a double sense. Knowledge of how to behave, formerly communicated orally, was now codified in writing. Cultural skills previously conveyed implicitly, by observation and example, were now conveyed explicitly and discursively. In traditional societies, correct behavior is not usually inculcated in writing but is rather a matter of demonstration and imitation. To put proper behavior in words and set it down in writing is tantamount to changing "propriety" from a matter of unthinking imitation to a consciously acquired, self-reflective way of life.[15] The principles of "right living" are thus transferred from the "mimetic" plane to that of "cultural memory."[16]

The texts codifying these norms are called instructions and invariably feature a father teaching his son. The instruction is both initiatory and testamentary in character. The aged father draws together the sum of his experience and passes it on to the son. Both father and son stand at the threshold of social and vocational existence, but while the father is about to depart, the son is about to enter. The father's instructions claim a general validity; they refer not to specific skills or "tricks of the trade" but to the totality of social existence—a codification of social competence, rather than a simple prescription.

Looking to Israel for a moment, we may remind ourselves that the Book of Deuteronomy has a very similar ambit. Moses, the teacher and lawgiver, stands at the threshold of death, just as the people of Israel—the tutelary collective—is on the point of crossing the Jordan and entering into the Promised Land. At this point, there is a recapitulation of the totality of commandments, regulations, and statutes designed to form the foundation of life in the Holy Land and make Israel "a wise and understanding people" (Deuteronomy 4:6). The fundamental difference between Israel and Egypt is that for the Israelites the commandments did *not* codify the norms prevailing in the world around them. The commandments came from Sinai; they were part of an extraterritorial, revealed order. Very different norms were operative in the land of Canaan. The Israelites were not only prohibited from adapting to those norms, but were instructed to set themselves apart in the strictest possible way, thus to live in accordance with extraterritorial norms. In Egypt, by contrast, the student scribes were initiated into the norms native to the world they were about to enter. Adaptation to the prevailing norms was the criterion of success.

In the ancient Egyptian world the implicit form of initiation into "right living" through imitation doubtless existed alongside an oral tradition of instruction explicitly conveyed by the fathers.[17] This traditional paternal practice provided the fictional framework for wisdom literature, allowing the content to be cast in terms of a familiar everyday situation. From this stock situation the authors could derive a number of features: the authority of the father, the wisdom inherent in a review of life on the threshold of death, the earnest nature of the initiation, the normative claim of paternal injunctions, and of course the intimate character of the father-son relation, which makes the "instruction" into something akin to a second act of procreation, now at the spiritual and intellectual level.[18]

The emergence of this kind of literature was an integral part of the project of reorganizing the Egyptian state undertaken in the Twelfth Dynasty.[19] Only then did instructions advance to the status of the central cultural texts of the Egyptian world. The decisive argument for dating them to the Twelfth Dynasty is that the ethics of integration and self-effacement espoused in them accord with the Middle Kingdom but not with the Old Kingdom. Further, the instructions are not our only textual evidence; we also have hundreds of biographical inscriptions in which tomb owners stand accountable for their lives. The social norms underlying these inscriptions are the same as those set out in a codified form in the instructions. In the Old Kingdom this motif of accountability only figures, and then very succinctly, in a comparatively minor subset of the inscriptions, the so-called ideal biographies. These inscriptions limit themselves to a rigid canon of identical concrete actions that stand—pars pro toto— for the whole sphere of moral integrity and social norms and conventions: bread for the hungry, clothes for the naked, a boat for the boatless, a coffin for the coffinless, in short the entire range of charitable, beneficial actions that, although by no means marginal, were only a part of the overall ethical system. The comparatively low degree of conceptual differentiation, abstraction, and explicitness displayed by the admonitions to "be virtuous" suggests that this aspect of moral instruction was still in a formative state. Most conspicuous by its absence is what I call "instruction of the heart," a theory of the inner man with a vocabulary of virtues, mentalities, and idealistic values, among which those pertaining to self-effacement were later to play the most important role.

The ethic of self-effacement, integration, and altruism is certainly fundamental to civilization in Egypt; and everything seems to indicate that the practical ethics of the Old Kingdom was already imbued with such values. But in the Old Kingdom these principles were imparted either orally in the form of proverbs and sayings or else remained implicit—simply presupposed as immutable and axiomatically valid. The collapse of the Old Kingdom called all these values into question. In the biographical inscriptions of the First Intermediate Period it is not selfless subordination that is praised, but "entrepreneurial" virtues. In the fore is the image of the patron who braves times of hardship and keeps his clients or even the whole nome alive; in short, alternative concepts of order are expressed that developed in the aftermath of the collapse of pharaonic rule. The First Intermediate Period was the heyday of the nomarchs, magnates, and condottieri of rival courts—an entirely different Egypt, which the Middle Kingdom and its program of restorative recentralization set out to combat. Wisdom literature, with its codification of social norms, was central to this project, intimately associated with the reorganization of the state as a monocracy and theocracy. Norms of social action and behavior are typically written out and codified at a juncture when the "mimetic tradition" has broken off and no models survive that actually embody those norms; when the validity of those norms can no longer be taken for granted; and when it becomes necessary to disseminate them beyond the immediate circle of those who continue to represent and sustain them.

These three points chart the dimension of the problems facing the Middle Kingdom. On the one hand, it was necessary to reestablish the norms of integrative ethics and self-effacement so radically challenged by the collapse of the Old Kingdom. On the other, these norms had to be universalized: the ethic of a tiny privileged minority had to be transformed into the ethic of a broad cultural elite representing Egyptian ideals and sustaining the existence of the state. Something akin to "education" was needed. Indeed, the Middle Kingdom was the first to find that it required a systematic education policy as part of its project of political restoration.

Solidarity and Memory

EGYPTIAN HAS A GENERIC TERM for the totality of all social norms: *ma'at*. As a translation of this term I propose "connective justice."[20] The principle of "connective justice" is not an achievement of the Middle Kingdom alone; it holds for Egyptian civilization in general. The Middle Kingdom was merely the epoch in which *ma'at* was first explicitly formulated in a way that was to become binding for all later epochs. The Old Kingdom certainly lived by the same semiology; the word *ma'at* recurs repeatedly in its "messages." But these inscriptions do not reveal the full meaning of *ma'at*, which was only developed discursively in the literature of the Middle Kingdom. A royal inscription from the Thirteenth Dynasty (ca. 1700 B.C.E.)

explicitly stresses the connective aspect of *ma'at* and presents a very serviceable definition:

> The reward of one who does something lies in something being done for him.
> This is considered by god as *ma'at*.[21]

Ma'at, then, is the principle that forms individuals into communities and that gives their actions meaning and direction by ensuring that good is rewarded and evil punished.

The concept of doing something for one another appears over and over in the texts of the Middle Kingdom and was clearly so well-defined that it had almost terminological status. By establishing a connection between doing-something-for-one-another and the human capacity for recollection, these texts further emphasize the temporal dimension of the connectivity brought about by *ma'at*. The wisdom texts contrast the mindful, just individual with the "covetous one," who thinks only of himself and needs no memory. Thus in the famous *Dispute of a Man with His Ba*, which has become the most frequently cited work of ancient Egyptian literature, we read the following: "There is no memory of yesterday, no one does anything for him who has done something these days."[22] Memory and mutually supportive action belong together; one is the condition for the other. Memory creates the space in which social action can unfold, while forgetting is synonymous with an inability to act, or in the Egyptian language, with "sloth/inertia." Without the past there is no action. In another text from the Middle Period, the *Tale of the Eloquent Peasant*, we read: "The slothful/inert [he who does nothing for others] has no yesterday"—no memory, no conscience, no responsibility, no past.[23] The ideal counterpole is the individual who can remember: "A good character returns to his place of yesterday, for it is commanded: Do something for him who does something in order to ensure that he remains active. This is to thank him for what he has done."[24] The "return to the place of yesterday" is a reference to memory, to responsible mindfulness of benefits received and obligations incurred. This is what it means "to have a yesterday." The imperative "do something for him who does/has done something" refers to the ideal of doing-something-for-one-another, of active altruism. The reward does not come automatically, but is a function of social action and thus, in its turn, of social memory:

Hide not your face from him you have known,
be not blind to him you have looked upon,
reject not him who turns to you for aid,
but desist[25] from this hesitation ["inertia"] to have your voice
   heard.
Act for him who acts for you![26]

This emphasis on time and memory gives the Egyptian concept of reciprocity, of doing-something-for-one-another, a markedly recollective quality. Action is remembering, inaction forgetting. The inactive loses sight of yesterday and the claims it has on today. In this connection, *ma'at* figures as the proper order of action in the dimension of time, a process kept in motion by the presence of yesterday in today. *Ma'at* guarantees that what was valid yesterday will hold good today, that a person will stand by what he said and did yesterday, that he will respond to what others have said and done. *Ma'at* is, thus, a consistency of action beyond the limits of the day, a form of active remembrance that provides the basis of trust and successful accomplishment. "All actions are interjoined," says the *Instruction for King Merikare:*

A blow is reciprocated with the same—this is the jointure[27] of
   everything that is done.[28]

A much later instance of this connection between memory and altruism as unfolded by the texts of the Middle Kingdom is found in the philosophies of Marx and Nietzsche. "Interest has no memory," says Marx in one of his early works, "for it thinks only of itself."[29] Those who live only to satisfy their immediate appetites and personal designs need no memory. Memory is not a part of egoism or self-preservation, but of altruism, thinking of others and the group as a whole, the community, society, humankind. Nietzsche enlarged on this connection between memory and human fellowship in his *Genealogy of Morals,* which is at the same time a genealogy of memory. Morality and memory develop as evolutionary partners in the breeding of people as cultural beings. We need memory in order to make promises and honor obligations. Memory is peculiar to the human being as the "animal with the right to make promises." Unlike Nietzsche, the Egyptians developed the concept of responsible action not from the special case of promises (with a view to the future) but from gratitude (with a view to the past). "Now this animal which needs to be forgetful, in which forgetfulness is a force, a form of *robust* health, has bred in itself an opposing faculty, a memory, with the aid of which forgetfulness is abrogated in certain cases—namely, in those cases where promises are made. This involves no mere inability to rid oneself of an impression . . . but an active *desire* not to rid oneself, a desire for the continuance of something desired once, a real memory of the will"; this, says Nietzsche, is "the long story of how responsibility originated."[30]

Like Marx, Nietzsche sees the individual as learning from this process of commemoration to stand back from himself and his own interests. The individual must sacrifice himself—this is the dictate of the "morality of *mores.*"[31] In return for the sacrificed individual self, he achieves a social self that, by virtue of possessing a memory, attains stability and reliability—a self that is the same tomorrow as it was yesterday and today. The mindful self is the locus where society inscribes its claims and obligations. A person brought up to aspire to human fellowship must remain true to this self, and by remaining so he will also be true to his group.

Nietzsche describes this quintessentially civilizing process in the grimmest of colors:

> One can well believe that the answers and methods for solving this primeval problem were not precisely gentle; perhaps indeed there was nothing more fearful and uncanny in the whole prehistory of man than his mnemotechnics. "If something is to stay in the memory it must be burned in: only that which never ceases to hurt stays in the memory"—this is a main clause of the oldest (unhappily also the most enduring) psychology on earth. . . . Man could never do without blood, torture, and sacrifices when he felt the need to create a memory for himself; the most dreadful sacrifices and pledges (sacrifices of the first-born among them), the most repulsive mutilations (castration, for example), the cruelest rites of all the religious cults (and all religions are at the deepest level systems of cruelties)—all this has its origin in that instinct that realized that pain is the most powerful aid to mnemonics.[32]

The Egyptians, by contrast, describe their concept of human fellowship—*ma'at*—as a gentle yoke. But they also proceed on the assumption that *ma'at* cannot exist among humankind without the state and its coercive rods. Some of Nietzsche's somber hues find confirmation in the police-state aspect of the Middle Kingdom. The state is there to enforce *ma'at* on earth, to guarantee the parameters within which *ma'at* can be taught and remembered in the first place. Thus the Egyptians regarded *ma'at* and its transmission not as something auto-poietic, which would spontaneously develop in the course of social interaction, but as a system that had to be imposed from outside, or rather from above, and that could be maintained only by the power of the state. Without the state and its sanctions on unmindfulness, the "laws of *ma'at*" would lapse into oblivion.[33] Here too, then, we can say that only that which does not cease to hurt will remain in the memory, the sole difference being that the Egyptians had already reached a stage of civilization where the pain of memory was not literally burned into the flesh but transposed into the symbolic forms of state institutions and laws, literary texts and school instruction—in short, a symbolic world of admonitory semiologies that no longer branded memory into the skin but imprinted it on the heart. Perhaps the state, with its attendant inequality and its hierarchical system of command and obedience, was the price people had to pay for the humanization of cultural memory. With the transposition of admonitory semiologies into the medium of writing, a concurrent change in the structure of affiliation, of "belonging," sets in. It becomes wide-ranging, abstract, and hierarchical. Egalitarian village communities are replaced first by chiefdoms and kingdoms, later by huge empires. The fellow-man is replaced by the subject.

Connective Justice

THE WORD "SUBJECT" evokes the image of pharaonic rule conveyed by the Bible: Egypt as a form of "oriental despotism," the very opposite of justice. It is an image of cowed masses pressed into service to build huge works of civil engineering and colossal pyramids, under the control of a labyrinthine bureaucracy and ruled over by a despot answerable to nothing but his own whims.[34] His power is absolute, and his will is performed on the spot. The toiling masses are a mindless entity, while the (absurdly inflated) sphere of officialdom is the instrument of the despot's all-powerful single will, whose sole aim is to assert and consolidate its own sway.

Accordingly, Emma Brunner-Traut defines ancient Egyptian society as an "aggregate" society, devoid of structure, an inchoate mass of individuals, the simple sum of a vast number of single enti-ties.[35] Despite the hierarchy imposed on this mass, no individual could "gain a comprehensive view of the whole and understand the close intermeshing of dependencies that kept it functioning." In her view, the Egyptians lacked not only alternatives, but even the mental pre-requisites for recognizing alternatives as such. Consequently, the hier-archical system never cohered into a "structure" but amassed itself into an "aggregation (Latin *grex:* herd) of individuals rather than an organic body in which the various parts interrelated and interacted and were bound together by horizontal and vertical bonds."[36] In par-ticular, Brunner-Traut notes the absence of "horizontal" social rela-tions, seeing Egyptian society as a purely vertical connectivity built exclusively around command and obedience.

The absence of horizontal social forms in Egypt can hardly be denied. Pharaonic monocracy permitted no forms of social organi-zation other than the professional groups of bureaucrats, priests, and (later) military men—no cooperatives, no associations, no collectives based on kinship or common interests, no nobility based on descent. Quite rightly, Brunner-Traut remarks: "Extended families such as we still find today in the East, including the Far East, did not exist, nor were there any tribal communities with collective identities across a series of generations."[37] Structures like these, which certainly existed in the predynastic era and resurfaced in the First Intermediate Period, were actively and programmatically discouraged by the state; hence the impression of an amorphous "mass."

But this impression is deceptive. The idea that there was an absence of political reflection, of conceptualizations of political coher-ence, and of social and political norms must be contested in the strongest possible terms. As we have seen, sources that articulate such reflections are abundant, though they have not formerly been inter-preted in this light.

In this conceptual universe, justice is what holds the world together, and it does so by connecting consequences with deeds. This is what makes it "connective." Justice links human action to human destiny and welds individuals into a community. In his studies on state law, Hans Kelsen has described the notion of an all-embracing idea of "tit for tat" as a precursor of the concept of causality.[38] Requital as causality, causality as requital: this formula is the most accurate expression of the "cosmic" aspect of this idea of justice. By linking up deeds with their consequences, connective justice knits the course of events, the scheme of things, and the world itself into a meaningful whole. Within such a view, instances of social disarray such as those described in the *Prophecies of Neferti* go hand in hand with disruptions at the cosmic level. When connective justice stops functioning, when evil goes unpunished and good no longer prospers, then the world is "out of joint."

But connective justice links not only consequence to deed but also the individual to his or her fellows. The Egyptians made the functioning of connective justice dependent on *ma'at,* on the reciprocity of human agency.[39] When solidarity falters, connective justice crumbles. The justice that makes the world go round is itself something that has to be "kept going." Justice is neither innate nor intrinsic, nor is it utopianly remote; rather, it is achieved by systematic maintenance. Thus the concept of connective justice relates precisely to that structure, that overall organic cohesiveness, that Brunner-Traut asserts to be absent from ancient Near-Eastern societies. In short, we are in the presence here not of amorphous masses but of societies welded into communities by a sociopolitical culture and by a system of education organized around justice.

The Egyptian concept of the *zoon politikon* (man as a political animal) differs most significantly from that of ancient Greece in that it refers not so much to a capacity for as to a dependence on community. In the ancient Egyptian view, people are "political" in the sense that they "can only live together." Without mutual support and guidance, human life is impossible. The ancient Egyptians developed an image of humanity that sees the aim of the individual not in the autonomy of independent self-fulfillment but in the development of social connection.

Life is fellowship or "connectivity"; death is loneliness, in the sense of disconnection, dis-integration. Loneliness is the fate of those who fail to realize connectivity, who fail to find their place in the whole. Living properly means making it possible for others to live with oneself. The ancient civilizations call this "justice"—in the Egyptian language, *ma'at.* Justice refers to a life in harmony with the connective structures that make community possible, both with one's fellows and with the gods. The great mystery of this connectivity in the eyes of the Egyptians was that it transcended death and promised immortality. Obdurate egotism and covetousness might tear at the fabric of this network, but not death.

This unrestrictedly positive attitude to connectivity is in accord with a concept of personhood, human and divine, that I propose to call constellational. Individuals—whether humans or gods—can live only in "constellations." Character, worth, and significance are attributes that grow solely from the roles and connections in which an individual is able to develop his own self. Everyone depends on everyone else: "The one lives when the other guides," says an ancient Egyptian proverb.[40] The gods and the dead need the offerings of the living, and the main reason for making the offerings is their symbolic expression of this all-embracing mutual dependence. In this world, autarchy is the quintessence of evil. Accordingly, Seth, the great countergod in the Egyptian pantheon, is described as follows:

He who is content with separation and hates fraternization,
he who [only] supports himself on his [own] heart among the
    gods.[41]

And a Ramesside dream book has this to say about the loner: "The god that is in him is Seth."[42]

9

THE POLITICIZATION OF
CONNECTIVE JUSTICE

Theory of the Heart

THE IDEA OF A CONNECTIVE JUSTICE that binds individuals into a community and their actions into the meaningful ensemble of a history is central to Egyptian civilization throughout its entire span. The Middle Kingdom is characterized by three specific modifications to this central idea: the "theory of the heart," the "loyalist reduction," and the Judgment of the Dead.

The Egyptian history of the heart divides into three major stages.[43] The first is the ideal of the "king-guided individual." At this stage, which is coeval with the Old Kingdom, there is no explicit mention of the heart. The individual (the official; we have no written testimonies of any other groups) sees himself as the executive organ of the royal will. The heart of the king thinks and plans for all.

The second stage, which is central to the image of the individual in the Middle Kingdom, is the idea of the "heart-guided individual." Here the heart plays a central role in biographical inscriptions and literary texts. The officials say of themselves that it was their heart that urged them into the service of the king. Loyalism, the "royal religion" of the Middle Kingdom, calls for (and to) the inner man:[44]

Venerate the king in the inside of your bodies!
Pledge allegiance to His Majesty in your hearts!
He is Sia, who is in the hearts,
his eyes, they pierce every body.[45]

So begins the *Loyalist Instruction,* an educational text designed to ensure the allegiance of the members of the upper classes to the new dynasty by appealing to their innermost selves. No longer a mere tool, the official should now be devoted to the king with hand and heart. Newly central are character, the moral profile, the inner virtues.[46]

> I was not drunken. My heart was not forgetful.
> I was not negligent in my actions.
> My heart it was that raised my station,[47]
> my character caused my top-rank position to endure.
> I achieved everything I did by being the favorite of my lady,
> and through my attentiveness I created prosperity.
> I performed all services by which a domain is administered,
> by putting up that which I found fallen.
> They say, do they not: "It is most beneficial
> for a man to exercise the excellence of his heart for his lady, that
> his monument be the taller for it."[48]

The idea of the Judgment of the Dead builds upon this concept of individual merit. The central image is the scale on which the heart is weighed against a figurine of the goddess Ma'at. Essential for success in this world and acquittal by the court of the dead on the threshold to the next is the *ma'at*-conformity of the heart. With a "heart full of *ma'at,*" the dead person stands before his judge:

> I have come to you and I know you and what you are
> and revere your underworld form,
> as you sit with Ma'at opposite you
> and judge the hearts on the scale,
> while I stand before you, my heart full of *ma'at,*
> no lie in my mind.[49]

If the candidate passes the test, Horus as Master of the Scales then says: "His heart was found just on the Great Scales."[50] Significantly, the object of attention is the *heart,* the *social* self for which people must exchange their *individual* selves, and as such the space where society inscribes its norms of "connective," civic behavior. This is the teaching of the Middle Kingdom.

The third stage is the ideal of the "god-guided heart," which is not the "heart full of *ma'at,*" but the heart that has taken god's guid-

ing will into itself. This image of humanity is central to the semiologies of the New Kingdom, and I will discuss it fully later. But at this
juncture I would like to cite a text from the early New Kingdom,
which although it adumbrates this new conception, still stands
squarely in the tradition of the Middle Kingdom:

> My heart it was that urged me
> to do [my duty] in accordance with its instructions.
> It is for me an excellent testimony,
> its instructions I have not violated,
> for I feared to trespass against its directions
> and therefore thrived greatly.
> Marvelously well I fared because of its inspirations for my
>   actions,
> impeccable was I through its guidance.
> [. . .] say the people,
> a divine saying it [= the heart] is in every body.
> Blessed he whom it has guided to the right path of action![51]

The Middle Kingdom sought to secure the network of connective
justice by lodging it within the individual. People were not defined
by external constellations, that is, by having their identities imposed
from the outside. Rather, they engaged in these constellations with
their innermost selves and based their membership in the community
upon the "virtues" of the heart.

Loyalism

IN LINE WITH THE MIDDLE KINGDOM's new emphasis on the
heart, loyalism required that the individual throw in his lot with the
king of his own accord. In loyalist teaching, service to the king is
prompted by the biddings of the heart. The theory of the heart is
intimately bound up with the rhetoric of decision, as is clear when
we look at the first verses of the *Loyalist Instruction:*

> Venerate the king in the inside of your bodies!
> Pledge allegiance to His Majesty in your hearts!
> He is Sia, who is in the hearts,
> his eyes, they pierce through every body.

He is Re, thanks to whose beams one sees,
an illuminator of the Two Lands, more than the sun.
A creator of greenery he is, more than a high flood,
he has filled the Two Lands with strength and life.
The noses stiffen when he lapses into anger,
one breathes again when he regains his composure.
He gives food to those who are in his retinue,
and feeds him who adheres to his path.
The king is Ka, Hu is his mouth,
all things that exist are brought forth by him.
Bastet he is, who protects the Two Lands,
who venerates him will be shielded by his arm.
Sekhmet he is to him who violates his commandment.
Whom he hates will be in misery.[52]

The *Loyalist Instruction* is one of a cycle of three Instructions designed
to instill loyalism in the hearts of their recipients.[53] Part of the same
educational program was the *Story of Sinuhe,* which has come down
to us on seven papyrus manuscripts and twenty-five ostraca. The
number of sources testifies to its canonical status: the *Story of Sinuhe*
was certainly one of the central texts that every educated Egyptian
knew by heart.

The *Story of Sinuhe* is composed in the manner of a biographical
inscription and indeed adheres to this form so closely that a number
of scholars were once convinced that they might some day discover
the tomb of the historical Sinuhe and find the original inscription.
The *Story of Sinuhe* is a fiction. But the concept of fiction is misleading, insofar as it suggests something invented, dreamed-up, unreal.
Some fictional texts—including *Sinuhe*—teach us a great deal more
about historical reality than do most of their nonfictional counterparts. Such texts are akin to models. They render reality in a fictional
mold. Thus the medium of literature established a new vantage in
Egyptian culture where the organization of the world was reflected in
the model of invented narratives. In this way the culture created for
itself an instrument of self-observation.

The plot of *Sinuhe* is quickly recounted. The first-person narrator is a courtier who accompanies Crown Prince Sesostris on a
military campaign to Libya. There he learns of the death of King
Amenemhet (Ammenemes) I and flees in panic. He explains his panic
as fear of internal upheavals, but that is only "half the truth," as we
learn later. The actual motives for his flight remain a mystery; the

text indicates only that a god has commanded him, or "given it into his heart," that he should flee. It is clear, however, that in "deserting" in this way Sinuhe risks the severest of punishments.

This portion of the narrative reveals something of the police-state nature of the Middle Kingdom, which is also evident in some of the "traces." In the surviving remnants of the files of a state institution named Central Prison or Labor House, "flight" is by far the most frequent reason given for incarceration. This offense refers not only to fleeing the country, as in the case of Sinuhe, but also to fleeing from the workplace. From the Middle Kingdom on, the "vagabond" dogged Egyptian civilization as a major problem. In the extant texts, he figures prominently as the inverse of the ideal subject, settled, hardworking, law-abiding, taxpaying. The police-state character of the Middle Kingdom is the inevitable institutional expression of a state that styles itself primarily as a bulwark against chaos, as a bastion of a civilization built upon law, order, and justice. Such a state will inevitably develop organs of control, surveillance, and punishment that curtail individual freedom of movement to the same degree as they afford protection.

Sinuhe makes his way to southern Palestine, wins the trust of a tribal chieftain, marries the chieftain's daughter, and makes a highly respectable career for himself. Thus the first part of the story progresses from Sinuhe's estrangement from home to his new life among strangers. The second part narrates Sinuhe's return to his homeland from that land of strangers. The crossover from the first section of the plot to the second is marked by an episode in which Sinuhe fights a challenger in single combat. This duel has a striking number of points in common with the biblical story of David and Goliath. With the consummate self-control of the civilized Egyptian, Sinuhe bides his time until his aggression-crazed, bloodthirsty opponent has used up all his weapons, then kills him with one arrow. At this climax of his Asiatic career Sinuhe is, however, seized by nostalgia for Egypt. Though the reason for his sudden longing is not set out in so many words, it would have been apparent to any Egyptian reader: Sinuhe has stared death in the face; he is filled with *horror alieni*. The dread of the foreign is a frequent theme of the inscriptions admonishing visitors to recite the prayer for the dead:

As truly as you love life and forget death,
your town gods shall praise you,
you shall never taste the horror of the foreign

but shall be buried in your tombs
and transfer your offices to your children.... [54]

This horror is not simply distaste for a place that is not "home," but centers rather on the fear of death and burial in such a place. For Egyptians this idea was absolute anathema.[55] Overcome by such fear, Sinuhe prays to the unknown "god who imposed on me this flight." His supplications are heard; a letter arrives from the king summoning him back to Egypt. The narrative ends with a description of the tomb complex accorded to Sinuhe in his homeland.

What this story impressed upon every Egyptian was that while one might perhaps live happily and successfully in foreign parts, it is absolutely unthinkable to die and be buried there. The path to immortality, to an eternity in the vicinity of the gods in the hereafter, and to continuing memory in this world, passes through the king, the "lord of burial." As in the Old Kingdom, the state of the Middle Kingdom was the generator of time and eternity.

The Proclamation of Pharaonic Kingship

IN THE STORY OF SINUHE there is a scene remarkable for the way it emblematically foregrounds the "propagandistic" function of literature in the Middle Kingdom, both at a political and a religious level. In their first encounter, Sinuhe is asked by Amunenshi, the Syrian chieftain who later becomes his father-in-law, about the state of things back in his homeland. The Egyptian asylum seeker extols the new king Sesostris as follows:

He is a god who has no peer;
no other has been born who could excel him.
A lord of knowledge he is, excellent in planning, effective in
    command.
One sallies forth and returns home at his behest.
He it is who subjugated the mountain lands while his father was
    in his palace;
he reported to him the fulfillment of his orders.
A hero he is who acts with his sword,
a warrior unequaled by any.... [56]

In more than forty verses the text paints the classic picture of a ruler who combines victorious military prowess with indulgence and leniency. The king is a god, a lord of knowledge, a hero, one who strides out with a stout heart, who smites the enemy, who rejoices in battle, a lord of grace, an increaser of those born with him, a gift of god, one who expands his frontiers.

The author of the *Story of Sinuhe* found the form of this praise song ready made and availed himself of it to compose a hymn to Sesostris I. He embeds the hymn in a situation that fully motivates both its subject and its form. The dramatic scenario reconstructs the question to which this hymn is the perfect response: who and what is the king of Egypt?

Amunenshi, who asks this question and is given the answer, lives outside Egypt and knows nothing of the king. Sinuhe takes his knowledge of the king out into the world, where he "propagates" it, in the original sense of "propaganda" as dissemination of the word to the heathens. From the Egyptian viewpoint, Amunenshi is a heathen, one who has to be won over to the cause of the pharaoh. The panegyric accordingly closes with good advice: send a messenger to the king, make your name known to him. He will not cease to do good to a foreign land that "is on his water."

A royal inscription from the early New Kingdom continues in this tradition and magnifies the king in particularly purple verses:

> Hearken, you dignitaries, priests, and subjects,
> all people that follow in the steps of that king:
> Proclaim his power to others,
> purify yourselves by his name,
> cleanse yourselves by his oath!
> Behold, a god he is on earth.
> Magnify him like Re,
> praise him like the moon,
> the king of Upper and Lower Egypt, Ahmose, who lives forever,
> who subjugates every foreign land.[57]

The political situation of Egypt illuminates the necessity of propaganda in the structure of pharaonic rule. Egypt was an empire within whose wide-ranging boundaries knowledge of pharaonic rule and its claims were very unevenly distributed. Neither the Sumerian city kings nor the Israelite and early Greek rulers were confronted with this problem. In Egypt the restoration of centralized pharaonic power after the collapse of the Old Kingdom required great efforts of political education and indoctrination. The *Story of Sinuhe,* the *Loyalist Instruction,* and in a broader sense the entire literature of the Middle Kingdom served the same purpose: to impose pharaonic rule not just as a political system, but rather as a religion, a doctrine of salvation and right living that pointed the way to harmony with the gods and one's fellows, as well as to immortality.[58]

10

WRATH AND LOVE: THE TWO FACES OF POWER AND THE RHETORIC OF DECISION

Righteous Wrath as a Political Virtue

THE DECLARED PROGRAM of the Twelfth Dynasty was to put a definitive end to "chaos." This program was formulated and disseminated in the *Prophecies of Neferti,* where the chaos of the First Intermediate Period is stylized into a classic memorial figure. Chaos can be banished only by effective political force, according to the principle that "politics and law are only possible if they can draw on physical force to assert themselves and effectively rule out counterforce."[59] Thus the Middle Kingdom asserts, for the first time in Egyptian history, the state's monopoly on the exercise of force, putting an end to the local militias of the nomarchs.

The chaos descriptions depict what the world would be like without the state. Their function is to hammer home the idea that not only peace, order, and justice, but the flourishing of nature and indeed the very meaning of creation depend on the existence of the state.[60] Order is not written into the fabric of the world, but must be achieved and maintained by human agency. This is the meaning and the mission of the state.[61] If the state were to crumble, so too would *ma'at,* the harmonizing force of connective justice that unifies all humans as well as animals, gods, the dead, and the cosmos. All common, shared things would disappear: language, knowledge, memory. And if memory were to disappear, then good would no longer be rewarded, evil no longer punished: the whole circle and circulation of meaning would break down. People would no longer understand each other, and brute force would take the place of communicative speech. The gods would avert their faces; nature would lose its nutritive, restorative energy, with famine and hardship as the result. On the human plane, violence and murder would hold sway: "Where three are walking along the road one would only find two: for the larger number kills the smaller."[62] All natural bonds would be terminated; fathers and sons would turn on one another; the Nile would flow red with blood.

The Egyptians identified covetousness as the root of all evil. Keeping it in check required an unremitting effort that derived its energy from "righteous wrath," one of the basic virtues of the king and his officials. At the installation of the vizier, the king addressed him thus: "You shall be angry about that which it is necessary to be angered by."[63] And in the *Admonitions of Ipuwer,* the collapse of justice is bewailed as follows:

> No people are to be found on the road,
> for fighting has arisen. They are banished as a result of the
>   wrong they have committed.
> There was no steersman in their hour.
> Where is he today? Is he perhaps asleep?
> Behold: one sees not his punitive power.
> When we were cast in mourning I could not find you.
> One cannot appeal to you as you are free of anger against it.[64]

There is no way to know who is being addressed here, the creator-god or his representative on earth. But the inability to summon up indignation at wrongdoing is clearly a characteristic of weak rulers, whether the creator himself or the king.[65] The concept of righteous wrath first appears in Egyptian instructions to the king. One text describes the pharaoh's anger thus:

> The noses stiffen when he lapses into anger,
> one breathes again when he regains his composure.[66]

The wrath of god only figures very much later, in texts from the Ramesside Period, when the function of an ethical authority, the lord and guardian of justice, had irrevocably passed from the king to god.[67] In the Egyptian view, greed, covetousness, mendacity, and other manifestations of evil are a characteristic of the world as it is. The Egyptians did not reject the world because it was "bad," for they had nothing to fall back on outside the world. For them the world was not rotten through and through, but ambivalent. The task of the king was to keep the world in a functioning condition by exercising a form of authority that itself had two faces: mild, gracious, and peaceable toward the law-abiding; merciless, death-dealing, and vindictive toward insurgents.[68]

The classic image of these "two faces of power" is the dual identity of the king as Bastet, the mild and gracious goddess, and Sekhmet, her cruel, avenging counterpart:

Bastet he is, who protects the Two Lands.
Who venerates him will be shielded by his arm.
Sekhmet he is to him who violates his commandment.
Whom he hates will be in misery.[69]

These verses from the *Loyalist Instruction* represent the rhetoric of decision. The individual cannot remain indifferent to the two faces of the pharaonic claim to power, but he must decide whether he belongs to those who "venerate" the pharaoh or to those who "violate his commandment."

Force and Justice

THE PUNITIVE FORCE OF THE KING, extending to the death penalty, is called *baw,* the plural form of the word we normally translate as "soul." *Baw* refers to a power that manifests itself in tremendous effects, or, vice versa, to tremendous effects in which an invisible power manifests itself. The most tremendous effect, of course, is death, and only the power of the king or the gods could mete out death. In Egypt killing was a strict state monopoly (though in Intermediate Periods the nomarchs also laid claim to it). Capital punishment was the preserve of the king, to be used very sparingly. These inhibitions had to do with the notion of *ba,* or "soul." In the Old Kingdom, the prevalent persuasion was that only the king had a *ba* that left the body after death and ascended to heaven. After the collapse of the Old Kingdom, this idea became universalized: every individual had a *ba* that traversed the threshold into the hereafter. Since every individual could now call his earthly judge to account in the hereafter if he had been wrongfully condemned, the death sentence could only be passed if there was absolute certainty of divine approval, not to say divine commission. The decisive text is found in the *Instruction for King Merikare:*

> Beware of unjust punishment.
> Kill not, for that cannot be useful to you.
> Punish with beatings and prison:
> by this the land will be well founded.
> Except only the rebel whose plan has been discovered,
> for god knows the rebel and god punishes with blood.
> . . .
> Kill no one whose spiritual strength is known to you,
> with whom you have sung the scriptures,
> who has read in the book of trial [. . .] before god
> and can walk freely in a secret place.
> For the soul returns to the place it knows
> and deviates not from its path of yesterday.
> No magic can hold it back,
> it reaches him who gives it water.
>
> The judges who judge the prosecuted,
> you know they are not lenient
> on the day when justice is passed on the wretched one,
> in the hour of the fulfillment of the prescription.
> [A lengthy passage follows on the Judgment of the Dead, at
>   which the king himself must justify his actions].[70]

A literary work of the late Middle Kingdom features a magician named Dedi who refuses to give a demonstration of the trick for which he is famed: reattaching a severed head. The king asks him to perform this feat on a human captive, but Dedi ventures to demur, with the words:

> But not on a human,
> O ruler, my lord!
> For see, it is forbidden to perform such a thing on the "noble
>   cattle."[71]

The king, the mighty Cheops himself, immediately concurs and has a goose produced instead for the demonstration. The long-lived persistence of such inhibitions regarding the death sentence is borne out by the trial records on the harem conspiracy to which King Ramesses III fell victim.[72] Once found guilty, the conspirators were not executed but condemned to commit suicide. These inhibitions were caused by the fear of the power of the immortal soul of the dead, the *ba,* to return to earth or to call its executioners to account in the hereafter.

The threat perceived in the ambivalent nature of man and the world provided the rationale for the state's power—indeed obligation—to kill. In a divided world, justice—the foundation of peace, order, and security—was constantly threatened by dissolution and could only be sustained by a form of rule that disposed of the deadly powers of fire and sword.[73] This punitive force (*baw*) is symbolized by the uraeus flaming with wrath. Still, in the eyes of the Egyptians, the pharaoh was but the earthly image of the creator-god, exercising a power continuous with that of god in heaven.[74] According to Egyptian notions, evil and chaos (the tendency toward disintegration) came into the world after it had been created. Only after the separation of heaven and earth and the withdrawal of the sun god into the heavens did the water dragon Apopis set out to thwart the circuit of the sun, with the consequence that the world took on the dualist or ambivalent structure central to the Egyptian image of the universe. At that point, "creation" merged with "kingship," the office charged with maintaining the course of the sun. In this divided world, the energies of the cosmos were no longer exclusively positive or life-giving, but—to sustain life—had to combat chaos.

Politics and Magic

IT WAS THE SPECIFIC task of the temple cult to thwart the evil designs of Apopis and so ensure the course of the sun and the continuation of creation. But notably in the Middle Kingdom annihilation rituals were directed not only against divine foes but also against the pharaoh's political enemies. These annihilation rituals are present in the archaeological record, where, as traces, they help to reconstruct the Middle Kingdom image of kingship.

Remains of pottery vessels on which the names of enemies are inscribed have been found at two major sites. The condition of the pottery fragments suggests that they were purposely smashed, in the course of a ritual known as the Breaking of the Red Pots.[75] But we also have finds from the Fifth and Sixth Dynasties and extending all the way through to the Late Period where the corresponding texts are inscribed not on vessels but on figurines.[76] These must have been connected with a ritual that had the same purpose as the Breaking of the Red Pots but was executed differently. Most of the figurines were found in pots made of burnt clay, though on two occasions they were discovered in a coffin, which indicates that they were actually buried.[77] The figurine texts name the target group at which these rites were leveled: foreign princes with their entourages and

> all Egyptians: men, eunuchs, women, and officials
> who will rebel, plan intrigues, or fight,
> who plot rebellion or battle, every rebel
> plotting rebellion in this whole land.

The final listing of "evil things," covered by this rite of execration, includes speeches, thoughts, plans, and dreams. Evil in the sphere of language and imagination is given greater prominence than bad deeds:

> All bad words, all bad speech, all bad imprecation,
> all bad thoughts, all bad plotting,
> all bad battle, every bad disruption,
> all bad plans, all bad things,
> all bad dreams, all bad sleep.

The ritual is intended to exert a magical form of power over a realm not otherwise susceptible to control: the image of the pharaoh in the words, thoughts, and even dreams of his subjects. Here again, and in ancient Egypt in general, magic is a supplement to what we would classify as rational forms of human action (in this case, surveillance and punishment) and not a substitute for them. Where the instruments of administrative justice and warfare cannot reach, magic takes over. Two aspects of this description of the potential foes of the pharaoh are especially noteworthy. First, the danger to be warded off by these rites comes from both outside and inside; foreigners and Egyptians, foes and rebels are all lumped together in one. Second, enmity or rebellion is latent; it exists either in the mind or in the future.

The category of "latent" or "potential" enmity imposes an important distinction. We must clearly distinguish "righteous wrath" from hatred for enemies and evil things. Anger is a reaction, hatred a basic attitude. "Righteous wrath" can be directed only at manifest wrongdoing, never at latent thoughts, plans, and attitudes, which are quite evidently objects of hatred. Hatred is also—and indeed especially—directed at the hatred imputed to the "other side." The rites are an enactment of hatred against those who "hate the king in their hearts." The manifest evildoer exposes himself to the righteous anger of the king. But the enemies designated as haters of the pharaoh are the object of his hatred. Hatred is leveled not at the miscreant but at the foe, whether "inside" or "outside," Egyptian or non-Egyptian. It is the pharaoh's claim to absolute power that generates this hatred. The Egyptians believed that there could be no rule without rebellion, just as there could be no light without darkness. As the sun cannot do without rays of devastating power, so the king cannot forgo symbolic and real force, the power and duty to kill.

In Egyptian iconography, the cosmologically and anthropologically grounded aggressiveness of kingship, its "Sekhmet" aspect, is allotted a system of imagery that could hardly be more violent (though one should add that in the royal texts from all epochs the peaceful aspects are in the majority). Indeed, no ruler could have afforded to play down the predatory ferocity intrinsic to the canonical image of the king. Even Akhenaten had himself depicted on a gigantic scale at Karnak slaying his foes. The king's deadly power is embodied not only in the falcon, lion, and wild bull, but also in the crocodile. This political symbolism was not confined to the Middle Kingdom but extends to the Egyptian image of the king throughout ancient Egyptian history. In the Poetic Stela of Tuthmosis III (Eighteenth Dynasty), for example, the god "shows" the king to the foreign peoples as a young bull, a crocodile, a lion, a falcon, a jackal.

I have come to have you trample the west lands,
Crete and Cyprus stand under the fear of you.
I show them your majesty as a young bull,
with stout heart and pointed horns, which one cannot attack.

I have come to have you trample the north lands;
the lands of Mitanni tremble for fear of you.
I show them your majesty as a crocodile,
the lord of dread in the water, which one cannot attack.

. . .

I have come to have you trample the Libyans;
the lands of Ethiopia are exposed to the force of your anger.
I show them your majesty as a raging lion,
how you make corpses of them in their valleys.

I have come to have you trample the ends of the earth [= the
    north];
what the ocean bounds is bundled in your fist.
I show them your majesty as "lord of the wing,"
grasping what it sees as the fancy takes it.

I have come to have you trample those who live at the beginning
    of the earth [= the south],
to have you bind the nomads as prisoners of war.
I show them your majesty as an Upper Egyptian jackal,
the lord of swiftness, the runner roaming the Two Lands.[78]

Generally speaking, the crocodile symbolized for the Egyptians the character traits they most abhorred: greed, aggression, brutality. But on the cosmic plane it was a sacred animal. The crocodile god Sobek is anything but an antigod, and the same applies incidentally to the goddess in lioness form, Sekhmet.

The images tell the same story. On the Narmer Palette, Egyptian kingship makes its earliest known appearance in history, with an act of punitive force. The unifier of the kingdom smites his enemies and triumphantly inspects ten decapitated princes with their heads between their feet. Comparable depictions of the underworld, in which the foes of god meet the same fate, are one and a half millennia to two millennia younger.[79] The assertion of ma'at, of a just order as the basis for a trustworthy and inhabitable world, does not shy away from killing; on the contrary, the resolve to kill is made particularly graphic.

But both the images and the inscriptions belong to the sphere of official representation, which makes inferences about their relation to reality fundamentally problematic. For it was normal practice to copy older texts and depictions as if one had done the same deeds and had the same historical events to record. This is not documentation but representation, the visualization of an image of the king with aggressive and violent features designed to intimidate would-be rebels and thus guarantee the protection of the loyal subjects.

The reality value of these images is analogous to that of the execration texts and the enemy figurines. They are iconic imprecations that place the surrounding peoples under the threat of potential destruction—to be on the safe side, as it were. Imprecation was a central instrument in ancient foreign policy. All contracts had to be sealed with a sacred oath; breaking that oath entailed consequences of the most terrible kind, which were explicitly depicted in the form of maledictions. The most impressive text of this kind is the one sealing the compact between Yahweh and Israel in the twenty-eighth chapter of Deuteronomy. These curses have the structure of potentially performative utterances: they are self-fulfilling, but only under certain conditions.[80] The same potentially performative status applies to our Egyptian images. The execution depicted is not a record of a historical event but a threat that, like the curses written into treaties, will fulfill itself under certain conditions. Therefore we must regard these images as symbolic acts of deterrence, of fending-off by magic, rather than as acts of subjugation, which would after all imply a form of inclusion in the Egyptian world.

The Idea of Frontier

THE SAME MAGICAL ATTITUDE to reality informs the strange habit of calling all non-Egyptians "vile enemies," even when there were bonds of amity—established by treaties or political marriages—with the ethnic groups thus designated. This habit accords with an Old and Middle Kingdom view that equates Egypt with the ordered world—a world, created by the sun god, in which the king puts *ma'at* in the place of *isfet*. Egypt's frontiers are imagined not as "frontiers between" but as "frontiers of." Beyond the "frontiers of" live not "others," with whom one might seek cooperative or even hostile relations, but absolute aliens with whom any relations would be unthinkable. The surrounding tribes are beyond the pale. No attempt is made to destroy them or convert them into Egyptians, only to keep them out. In the *Instruction for King Merikare,* the Asiatic is described as follows:

The wretched Asiatic, he is truly plagued
by the place in which he lives:
scarce in water,
inaccessible despite all the paths that lead thither,

hard through the mountains.
He cannot live in one place,
lack of food drives his feet onward.
He has been fighting since the time of Horus,
he does not overcome, nor can he be overcome,
for he does not announce the day of battle,
like a robber cast out by the community.[81]

Such an image of foreigners negates any possibility of "foreign policy."
Alliance with them is as impossible as victory over them. Foreigners
are neither friend nor foe. The foe announces the day of battle,
whereas the foreigner is in a constant state of "fighting" and therefore
has to be thwarted, intimidated, shut out. Here Sesostris III justifies
his policy toward the Nubians:

I have set up my frontier by penetrating farther south than my
    forefathers,
by going beyond what was enjoined on me.
I am a king who speaks and acts;
what my heart plans, that is done by my hand.
[. . .]
one who attacks the attacker and keeps silent when all is quiet,
who responds to speech in accordance with its meaning,
for to keep silent when one is attacked would mean provoking
    the enemy to violence.
Attack is strength,
but withdrawing means weakness.
A coward is he who lets himself be driven away from his
    frontier.
The Nubian hearks, and falls at the first word;
answering him means driving him away.
If one attacks him, he shows his back,
if one withdraws, he becomes aggressive.
For these are not people who merit respect,
but wretches they are with broken hearts.[82]

In this view of the world, foreigners do not qualify as political partners. They are like timorous wild animals that immediately retreat
when attacked but that are always ready to return and strike when
terrain is yielded:

The Asiatic is the croco[dile] on its bank:
It snaps from the isolated path
but it does not raise its head near the busy quay.[83]

It is important to note that the foreigner is not evil, nor does he count as a rebel. He simply does not figure at all in the ordered, legally administered landscape created by *ma'at*, in which it is possible to distinguish good from evil. He has to be deterred and intimidated, but not punished.

The *Story of Sinuhe*, which I discussed earlier, takes a dialectical view of this issue. On the one hand, it stresses the ultimately uncrossable nature of the frontier. While Sinuhe has great difficulty in getting past the political boundary, he discovers the geographical bounds to be even more difficult to overcome—he almost perishes in the no-man's-land between Here and There. And the cultural frontier turns out to be entirely insuperable. Sinuhe returns once he realizes that Egypt is the only place where he can die; it is in this text that Egypt first appears as a chronotope of immortality, a sanctuary of permanence. On the other hand, the *Story of Sinuhe* transcends the ideological boundary by advancing the possibility of proclaiming pharaonic power to the "heathens" and of integrating foreign princes and chiefs into the radius of Egyptian loyalism.

Equality and Justice

"BETWEEN THE WEAK AND THE STRONG," Rousseau says at the beginning of *The Social Contract*, "freedom is the oppressive and law the liberating principle."[84] It would be impossible to give clearer expression to the liberating aspect of the Egyptian concept of *ma'at*. The state of the Middle Kingdom was coextensive with the ordered world; it created and guaranteed a sphere of security and peace in which the laws of *ma'at* were valid. *Ma'at* is the law liberating the weak from oppression at the hands of the strong. The idea of liberation from the oppression caused by inequality is informed at least to a rudimentary extent by the idea of the equality of all human beings. As far as I can see, there is only one known Egyptian source that explicitly addresses this idea, but I believe this text to be representative of the Egyptian view. The text is an apologia by the creator and sun god, justifying his creation in order to "allay the indignation among the crew of the bark." The sun god sums up his work of creation in the form of four deeds. He has created wind and water for all alike, he has instilled the fear of death into all human hearts, and above all he has made all men the same:

> I have made each man the same as his neighbor
> and have prohibited that they should do wrong.
> But their hearts have violated my commandment.[85]

It cannot be emphasized sufficiently that for the Egyptians inequality was not inherent in the creation or continuation of the world. Quite unlike, say, the Vedic view of the world, which understands caste hierarchy as the divine scheme of things, or ancient Greek anthropology, which regarded the difference between free citizens and slaves as entirely natural, the Egyptians did not see existing differences— between rich and poor, strong and weak—as part of the order of creation. For the moment we can disregard the idea of inequality between Egyptians and non-Egyptians implicit in the unreflecting ethnocentrism of the Old and Middle Kingdoms, whereby the Egyptians designated themselves as "humans" and equated their world with the ordered world in general. Of interest for us is the structure of that ordered world itself, and here it is quite clear that inequality is not an intrinsic feature. It is not divinely ordained, but is the fault of human society; its existence is traced back to the "heart"—to human free will. Inequality is a product of covetousness, the "greed of the heart." This point is crucial, as it proves that inequality is in fact a product of disorder, not order. This "heart-produced" inequality is manifested in the fact that there are strong and weak, rich and poor, a primitive condition that cannot be tolerated and that must be transformed into a civilized state, so that the earth itself can be rendered inhabitable.[86] *Ma'at* or justice is the order that has to be imposed on the disorder that reigns naturally on earth. And as this disorder manifests itself as inequality, *ma'at* creates a form of equality.

The king is advised to appoint his officials solely on the criterion of ability: "Make no difference between the son of a [noble] man and a lowly man. Appoint a man according to his abilities, so that all arts be cultivated."[87] But the most crucial requirement is that all be equal before the law. Judges emphasize that they have made no distinction between rich and poor, strong and weak, those they know and those they do not know. One vizier is described as having such fear of being thought partial that he "disadvantaged people from his family against others more remote from him," and in so doing practiced a form of inverse partiality. "This is more than *ma'at*," the commentary runs; and "partiality is abhorrent in god's eyes."[88]

Though inequality is not abolished, it is offset by a political distribution of rule. For the unequal distribution of power is not only not god-given, but is actively opposed to god's will. Against the background of this view of the world and of human beings, the connection between judging and saving clearly emerges. Passing judgment on persons is an act of salvation that protects the weak from oppression by the strong. Hence, in the Coffin Text cited above, the creator-god concludes his apologia as follows: "I judge between the strong and the weak."[89] The creator, while not answerable for wrong, is far from leaving the world to the depredations of wrongdoers. On the contrary, he is determined to intervene by means of judgment and salvation in order to restore equality, order, and justice wherever the obduracy of the human heart has sought to undermine their sway.

The creator-god effects this world-sustaining intervention by means of the state, which rescues and protects the weak. In the *Installation of the Vizier*, we are even told: "The ruler loves the timorous more than the stout of heart."[90] The Egyptian state is the implementation of a legal order that precludes the natural supremacy of the strong and opens up prospects for the weak (the "widows and orphans") that otherwise would not exist. The political hierarchy of the state is the means by which the ruler "saves the weak from the hand of the strong" and thus keeps the world inhabitable.

Before we start lamenting the absence of social revolutions or at least reforms in ancient Egypt, we should bear in mind that the role of social reformer and "good shepherd" was a part of the official image of the king. The king succeeded as a ruler by imposing justice upon his kingdom; the measure of his success was not the well-being of the powerful but of the proverbial widows and orphans.

There is much evidence that this image of rulership did not originate with pharaonic monarchy but first developed among the nomarchs of the First Intermediate Period, after the collapse of the Old Kingdom. The virtues of the just king were originally those of the magnates, of patrons who kept their clients and indeed their nomes alive in times of hardship. The kings of the Middle Kingdom thus combined the god-king idea of the Old Kingdom with the image and the virtues of a "great patron" of the First Intermediate Period.

As the concept of rule developed by the patrons, magnates, and nomarchs did not aim at establishing an alternative political system, it was easily adopted into the pharaonic image of rulership. Thus from the precedent of the patrons the image of the "good shepherd" took shape, protecting his charges not so much from hunger and misery but from oppression and exploitation by the mighty.

The argument is a familiar one: a strong state is legitimized by reference to human frailty.[91] The special aspect of the Egyptian version is that it appeals to the idea of human frailty not only to justify the state but also to substantiate the necessity of education. The operative assumption in Egypt is that people can be brought to respect the law and spare the weak not just through threats of punishment but also— and above all—through education. Human beings may not be just by nature, but they do have an innate leaning toward the idea of justice and (with the exception of incorrigible rogues) can be educated by appeals to that instinctive proclivity. The natural vertical discrepancy between rich and poor, vilified as chaos or injustice, is offset by the vertical hierarchy of superior and subordinate, patron and dependent. Natural verticality comes about through covetousness— the instinctual drive of the heart—whereas the hierarchical variant is based on solidarity, "vertical solidarity," an awareness of cohesion and responsibility. This awareness can be instilled in people by education.

Thus the wisdom literature, such as Neferti lamenting the collapse of justice, refers mainly to the disappearance of solidarity, the breakdown of verbal communication, and the ascendancy of autonomous force.[92] A close relationship is seen between political and ethical disaster; the state is starkly foregrounded as the institutionalization of social virtues. These laments are not designed only, or even primarily, to affirm that people cannot exist without a state order. They are at least equally concerned to show that human society is impossible without a sense of public spirit, without the virtues, mentalities, and attitudes implicit in the concept of justice.[93]

11

THE FOUNDATION OF
CONNECTIVE JUSTICE IN
THE HEREAFTER: THE
JUDGMENT OF THE DEAD

The Hereafter as a Moral Institution

THE SPREAD OF THE RELIGION of Osiris and, inextricably bound
up with it, the emergence of a universal Judgment of the Dead constitute the most significant new paradigm in the Egyptian history of
meaning to arise between the Old and the New Kingdoms. In the
Old Kingdom, the notion of life after death centered on eternal continuation in the tomb. The dead, with the exception of the king, did
not ascend to heaven, nor did they descend into the underworld.
Instead they crossed to the "beautiful West," the city of the dead, in
which by virtue of monumental memorials and cultic ritual they
hoped to maintain a place for themselves in the memory of society.
The mystery of the grave and the corpse was, as it were, "of this
world." The dead inhabited the *hrt ntr,* the divine city around the
pyramid in which the dead king ruled as the Great God over "those
with secret seats." Only the king crossed the great divide; he ascended
to heaven. At the same time, however, his mortal coil remained in
the secret precincts of the pyramid, where it received ritual offerings.
But whereas the mortuary service in private tombs addressed itself to
the dead person who was thought to inhabit it and thus only had to
overcome the distance between above and below, the pyramid mortuary cult had to summon the dead ruler from the "other side" and
thus bridge a gap of an entirely different caliber. The insistent use of
deixis and demonstrative pronouns in the Pyramid Texts reflects the
gradual development of the awareness of this gap. What was "here"

and "this" in the older texts gradually turned into "there" and "that." The world that the dead ruler was imagined to inhabit receded farther and farther into the distance.[94] The appeal to the dead ruler to help himself to the offerings on the offering table was preceded more and more insistently by ceremonial proclamations designed to clear a path to them: "[the] wings of the heavenly door open, the gates of the cool are flung wide." Whether the doors referred to are those of the statue shrine or those that lead to heaven, the proclamation itself is a typical form of symbolic representation, where everything involved in the practice of the cult at the same time takes on an otherworldly meaning.

The hereafter developing at the end of the Old Kingdom in the sphere of nonroyal death beliefs was of a different kind. It was not only "subterranean" as opposed to "heavenly," "Osirian" as opposed to "solar," but was above all extremely moral—that is, configured in terms of good and bad. In the Coffin Texts, the justification of the dead person, his victory over adversaries, plays a much greater role than in the Pyramid Texts. In the Old Kingdom, the tomb was already a moral institution, though one that foregrounded the things of this world. The owner of the tomb protested that he had abided by *ma'at* on earth and that he expected cultic purity and decent behavior from visitors to the tomb. Failure to comply with these expectations was sanctioned with formulaic menaces.[95] In the Middle Kingdom these threats became a great deal more extensive and painted a luridly explicit picture of hellish retributions;[96] at the same time, the tomb owner's apologia developed the subject of his uprightness on earth in anticipation of his appearance before the tribunal that awaited him on the other side.[97]

In contrast to the Old Kingdom, the tomb of the Middle Kingdom was now no longer the place of the dead, but had become a point of potential access, of symbolic contact, between this world and the hereafter. The dead no longer lived in the tomb. "That place where I am";[98] "in that holy land where he now is":[99] phrases like these, frequently found in the texts of the First Intermediate Period and the Middle Kingdom, do not refer to the tomb and the burial chamber. A whole new dimension of meaning has accrued.

In the Old Kingdom, the world beyond, the "beautiful West," was a continuation of this world. The tomb was a place of symbolic perpetuation of the human sphere, ensuring permanence beyond death. The dead person took the world of the living into the next life, in the form of grave goods and mural images. Then, toward the end of the Old Kingdom, the imaginary geography of the underworld began to develop, the kingdom of Osiris. It is an otherworldly sphere of the greatest mystery and inaccessibility, divided from this world by a zone full of dreadful fiends and deadly dangers. Now, the hereafter began to develop "a life of its own," with particular potentialities and forms of existence. The emphasis switched from perpetuation to transition. Though the idea that the dead could take the world of the living with them in symbolic form persisted in such customs as the soul houses and servant figures that were put into the tomb, the mortuary literature of the Middle Kingdom also features spells designed to enable the dead man to build a house for himself in the hereafter.[100]

The idea of the Judgment of the Dead is crucial both to Osirian religion itself and to the new semiology of the Middle Kingdom. In the early stages of its evolution, the Judgment of the Dead was modeled on the mythical trial in which Osiris urged his claims successfully against his murderer, Seth, and thus overcame death. Every dead person hoped to find similar vindication after death and to follow Osiris into the realm of immortality. Some texts even have the tribunal convening in the sacred site of Osiris in Abydos—the "Great Stairway."

The processional festival of Osiris at Abydos gradually became a cult site of such importance that it attracted pilgrims from all over Egypt. High officials who were able to afford the costs had memorial chapels erected on the processional route, so that after death they might still participate in this festive event and inhale the fragrant incense. These chapels are if anything even more intensively inscribed with self-justificatory apologias than the tombs. In the context of the Osirian doctrine of self-justification, autobiographical discourse rose to spectacular new heights and confirmed the emphasis on the inner man, virtue, and character—in short, the heart.

Osiris is the crucial indicator of the fundamental significance of death in the history of ancient Egyptian systems of meaning. In the Old Kingdom the great project of articulating the cultural meaning of death through monumental tomb architecture had, as yet, nothing to do with Osirian religion. Osiris was a newcomer who only started making real progress as a "cult figure" in the Fifth Dynasty. The advent of Osirianism opened up a new path to salvation over and above the lithic route of Imhotep. Monumental tombs continued to be part of the Osirian faith, but now alongside such dicta as "The [true] tomb is built by doing right" or "The [true] monument to a man is his virtue."[101]

Judgment of the Dead and Virtue in Life

I WILL NOT HERE ENLARGE in any great detail on the idea of the Judgment of the Dead.[102] My present interest is in the contribution of the Middle Kingdom to the idea of a postmortem verdict, and the extent to which that idea influenced the Egyptians in the conduct of their lives and the formation of a specific political order.

We can identify two basic forms in the history of this idea. The first is substantially older than the Middle Kingdom and is discernible in the inscriptions of the Old Kingdom, while the second only acquires its canonical form in the New Kingdom, in the *Book of the Dead*. The Middle Kingdom thus represents an interim period.

In the early Old Kingdom the postmortem tribunal is modeled on an earthly court of law. This tribunal, it was believed, sat in judgment only whenever a case was submitted or an action was brought. What effect did such an idea have on the conduct of life in the world of the present? The dead person had to anticipate all kinds of accusations—a final reckoning not only with fellow humans but also with the dead and the gods. The only preparation for such a tribunal was extraordinary circumspection in the life one led on earth, the avoidance of strife and wrongdoing, and the achievement of a maximum degree of harmony. In addition, it was expedient to anticipate such a wide-ranging arraignment by operating from as impregnable a position of strength as possible. The Egyptian term for this position of strength—and an obvious reference to magic lore—was that of an "excellent transfigured one who knows his spells." The *Instruction for King Merikare* tells us that magic was given to human beings by the creator as a weapon "to fend off the blow of events."[103] Magic was the way of coping with complex situations and unforeseeable blows of fate.

The classical form of this idea, which attained canonical status from the fifteenth century B.C.E. at the latest, was very different indeed. Judgment was no longer modeled on earthly tribunals, but rather on initiatory ceremonies of trial and purification. The tribunal before which the dead had to appear was constantly in session, and every dead person had to appear there whether accusations had been brought against him or not. The tribunal was the threshold everyone, including the king, had to cross after death in order to gain entry to the hereafter. The terrors of this idea were compensated by the prospect of not having to spend all eternity as a pale ghost in the realm of the dead but of perpetuating life with one's individual identity intact in the world of the gods. The divine tribunal had the power to stamp the seal of eternity on the personhood of the defendant, provided of course that he or she was not found wanting.

A tribunal of this kind reduced the unpredictability of the unpleasant eventualities that might be lying in wait, for the prosecution was represented not by potential enemies but by an omniscient god. The demands of such a god were common knowledge. The one hundred twenty-fifth chapter of the *Book of the Dead* systematizes the confessions to be recited by the dead in the form of a negative litany of possible sins. By asserting that he had not committed any of these sins, the dead person professed allegiance to the prevailing moral code. Each of the sentences beginning with "I did not" was an exact counterpart of the commandments stipulating "Thou shalt not. . . ." It was not sufficient, however, merely to deny having done these things. The confessional opening of one's heart to an omniscient god was symbolized by the ceremony of psychostasia, the "weighing of the heart." While the defendant recited his protestations of innocence, his heart was laid on a scale and weighed against the figurine of Ma'at, the goddess of truth. Every lie caused the pan with the heart on it to descend. If in the final reckoning the heart was found to be too heavy, it was devoured by a monster. The dead defendant would then disappear as a person, in contrast to the preserved personhood of those able to urge their case successfully.[104] This wonderful image was not the representation of any real weighing ceremony, but a symbolic way of rendering the invisible visible: the relation between human conscience, symbolized by the heart, and the will and knowledge of god, symbolized by the figure of the goddess Ma'at.

The *Book of the Dead*, in which these concepts are codified, belongs to the genre of mortuary literature. Yet this emphasis on the magical equipment of the dead does not contradict the view that the postmortem tribunal with its precise list of don'ts already had significance for the conduct of living. The best way to prepare for an otherworldly grilling was to examine the eighty offenses listed in the "negative confessional litany" and to avoid committing them. The *Book of the Dead* was thus a guideline for the moral investments that necessarily accompanied the material expenses of tomb building if a person was to be reasonably sure of life after death. A stela with a biographical inscription from the fourteenth century B.C.E. explicitly states that its

author, a nobleman named Baki, made the "laws" of the postmortem
tribunal the principles around which he organized his life:

> I am a noble who is fortunate in Ma'at,
> who sought to fulfill the laws of the "Hall of the Two Ma'ats,"
> for I planned to gain entrance to the realm of the dead,
> without my name being linked with a shameful act,
> without having done people any harm
> or anything that the gods deprecate.[105]

What Baki here calls the laws of the "Hall of the Two Ma'ats" are the
eighty items on the list of negative confessions. Once again the
Instruction for King Merikare makes clear how the individual, aware
that he would have to answer for his acts before the divine seat of
judgment, could gear his life to the requirements of the divine tribunal:

> The judges who judge the prosecuted,
> you know they are not lenient
> on that day when judgment is passed on the wretched one,
> in the hour of the fulfillment of the prescription.
> Terrible is the prosecutor, who is a knowing one.
>
> Count not on the length of the years!
> They see a lifetime as an hour.
> What is left of the man after the landing [death],
> his deeds will be laid beside him in their sum.
>
> But being there lasts forever.
> A fool is he who does what they deprecate.
> Who comes to them without crime,
> he will there be as a god,
> striding free like the lords of eternity.[106]

The Judgment of the Dead as the Foundation
for Justice

FOR AN EGYPTIAN, two ideas had to be accorded axiomatic status
if justice was to reign on earth: the immortality of the soul and the

existence of a punishing or rewarding authority who decided on the fate of that soul. These were the two ideas that made Egypt interesting for the western world long before the hieroglyphs were deciphered. Without recourse to revealed law, the Egyptians had succeeded in building a state and a society as fabled for their stability as for their wisdom, justice, and piety. What was in fact known about the Egyptian idea of the Judgment of the Dead before the hieroglyphs were deciphered and the *Book of the Dead* could be made to yield up its secrets?

The source of western knowledge about the Judgment of the Dead was Diodorus. But his description was markedly different from the contents of the *Book of the Dead*. In Diodorus' account, the Judgment of the Dead took place between embalming and burial. The corpse was rowed over a pond to a place where a tribunal of forty-two judges sat waiting to pass judgment. Anyone who had accusations to bring against the dead person could now do so. If the defendant was found guilty, the corpse could not be buried. But if there were no accusations or the accusations proved unfounded, the dead person was glorified by all present and subsequently buried with full honors. Reinhold Merkelbach has compared this account with the texts in the two Rhind mortuary papyri, which he interprets as being the record of the burial ceremonies for Menthesuphis and his wife, who both died in the year 9 B.C.E.[107] The papyri give a graphic account of the ceremonies, which took the form of a dramatic performance, with the priests assuming the roles of the gods. Taken together, this account and the descriptions by Diodorus suggest a "Baroque spectacle."[108] Indeed, the Baroque age was much impressed by Diodorus' account. In his *Discours sur l'histoire universelle* (1681), Jacques-Bénigne Bossuet makes lengthy reference to it, while Abbé Jean Terrasson drew on it for his novel *Séthos* (1731).[109]

Bossuet and Terrasson point to the close links between the idea of the Judgment of the Dead and the state. The Egyptians were the first to postulate that a state could be founded only on the basis of an unshakable faith in the immortality of the soul and the prospect of future judgment, ideas that are also central to Christian religion. The Egyptian concept of the verdict passed on the dead bears some comparison to the early Christian notion of divine judgment as set out in chapter 25 of the Gospel According to St. Matthew. Instead of the Egyptian tribunal, the gospel offers the Last Judgment, instead of individual lifetimes the lifetime of the world; the "House of Osiris" into which the vindicated Egyptian dead were admitted is replaced by the Kingdom of God. And here too, admission to everlasting bliss depends upon the dead person's compliance with the norms of human fellowship; in the hereafter, those transgressions not susceptible of retribution on earth are accorded the ultimate sanction of eternal damnation.[110]

The Old Testament, by contrast, is devoid of any concept of life after death or reward and retribution in the hereafter. In Israel, destiny and history, equated with the will of God, were the main spheres in which connective justice made its mark. In Deuteronomy and Deuteronomic historiography, the history of the Israelites is intimately bound up with their loyalty to the law. History and law are inextricably intertwined. Historical disaster is a product of transgression. The greater the disaster, the greater the transgression needed to explain it in terms of connective justice. As there is no hereafter, reckoning takes place in this world. And as it is very rare for this reckoning to be apparent in the lives of individuals, the idea of collective guilt gradually asserts itself. The sins of the fathers are visited upon the children, and the whole nation must atone for the misdemeanors of heedless and unmindful kings. As J. Taubes writes: "In tribes and primitive peoples, crime and punishment passed on down the chain of generations is the mythic brace holding together the logic of events between man and the gods."[111] Taubes points to Ezekiel as a turning point. Here the prophet comes out against the principle of genealogical collective liability, as expressed by the proverb "The fathers have eaten sour grapes, and the children's teeth are set on edge" (Ezekiel 18:2; see also Jeremiah 31:29). Rather, he sets out a new principle of individual liability:

> As I live, saith the Lord GOD, ye shall not have occasion any
>   more to use this proverb in Israel.
> Behold, all souls are mine; as the soul of the father, so also the
>   soul of the son is mine:
> the soul that sinneth, it shall die.[112]

But without a concept of a tribunal in the hereafter, this conception of connective justice leads to duress and paradox, as set out notably in the Book of Job. If the reckoning must take place on this side of the great divide and if the sway of connective justice must be evident both in the history of the nation and the destiny of the individual, the resulting pressure for history and personal destiny to display a meaningful contour can become excessively high. For this reason various versions of ancient Judaism, including Christianity, develop concepts of a life after death and justice in the beyond.

What Taubes calls the "mythic brace" was alien to the Egyptians, for whom the Judgment of the Dead favored the individualization of guilt. Belief in this judgment worked to fashion the Egyptians into social beings, fellow humans. The trouble with social norms, the agreed-upon conventions that regulate communal living, is that they cannot ultimately be enforced. They are not based on laws that allow for appeal to an independent court, where severe sanctions might be imposed. Rather, they are obligations of a moral nature; these obligations can be ignored with complete impunity because they come "from above." The covetous and hard-hearted, the selfish and the megalomaniac are not answerable to any earthly court. From this absence of accountability on earth came the concept of judgment in the life to come. In the list of offenses punished by the Egyptian postmortem tribunal, most prominent are sins against human fellowship, transgressions of the moral obligation to help and protect, to be considerate and public-spirited, modest and self-effacing:

> I was not covetous; I did not steal;
> I have never killed anyone [or: I have not killed, not commanded
>   to kill], I have not killed the "divine cattle" [= people];
> I have not increased the prescribed workload at the beginning of
>   each day, I have done no orphan any harm in his property.
> I have not robbed portions, nor practiced grain usury, I have
>   only been interested in what is my own;
> I have not lied, not scolded, I have not quarreled, sued,
>   terrorized, spoken unnecessary words, raised my voice, nor
>   spoken rashly.
> I have not secretly listened to others, nor winked my eye at
>   them, I have not puffed myself up or raised myself above my
>   station,

> I was not heated [or: "hot-mouthed"], not choleric, not violent,
> I have not turned a deaf ear to the words of truth. I have not
>   denigrated anyone to their superiors.
> I have inflicted no pain, I have not let others go hungry, I have
>   not caused tears, I have done no one any harm.[113]

Most of these misdemeanors are outside the scope of legal sanctions, and even where cases of punishable crimes are concerned—such as murder and manslaughter, robbery, theft, perjury, lèse-majesté, or blasphemy—the postmortem tribunal would limit itself to those cases undiscovered or unatoned for in this world. When the dead person underlines his worthiness to pass into the hereafter in an affirmative form, he makes use of the topoi of autobiographical inscriptions:

> I have done what people advise
> and what gratifies the gods.
> I have made god content by doing what he loves:
> I gave bread to the hungry,
> water to the thirsty,
> clothes to the naked,
> a boat to the boatless.[114]

The tomb inscriptions are likewise apologetic; they too presuppose an otherworldly jurisdiction over immortality.

The idea of a Judgment of the Dead also formed the Egyptians as political beings and as subjects of the king. In the Coffin Texts of the Middle Kingdom, a strikingly large number of authorities of surveillance and punition appear. A spell from a mortuary liturgy in the Coffin Texts offers the following judgment scene:

> O Osiris N here, you will not be put to the test, you will not be
>   locked up, you will not be taken prisoner,
> you will not be bound, you will not be put under guard,
> you will not be put on the scaffold on which the rebels are put,
> you will not have sand laid on your face,
> to prevent it weighing on you.
> No bars will be put before your face,

The Judgment of the Dead
Thebes, Tomb 41 (ca. 1300 B.C.E.)
(from J. Assmann, Das Grab des Amenemope, *Mainz, 1991, pl. 41)*

to stop you from going out.
Take your staff,
your raiment, your sandals,
and your weapons for the road!
May you cut off the head and sever the neck
of your foes male and female,
who speed your death, divert your coming,
who say to god: "Bring him here," on the day of execution.[115]

It is difficult to avoid the impression that these notions of an otherworldly police, of prison and scaffold, of denunciation and intrigue
reflect the experiences of the real world. The Coffin Texts are full of
demons who spread an atmosphere of surveillance and punishment
in the afterworld; the dead had to protect themselves from these
demons at least as much as they depended on them for protection.
All these disquieting beings are, of course, a product of the longing
for safety. These demons evoke the same dialectic of protection and
deterrence that informed the semiologies developed by the Twelfth

Dynasty in response to the experiences of the First Intermediate Period. Reflecting the pharaonic state, the hereafter is also constructed as a police state, where the ruling authorities offer security only to the degree that they also threaten to monitor and punish the individual.

12

THE TWO WORLDS AND THE
LANGUAGE OF DESPAIR

Doctrines of Two Worlds

THE TEXT OF THE PAPYRUS known as the *Dispute of a Man with His Ba* (Berlin 3024) contains the only chaos description up to this point that trains its gaze—averted from the chaos of this world—not on the past or on the future, but on the hereafter. In the world after death the principles of human fellowship and love that have disappeared from "this" world are still valid.

From a Christianized vantage, accounts of "this world" as a vale of tears and a place of unholy corruption, redeemed only by death, sound suspiciously familiar. The following text from a cantata by J. S. Bach can stand for countless others:

> False world, I trust thee not!
> Here I must live among scorpions
> and false serpents. . . .
> Honesty is banished from the world,
> falsehood has driven it out.
> Now hypocrisy remains in its place.
> The best of friends is untrue:
> O lamentable state!
>
> And yet,
> although I am cast out,
> still God remains my friend,
> His friendship is sincere.[116]

169

The text of the cantata makes clear what is meant by this "false world"—not cosmic realms, but social spheres, the worlds of community, of shared communication. This is also the subject of the Egyptian lamentations. The world whose decline is being mourned is the one founded on communal remembrance and animated by active solidarity. Of course the Egyptian texts—particularly the literature of the dead—are replete with "here" and "there," "this side" and "beyond," "heaven," "earth," and "underworld." But it is absolutely clear that while these refer to strictly separate cosmic realms, there is only one all-inclusive social sphere. This sets the Egyptian concept of "this world" in sharp contrast to the Christian vision, as illustrated in the text of the cantata, which clearly refers to two separate social spheres. Though I am "cast out" of one sphere, "still God remains my friend." This friendship represents a distinct and reliable sphere of belonging. Such a distinction was not accessible to the Egyptians.

Death represented the threshold between "this" world of indirect proximity to god and "that" world of direct communion with him. A harper's song from Theban Tomb No. 50 proclaims:

Every god you served on earth
you [now] see face to face.[117]

But in pharaonic Egypt this distinction between "on earth" and "there" never took the form of negation of "this world." The Egyptians never believed that they belonged in "that" world, where death would be a "homecoming." "Here" and "there" remained completely integrated into one single sphere of belonging. The gods were part of this community even though they were not directly accessible in this world. Hence in Egypt the worldly and the spiritual were never played off against each other as in the Bach cantata; one single sphere was shared by gods and humans alike and governed by the same laws of harmonious togetherness. Ma'at, the quintessence of the laws that welded humans into a community, was regarded as the holiest of the holy, the supreme essence of all life-serving and salvational values. When harmonious living on earth was disrupted, major disruptions of human contact with the world of the gods were certain to follow, and vice versa. If the rites were not performed properly, rebellion and internecine strife would break out, solidarity and justice among men would wither, the gods would turn away from human offerings. It is humans who bear the responsibility for maintaining the connectivity that binds them to one another and to the gods.

Lamentation over the collapse of such harmonious coexistence is the theme of the chaos descriptions, which revolve around the isolation of the individual unable to find community in the world. It stands to reason, then, that these lamentations typically take the form of communion with the self. They are enacted as dialogues with the author's own heart. The *Lamentation of Khakheperreseneb,* for example, is constructed as a dialogue between the author and his heart:

> A brave heart in situations of wretchedness
> is a companion for its lord.
> Had I but a heart that knows how to suffer!
> Then I would rest upon it.
> Then I would heap on it words of wretchedness,
> so that it would drive away my suffering.[118]
> He spoke to his heart: Come, my heart, that I may speak to you
>   and that you may respond to what I say and explain to me
>   what is going on in the land.[119]

Neferti begins his prophetic lament with a call to his own heart:

> Rouse yourself, my heart, and bewail this land from which you
>   come![120]

The form of interior dialogue with the appeal to the heart expresses the marginal status of the isolated individual. But it also fulfills an entirely different literary function. In the text quoted above, there is no genuine dialogue: the heart makes no response. Rather, the call to the heart is an opening gambit, comparable to the appeal to the Muse familiar in western literature. But whereas the Greek bard received his inspiration from without, from a long-existing oral tradition, the Egyptian "author" looked within for his inspiration, for he was expected not to reproduce but to produce, to bring forth new, unprecedented speech: The author of the *Lamentation of Khakheperreseneb* wishes, "O that I might find unknown phrases, strange expressions, new speech not yet uttered, free of repetitions, not sayings such as the ancestors used."

The dialogue between "self" and "soul" in the *Dispute of a Man with His Ba* has nothing to do with this opening topos. Here the dialogue form is authentic: the soul responds. The colloquy takes the form of a dramatic dispute in the course of which positions diametrically opposed to begin with are gradually reconciled.[121]

The Dialogue between "Self" and "Soul"

THE *DISPUTE* IS THE ONLY WORK of Egyptian literature that has achieved any kind of familiarity outside the ranks of Egyptologists.[122] The soul—Egyptian *ba*—is the vital energy incarnated in the body during a lifetime and released after death.[123] In the first part of the *Dispute* (whose opening section is lost), the self and the *ba* argue about the right way to die. In the largely lost speech with which the extant section begins, the *ba* says, "Their tongue is not partial"—a reference to the judges presiding over the postmortem tribunal. This gives us an important indication about the scenario. Egyptians saw death not as an end but as a transition. Physical death would place them in the immediate neighborhood of the gods, who are only indirectly present on earth. Thus in a text from the same period, one litigant who has vainly attempted to gain his rights from an earthly judge concludes: "Behold, I address myself to you with a legal plaint and you will not hear me. I shall go hence and complain to Anubis about you."[124] The litigant is not saying that he will offer a prayer at the nearest temple of Anubis; rather, he is threatening to commit suicide so as to cross the threshold between indirect and direct access to the gods and thus appeal to divine justice. Before this same threshold the dispute between the man and his *ba* takes place.

The self responds with a complaint: "My *ba* does not speak to me" (5–6). Like the plaintiff before the court, the *ba* has threatened to break off discussion with the self and to turn directly to the impartial tribunal of the gods, a move which can only be achieved via separation, death, "going hence." The self takes up precisely this point: "My *ba* shall not go hence, but rather stay and vouch for me" (7) and "my *ba* shall not let it happen that he [the *ba*] go hence on the day of misfortune" (10).[125]

"Behold," the self continues, here apparently already addressing the divine judges, "my *ba* opposes me, but I listen not to him. He drags me to death before I have come to it." The desire of the self is that

he shall stand on that side [i.e., "wait"]
as Nehepu does.
One such is he who goes out to bring himself back.

Though the concrete sense of these verses remains elusive, their clear
intent is to prevent the "going hence" envisaged by the *ba*. At issue
is the separation of self and *ba* in death; the *ba* wants this separation,
while the self wants to prevent it. The self continues:

My *ba* is foolish to rail at [?] the sorrow of life.
[The self then addresses the *ba:*]
Keep me back from death before I have come to it.
Make the West pleasant for me.
Is it then a misfortune?
Life is a span of time.
[Even?] trees fall.
Tread on the lie if my wretchedness continues!

Finally the self also speaks of the postmortem judges whose impar-
tiality was lauded by the *ba* and asks for their verdict:

May Thoth judge me, who appeases the gods,
may Khonsu defend me, who writes in truth,
may Re hear my statement, who points the sun-bark to rest,
may Isdes defend me in the sacred chamber.[126]

The *ba* replies:

[...]
What do you want to accomplish
by caring about life like a possessor of treasures?

The word *km* ("accomplish, bring to an end") resumes the theme of
time, which was initially addressed by the self with the statement "life
is a span of time." The self advocates time, delay, waiting, and
patience, while the *ba* advocates the Now. With its response, the self
clarifies the values it upholds and what is meant here by "life":

I said: I shall not go hence as long as the hereafter is neglected.
Verily you hurry away without giving thought.
[...]

Even when you are dead, your name still lives on.
A place of rest is the hereafter,
whence the heart takes one.
A haven is the West,
when navigation is difficult [...]
If my *ba* hearkens to me without wrongdoing
and his heart agrees with me, then he will be happy.
I shall ensure that he reaches the West as a tomb owner ["one
    who is in his pyramid"]
after his descendant appeared at his burial.
I shall make a shelter over your corpse
so that you will make envious another *ba* that is weary.
I shall make a shelter that is not too cold
so that you will make envious another *ba* that is hot.
I shall drink water at the place where it is scooped, and put up a
    shade,
so that you will make envious another *ba* that is hungry.
If you drive me away from such a death,
then you will find no place on which to set yourself down.
Have patience, my *ba*, my brother,
until an heir is present who will bring offerings,
who will stand at the tomb on the day of burial
so as to stand guard over [or: stretch out] the bier.

In these verses both the self and the *ba* seek death. The only controversy between them is over the form and the idea of death. The self
imagines death as the continuation of the vital union between self,
body, and *ba* under changed conditions. For the *ba*, death signifies
the termination of that union. Death as envisaged by the self requires
time and preparation, so the self advocates time, delay, postponement.
For the *ba*, this concern for the hereafter as perpetuation on earth is
illusory. Though in no sense challenging the notion of crossing over
to the world of the gods after death, the *ba* forcefully denies the
concept of the "West," the idea of remaining on earth after death, in
one's tomb, as a tomb owner, as a member of society. Death is the
end; there is no return. The tombs fall into desuetude and their owners are just as surely forgotten as the poor who sink down by the
riverside path and with whom the fish now converse.

The "hereafter" of which the self dreams is pure illusion; this
response from the *ba* is the most stunning and brutal negation of

supreme values conceivable.[127] For an Egyptian these were indeed "Satanic verses." What the *ba* pillories as illusion was the very heart of Egyptian religious conviction: the permanence of the mummified corpse in the burial chamber, the posterity of the name on the tomb, and immortality in the light of the sun. That a literary work should have imagined such a radical counterposition to the central values and norms of the Egyptians' own faith provokes both admiration and pause. Dogmatic religions cannot afford to countenance such an antagonism.

Immediately after these shocking words, the *ba* abruptly changes its tack and relates two parables. The first is about a man who plows his field, loads his harvest onto a boat, and sails home with his family. At sunset a storm springs up, the boat capsizes, and his wife and children are devoured by crocodiles. The man sits on the bank of the river and laments: "I weep not for her who was born and that she cannot come out of the West for another [life] on earth. I weep for her children that were smashed in the egg and have to see the countenance of the god of death before they have lived." The moral of the parable: "What is worse than death? Never to have lived." This conclusion is the negation of the tragic wisdom of the Greeks and of Koheleth: "The best thing for Man is never to have been born."

We also find this latter motif in *Ipuwer:*

Behold, great and small say: "I wish I were dead!"
Small children say: "Had he but not let me live!"[128]

This is the view imputed to the self by the *ba,* which as the embodiment of vital energy goes on to assert that not being born is the greatest misfortune imaginable: "I weep not for those who have lived but for those who have never come to life." With this statement the *ba* gives its own amoral vitalism a paradoxical twist that leads to a reductio ad absurdum.

The second of the parables centers on the motif of time, delay, and postponement. A man calls for his supper although it is early in the day. His wife tells him he must wait until evening. He departs in anger. In the evening, however, he returns completely changed. But his wife knows him as one who does not listen to those who admonish him and is "empty of heart" (obstinate) with respect to what they tell him. The *ba*'s position is mirrored in the behavior of the "man," who wants his supper "now," while the self represents the position of the wife, who knows that everything has its right time. The *ba* is obstinate, it "does not listen." The fact that the *ba* is the one telling the story is surprising. With these two parables it represents not only its own position but also that of the self.

Once the *ba* has forsaken the level of argumentative dispute and told these two parables, the self also changes its point of view and tops the *ba*'s parables with four lyrical songs. The first song has eight short stanzas, each beginning with the phrase "Behold, my name stinks because of you," followed by a "more-than" comparison: more than the stench of vultures, of fish, of birds in the thickets of swamps, of fishermen, of crocodiles, more than the name of a woman accused of adultery, more than the name of a child accused of being born out of wedlock, more than the name of a rebellious city. These charges are the response of the self to the *ba*'s shocking amoralism and skepticism with regard to the hereafter. The *ba*'s position has turned all the Egyptian values and norms upside down. Is that not reason enough for the man's name to "stink"?

In Egyptian, "behold" and "because of you" are homographic and so we cannot rule out the possibility that the passage was intended to read as follows: "Behold, my name stinks, behold, more than the stench of vultures." In this case, the chant would not be describing the consequences incurred by the self as a result of following the *ba*'s recommendations, but rather the situation that drives an individual—self "plus" *ba*—to suicide.[129] In my view, this interpretation seems unlikely. The "I" of the dialogue has not fallen into disgrace with his fellows as a result of some heinous undiscovered crime; rather, the issue is the fate of one's name after death. The self has already reminded the *ba* that the name lives on after death and that the individual must therefore take personal responsibility for his life and for his preparations for death. If these preparations are neglected, the name will be "noisome," abhorred by posterity. At the Judgment of the Dead, the deceased conjures his heart, as it lies on the scales, not to make his name "noisome before the councils that turn human beings into [the] sums [of their actions]."[130] In the *Instruction of Ani,* we hear: "Do not go away when the superiors enter, so that thy name does not stink." This is an obvious reference to slander. The self makes clear to the *ba* that its amoral view of death will provoke slander.

The second song is a chaos description. Of the three traditional aspects of chaos usually thematized—collapse of the cosmic order, inversion of social relations, dissolution of interpersonal bonds—this version concentrates exclusively on the third, the disappearance of "love." Everything centers on the purpose of living in a world where covetousness prevails rather than love. The Middle Kingdom had elevated "connective justice" to its central semiology by linking it with the idea of the Judgment of the Dead as that of an ultimate, transcendent, and supreme authority. In the *Dispute of a Man with His Ba* this semiology is probed and tested to its very foundations. In a world bereft of memory and no longer welded into a community by connective justice, can man adhere to those values that derive their prescriptive force from a belief in life after death? Or will he lose his moral identity and succumb to the general process of disintegration? The self's second song describes a world devoid of human bonds:

> To whom can I speak today?
> The brothers are evil; the friends of today, they do not love.

> To whom can I speak today?
> The hearts are greedy; everyone takes the goods of his neighbor.

> To whom can I speak today?
> The kind are doomed; the violent come down on everyone.

> To whom can I speak today?
> The face of evil is content; goodness is cast to the ground
>   everywhere.

> To whom can I speak today?
> He that should arouse anger by his badness
> makes everyone laugh though his crime is vile.

> To whom can I speak today?
> Robbery rules; everyone steals from his neighbor.

> To whom can I speak today?
> The traitor has become one's intimate,
> the comrade an enemy.

To whom can I speak today?
There is no memory of yesterday; today nothing is done for him
  who did something.

To whom can I speak today?
The brothers are evil, one seeks refuge with strangers for
  affection of the heart.

To whom can I speak today?
The faces are averted; everyone turns his gaze to the ground in
  the face of his brothers.[131]

To whom can I speak today?
The hearts are covetous; there is no heart one can rely on.

To whom can I speak today?
There are no just men; the land is left to the despoilers.

To whom can I speak today?
There is no one to confide in; one takes refuge with a stranger to
  vent one's sorrows.

To whom can I speak today?
None are content; he with whom one walked is no more.

To whom can I speak today?
I am weighed down with wretchedness for want of a friend.

To whom can I speak today?
Wrong roams the land and there is no end of it in sight.[132]

Sixteen images of the disintegration of human fellowship evoke a
"false world" that isolates the author through no fault of his own. As
in the text cited above from Bach's Cantata No. 52, the gaze of the
self turns away from this uninhabitable world and toward the
hereafter. This averted gaze turns everything upside down. The Egyptian word for death, normally avoided and circumscribed by such
euphemisms as "landing," now insistently appears, in the famous
third song, as a salvation:

Death stands before me today
[like] a sick man's recovery, like going outdoors after
   confinement.
Death stands before me today
like the fragrance of myrrh,
like sitting under a sail on a breezy day.
Death stands before me today
like the fragrance of lotus blossoms,
like sitting on the shore of drunkenness.
Death stands before me today
like rain going away [or: like a well-trodden path],
like a man's return from war.
Death stands before me today
like the clearing of the sky, like a man enlightened [?] about that
   of which he was ignorant.
Death stands before me today
like a man's longing to see his home
when he has spent many years in captivity.

The inversion of normative values is central to the unique force of this text. Just as the *ba* has upended the most sacrosanct values of Egyptian religion, so here the self turns man's most instinctive fears on their head. Death appears as a cure for disease. The dying Socrates is reported to have said: "Do not forget to sacrifice a cock to Asclepius." In Greece it was customary for someone who had recovered from a severe illness to sacrifice a rooster to the god of medical skill. The self's insight in this third song is of comparable power.

The fourth song directs its gaze firmly at the other world. The "there" that is "not here" appears as a rescue from an unholy present:

But who is there will be as a living god,
who punishes transgression on him who commits it.
But who is there will stand in the [sun] bark
and distribute offerings from it to the temples.
But who is there will be a wise man who cannot be debarred
from appealing to the sun god when he speaks.[133]

The confrontation between "here" and "there" could hardly be more marked. The activities of the one "who is there" are those of connective justice: punish transgression, ply the temples with offerings, speak as a wise man. Their realization reflects what is impossible "here." The connectivity or *ma'at* that has disappeared in this world can be found "there," as can the peaceful, supportive coexistence no longer possible on earth.

The text concludes with the words of the *ba*, which now speaks a completely transformed language, the language of love and reconciliation:

> Desist from your complaining,
> my nearest, my brother!
> May you bring burnt offerings
> and get close up to life as you see it.
> Love me "here," now that you have postponed the West,
> but long indeed to reach the West,
> when your body touches the earth.
> I will lay myself down when you are spent.
> Then shall we dwell together.

With these words the *ba* concedes everything the self has been urging from the outset: to wait patiently together until the time has come to die, to prepare for the "West," and to maintain a shared identity beyond the threshold of death (the word "we" appears for the very first time in the last line, thus forming an indubitable climax). The *ba* enters into the full communion with the self that it had declined in the initial, lost part of the text. Within the dialogue's setting of complete isolation, man finds support and solace in himself as long as he succeeds in maintaining the values and norms that, although temporarily "vanished" from this earth, still have validity in the hereafter, as the Judgment of the Dead warrants.

    In her impressive study of this text, Odette Renaud contends that it describes a psychopathological condition, "the first neurosis in world history." I myself would speak of despair. In a world where "connective justice" is the cardinal paradigm, solitude is a crisis that plunges the individual into the severest despair. As in the Book of Job, the text gives expression to the experience of despair, then overcomes it by setting the gaze free to move to a wider horizon that promises to the isolated self communion with his own soul and with the gods who inhabit a world beyond this one.

The *Dispute of a Man with His Ba* is not about the world as it is but about a catastrophic situation. It belongs to the genre of lamentations or chaos descriptions. In the experimental laboratory of literary fiction, connective justice as the cardinal semiology of the Middle Kingdom is subjected to a radical test of strength. In this work, literature reveals itself as an instrument of social and anthropological self-illumination with which a culture might assure itself of the resilience of its own supreme values. Whereas other works of the same genre (the *Admonitions of Ipuwer* or the *Prophecies of Neferti*) are primarily concerned with the fate of the state if connective justice breaks down, the *Dispute* centers squarely on the fate of the individual, more specifically on the problem of solitude. Its message is not that man is alone in this world, but rather that without *ma'at* he is bound to become more and more isolated.

Suspicions that the *Dispute* might represent a form of gnosis are allayed by the realism of the chaos descriptions, which invariably refer to a temporary situation and do not advance a diagnosis for all time. The world is not rotten and corrupt by nature, nor is man an alien in an evil world. Rather, the chaos descriptions reflect the insight that the ordered systems that make this world habitable and allow man to feel at home in it are fragile and not to be taken for granted. Man has no other home; the world of the gods is not "another world." However, the divine realm and the Judgment of the Dead represent both a frame of reference and a touchstone. As such, they are also a sanctuary to which the principles that impose order on this world may retreat when they are banished from "here."

A chaos description from a much later epoch, the *Tale of Woe,* also delineates the distress of an isolated man, and again trains its gaze on the hereafter and communion with the sun god:

Had there but been a message to comfort my heart
when misfortune came.
But there was never any inquiry after how I might be faring
in all the course of my wanderings.
When bones and flesh are forsaken at the edge of the desert—
who will bury them?
There was no message of concern about me.
Behold, neither the dead nor the living concerned themselves
with my cares.
Of what significance will my sufferings be in later times,

when I am in the realm of the dead and in contemplation of the horizon-dweller?[134]

Again the text is not a diagnosis of the world as it essentially is but the portrayal of a situation of complete isolation in which the prospect of communion with the sun god in death is the only form of community for which the lone wanderer can hope.

Pharaonic Egypt never developed a radical two-worlds theory comparable to those of Christianity, Judaism, and Gnosticism. The Judgment of the Dead connects the norms of this world with those of the next. What is valid here will be valid there. The attitudes and behaviors that lead to happiness, fulfillment, and success in this world will find equal favor in the next. Classical Egyptian texts make no mention whatsoever of the idea of inversion by which in the next life the poor shall be made rich and vice versa, or those that travail and are heavy laden will be compensated for everything they have been made to suffer. The Judgment of the Dead is not the great divide between this world and the next, quite the contrary; rather, it binds both worlds together inseparably.

13

REPRESENTATION, MEDIACY, THE "RIVEN WORLD," AND THE PROBLEM OF EVIL

Representative Theocracy

IN THE RETROSPECTIVE VIEW of earlier periods—and of our own—Egypt has always appeared to be a land with a special proximity to its deities. The gods inhabited and ruled the country in the form of cult images and temples, the "settlement density" of the divine was singularly high. A veritable army of priests was devoted to serving the divinities intensively and unremittingly. The gods had to be anointed, clothed, and fed; they had to be praised three times a day. It hardly surprises that in late antiquity Egypt was regarded as the "holiest land" and the "temple of the world."

But such references describe a form of Egyptian religion that had taken shape gradually over thousands of years. In the Old Kingdom the temples were small, local, and insignificant. The kings invested in their own personal mortuary cult complexes, not in the regional temples of the gods. Indeed, in the Old Kingdom the mortuary cult of the kings was the true state-organized form of religious worship. Only in the Middle Kingdom did the rulers become builders and cult lords of temples for the gods. In adopting this role, the Middle Kingdom rulers emulated the magnates and nomarchs of the First Intermediate Period. Since the nomarchs could not present themselves as the commissioners of a central power, they had to look for a different kind of authority to legitimize their rule. To this end they appealed to the gods (something the kings of the Old Kingdom had no need to do), and the gods they turned to were the local deities of the respective nome capitals. Thus we read in the inscriptions of Ankhtifi of Mo'alla:

> Horus has brought me to the nome of Edfu
> for the sake of life, salvation, and health, that my name order
> it [anew]
> But Horus had the wish to order it anew,
> because he fetched me to it [the nome] to order it anew.

For a god to take this kind of initative was entirely new. Horus of Edfu appears here in precisely the same role as a ruler of the Old Kingdom: the commissioner who initiates and legitimizes the activity of his official. The nomarchs no longer saw themselves as officials of the king and representatives of a central power but as agents of the local deity, who was the real ruler of the land. This model of legitimate rule developed by the nomarchs of the First Intermediate Period was taken over by all subsequent rulers. Kings were now the chosen, appointed agents of the state god, the stewards of the creator, who was the real lord of the world.

This new relation between god and king resembles the Mesopotamian model of rule more than it does the Old Kingdom's. True, no texts have survived from the Old Kingdom to testify to the ruling practices of the time. But the royal titularies,* the architecture, and the iconography are eloquent enough. The god of the state was the dead king; all architectural and ritual endeavors were devoted to his cult. The living king was the lord of this cult. The king bore the name of Horus as his most important title and was regarded as the living incarnation of that god (not merely as his representative on earth). In the course of the Old Kingdom, this "incarnatory" model was joined by another, which I call constellational. The incarnatory model expressed in the Horus title—and hence identifiable as early as the Naqada period—saw the pharaoh as the embodiment of the supreme god. The constellation model saw in him the son of the sun god Re. In this model the supreme god is not embodied in the king but begets the king—the "son of Re"—with a mortal woman. This change from direct to representative theocracy achieved canonical status with the kings of the Fifth Dynasty, and remained squarely rooted in Egyptian

---

*refers to the five names—including the throne name, Horus name, and Golden Horus name—assumed by an Egyptian king at his ascension.

cultural memory. The myth that dramatizes this shift appears in a major literary work of the late Middle Kingdom.

King Cheops, so the myth runs, was possessed of the desire to know the number of secret chambers in the temple of Heliopolis. A sage was consulted but announced that not he but three future kings would give Cheops the knowledge he wanted. These three kings, the successors of Cheops' grandson, were triplets begotten by the sun god himself with the mortal wife of one of his priests. They would build temples for the gods and fill them with offerings. The sage's implication is that Cheops was so preoccupied with the construction of his own immense pyramid that he had omitted to honor the gods with offerings. Cheops is suspiciously interested in the exact details regarding the triplets and is clearly determined to do away with his prophesied successors. Nonetheless, these kings are born unharmed and receive the names that have been handed down to us on the king-list of the Fifth Dynasty; here, and only here, a mythic narrative refers to names that likewise figure on the king-list.

The archaeological and epigraphic evidence from this period corroborates the myth. From the Fifth Dynasty onward, all the kings actually did call themselves "son of Re." The kings of the Fifth Dynasty even erected solar sanctuaries alongside their own mortuary temples, a tradition abandoned by their successors. The "son" title ushered in a new age in Egyptian history, in which the king's image was determined by his filial descent from the creator and state god, Re. As son, the king acted on behalf of the father, understood as the totality of fathers and mothers. To keep these ancestors placated, he built temples and kept them supplied with offerings; on behalf of his ancestors, the king ruled over his subjects and engaged in warfare. We must still ask ourselves, however, whether the switch from direct to representative theocracy really did set in as early as the Fifth Dynasty. For the conception of the king as the titular son and ordained representative of the gods, and as mediator between the human and divine spheres, corresponds only to the much later, Middle Kingdom image of the king. What this myth does is to transpose the image back into the late stages of the Fourth Dynasty, much as the *Prophecies of Neferti* were transposed to the age of Snofru. The legitimacy of the Twelfth Dynasty derived from its view of itself as a turning toward salvation. But that turning was not only a turning away from the chaos of the First Intermediate Period to the orderliness of the Middle Kingdom but also from the direct theocracy of the Old Kingdom to the representative theocracy it ascribed to the Fifth Dynasty.[135]

The model of representative theocracy determines the worldview of the Middle Kingdom, although its precursors dated back to the Fifth Dynasty. Underlying this model is a distinctive conception of human nearness to god. In the Egyptian view, divine presence was by no means a natural, given fact of life. The Egyptians did not feel close to their gods in the same way as the Greeks did, at least if their literary works are anything to go by. They were not in a constant state of anticipation about encountering some god in the shape of a brook or a tree, a bird, a dream, or a man. The gods were remote and concealed from view on account of the tragic dissociation described in the *Book of the Heavenly Cow*. According to the myth, gods and men inhabited the same world at first. But then the humans organized an insurrection against the rule of the creator and sun god. To punish them, the creator almost decided to annihilate them, but then opted for a different solution. He spanned the heavens above the earth ("down below") and retired there with the other gods. On earth he set up his son Shu, the god of the air, as his successor.[136] As the personification of the state, Shu is charged with keeping the heavens arched high above the earth, thus maintaining both the remoteness of the gods and the link between gods and men. In a text from the early Middle Kingdom, Shu describes himself thus:

> I am he that instills the fear of him [the sun-god] into those
> who inquire after his name.
> I am he that is in the midst of the millions and hears the speech
> of the millions.
> I am he that causes the words of the self-born [= sun god] to
> reach his multitude.[137]

Shu guarantees the inscrutability of the remote sun god and at the same time institutionalizes communication between the sun god and his creatures. He is the model for all the kings later established by the sun god as his representatives. Hence the state both presupposes remoteness on the part of the gods and at the same time compensates for it. Or, to put it more trenchantly, if the gods were present, there would be no state. But because the gods are remote, there has to be an institution that ensures contact with the divine world even under conditions of remoteness. From now on, gods will be manifest on earth only through a structure of representation. In their myths the Egyptians describe themselves as inhabiting a disenchanted world; the present state (in both senses of the word) is both the healing of a breach and a compensation for a loss, the loss of corporeal closeness to the gods. Real presence is replaced by representation. By virtue of their symbolic power, state and cult, temples, rites, statues, and images make present the divine and establish an irremediably indirect contact with the gods. Whereas the myths once narrated and imagined the direct propinquity of the gods, divine presence now depends upon the culturally formed possibilities of symbolic mediation and representation. The state is the institution of this closeness. The pharaoh rules as the representative of the creator god. The primal model of legitimate rule is that of the creator over his creation. After the insurrection of the creatures, the direct theocracy of the myths is transformed into the representative dimension of historical rule.

The locus classicus for the representative theology of pharaonic kingship in the Middle Kingdom and the mediator role of the king is a text that, although only traceable as far back as the reign of Hatshepsut, probably stems from the Middle Kingdom. The king is presented as worshipper of the sun god:

> Re has set up the king
> on the earth of the living
> for ever and ever
> to speak justice to the people, to satisfy the gods,
> for the generation of *ma'at,* for the destruction of *isfet.*
> He [the king] gives the divine offerings to the gods
> and mortuary offerings to the transfigured.
> The name of the king
> is in heaven like [that of] Re.
> He lives in joy
> like Re-Horakhty.
> The dignitaries rejoice when they see him.
> The subjects give him ovations
> in his role of the child.

The acts of the king are paired like the correlative concepts men/gods and *ma'at/isfet.* The first pair is concrete, the second abstract. Obviously the relation between the two pairs is explanatory, not merely additive: the second pair explains the first, the first concretizes the second. To paraphrase the propositions in reverse order:

The task of the king on earth is to realize *ma'at* and drive out *isfet*.

In concrete terms, that involves jurisdiction over men and satisfaction of the gods.

Thus the concept of *ma'at* can be specified as justice—an ordered legal system among men, to be established via jurisdiction; satisfaction or harmony among the gods, to be established via cult (veneration and offerings).

The concepts "jurisdiction" and "cult" can be specified more closely if we draw on chapter 126 of the *Book of the Dead,* which deals with the same notions of representation and mediation. The deceased turns to "the four baboons at the bow of the sun bark"

> that let *ma'at* ascend to the lord of all,
> that speak justice between the weak and the strong,
> that satisfy the gods with the breath of their mouths,
> that give the gods divine offerings
> and the transfigured mortuary offerings.[138]

This text replaces the terse formulas "speak justice to the people" and "satisfy the gods" with the more detailed phrases "speak justice between the weak and the strong" and "satisfy the gods with the breath of their mouths" (reciting sacred formulas). The first of these refers to the Egyptian concept of justice as a salutary institution of equality in a world in which not only are there weak and strong, but also the strong oppress the weak if the state does not intervene.

But the text is also important in its linkage of the motifs of "saving justice" and representation. Just like the king and god Shu in the earlier passage from the Coffin Texts, the baboons appear here as agents of justice and communication. In a world become wide-ranging and complex, the baboons maintain the links between above and below. They "let *ma'at* ascend" and also disseminate it downward. In a situation of remoteness and separation from the gods, they ensure that community is maintained and that the weak are looked after even in a world marked by greed and main force.

Theodicy: Semiologies in the Face of Evil

HOW IS IT THAT THE WORLD, a place of divine origin, is riven by greed and violence? How did evil come into the world, and with it the separation of heaven and earth, gods and men?

The biggest challenge facing any construction of meaning is posed by experiences of imperfection, evil, and failure. And the semiologies of the Middle Kingdom were confronted primarily with the problem of giving a meaning to these experiences. The purpose of the state is the aversion of "chaos," and this chaos is represented as the quintessence of all evil. But this idea of chaos should not be confused with cosmogonic chaos, the primal state of the fore-world from which sprang the order of creation. Cosmogonic chaos is amorphous primal matter devoid of any connotations of evil or imperfection (such as those that resonate in the biblical *tohu-bohu*). The chaos that the Middle Kingdom pits itself against is not cosmogonic, but "cratogonic": the opposite of chaos is not the birth of a world but the establishment of rule.

For the Egyptians, cosmogony was a complex process combining the two aspects of intransitive unfolding and transitive creation. By contrast, their ideas on the origin of rule were unequivocally transitive: once the world had come into being, it had to be actively maintained by the exercise of power. The Egyptian understanding of evil belongs within this context. The creator, in the form of the sun god and wearing the deadly insignia of kingship, contests evil. The sun god disseminates light—that is, justice, the life-giving force that guarantees order and "meaning" against the ubiquitous threat of evil, embodied in the form of a monstrous water serpent.[139] This dramatic view of the world extends the ideological foundations of the Egyptian state into a cosmic dimension.

The central semiology of the Middle Kingdom is predicated on the imperfection of the world and the experience of evil. Like most other religions, Egyptian belief attributes this imperfection to a rebellion of man against his creator. The *Book of the Heavenly Cow* presents one instance. The *Instruction for King Merikare* also thematizes human insurgence. The experience of evil is juxtaposed with the premise that the world is fundamentally well ordered and well provided:

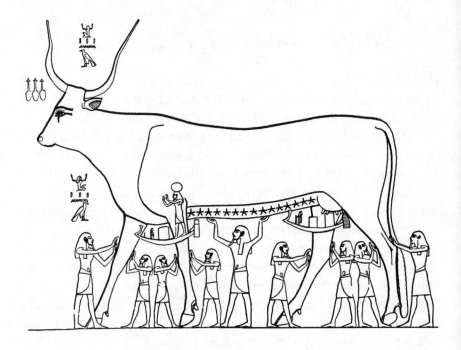

The Heavenly Cow
Wall relief in the tomb of Sethos I (ca. 1290 B.C.E.)

Well provided are the humans, the herd of god.
For their sake he created heaven and earth,
he thrust back the greed of the water
and created the air that their noses might live.
They are his images, they have come forth from his body.

For their sake he rises in the heavens,
for them he created the plants and the animals,
fowl and fish, so that they might eat.
[But] because they plotted rebellion,
he killed his enemies and wreaked violence on his children.
For their sake he let there be light,
to see them he sets forth [across the sky].
For their protection he set up a chapel for himself;
when they weep, he hears.

He created for them rulers "in the egg"
and commanders to strengthen the backs of the weak.
He created for them magic as a weapon,

to fend off the blow of events,
watching over them night and day.

That he slew the "crooked-hearted" among them
was as a man slays his son for his brother's sake.
God knows every name.

This text lists twelve works of the creator. Ten of them are especially designed for man's well-being, thus "for them" and "for their
sake" prefaces these works. Two of the works, however (where the
phrase "for them" is absent), are directed—with punitive, judgmental force—against mankind. Significantly, the creator has made a
distinction between men. He has slain the evil, not "for their sake,"
but for the sake of the good. This text addresses the same theme as
the myth of the near destruction of the human race in the *Book of
the Heavenly Cow*. In both narratives, the establishment of the state
("rulers in the egg") and the creation of magic are understood as
compensatory measures taken by the creator to guarantee a sphere
of order and providence in a world threatened by evil. Without the
state the weak would be lost; without magic, the unfortunate utterly
cast down. The punitive force of the creator against his own children is the indispensable precondition of their well-being. It does
not occur blindly, nor does it have anything to do with the "blow
of events" (against whose force man was given magic). The "blow
of events" is absurd and outside the horizon of connective justice;
the blow dealt by god is pertinent and meaningful. God slew his
children "because they plotted rebellion"; he killed the "crooked-
hearted" among them "as a man [i.e., a father] kills his son for his
brother's sake."

The texts that hark back to the First Intermediate Period also
speak of killing and dying. But it is not the "crooked-hearted" who
are slain but the weak, the few, the children; likewise, the people dying
of hunger are also without fault. The horror of this scenario is its
very meaninglessness. The reproach flung at god in *Ipuwer* can be
read as the inverse of this hymn to the creator god. In *Ipuwer* the
herd of god is "scant" because men are killing each other, nor are
"the timorous distinguished from the violent." In no way does god
guard over mankind. On the contrary: "There was no steersman in
their hour. Where is he today? Is he perhaps asleep? One sees not his
punitive power." These are the challenges that the semiologies of the

Middle Kingdom had to contest. Chaos, in the sense of absurdity and meaninglessness, is banished by the state. Creation itself does not banish chaos. Nor does creation guarantee the presence of meaning and order. Man must actively ensure that meaning and order are present in the world.

Chaos threatens man from within, as the Coffin Text spell 1130 makes clear:

Thus spoke he with the secret name.
The lord of all said, when the rebellion of the bark crew had to
    be quelled:
Be whole and at peace!
I will proclaim to you the four good deeds
that my own heart did to me in the encircling snake
so as to reduce wrong to silence.

I have done four good deeds in the portal of the land of light:
I have created the four winds,
that everyone can breathe in his time.
That is one of the deeds.

I have created the great flood of water,
That the poor may dispose of it like the rich.
That is one of the deeds.

I have made each man the same as his neighbor
and have prohibited that they should do wrong.
But their hearts have resisted my commandment.
That is one of the deeds.

I have ordained that their hearts cease to forget the West [i.e., "I
    have created the fear of death"],
so that the local gods be brought offerings.
That is one of the deeds.

[...]
I judge the rich and the poor.
I proceed equally against those who do wrong.
Mine is life, I am its lord,
No one will rob me of rule.

In order "to reduce wrong to silence" the sun god and creator affirms the principle of rule. Chaos comes from the human heart. The sun god cannot prevent his commandments from being violated, but he can, and will, punish transgression. He kills for the sake of life. He holds the scepters of life and rule: "There is no end to the day of the tribunal."[140]

This is the god whom the king represents on earth. The state translates the life-giving and judgmental rule of the creator god into earthly equivalents. The riven world is held together by connective justice. The Egyptian semiology of a divided or riven world does not hold out hopes of "another" world in the hereafter, but points to the pharaonic state as the eminently "this-worldly" compensation for worldly imperfection. The Egyptian civilization needs no Redeemer, only a "good shepherd" protecting his sheep from the wolves.

PART FOUR

The New Kingdom

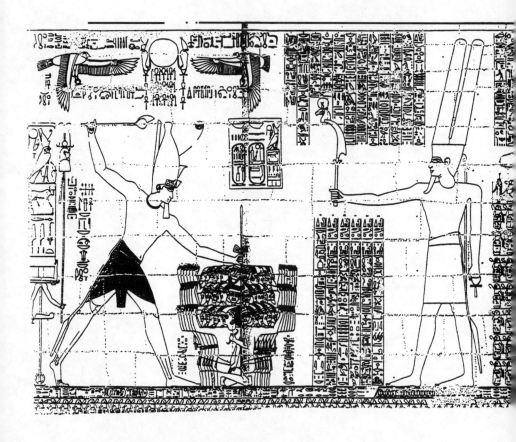

Ramesses III Smiting the Enemies (traditional motif)
(from S. Schoske, Das Erschlagen der Feinde: Ikonographie und Stilistik der Feindvernichtuung im alten Ägypten, *Ann Arbor, 1994, fig. 174, p. 66)*

14

HISTORICAL OUTLINE

THE NEW KINGDOM BEGINS with the wars of liberation against the Hyksos, whose seizure of power in Egypt marked the end of the Middle Kingdom and its inglorious aftermath.

"Hyksos" is the Greek version of the Egyptian term for "the chiefs of foreign lands." The six kings of the Fifteenth Dynasty bore this title and they are referred to as such in the king-list. They were foreigners of Asiatic origin and ruled for over a hundred years (1650–1540 B.C.E.). This was the first period of foreign rule in the history of pharaonic Egypt. The experience of foreign rule and of liberation was crucial for the further course of the New Kingdom; it had major repercussions on politics, the structure of society, and even on the Egyptian worldview, in which the idea of the foreign now took on an entirely new significance.

Excavations at Tell el-Daba (in antiquity Avaris, the Hyksos capital) have revealed a purely Palestinian culture. The evidence suggests that in the seventeenth century B.C.E. a Palestinian empire had formed, which penetrated first to the eastern reaches of the Delta and from there laid the entire Egyptian kingdom under tribute. Written sources tell us that there were intensive diplomatic relations with Nubia. In Manetho's list, all six Hyksos kings forming the Fifteenth Dynasty have throne names that feature the sun god Re and thus indicate conformity to the Egyptian tradition. Manetho describes Hyksos rule as a reign of terror and says that it lasted 517 years, much longer than was actually the case. This indicates the immense significance the period had gained in Egyptian memory. Manetho is ignorant of the origins of the Hyksos, calling them people "of insignificant

Ramesses II Taking a Syrian Town (Ramesside battle picture)
Ramesseum (ca. 1250 B.C.E.)
(from H. Müller-Karpe, Handbuch der Vorgeschichte IV, *Munich,*
1980, pl. 54, D)

descent." Flavius Josephus, his most attentive reader, identifies the
Hyksos with the Jews, and this identification is found throughout the
written tradition of antiquity, with the notable exception of the Bible,
which contains no reference to rule over Egypt, reporting solely captivity and servitude.

The New Kingdom, then, begins with the wars of liberation
against the Hyksos. These wars, which lasted from circa 1570 to 1540
B.C.E., were of decisive import for the nascent kingdom and left a
lasting imprint on its political symbolism and long-term political
objectives. Indeed, the wars of liberation were as crucial to the semantics of the New Kingdom as the chaos of the First Intermediate Period
was to the semiologies of the Middle Kingdom. In retrospect, the
Middle Kingdom equated the First Intermediate Period with internal
chaos and explained this chaos in terms of an absence of *ma'at*.
Accordingly, the Middle Kingdom constructed its formative semiologies around the ideology of *ma'at*, of "connective justice" and "vertical solidarity." In the collective memory of the New Kingdom, the

experience of the wars of liberation was summed up in the formula of "external menace." Thus, whereas the main concerns of the Middle Kingdom centered on domestic policy, those of the New Kingdom focused on foreign policy.

Within the cyclical structure of Egyptian history, it is of the greatest significance that the early rulers of the Eighteenth Dynasty— who ushered in the New Kingdom—modeled themselves closely on the Twelfth Dynasty in the style of their inscriptional and artistic self-representation.[1] As the Twelfth Dynasty had elaborated the memorial cult of the nomarch Heqaib of the Sixth Dynasty into a major sanctuary at Elephantine,[2] so the New Kingdom venerated Sesostris III of the Twelfth Dynasty with a temple in his honor at Buhen (Nubia).

But even apart from such parallels, a more pervasive cultural continuity clearly distinguishes the Second Intermediate Period from the First. In the south of the country, notably in Thebes, there appears to have been no breach whatsoever in cultural tradition. Various important manuscripts stem from this age and region, including the medical manuals of Papyri Smith and Ebers, the mathematical Papyrus Rhind, Papyrus Prisse containing the best and most complete version of the *Instruction of Ptahhotep,* Papyrus Westcar with *King Cheops and the Magicians,* and the statuette bearing excerpts from the so-called *Cairo Hymn to Amun,* the earliest genuinely theological text that we have from Egypt.[3] The manuscripts from the Eighteenth Dynasty with the *Prophecies of Neferti,* the *Instruction for King Merikare,* the *Instruction of Amenemhet I* (Papyrus Millingen), and other works of the Middle Kingdom extant in this later form are further examples of the outstandingly rich written heritage that has come down to us from this period. In cultural terms, the first genuine breach or clearly distinctive threshold to a new epoch does not occur until the Amarna Period and the early Ramesside age (1350–1270).

It bears noting, however, that the ousting of the Hyksos was interpreted and commemorated in terms of the myth of Horus and Seth—the essential myth of state that established the foundational vocabulary of the Old Kingdom and served as a prototype for future myths. From the reverse perspective, it is equally important to note that the myth of Horus and Seth was itself reinterpreted in the light of the historical experience of the wars of liberation. Accordingly, the operative opposition was no longer law versus force, or culture versus savagery and nomadism, but Egypt versus Asia. Seth was transformed into the god of the Hyksos and hence into an Asiatic. Egyptian policy was now oriented toward an image of the foe defined in religious terms; as a result, that policy became both aggressive and expansionary. Seth was not, however, demonized or ostracized. On the contrary, his new role as the representative of the Asiatic world guaranteed that alien things could now be translated into domestic terms. Foreigners were no longer simply thought of as belonging to the realm of chaos and thus beyond the pale; they were now seen as instances of "otherness," who qualified for consideration as (potential) adversaries or partners, either to be subjugated as tributary vassals or won over by means of alliances and political marriages. In Egypt, foreign gods were now either worshipped in their own right or assimilated to existing deities; for example, the equation of the Hyksos' Baal with the Egyptian Seth. The New Kingdom's image of the world no longer opposed the Egyptian cosmos to external chaos; rather, the world created by the sun god was now understood to contain many different peoples. The assertion of a new "ecumenical" orientation may seem paradoxical, given what we have said about "foes" and "aggression." But conflict is, after all, a species of relationship, albeit an antagonistic one. In place of Egypt's earlier almost total lack of dealings with the complex and tension-ridden political structure of the Near East, we now see the emergent awareness of an overarching political universe full of relations and conflicts from which Egypt could no longer hold itself apart.[4]

The so-called Ramessides, who formed the Nineteenth and Twentieth Dynasties, originated from Sile, a frontier fort in the eastern Delta, and ruled Egypt from Pi-Ramesse, their newly built capital close to Avaris. They felt a special allegiance to Seth. Some of these kings even had the god in their names: Sethos I, Sethos II, Sethnakhte. Ramesses II's Stela of Year 400, a unique instance of historical commemoration, marks the four hundredth jubilee of the establishment of the Seth cult in Avaris, the Hyksos' capital city. The text shows clearly that for the Egyptians of the period the Seth cult of the foreign interlopers did not represent anything alien, still less anything evil. Seth was still a major deity, who helped the sun god keep the world in good functioning order. The new military and aristocratic semantics of this age gave Seth the attributes of a war god. Thus in the New Kingdom the Horus-Seth myth was still inclusive rather than marginalizing. Not until the Late Period, when the experience of alien rule became painful and oppressive, did the image of Seth take on a diabolical aspect.

Liberation and expulsion are two sides of the same coin.

Wherever a political semantics develops from the experience of liberation, it also incorporates the aggressive connotations of ejection. In the New Kingdom, militarism and imperialism flourished to an unprecedented degree. The kings of the Eighteenth Dynasty systematically prolonged the wars of liberation, discovering in them an instrument for the accumulation of both material *and* symbolic capital. From now on, the victorious general figured prominently among the roles of the king, ultimately advancing to the dominant symbol of legitimization via merit. "Expanding the frontiers" became the foremost political objective.[5] In campaigns of conquest far exceeding the defensive aims of the "wars of liberation," Tuthmosis I penetrated as far as the Euphrates. Tuthmosis III replaced the strategy of military conquest with a policy of annexation: conquest was followed by occupation, the establishment of garrisons, the appointment of commandants, stewards, and vassals, the delivery of tribute, the foundation of economic and cultic institutions, ports, supply bases, and communication networks. Year after year, military campaigns were undertaken as a demonstration of power to intimidate vassals, to consolidate annexed territory, and to extend the infrastructure. This political program developed such an impetus that the kings of the Eighteenth, Nineteenth, and Twentieth Dynasties were unable to extricate themselves from it, despite attempts by some like Queen Hatshepsut and the revolutionary Akhenaten. Tuthmosis III stood unassailable as the incarnation of successful political leadership.

But warfare and subjection were not the only methods employed in Egyptian foreign policy. Tuthmosis IV terminated the warfare against the Hurrian empire of Mitanni, securing peace and political alliance by means of a diplomatic marriage with a Mitannian princess. Amenophis III followed his example. After the forcible caesura of Egyptian foreign policy in the Amarna Period, however, kings Sethos I and Ramesses II of the Nineteenth Dynasty returned to the systematic policy of aggression and subjugation pursued by Tuthmosis III. The new adversaries were the Hittites. The famous Battle of Qadesh, in which the Egyptians were ambushed and Ramesses II only just escaped capture, brought a turning toward peace, alliance, and diplomatic marriage. But that process took a further thirty years to engineer. After the demise of the Hittite empire, a convincing justification for the continuation of an aggressive policy toward Asia proved difficult. Other conflicts, such as Merneptah's wars against the Libyans

or Ramesses III's defensive actions against the Sea Peoples, were artificially inflated to the scale of the Asiatic wars.

The extent to which this policy, the semantics underlying it, and
the concept of history sustaining it were peculiar to the New Kingdom
is demonstrated by the development of entirely new forms of historical representation, which themselves disappeared with the New Kingdom. Chief among these is the depiction of scenes of battle that show
the king in his chariot taking an Asiatic fortress by force. The earliest
of these is to be found on a chariot of Tuthmosis IV, while the second
decorates a chest in the grave treasure of Tutankhamun. From the
Nineteenth Dynasty onward, this form of depiction became dominant
in the portrayal of royal deeds of derring-do on temple walls. The
high point of this development was reached with the representations
of the Battle of Qadesh under Ramesses II, which show the king and
his chariot in a maplike depiction of the terrain, supplemented by a
sequence of other scenes that amount to a graphic narration of the
battle. This quintessential example clearly reveals the real significance
of this representation: nothing less than the replacement of the hitherto purely formulaic pictograms of the king as warrior (exemplified
since time immemorial by the image of the king "smiting his enemies") by a graphically realistic portrayal of one actual event in all
its historical uniqueness. This process was tantamount to a deritual-
ization of the historic feats of the king, which were no longer regarded
as the consummation of an ancient prescription but as the accomplishment of deeds unique in themselves. It was the event that
counted, not the ritual repetition.

The wars of the New Kingdom were waged at the behest of
Amun or Amun-Re, the god of Thebes. Kamose, one of the earliest
liberation fighters, already saw himself as setting forth in the name
of the Theban god.[6] In the course of time the religious justification
for military action became increasingly insistent and pervasive, and
the religious symbolism of war increasingly rich. The Battle of Qadesh
represents a high point in this regard as well, the reversal of fortunes
at the crucial juncture being attributed to the intervention of Amun
himself. But Merneptah's account of the Libyan wars goes even further. He describes his own divine commission as vouchsafed by a
dream-oracle in which Ptah "in person" entrusted the scimitar of war
into his hands. In addition, the earthly battle is preceded by a heavenly lawsuit in which the Libyan adversary is condemned by the gods,
so that Merneptah's battle is nothing other than the execution of a

divine sentence—a "holy war."[7] In the New Kingdom, war and religion became ever more indissolubly linked. Ideologically, this combination generated a theology that represented history as the product of the strategic interventions of god. Naturally, this conjunction also had an institutional aspect. Wars were financed from the temple treasury, and the spoils of war flowed largely back into that treasury. But the link between religion and warfare was stronger still. The two social groups imposing themselves more and more obviously in the course of the New Kingdom were the military and the priesthood. We have no way of knowing which of them finally gained the upper hand. The end of the New Kingdom was ushered in by a revolt on the part of the high priest of Thebes. And ultimately it was a general, Herihor (ruled 1080–1073 B.C.E.), who not only took over the office of high priest but also ascended the throne in that very capacity.

The seizure of power by Herihor triggered the collapse of the unity of the state. It marked the end of the New Kingdom and the onset of the Third Intermediate Period. Geographically, the old north-south dualism was restored. Politically, however, the conflict underlying the schism—military versus priesthood, war versus religion—was an entirely new one. In the north, a Libyan dynasty of military leaders ascended the throne—now moved from Avaris to Tanis—and reigned over Lower and Upper Egypt in accordance with the traditional system of pharaonic kingship. In the south, a kind of "god-state" or theocratic regime emerged, centered in Thebes. There the god Amun reigned by means of oracular proclamation. This form of direct theocracy was nothing other than the institutionalization of a "theology of will," the Ramesside theology that imputed the course of history to divine volition. From now on, the will of god as proclaimed by the oracle dictated not only the acts of government but also the conduct of everyday life. Religion attained a new and much more comprehensive status, advancing from an important aspect of Egyptian culture to a decisive historical factor and an agent of thoroughgoing change. From here it was only a small step to what was to begin a little later in Israel and subsequently revolutionize the face of the world.

15

COSMOTHEISM AS A FORM
OF KNOWLEDGE

The Cosmos and the Dimensions of the Divine Realm

THE TERM "COSMOTHEISM" was coined by Lamoignon de Malesherbes in his edition of Pliny the Elder's *Natural History* to designate the ancient, and particularly the Stoic, worship of the cosmos as Supreme Being. In my inquiry, I adopt the term in a somewhat broader sense, one that encompasses polytheistic religions that worship the cosmos as the collective manifestation of various different deities. In the religious history of the New Kingdom, cosmotheism materialized in three different forms: traditional polytheism, revolutionary monotheism (which acknowledged the sun and light as one sole divinity but thus remained within the framework of cosmic worship), and finally pantheism, which regarded the supreme god of the pantheon as the embodiment of all other deities and of the oneness of the universe.

Polytheistic religions worship not one single god but a world of gods. This divine world is not merely a chaotic jumble of various deities but has a specific structure. In Egyptian religion, three structural parameters imposed order on this collectivity. First, language, through the narrative structure of the myths, placed the gods in systems of kinship and related their actions and destinies to each other. Second, the cosmos itself represented a model for the collective agency of various different powers. Third, the organization of the polity assigned the gods divine rule in temples and cities and interpreted the human exercise of power as a form of divine rule by proxy. In this dimension, political community took the form of cultic community or congregation.

These three parameters and the structure they imposed can also be seen in the various aspects that divine beings displayed. Gods had names, genealogies, and a mythically revealed spectrum of roles; they had a "portfolio," a sphere of cosmic, vegetative, or cultural competencies; and finally they had cult locations from which they exercised their earthly rule. In human terms, these categories also represent different dimensions of religious experience. Egyptians would come into contact with the divine first in the myths, divine names, and sacred formulas and recitations: second in cosmic, natural, and cultural phenomena; third in temples and cults.

Revealed religions of a monotheistic nature break completely with this structure of multiple names, myths, and points of contact. Tribal religions, by contrast, have yet to develop such a structure. In short, this structure defines the various instances of polytheism as a religious form specific to the ancient world.

The sociologist Talcott Parsons refers to these polytheistic communities with the blanket term "cosmological societies."[8] A cosmological society lives by a model of cosmic forms of order, which it transforms into political and social order by means of meticulous observation and performance of rituals. But there are, of course, various kinds of participatory observation. The Mesopotamian model (like the Roman and ancient Chinese) was divinatory; the cosmos was observed for signs in which the will of the gods manifested itself. In divinatory cultures, signs are exceptions to the rule. The regular, predictable, and recurrent forms the ground against which exceptions stand out as significant.[9] In Egypt, the reverse obtained. Regularity, recurrence, and predictability attained significance against the background of the contingent, unique, and deviant. In divinatory cultures, rainbows, earthquakes, and eclipses of the sun and moon were carefully observed and recorded; in ancient Egypt, such phenomena were passed over in silence. In Egyptian religion the will of the gods was bound up with the maintenance of the cosmic process. The lot of the gods was to forever play their part in the daily drama of the cosmic process. The ritual reenactment of this process was designed not only to adapt the order of the human world to that of the cosmos but also, and indeed primarily, to keep the cosmic process itself in good working order.

The Egyptians regarded the cosmos less as a well-organized space than as a functioning process. Creation was not over and done with on the seventh day, but continued indefinitely. Cosmogony began not so much with an intentional act of creation as with a kind of initial ignition, a "First Moment" that the cosmic process everlastingly reiterates. The First Moment separates preexistence from the cosmogonic process of cyclical time, not from a perfect, complete cosmos. The cosmogonic process, though cyclical, must be constantly reinforced by unremitting efforts that wrest the cosmos from its persistent gravitation toward chaos. This is the task of the gods, above all of the sun god; the rites performed on earth make their own contribution to the cyclicalization of time and the cosmic process.

The historian and political philosopher Eric Voegelin, whose monumental five-volume *Order and History* appeared between 1956 and 1985, saw this dramatic aspect of the cosmotheistic view of the world very clearly and suggested that for peoples for whom myths were a form of living truth, time threatened the cosmos with destruction; they consequently pitted the ritual repetitions of their cosmogonies against the irreversible march of time, hoping thus to sustain the sensitive equilibrium between origin from nothingness and disappearance into nothingness.[10] One or two emendations of this view are necessary, however. For the Egyptians, the cosmos was not suspended between nothingness and nothingness, nor did it emerge from nothingness. Surprisingly, the Egyptian concept of "nothingness" is not a part of the extracosmic or precosmic sphere but of the "inner cosmic." In Egyptian thought, the distinction between being and nothingness could only be understood in terms of the existing world, the ongoing process. In fact, this distinction represented the primary cosmogonic condition for a universe to take shape at all. The Egyptians believed the cosmos to have originated not from nothingness but from oneness, from an undifferentiated unity to which it would also revert at the end of time. This oneness (Atum, the god of preexistence, floating in Nun, the primeval ocean) was not the counterforce that threatened the cyclical course of the cosmos with irreversibility or entropy. That threat was posed, rather, by nothingness. This fundamental Egyptian distinction is masked by the terminology of religious historians, with their inflationary use of the term "chaos." The Egyptians were rather more precise on this point; at the very least, we may say they distinguished *two* kinds of chaos. Their world came forth from Nun, the primal waters (Chaos I or "oneness"). The sun god repeats the cosmogony of the First Moment by rising up from the primal waters anew each morning. One hymn to the sun even presents the belief that in sleep humans dive down into the primal waters, from which they emerge refreshed and rejuvenated the next morning "to put off the old person and put on the new."[11] This is the mystery of cyclical time, the mystery of renewal. In Egyptian cosmography, chaos—the force of irreversibility and entropy against which the sun god must constantly reassert the cyclical nature of time and with it the regeneration of the cosmos—takes the form of a huge sea serpent that threatens to drink the primal waters dry (Chaos II or nothingness, destruction, entropy). This figuration of inner cosmic chaos (II) is thus the exact opposite of precosmic and extracosmic chaos (I). The latter sustains and regenerates the world; the former threatens it with destruction.

Cosmohermeneutics: The Mystic Meaning of the Circuit of the Sun

THE EGYPTIAN CONCEPT OF THE COSMOS as an indefinitely repeated cosmogony has its foundation in the idea of the "circuit of the sun," the apparent motion of the sun around the earth. The Egyptians imagined this motion as a journey by boat. In two barks, one for day, the other for night, the sun god traverses the heavens and the underworld. The course of this voyage involves almost all the important deities of the Egyptian pantheon, alongside an abundance of minor, "specialized" deities. My present concern is not with the mythology of the sun god but with the superordinate image of the cosmos. Other gods enter into relations with the sun god in accordance with defined patterns and "constellations." Each phase in the circuit of the sun is characterized by different constellations: birth by the mother, rearing by divine nurses, ascent of the throne by acclamatory worshippers, confrontation with the enemy by adjuvant gods, sunset as return to the womb. The model for correct dying leads to regeneration by way of a netherworldly union with Osiris, with a consequent rebirth in the morning from the primal waters that itself repeats the initial cosmogonic ignition, the First Moment. Each phase also has its own meaning and drama and requires specific efforts to ensure the triumph of the light. For time is not cyclical "in itself." Cyclicality is rather a cultural form imposed on the world by semantic and ritual efforts. The world is "kept going" by cult in general and by the "hour ritual" in particular, accompanying the circuit described by the sun with hourly recitations.

In the cult of the sun, language plays a crucial role. It functions as an "interface" that couples cosmic and earthly processes and that (like the air god, Shu) establishes the link between above and below. The Egyptian expression for this coupling process is "letting *ma'at* ascend."[12] *Ma'at* is not only justice done but also "truth" told. Both are aspects of connective action and behavior, one linked to deeds, the other to communication. "Letting *ma'at* ascend" is a language offering. The sun god is worshipped primarily by recitation sent up on high. The truth he is told is an interpretation of the cosmic processes in terms of their mystic or salvational meaning. The salvational quality of the sun's journey is remarkably close to the "theology of the heathen" about which the physician Sir Thomas Browne wrote in 1642 with astonishing perspicacity: "The natural motion of the sun made them more admire Him than its supernatural station did the children of Israel. The ordinary effects of nature wrought more admiration in them than, in the other, all his miracles. Surely the heathens knew better how to join and read these mystical letters than we Christians, who cast a more careless eye on these common hieroglyphics, and disdain to suck divinity from the flowers of nature."[13]

The solar hymns that the Egyptians sent up on high as *ma'at* to the sun god imply just such a reading of the "mystical letters" of the universe. Their language is a species of commentary, which I have called "sacramental interpretation," that teases out the homology between heavenly and earthly events. The essence of the commentary is to highlight the salvational relevance of an event or process. These hymns-as-commentaries elucidate aspects of the cosmos in terms of three different dimensions of meaning. In the governmental and political dimension of rule, the salutary aspect of the circuit of the sun lies in its affirmation of order over chaos through the victory of light over darkness and motion over standstill. In the social dimension, the salutary meaning of the course of the sun lies in the love with which god infuses the world. On the individual plane, it is the cycle of death and rebirth, aging and rejuvenation that makes the course of the sun the model of hope for the hereafter. The circuit of the sun thus stands as an aggregate model for earthly life. The cultic recitation of this "solar discourse" draws on sacramental interpretation to translate the cosmic processes into a design for human living.[14] The effects of this translation are anything but negligible. "I have overthrown Apopis for you and procured free passage for your bark so that it does not run aground on the sandbank of Apopis on its great journey," the king as sun priest says to the sun god (Apopis is the archenemy of the sun god, a huge sea serpent threatening to arrest the progress of his bark).[15] The king is "the protector of Re-Horakhty, felling his foe with the power [= salvational effect] of his speech, which enables the bark to glide on its way in joy."[16] In this cyclical cosmology the concept of salvation has to do not with redemption, but with renewal and "keeping things going." Salvation is the overcoming of the forces of stasis and dissolution. And once again, connectivity, in the form of continuity on the temporal plane and solidarity on the social, "unifies the hearts and creates order."[17]

It is the *salvational efficacy* of this process that gives it meaning in the first place and that marks the linguistic accompaniment as an interpretation. Of central moment is the idea of a dual overcoming: the overcoming of evil, personified by Apopis threatening the bark with standstill, and the overcoming of death. Both are manifestations of chaos, two aspects of the same process. The overcoming of evil is the active, transitive aspect, directed at the external world. In this dynamic, the sun god figures as the god of the world, whose word creates order, speaks law, ensures livelihood, and "drives out evil." The circuit of the sun is a proceeding in the legal sense, a judicial conflict in which accounts are settled with evil and the sun god is vindicated; thus, the "split" world, a world riven by the presence of evil, is constantly restored—that is, governed, made safe and inhabitable.

The overcoming of death is the passive or intransitive aspect of the nightly journey. This process takes the form of a life span that the sun god traverses, aging and dying in order to be reborn. The mystery of solar rebirth is in fact the central salvational element in Egyptian religion. Whereas the Greeks were fascinated by the harmony of the whole, the Egyptians fixed their attention upon the process of ongoing vindication and rebirth. To them the cosmos appeared as the quintessence of the death-defying fullness of life, as well as a chaos-banishing force for order.

This salvational meaning forms the *sensus mysticus* of the cosmic processes deciphered by the priest and sent up on high to the sun god in hymnic recitation. The visual recognition of the circuit of the sun becomes an act of understanding by identification. Human beings recognize themselves in the cosmos. It is *their* death that is overcome, *their* ambivalence about good and evil that is oriented toward the good, *their* disorder that is tamed, *their* rule that is exercised. They have no interest in cause and effect, the logic that informs and explains the process; rather, their interest is in the salvational meaning of processes interpreted in terms of action and lived life. The cosmos is not explained, it is interpreted. It contains a message that humans can relate to themselves, a meaning that they can activate in themselves.

From what we have said so far, it should be apparent that we are in the presence of a concept of immense complexity, a whole edifice of knowledge that priests had to master in order to intervene in the circuit of the sun with their recitations. Some instruction about the nature and meaning of this cosmological knowledge is provided by a text already quoted from in chapter thirteen (p. 187). The first two stanzas describe the king's knowledge and how it empowers him to embark on his world-sustaining interpretation of the solar circuit.

The king
worships the sun god in the early morning
upon his emergence when he "opens his orb,"
when he flies up to heaven as scarab
—he enters the mouth,
he emerges from the thighs,
at his birth in the eastern sky.
His father Osiris raises him up,
the arms [of the air gods] Hu and Hauhet receive him.
He sets himself down in the morning bark.

The king knows
this mysterious speech that the "eastern souls" speak,
when they make jubilant music for the sun god
at his ascent, his appearance on the horizon
and when they open for him the wings
of the gates of the eastern horizon
so that he can voyage forth on the ways of the heavens in his
    boat.

He knows their aspect and their incarnations,
their mansions in God's-Land.
He knows their locations,
when the sun god goes forth at the beginning of his journey.

He knows that speech uttered by the crews
when they pull the bark of the lord of the horizon.
He knows the birth of Re
and his transformation in the flood.
He knows that secret gate through which the great god comes
    forth,
he knows him who is in the morning bark,
and the great image in the night bark.
He knows his landing places on the horizon
and your steering equipment in the heavenly goddess.[18]

This text enumerates everything the king must know for the worship of the sun god in the morning: the nature of the cosmic process, its various stages, its scenic and constellational arrangements, and its salvational meaning as rebirth; he knows the deities involved, their actions, their speech, the circumstances of their lives; and he knows the spatial framework of the process—heavenly gates, barks, landing places, steering equipment. The king must know all this precisely in order to be able to intervene effectively in the cosmic process with his worshipful speech. His fears are less that one day the sun might no longer rise than that the salvational meaning of the process might be lost or forfeited. The king, then, performs an *officium memoriae*. He must summon all his mnemonic power to keep this salvational knowledge present. The world thus maintained is a world of meaning, of language, of knowledge, of relations and reflections, an anthropomorphic reading of the universe with a correspondingly cosmomorphic image of human order. The hourly ritual bans cosmic chaos, and with it the chaos in man himself.

Cosmotheistic "natural science" is a matter of speculative identification. Man's worship of the ordering powers effective in the cosmos mobilizes the cosmos within himself. He interprets the world by investing it with his own self; his goal is full participation, as a part within the whole. "Who knows this, is an image of the great god," says the *Amduat,* the oldest Egyptian book of the underworld: *eritis sicut Deus.*[19] But there are also variants of this promise that say "Who *does* this . . ." Knowledge and action (gnosis and praxis) are interchangeable. Cosmotheistic knowledge is geared to action; it is savoir-faire, a knowledge of the rites that keep the world in working order. The universe is not only interpreted in terms of divine acts, as a ritual celebrated by the gods: this interpretation is itself also staged as ritual.

This cosmotheistic form of knowledge is not peculiar to the New Kingdom; it informs ancient Egyptian civilization in general and makes it a "cosmological society" in Parsons' sense of the term. In the New Kingdom, however, this cosmotheistic knowledge became uniquely dynamic and central to the collective experience of the Egyptians. This new development is primarily reflected in an unparalleled spate of hymns to the sun. Several hundred such hymns have come down to us from the New Kingdom. Some of them are reproductions and variations of standard texts; some are entirely new compositions. As almost all of these inscriptions can be accurately dated, they can document the history of a discourse. And this discourse reflects a thoroughgoing change in the meaning the Egyptians gave to the circuit of the sun.

The New Solar Theology

THIS CHANGE CAN perhaps be most trenchantly described as a shift from joint to individual action. In the classical conception, the sun god ran his course in an overarching pattern of changing constellations that involved the whole confraternity of the gods. His role was sometimes active and interventionist, sometimes passive and receptive, but in all cases he was centrally integrated into a collective system of divine roles. All the deities participated in one way or another in the circuit of the sun, and hence in the salvational function bound up with it. The cosmos itself was synonymous with this concerted effort by the gods.

In the new conception, the sun god is alone as he traverses the sky and the underworld:

You have shown yourself in the sky, where you are alone.[20]

It is impossible to overestimate the crucial and radical change that this new conception represents. In traditional Egyptian religion, a "lonely god" could be imagined only in the context of preexistence, of primordial oneness. In the world that was subsequently created, loneliness was untenable, not only for men but for gods. Life was crucially and invariably connective and constellational. But in the new solar theology, the sun god runs his course alone. The new texts are suddenly devoid of all mythic imagery: no serpent foe, no mother in heaven, no father in the underworld; moreover, the course of the sun has nothing more to do with birth and death, justice and rule, or other essential existential elements of human life. The idea of the connective nature of human justice disappears along with the constellational understanding of the sun's course. Cosmic and earthly meaning no longer mirror each other.

The repercussions of this cosmo-theological revolution on the entire cultural semantic system were enormous. The focus of cosmic life on one single source puts god and the world in an "over-and-against" relationship that nullifies the traditional notion of *ma'at* as a constellational linking of all living things. This sea change is reflected most eloquently in the newly transitive verb forms used to describe the deeds and works of god. In traditional accounts, the gods "live" and their life and interaction constitute reality. But now the collective quality of divine and cosmic life is pared down to the "life-giving" action of the one world-creating and world-preserving god. The course of the sun is no longer synonymous with the collective convivial community of a world of deities, but has become the life-giving deed of the one and only sun god, performed anew each day. From here it is only a small step to a "theology of will" that derives time from the life-creating act of the sun god and that, indeed, attributes to the god everything that happens in the temporal dimension—that is, the history of the land and the destinies of individuals.

This "new solar theology," this anticonstellational view of the course of the sun, is not, however, monotheistic. The hymns continue to refer to all kinds of gods. The difference is that now, almost without exception, the gods figure as a collective group, on a par with men and animals. They belong to a world set apart from the remote, solitary sun god who still shines, gives life, creates and sustains, but *from afar.*

This new conception of the sun god might have remained an insignificant quirk of history had it not culminated in the revolution triggered by Akhenaten, one of the most astonishing developments in the annals of ancient Egyptian civilization. For it is nothing other than the very first attempt in the history of humanity to found and establish a counterreligion.

16

AKHENATEN'S REVOLUTION

The First Counterreligion in History

TWO ASPECTS OF AKHENATEN's religious revolution are especially astounding: its incredible speed and radicalism, and the total
obliteration of all traces of it in the aftermath.[21] Founding the new
religion and completely doing away with the old was the work of only
a few years, from 1352 to 1338. The reasons for this volte-face are a
subject of major controversy. Some trace Akhenaten's reform to an
economic test of strength between the king and the Amun priests of
Thebes. The colossal spoils of the Tuthmosid wars, so the argument
runs, had so increased the property of the Temple of Amun of Karnak
that the latter had become a state within the state, with increasing
political influence. This theory can point to parallel processes in the
late Twentieth Dynasty, when conflicts between the Theban high
priests and the Tanite kings did indeed usher in the end of the New
Kingdom.

There is, however, no documentary evidence of such a conflict
in the pre-Amarna age. In fact, it is difficult to imagine that, at this
relatively early stage, the king's access to the property of the Theban
Amun temple could have been restricted. In Egypt the temples were
organs of the state, not institutions of a "church" in any way independent of the state. The wars that filled the temples' coffers in such
heaping measure had been financed from precisely those same coffers
and had been, after all, undertaken at the behest of Amun.

A different theory, first advanced—if I am correct—by the

214

American Egyptologist James Henry Breasted, proceeds on the assumption that the imperialist policy of the Tuthmosids had brought about a drastic change in Egypt's conception of the world.[22] Egypt could no longer perceive itself as coextensive with the civilized world. The Egyptians' recognition that they were part of a world containing many different peoples brought about a change of Copernican dimensions; the ensuing cognitive dissonance triggered a crisis in the polytheistic image of the universe. The new "ecumenical" worldview found its religious expression in the idea of the sun god creating and sustaining all peoples with his world-spanning circuit and life-giving beams. One of Breasted's most attentive readers, Sigmund Freud, identified this political universalism of the Eighteenth Dynasty as the source not only of Egyptian but also of biblical monotheism.[23]

The second remarkable aspect of Akhenaten's revolution is its complete disappearance from the collective memory of Egyptian civilization. The discovery of a monotheistic counterreligion in the New Kingdom dates from as late as the 1880s.[24] By fifty or one hundred years after Akhenaten's death, all memory of him had been expunged. His name was struck off the king-lists, his inscriptions were scratched out, his buildings were torn down, and nothing was left to commemorate this revolutionary intermezzo that turned Egyptian life and thinking upside down, if for a period of twenty years at most. In a legal document from the reign of Ramesses II, there is one single mention of "that fallen foe from Amarna," no doubt because a concern for accuracy made it unavoidable.[25] Neither the king's famous *Great Hymn to the Sun* nor other hymns from this period left any trace whatsoever on later Egyptian hymns to the sun. In Egypt, monotheistic religion died intestate; there was no surviving tradition, no history of reception, only complete and utter oblivion. Between circa 1340 B.C.E., when the text of the hymn was set down in the Tomb of Ay, and circa 1884 C.E., when an Egyptologist presented it to the public for the first time, no one had set eyes on it. This history of oblivion is fundamental to a full appreciation of the significance of the rediscovery. True, the *Epic of Gilgamesh* was also rediscovered after thousands of years, but within the history of its own culture *Gilgamesh* had enjoyed a prominent place. Akhenaten's *Great Hymn* was neither interpreted by any scribe in its own time nor passed on to posterity. Immediately after its initial circulation, the *Great Hymn* disappeared.

It is, then, doubly remarkable that upon its rediscovery this hymn was accorded an importance unmatched by any other Egyptian text. The radical monotheism of Akhenaten's hymn negates other gods; indeed, it avoids the use of the very word "god" whether singular or plural—in this, it far exceeds even the Bible. Akhenaten's monotheism, in stark contrast with the religion of the Bible, remains cosmotheistic: it worships a *cosmic* power that manifests itself in the form of the sun, of light and time, of radiance and motion. The revelation offered by Akhenaten consists not in moral laws and historical action but in the conviction that *everything*—visible and invisible reality in its entirety—is a product of light and time, and hence of the sun. Akhenaten believed that he had discovered the *one* divine principle from which the world had initially originated and originated anew every day. And as this unique principle was the source of all others, it followed that there could be no other gods but this one. This was no question of "loyalty" or "jealousy," as in early biblical henotheism, but of knowledge and truth; Akhenaten's vision was a *cognitive* breakthrough. As a thinker, Akhenaten stands at the head of a line of inquiry that was taken up seven hundred years later by the Milesian philosophers of nature with their search for the one all-informing principle, and that ended with the universalist formulas of our own age as embodied in the physics of Einstein and Heisenberg.[26]

But this new formula was experienced by the king as a *religious* revelation, which he set about putting into practice with the utmost radicalism. All traditional cults were closed; the only worship permitted was that of the new god, the Aten (sun disk), and this itself was largely restricted to Amarna, the new capital, which Akhenaten erected in Middle Egypt on virgin soil, in a plain opposite Hermopolis. As a religious founder, Akhenaten stands at the head of a lineage very different from his predecessors', one represented after him by the Moses of legend, and later by Buddha, Jesus, and Mohammed.

The new god was the sun or, in the Egyptian term, "the *living* sun," whose motion brings forth time and whose radiance brings forth light and hence all living things. This new image of the circuit of the sun was antimythical, anticonstellational, and antianthropomorphic. Nothing was imputed to this god but what the inquiring eye and the thinking mind of the king could descry as effects of the light and the motion of the sun. In short, it was a strictly heliomorphic theology.

Akhenaten was enlightener and iconoclast in one. The upheaval caused by his new religion is more apparent in what it negates, discards, and excludes than in what it positively represents. But the new religion's negative thrust was not limited to linguistic censorship; it also found expression in a large-scale organized campaign that makes Josiah's religious reforms in Israel six centuries later appear halfhearted in comparison. Police and military ranged through the country in a bid to erase all the inscriptions of the hated god Amun (the precise reason for this hatred is unknown) from the face of the earth.[27] The old religion was to be reduced to utter silence, and this objective was pursued with the same thoroughgoing radicalism as the new religion itself was to suffer only a few years later. The enormous number of traditional temples and cults, rites and festivals, myths, hymns, and images were replaced by a handful of hymns celebrating the new religion, a puritanical cult devoid of magic and symbolism, and the massive presence of the royal family. Of course, if this religion had survived at least for a few centuries, it would certainly have been elaborated upon. The texts we have represent this dogma of Akhenaten's religion in its initial stages only—a state of evidence unique in the history of religion. In all other cases we can only speculate on religious origins from later accounts and systems of dogma. But with the Amarna religion there is no "later," no tradition (which, after all, is invariably a falsification), no reception, no redaction, no elaboration, modification, conversion, no interpretation, no adaptation. Akhenaten speaks to us in the pristine freshness of his first revolutionary pronouncements.

It is fascinating to speculate about what this religion might have become had it survived. The Amarna religion would certainly have generated a corpus of religious and dogmatic texts, for how could the traditional religion have been permanently ousted without explicitly castigating it as a concoction of lies, ignorance, and heathenism? Akhenaten's revolution marked the advent of the categories "true" and "false" in the history of religion. Wherever such distinctions appear in later periods, they are invariably codified in normative texts. Orthopraxis, based on the distinction between right and wrong in human action and behavior, can be found everywhere; orthodoxy, with its distinction between true and false, exists only in religions of the book. Hence Akhenaten's new religion would surely have produced a corpus of canonical texts. The emphasis in Egyptian religious life would have shifted from rites (relegated to a comparatively minor role in Amarna) to "scriptures."

These scriptures would probably have centered on the subjects of state and cosmos, and would have concentrated on the role of the king as mediator, for in Amarna the divine was personified—and hence addressable—solely in the guise of the king. For ordinary mortals the Aten was the sun and Akhenaten the god. At the same time, Akhenaten was the son of Aten, who engendered him every day anew with his rays. Fully in line with the loyalism of the Middle Kingdom, the inscriptions of the Amarna Period eulogize the king as a disaster-averting bringer of salvation, and also refer throughout to his "teachings," which apparently propagated such views.[28] The cosmologies are even more readily imaginable. The so-called *Great Hymn* is a philosophy of the cosmos that contains the seminal potential for a whole series of major tractates.

One particularly tantalizing question is whether the Amarna religion, if it had succeeded, would have revolutionized the world as Moses' religion in Israel did. What would the world look like if the global monotheistic and metaphysical revolution had come about under the auspices of Egyptian cosmotheism rather than Israelitic transcendentalism; that is, if this revolution had been ushered in by an act of deistic enlightenment rather than theistic revelation?

I myself do not believe that Akhenaten's religion of light could have revolutionized the world in this way. True, it was a radical counterreligion capable of toppling established Egyptian traditions, if only briefly. But to generate a revolutionary potential above and beyond that, Akhenaten's religion would have needed the antagonistic force unique to *redemptive* religions—which it did not have. Redemptive religions do not aim to give man a home in the world, but rather set out to alienate him from the world by appealing to a transcendental self within, a "soul" that is the nucleus of being and that makes possible self-awareness and individualization.

The aim of the Amarna religion was the exact opposite. Man was incorporated into the world, reminded of his dependency on light and time by analogy with plants and the beasts of the field. The Amarna religion, precisely because of its cosmotheism, had no potential to offer man redemption. And so, for all its monotheism, it would have been overrun by the redemptive religions—as were all the others of its kind. History was to take a different course. In Egypt, the Amarna religion disappeared immediately after the restoration of the traditional forms it had set out to obliterate.

The Great Hymn

THE *GREAT HYMN* COMPRISES THREE SECTIONS.[29] The first is a description of the circuit of the sun. The polytheistic constellations that were evoked in mythical images by the traditional, pre-Amarna songs are gone. Instead, the *Hymn* presents a confrontation between god and the world. No mother giving birth to the god in the morning, no nurses to suckle him, no foe to be bested, no realm of the dead to receive the god in the night; over and against the one god stands the one world, the object and receptacle of his life-giving energies. The religious vision and poetic greatness of the text coalesce in the wealth of loving detail that depicts the god's bestowal of life. Men and women rise, wash, dress, and repair to their work, animals rouse themselves, birds take wing, fish dart around in the water, boats travel upstream and down. The theological import of this description lies in the fact that vital energy is in itself a paean of praise to the divine intoned by all creatures every morning, a hymn in which humans join as one voice among many. The praise of the created world expresses itself not in words but in the way all creatures turn their faces to the sun. Nor does god speak; he shines. The religious mystery, the salvational meaning, no longer resides in mythical imagery that points up the connection of human and cosmic destinies, but in the biophysics of natural processes.

The second section is a song to creation. In its traditional form, this was a mythical motif, an account of the primordial age. Akhenaten restricts himself to the present, to the world accessible to the senses, treating creation on the one hand as an embryogony (the origin of life in the womb) and on the other as an ecology (the wise arrangement of the world, where all are provided for according to their needs). In contrast to earlier texts, the *Hymn* does not equate the world with Egypt, but understands it as embracing many lands and peoples, who differ in skin color, language, and conditions of life. Only Egypt thrives on the water that comes from the depths; all others live off the rain, the "heavenly Nile."[30]

The third section of the *Hymn* is the most innovative and unprecedented of all. It revolves around an Egyptian concept that we might gloss as "transformation, incarnation, emanation," and that derives from the word for "become, originate." The scarab is the symbol of this primal force of becoming, which fascinated the Egyptians as much as the Greeks were intrigued by the principle of "being." This section narrates the "becoming" of the sun, which by virtue of its radiance and motion becomes that which it brings forth and makes visible. The visible sun is itself also an incarnation of god in the heavens, while the created world is his myriad embodiment on earth. The boundaries between creator and created are blurred. Everything visible in the light comes forth from him, as an embodiment of him. The world that the light reveals as ordered and inhabitable—towns and villages, fields, paths, rivers—is itself the embodiment of god.

Though god and his creation are intimately linked in the process of illumination and visual perception, this link is not established by language or by the apprehending minds of mortal beholders. The connection with god is the preserve of the king alone. Creatures have eyes to look on god, but only the king has the knowing heart that enables him to recognize, to "know" god. His heart is the sole constant in this regular alternation of light and dark, life and death, becoming and declining, the only place where god is also present at night. For the world comes into being at god's bidding, as he created it:

When you dawn, they live.
When you set, they die.
You yourself are the time in which and through which one lives.[31]

This is Akhenaten's great discovery. Others before him had recognized that the world lives from the sun and its light, but the idea that *time* originated from divine light was revolutionary; all was now explicable as the work of god. In the two canonical hymns (the *Great Hymn* and the *Shorter Hymn*, probably both by Akhenaten), there are indications that god himself instructed the king, that is, revealed himself to him. In the words of the *Great Hymn*: "You apprise him of your plans and your powers."[32] Another hymn reads: "Your might and force are firm in my heart."[33] God has opened up his being to the king by vouchsafing him insight into the entwined nature of light and time as the all-encompassing "formula of the world."

The revelation effected by Akhenaten's god is more an act of enlightenment than the establishment of a new religion. Akhenaten's key insight is that god is *only* light and time; all reality, visible and invisible, can be traced back to light and time. But does not the true nature of god, as represented in the many deities of traditional Egyptian religion, go far beyond visible and invisible physical reality?

I refer to two religious ideas absolutely crucial for the Egyptians and conspicuous by their complete absence from Akhenaten's hymn, having fallen foul of Amarna's censorship: (regenerative) immortality and justice. Truth and justice were now identical with the will of the king and his teachings. It was not god but the king who "lived on *ma'at*" at Amarna. To live in *ma'at* no longer meant solidarity in thought, speech, and action; it now meant casting in one's lot with the king and following his teachings.

The traditional vision of the circuit of the sun was the authoritative guide to personal "salvation" for the ancient Egyptians. Each hoped to become an Osiris after death and to partake in the life of the cosmos through the midnight union with the sun; each hoped that his *ba* would follow the course of the sun god and be allotted a place in the bark of the millions.[34] In the mortal world, the hopes of the Egyptians hinged on the idea of justice. As the sun god fought evil in heaven, so he would stand by the needy and oppressed on earth.[35] An earlier hymn puts it thus:

Hail, Re, lord of justice,
who keeps his shrine concealed, lord of the gods,
[...] who hears the pleas of him who is in distress,
well-inclined of heart to him who calls to him;
who saves the timorous from the hand of the violent
and judges between poor and rich.[36]

Nothing of the sort is to be found in Akhenaten's hymn. For him, god is nothing but light and time. He overcomes neither evil nor death, as neither has any place in this new vision of the world. Akhenaten's vision was the most consistent Egyptian attempt to transcend the idea of a "riven world." But Akhenaten's emphatically *undivided* world has no place for the moral aspect of the divine and the claims that attend it. Even so brief an outline of Akhenaten's vision makes it apparent that his monotheism has very little in common with the biblical variety—the one notable exception being its antipolytheistic impetus. In the fourteenth century B.C.E. this impetus fleetingly presaged the conflict in which the One and the Many were later to form irreconcilable opposites. For Akhenaten, the One appears in a cognitive, rationalist guise: the Egyptian king has no need of many gods because he believes he can refer back to one controlling principle and agency the energies that create and sustain the world. In the Bible the antipolytheistic impetus takes on a political form, as fidelity to the covenant with the one and only God. Akhenaten's monotheism is cosmological, a philosophy of nature in religious garb. Biblical monotheism is historical, political, and moral; its main vehicles of expression are historical narrative, legislation, and constitution.

Both monotheisms were revolutionary. They did not evolve from earlier religious developments but owed their existence to what Erik Hornung calls a "complete about-turn in thinking."[37] Both innovations were imposed by military force. In Egypt, we can still see the traces of that force on the monuments; in Israel, we hear its echo in the biblical account of Josiah's religious reforms. It was in the exercise of such force that the antipolytheistic impetus manifested itself.

The Trauma of Amarna

IN CONTRAST TO ISRAEL'S, the Egyptian monotheistic reform failed to take root. After the death of its originator, the Amarna religion was rigorously suppressed. The destruction of all memory of this epoch is not simply an official *damnatio memoriae*, but has the intensity of a *traumatic* experience. Such experiences do not lend themselves to representation in the symbolic forms of cultural memory. They are not simply passed over in silence, but are so supremely dreadful as to actively resist any representation at all. As it is impossible to come to terms with such traumatic experiences on the symbolic plane, they remain stubbornly "indigestible," an unmitigated shock, a suppurating wound. The memory of Amarna was not merely obliterated; it was repressed or, to use the psychoanalytic term, "encrypted"; Amarna represented a "crypt" in collective remembrance and was thus inaccessible to conscious cultural symbolization.[38] In the following I restrict myself to a brief discussion of this point, as I have enlarged on it elsewhere.[39]

In my view, the following features justify referring to the experience of the age of Amarna as traumatic: the symbolic, and possibly physical, violence with which the new religion was enforced; its absence of meaning for the majority; the internal and external political crises with which the period ended; and the psychohistorical consequences of collective repression, which took the form of distorted memories, legends, demonization of foes, and various forms of explicit cultural abhorrence.

To illustrate the first point it may suffice to engage in a thought experiment. Let us imagine a traditional society convinced that not only the political and economic welfare of the country but the very survival of natural life depends on the celebration of three religious services every day in all churches through the length and breadth of the nation. Let us further imagine that as a result of a revolution "from above" all churches are suddenly closed, all scriptures destroyed, and all consecrated objects smashed. How would such a society come to terms with this catastrophe?

Though the average Egyptian had no access to the temples and might not have been much troubled by their closing, Akhenaten's ban on traditional religious activity extended to the festivals—a prohibition whose impact can hardly be overestimated.

The festivals were the very foundation of the individual Egyptian's social identity. His allegiance was in the first place to a town and its deity, and the fundamental structure of his social and religious integration was dramatized in the major processional feasts particular to each town. The ban on religious feasts must have been experienced as an eradication of meaning, as is indeed attested by the *Graffito of Pawah*, written in the seclusion of the tomb of Pairi. The text begins: "My heart longs to see you," a reference to the author's yearning for the sight of the deity as made manifest and tangible in religious processions.[40] For the majority of Egyptians, the age of Amarna was one of destruction, persecution, suppression, and godlessness—of "darkness by day," the formula used to refer to the experience of divine absence. The gods had turned away from Egypt.

The experience of being forsaken by the gods as a result of a heinous crime, unspeakable in the truest sense of the word, found apparent confirmation in the severe crises that beset Egypt toward the end of the age of Amarna. The Restoration Stela of Tutankhamun refers to this desolation, resorting to the traditional form of chaos description:

> The . . . were desolated,
> their holy places were on the verge of disintegration,
> they had become piles of rubble,
> overgrown with thistles.
> Their chapels were as if they had never been,
> their temple precincts were trodden roads.
> The land was in grave illness,
> the gods had turned their backs on this land.

If one sent soldiers to Syria,
to extend the frontiers of Egypt,
they had no success.
If one appealed to a god for succor,
he did not come.
If one besought a goddess, likewise,
she came not.
Their hearts had grown weak in their bodies,
for "they" had destroyed what had been created.[41]

Forsaken by the gods, the land lapses into "grave illness" and suffers from foreign attacks. Those to blame for these catastrophes ("they") are not mentioned by name, as is consistent with the systematic suppression of their memory. The text's term for "illness" must be understood metaphorically; it figures in literary texts in the same sense and is part of the symbolic topology of chaos description.[42] There are, however, a number of Hittite sources indicating that a plague actually did break out at the end of the Amarna Period. Egyptian soldiers captured by the Hittites during a raid on Syria brought with them a plague that raged for twenty years in Anatolia and extensive areas of the Near East. It is not likely that Egypt itself would have been spared.[43] If, indeed, there was an epidemic in Egypt, it would not have been experienced as one of those "mishaps" against which, in traditional Egyptian semantics, the creator had provided humans with magic as a defense. In the light of a theology of will that imputes the course of history to divine volition, a plague could only have been interpreted as an expression of the ire of the gods. The idea that the gods would turn away from a land that breaks with its own system of order can already be found in the *Prophecies of Neferti*, but the idea of punitive wrath was previously unknown. This motif bears the seeds of a new semiology that was to assert itself in the subsequent period and would indissolubly link good fortune and prosperity with the favor of the gods.

But the clearest indication of severe crisis at the end of the Amarna Period is supplied by two events that under normal circumstances would almost certainly qualify as measures of desperation. The first was the petition to the king of the Hittites by an Egyptian queen, the widow either of Akhenaten or Tutankhamun, beseeching him to send her a prince to marry. The second was the assumption of power by a military man, Horemheb, the commander-in-chief of the Egyptian forces, whose unique combination of titles before his accession to the throne indicates the onset of a state of emergency. We shall return to him later. Both internally and externally, Egypt was traversing a major political crisis that heightened the traumatic character of the Amarna experience.

Unlike the First Intermediate Period, whose memory was actively drawn upon by the Twelfth Dynasty, the Amarna Period was not stylized as a chaos description legitimizing the military rule of Horemheb and the family of officers from Sile designated as his successors; Horemheb's rule was not proclaimed a "turn to salvation." The only trace of such a retrospective is found in a stela erected in Abydos by Sethos I for his father, Ramesses I. It begins with a chaos description which unfortunately has only survived in very fragmentary form:

> . . . raged like the youths at the time of Re.
> None turned in their tracks.
> The necropolises, no one looked after them,
> like water that [indifferently] flows past the shore.
> The underworld and its constitution had become unknown
> through [oblivion] . . . [44]

Earlier interpreters also saw an allusion to Akhenaten in a stanza of a literary prayer to Amun:

> The sun of him who mistakes you has set, Amun,
> but who knows you says: It has risen in the forecourt!
> Who assails you is in the dark,
> though the whole of the land lie in the sun.
> But everyone who gives you into his heart,
> behold, his sun has risen![45]

For these verses to refer to Akhenaten, however, all the verbs would need to be put in the past tense ("who mistook you," "who assailed you"), which, although possible, is unlikely. What we have here is, rather, a reference to the doctrine of loyalism prevalent in the pre-Amarna period: the loyal walk in bright sunlight, the disloyal in darkness. In the Ramesside Period, this topos—and, indeed, loyalist discourse in general—was extended to the relationship between god and man. Thus the hymn to Amun is unlikely to be a conscious, explicit reference to Akhenaten. In a more general sense, however, it is precisely that. The extension of the traditional relationship between king and loyal subject to that between god and the pious shows most clearly that the Amarna experience had deprived kingship of the symbolic capital by which the ruling king was represented to Egyptians as their god, the source of their lives' meaning, and the lodestar that guided their destinies. The dreadful aberration of Amarna tore a gaping hole in the semantic fabric of the entire Egyptian civilization, a hole that the kings of the Ramesside Period could no longer fill. Only the gods could mend that hole, chief among them Amun.

The memory of the Amarna Period was effectively erased by blotting out all trace of its works and by rewriting history. The names of the Amarna kings were struck off the king-lists and their regnal years were tagged on to the reigns of Amenophis III and Horemheb. What could not be erased were the memories of the traumatic experience that had dealt such a crippling blow to the Egyptians' system of meaning. The trauma persisted and led to the emergence of a legend transmitted by Manetho, and which also figures in numerous Greek and Latin accounts of the origins of the Jewish people.

Manetho's version is the most detailed. He recounts that King Amenophis (Amenophis III) once expressed the desire "to see the gods." The sage Amenophis, son of Hapu, tells him how to accomplish this. He would first have to purge the land of all lepers and "sullied ones." The king rounds up eighty thousand people, some of them priests, and compels them to forced labor in the quarries. Appalled by this display of cruelty, Amenophis the sage anticipates retribution from the incensed gods. He has a premonition that the lepers and their allies will rule over Egypt for thirteen years. Fearful of directly telling the king this prophecy, he writes it down and then commits suicide.[46] The lepers request the forsaken Hyksos residence of Avaris from the king and he accedes. In Avaris they organize a leper colony and elect the priest Osarsiph as their leader. Osarsiph makes all his followers swear an oath of allegiance and then issues a series of laws that are the precise opposite of traditional Egyptian mores and customs. The first commandment is not to worship the Egyptian gods and to deny reverence to their sacred animals and other dietary taboos. The second forbids any contact with outsiders. Thus organized, the lepers turn Avaris into a fortress and enter into an alliance with the Hyksos, who were driven out of Egypt two hundred years before and are now living in Jerusalem. The Hyksos send military assistance to Avaris in the form of two hundred thousand men.

Pharaoh Amenophis recalls the prophecy of the sage and immigrates to Ethiopia with sacred animals previously rounded up from all over the country. Before he leaves Egypt, he orders the images of the gods to be carefully hidden. The Ethiopian king grants the Egyptians refuge for a period of thirteen years. During this period the lepers and the Jerusalemites reign over Egypt so ferociously that in retrospect the reign of the Hyksos looks like a Golden Age. Not only are the cities razed, the temples torn down, and the images of the gods destroyed, but the sanctuaries are turned into kitchens and sacred animals are roasted on the spit. Finally Osarsiph, the lepers' leader, assumes the name Moses. At the last, however, Amenophis and his grandson Ramesses join forces against the lepers and their allies and expel them from the land.

Three different interpretations have been proposed for this story. The first sees in it a legend that is a disguised reminiscence of the age of Amarna.[47] A number of details support this theory: the persons involved (Amenophis III, Amenophis son of Hapu), the thirteen years, the destruction of the temples, and, above all, the religious character of the conflict, beginning with the desire to see the gods and ending with the eating of the sacred animals. The second interpretation understands the story as a reference to the rule and ultimate expulsion of the Hyksos. The location (Avaris), possibly the name Osarsiph, and the Asiatic associations of the story support this interpretation.[48] The third theory contends that the account refers to the Jews. In this view, the narrative is a conscious "counterhistory" to the description of the Exodus in the Bible and so represents an expression of Egyptian Judeophobia.[49] Evidence for this view includes the commandments ordained by Osarsiph, especially the ban on associating with outsiders. "Impiety" and "misanthropy" were the clichés central to the image of the Jews in antiquity.[50]

But all three interpretations have their weak points. The Amarna theory has no explanation for the name Osarsiph, the Asiatic associations, or the ban on outside contact. The Hyksos theory cannot account for the religious character of the conflict, nor are the names (except, perhaps, Osarsiph) consistent with the Hyksos Period; also, Manetho clearly distinguishes the episode from the period of Hyksos rule. The Jewish theory is faced with the problem that Manetho was drawing on sources that were probably a great deal older than the Septuagint.

The trauma theory satisfyingly reconciles all three explanations by relating to the Amarna Period not the details of the legend but the impulse that led to the legend's birth. The Amarna trauma was the motive for recasting memories of the Hyksos Period in the form of a story of religious conflict. These memories had not been banished from official commemoration; they were an available and highly suitable vehicle for an oblique representation of the trauma of extreme religious otherness. The historical Hyksos were probably not adherents of a religion radically different from that of Egypt. Though they worshipped other gods with other rites, their practice was not regarded as an alien religion but as a sign of an alien culture, in which the deities were, in fact, the least foreign element, as is borne out by their rapid assimilation into the Egyptian pantheon. The Amarna religion, on the other hand, was entirely alien, not only defying translation into traditional views but actively negating and seeking to destroy that tradition. In Ramesside retrospect the Hyksos were transformed into monotheists worshipping Seth:

King Apophis chose the god Seth as his lord
and worshipped no other deity in the whole land except Seth.[51]

But the Amarna trauma did not only retrospectively transform the memory of the Hyksos, it also marked Egyptian views and experience of things foreign, and Asiatic in particular, in the age to come. Thus the legend of the thirteen-year rule of the lepers can be seen as collapsing reminiscences of Amarna with memories of the Hyksos, experiences of Assyrian conquest, Persian and Greek rule, and ultimately the encounter with the Jews.

17

PERSONAL PIETY AND THE
THEOLOGY OF WILL

Taking God into One's Heart

THE RELIGIOUS HISTORY OF THE NEW KINGDOM is marked by two developments of the utmost significance. The first is the crisis of the polytheistic worldview that culminates in the revolution of Amarna. The second has come to be known by the name of "personal piety."[52] This blanket term stands, however, for four different phenomena (that these are often confused frequently leads to serious misunderstandings): local forms of religion (for example, the Heqaib cult at Elephantine) as distinct from the official supra- and interlocal state religion;[53] domestic and individual forms of religiosity (for example, the private cult chapels at Amarna and Deir el-Medina) as distinct from priestly temple religion;[54] popular religion (for example, amulets, Bes figurines, magic objects, as well as graffiti and votive figures in sanctuaries) as distinct from the religion and theology of the literate elite;[55] and new forms of religiosity peculiar to the New Kingdom, as distinct from traditional religiosity. The following section is devoted exclusively to this last group.

There is no ancient Egyptian term for "personal piety," no word for the new religiosity that spread in the New Kingdom with the celerity and dynamism of a veritable religious movement. This lack is hardly surprising; there is no Egyptian word for "religion" at all. There are, however, certain unambiguous formulae and expressions that clearly convey the spirit and program of this new religiosity. Chief among these expressions is "to put god into one's heart," also rendered as to "place" or "give" god into one's heart. This expression is so typical of the new movement that we can legitimately accord it the rank of a self-designation and equate personal piety with "giving god into one's heart."

The active embrace of god is the third stage of the "history of the heart" discussed in chapter nine. In the New Kingdom, the interventions of the deities into human affairs were no longer considered to be restricted to warfare or political history in the broader sense of the term. They extended into all aspects of personal life. Cases of miraculous healing, as well as of sudden sickness and misfortune, came to be interpreted as manifestations of divine power; life as a whole came to be seen as the object of divine attention and guidance. Personal piety and the belief in divine intervention are both aspects of that new religious orientation I have termed "theology of will." Accordingly, the Middle Kingdom ideal of the "heart-guided" individual is replaced in the New Kingdom by that of the "god-guided heart." The heart is no longer inscribed by society with the norms of *ma'at*, but has taken god into itself. This ideal reflects a structural change in the concept of *ma'at* within a transformed religious context that now sets god and the world against each other and that sees the world as emanating from the creative, animating, and destiny-forging will of god. *Ma'at* no longer refers to the principle of immanent connective justice, but is now the expression of a form of connectivity stemming from god's will. "Being just" no longer means integrating oneself into the network of the community via self-effacement and solidarity, but now requires giving oneself up in humility and obedience to the will of god, who, as Amenemope declares, "gives *ma'at* to whom he pleases."⁵⁶

The teachings of Amenemope, from the later Ramesside Period, clearly express the ideal of the god-guided heart:

Make yourself heavy in your heart, make your heart steadfast,
do not steer with your tongue.
[True] the tongue of man is the rudder of the boat,
[but] the god-of-all is its steersman.⁵⁷

But from as early as the Eighteenth Dynasty, in the reign of Tuthmosis III, comes a striking example of the formula of "putting god into one's heart":

[Amun is] father and mother for him who gives him into his
   heart,
but he turns away from him who passes by his town heedlessly.
Who is guided by him cannot go astray.[58]

A prayer ostracon from the period of Amenophis II reads:

I have given you into my heart because you are strong,
. . . [you] protector,
behold: I no longer know fear.[59]

The Festival as the Source of Personal Piety

THIS OSTRACON IS ONE of a series of similar pieces that were
found in the Theban necropolis. All date from the middle of the
Eighteenth Dynasty and provide important indications about the
source of the new religiosity. In later periods, too, Thebes remained
the stronghold of this new religion, which must be in some way connected with the nature of the god Amun. The prayer ostraca, with
these earliest texts of personal piety, offer evidence of specific religious
practice and purpose. They were placed in the path of the god as he
set out on his procession; thus, individuals could address the god "in
person" (that is, his processional image) without the mediation of
cult and state. The framework for this means of religious communication was the festival, specifically the Beautiful Festival of the Valley,
during which Amun proceeded from the eastern to the western bank
of the Nile at Thebes, visited the mortuary temples of the kings, and
in so doing also passed through the necropolis of the officials. In
Egypt, the festivals were the only occasion for the common people to
take an active part in religious life, the sole opportunity for "seeing
god." The prayer ostraca from Sheikh Abd el-Qurna prove, with reference to the Valley festival, that as early as the reigns of Tuthmosis
III and Amenophis II individuals could address prayers for succor
and other petitions to the deity on the occasion of the religious festival.
   The "riven world" was made whole for the duration of the festival. The Egyptian religious feast centered on the belief that (within
certain limits) the rift between heaven and earth might be suspended
and the gods could walk the earth once again in person. Representation was transformed into real presence. The feasts reenacted the

primordial era when the gods were directly present to people and the sun god ruled over gods and people alike. Festal hymns speak of heaven and earth reuniting, or of both being caught up in jubilation at the immediate presence of god:

> Heaven and earth are full of his beauty,
> flooded by the gold of his rays.[60]

They all begin with the apostrophization of heaven and earth:

> Rejoicing in heaven,
> joy on earth![61]

The festivals not only permitted individuals to enter into direct personal relations with god, they also defined the individual's social and political membership. Egyptians avowed their allegiance not to a nation or a people—the concepts are anachronistic—but to a town or city. The individual's political membership was bounded by the town or city where he was born and hoped to be buried. But the outward and visible representative of this affiliation was not the mayor of the community but the likeness of the local deity, whose presence was immediately experienced and celebrated at the festivals. The individual further belonged to the urban community of fellow citizens, which was itself synonymous and coextensive with the festal congregation of the local deity. This same community also had a quite secular and pragmatic aspect, for the Egyptian state was dependent on its citizens as a source of corvée manpower. Each and every person had to be available at all times. The state's access to its citizens was organized via the temples.

Beginning in the New Kingdom, the individual's identification with his native town or city underwent a process of theologization. Civic loyalty was transformed into religion. In Egypt, significant shifts of this kind were typically reflected in the identity of the "lord of the burial," who ensured life after death. Up to the New Kingdom, and very conspicuously in the age of Amarna, the lord of the burial was the king. But in the course of the New Kingdom, the king was replaced in this capacity by god, more specifically by the local deity. Thus chapter 183 of the *Book of the Dead* reads:

Today I came from the city of my god: Memphis.
It is the true one [= the original, authentic one] of all the
    beautiful nomes in this land.
[. . .]
Blessed he who works justice for the god who dwells there!
Who does this will be given old age,
the advancement to a tomb owner,
and at length a happy funeral
and burial in the Sacred Precinct.[62]

In Memphis, Ptah was the lord of the burial, in Thebes Amun, in
other cities various other local deities. Hence the local deity was
thought of, as one late wisdom text puts it, as "he by whose command
are the death and life of the people."[63]

Service and loyalty to the king were replaced by service and
loyalty to god. Keeping faith with god required staying in one's native
city. Accordingly, in the text just cited (our earliest testimony of taking god into one's heart), the deity is hailed thus:

[Amun is] father and mother for him who gives him into his
    heart,
but he turns away from him who passes by *his town* heedlessly.

Piety entailed remaining faithful to the town or city of one's god. The
reward for such a life was a fine burial, provided for by the god. A
Ramesside hymn says of Amun-Re:

His reward is a fine burial
for a heart content with *ma'at*.[64]

A biographical inscription from a later period extends the idea:

Who follows him will be a tomb owner,
death reaches him not.
He dies sated with life and reaches the burial
who walks on his water.
One recognizes the praised one by his great name,
his reward is that of a blameless transfigured one.[65]

Fidelity to one's own city coexisted with "pilgrimages" to other cities—possibly by citizens living at some distance—to take part in their festivals. In hymns of the Ramesside Period we read:

> I am a weak one of her place,
> a poor one and a pilgrim of her city.[66]

> Every one who goes on a pilgrimage to your city says, when
>   leaving you:
> Fortunate he who joins you![67]

Thus the idea of personal allegiance to a deity had its origins in the Egyptian institution of the religious festival. During the New Kingdom, this allegiance was expanded and generalized to the point that it became a new religion, which might legitimately be termed "god-loyalty." The striking formula "walking on someone's water" as a profession of the servant's loyalty to his master was now transferred to the divine plane:

> who gives air to breathe to him who worships him
> and makes the lifetime excellent of him who walks on his water.[68]

God as Patron: Piety as Loyalty to God

THIS, THEN, IS THE NEW DEVELOPMENT: god succeeds to the role played by the king in the Middle Kingdom and by the patron in the First Intermediate Period, while pious individuals are cast in the role of the weak, poor, and vulnerable, regardless of their actual social position.[69] From the New Kingdom, the deity was father and mother to all: father of orphans, husband of widows, refuge for the persecuted, protector of the poor, good shepherd, judge of the poor.[70] Correspondingly, the pious were characterized as poor, persecuted seekers of protection. Protection was no longer sought from one's fellows, but solely from god. After the age of Amarna, the texts frequently offer sentences of this kind:

> I have not sought for myself a protector among men,
> god [Amun, Mut, etc.] is my defender.[71]

Trust in the justice that liberates from fear no longer had any basis in the human world, but was now invested entirely in the deity. This "trust," for which Egyptian has no word, was now expressed through the metaphor of silence. Originally the central virtue of human fellowship—taking the form of discipline, moderation, and subjection to the community—silence now became the central virtue of piety.[72] The silent were those who submitted themselves to god's will and trusted implicitly in the protection of the deity or, as the Egyptian phrase has it, who "place themselves in the hand of god."[73]

Just how concrete a form this transfer of trust from the human to the divine sphere could take is illustrated by the case of Zimut-Kiki, who bequeathed his entire fortune to the goddess Mut, thus making her his patroness during his lifetime and enlisting her support for his burial and mortuary cult.[74] Kiki gives an account of this devotion in his tomb, situated in western Thebes:

There was once a man from southern Heliopolis,
a true scribe in Thebes;
Zimut was his name from his mother,
called Kiki, justified.

He had been instructed by his god
and made wise in his teachings,
he put him on the path of life
to preserve his limbs.
The god had recognized him as a child.
Food and precious things were allotted to him.

And he bethought himself
that he should find a patron;
and he found Mut at the head of the gods,
fate and fortune in her hand,
lifetime and the breath of life are hers to command.
Everything that happens, happens at her command.

He said: I will give her my fortune and all my revenues,
for I recognize her power with my eyes,
her unique agency.
She has made my fear vanish
and protected me in the moment of need.

She came, preceded by the north wind,
when I called her by her name.

I am a weak one of her place,
a poor man and pilgrim of her city;
I dispose of my fortune so that she be rich
and I in exchange have the breath of life.
No one of my house shall have a share of it,
it shall belong to her *ka* [life force, personality] in peace.

[...]
I have not chosen a protector among men.
I have not [sought] myself a [patron] among the great.
It is no son of mine that I have found
to [arrange] the burial [for me].
The burial lies in your hand alone.
You are also the birth goddess who provides for me
with an immaculate mummy when I come to die.

[...]
I exult in your strength,
because you are so much greater than any other god.
My heart is filled with my lady
and I fear no man.
I spend the night sleeping peacefully,
for I have a protector.

Who makes Mut his protector
no god can attack him;
he stands in the favor of the king of his time,
until he achieves venerability.

Who makes Mut his protector
no ill can befall him;
he is sheltered all his days
until he is one with the necropolis.

Who makes Mut his protector,
how beautiful is his lifetime!
The favor of the king penetrates his body,
the body of him who has given her into his heart.

Who makes Mut his protector
he comes as a praised one from the womb;
he is assured of good on the birth brick [a kind of birth stool
    formed by bricks],
he will be a tomb owner.

Who makes Mut his protector
blessed he who longs for her!
No god will cast him down
as one who does not know death.[75]

With this decision to confer his fortune on Mut, Kiki became the
"client" of the goddess. Regardless of how many others actually went
to such lengths, the fact that for Egyptians of the Ramesside Period
such a deed was within the realms of possibility shows that the
inscription's reference to the deity as a patron, as a refuge and stronghold for the persecuted, was not mere metaphorical verbiage. The
text presents a real model, an existing institutionalization of the relations between god and man. By transferring his worldly goods to the
god, the worshipper bought his way into the patronage of a deity; he
became the god's client. When he praises god as his patron and
defender and adds that he has not sought himself a patron among
men, this worshipper eschews social patronage in favor of its religious
counterpart. The trust "invested" (in the literal sense) in the deity by
the pious was withdrawn from the human dimension. Piety was not
an extension of *ma'at,* but a substitute for it. *Ma'at* was replaced by
the will of god.

The Theologization of Connective Justice and the Readability of History

RELIGION THUS ESTABLISHED A NEW FORM of connectivity.
Whereas the Middle Kingdom made the integration of the individual
depend on the capacity of his heart to hearken and remember, now
the relation between man and god became the crucial social bond
that integrated the individual into the community. When Egyptians
of the New Kingdom say that they have "given god into their hearts,"
it is this bond that they refer to. In a world broadened by this dimension of connectivity, experiences of radical isolation as thematized in
the *Dispute of a Man with His Ba* are simply no longer possible.

In the light of this new sense of piety, fate and history attained a new readability. The idea of personal piety brought structure and meaning into spheres of existence that were formerly contingent and inscrutable. As we have seen, structure finds its way into the numinous world through the parameters of language, the cosmos, and political order. But the reverse is also true. The world of the gods, having acquired structure and cultural form, brings structure to language, the cosmos, and the sociopolitical sphere. The divine world renders this world intelligible. The "solar discourse" discussed earlier is an outstanding example of such a "reading" of the world—one that enabled the Egyptians to identify the course of the sun as a "text" of the utmost relevance to their personal and political salvation. The focus on the Nile flood cycles illustrates the same phenomenon. For the Egyptians, it is the cosmic dimension of divine presence that makes the cosmos itself intelligible. A similar process operated on the level of language. Because language constituted a dimension of divine presence, hieroglyphic script was canonized as "divine speech" and "holy scripture," and Middle Egyptian was elevated to the status of the cult language. Linguistic polysystemics is typical of all cultures where language is a factor of divine presence.[76] As for the political and cultic dimension, urban festivals clearly reveal the structuring power of polytheistic religion. Polytheism was thus the determining factor in the topological organization of the land and the affiliation structure of its inhabitants.

But what both modern civilization and the Bible (for example) consider to be the decisive dimension of reality apparently had no place in the Egyptian system. That dimension is time, as experienced, remembered, and interpreted by human beings, at both the level of individual biography and that of political history. Was time, in the sense of biography and history, unreadable for the Egyptians? Of course not. But what, if not the ordering parameters of the polytheistic worldview, did in fact structure time for the Egyptians?

In Egypt, the cultural construction of biographical time was determined by the idea of connective justice, the idea that there is a connection between doing and faring.[77] This reciprocal relation made biographical history readable by giving it meaning and direction. While Ma'at, as the personification of connective justice, was indeed worshipped as the goddess of law and truth, she never figured as a deity dispensing reward or retribution. The Egyptians of the Middle Kingdom did not theologize this function. Connective justice was the business not of the gods but of man; as we have seen, connective justice took the form of social memory enabling men to "act for one another." The actions of one's fellow citizens, not the goddess Ma'at, counted for one's welfare on earth. The connection between doing and faring lay completely in the sphere of human responsibility; it was not a function of divine presence. "Doing and saying *ma'at*" did not bring men any nearer to god. Only in the Judgment of the Dead did the heart of the just prove worthy (or not) of swelling the ranks of those who would have congress with the gods in the afterlife.

By contrast, the theology of will represents a theologization of connective justice: doing good becomes an act of piety. The just man has given god into his heart and walks on his water. From the New Kingdom on, *ma'at* makes proximity to god possible not only after death but also in this life. The change undergone by the idea of guilt is especially striking. Where guilt and sin were concerned, Egypt took an entirely different line from other Middle Eastern civilizations. When beset by misfortune, the Mesopotamians attempted to find out the name of the incensed deity by divination and then set out to mollify that deity with offerings. Here religion did indeed render one's own history readable, making it possible to offset mishaps such as illness, accidents, and losses via specifically religious measures. The problem with this form of interpreting reality is obvious, however. When every misfortune is read as a punishment for some misdeed, the case of the innocent sufferer defies readability and resolution. In Mesopotamia a large body of literature wrestled with the problem of the innocent sufferer. The biblical Book of Job also stands in this tradition.

In Egypt this problem was nonexistent. The Egyptians had no trouble at all with the idea that a blameless individual could be struck with misfortune. For them, mishaps and misfortune—"that which happens," as the Egyptian expression has it—had nothing to do with the connection between doing and faring but with the external dimension of contingency. Misfortune was not the manifestation of an incensed deity but of the power of evil, of chaos, of nonbeing. Against this power, a man might protect himself by throwing in his lot with a powerful patron who guaranteed his adherents that "never would misfortune come over them." But patrons were, of course, powerless in the face of illness and other random misfortunes. Then the remedy was magic, which harnessed for the individual's benefit the cosmogonic powers that kept the world in motion. It was the

Egyptian way of coming to terms with contingency; it was given to men—as the *Instruction for King Merikare* has it—"to fend off the blow of events."[78] Misfortune lay outside the province of social action, and only this latter was constituted by the link between doing and faring, the connective justice of *ma'at*. The Egyptians confronted misfortune with pessimistic skepticism: "One cannot know what happens, so that one can envisage the morrow," says the *Instruction for Ptah-hotep;*[79] so, too, the *Instruction for Kagemni:* "One cannot recognize what happens."[80] The *Tale of the Eloquent Peasant* counsels:

Gird yourself not for the coming day before it has come:
one cannot know what misfortune it brings.[81]

A letter to the dead, written during the Middle Kingdom, includes the sentence "There are no limits to what happens."[82] Epistles from the New Kingdom contain the formula "Today I am fine but I know not my condition tomorrow."[83] Because man has no way of knowing the future, he must not forge plans in the delusion that the morrow will be at his disposal. Thus in Egyptian, concepts like "future" (*iyt*, "the coming") or "history" (*hpryt*, "the occurring") have connotations of potential misfortune.[84] "Mishaps" (such as illness, solitude, impoverishment, or persecution) have nothing to do with "faring"; they cannot be interpreted as punishment for previous blameworthy actions, and so remain unintelligible in this light.

The advent of personal piety transformed precisely this situation. The god now figured as the authority who dealt reward or retribution, and in this capacity ousted the notion of an immanent form of connective justice based on social solidarity. God himself guaranteed the connectivity of one man acting for another:

For this does not mean that he who acts, acts for one who does
    not act.
It means [rather] that Re acts in heaven
and sees him who acts. He gives his reward for the deed to him
    who performed it.[85]

Or, in more general terms, "Who does something good is rewarded by god."[86]

Phenomena that had previously belonged to the external sphere of contingency became readable in religious terms. God now guaranteed a discernible link between doing and faring, and his presence was experienced through his rewarding or punitive interventions.[87] A new dimension of experiential nearness to god had opened up, accurately described as revelation and indicated by concepts of "finding" and "coming."[88] One instance of this dates from the close of the Amarna Period of persecution. A hymn to Amun uses the language of revelation to express yearning for the expelled deity:

> How good it is to follow you, Amun:
> a lord great in "being found" for the one who seeks him.[89]

In later texts of personal piety, "being found" usually refers to the saving intervention of the deity:

> May Amun be found by his coming,
> sweet breaths of air preceding him.[90]

> I found her as she had come with a sweet breath of air.[91]

The most celebrated instance of such a revelation is found in the poem on the Battle of Qadesh (which I shall discuss in the next section). At the moment of ultimate danger, Ramesses II prays to Amun:

> My voice echoing in Thebes,
> The moment I called to him, I found Amun came.[92]

Amun intervenes in the battle by "giving his hand" to the king and, at the last minute, saving him from death or captivity. Amun's aid is not described in magical or mythic terms as a theophany on the battlefield, but in completely realistic terms: at the last moment an Egyptian elite squad comes to the rescue of the beleaguered king. This squad had been sent off on a different route to perform some special task and now returns to join the main body of the army. An accurate rendering of the course of the battle becomes readable as divine intervention: the new construction of reality dependent on the presence of god. Amun does not manifest himself in person but in the medium of history, of "events." As before, we remain within the framework of mediate presence. Not until the advent of mysticism is an attempt made to pierce these veils of indirect divine presence—and no such attempt is to be found in pharaonic Egypt. But within the bounds of mediate presence, history now became transparent in divine terms for him who "has given god into his heart."

According to classical Egyptian belief, god acted through the medium of the king, who was the agent of his will. This is neither a genuine theology of will nor a theology of history, but is a form of "representative theocracy." In the Qadesh *Poem*, however, god does not act through the medium of the king, but through the intervening troops. God acts himself and not by proxy, for the soldiers do not "represent" him. Only such personal action on the part of god, unmediated by the representative agencies of cult and kingship, can be strictly regarded as an "intervention" or "revelation." Only here can we genuinely speak of "historical action" on the part of god.

An important distinction now emerges. On the one hand, "manifestations of power" like the rising of the sun keep the world in motion. These repeated actions have a ritual character and belong in the category of cyclical time, *neheh*. On the other hand, events of a unique, discrete nature belong to the category of linear time and qualify as "epoch-making," in the sense of dividing history into a before and after. The Battle of Qadesh was experienced by the Egyptians in just this sense. History was no longer "festival" but event.[93]

I venture that a king from an earlier period would not have placed much emphasis upon the near disaster at Qadesh. In his victory report he would have passed over his peril and rescue in silence. The only significant events were those that confirmed the regular and the ritual; events outside that framework—defeats, palace revolts, and so on—were allotted to the sphere of contingent manifestations of chaos and found unworthy of mention. In the New Kingdom, the relation between figure and ground begins to reverse. Events now stand out against the backdrop of the eternally recurrent, like the writing on the wall.[94] This corresponds to the Mesopotamian model. There the will of the gods was not (as in Egypt) completely absorbed in the business of "keeping the world going," but also affected human history, action, and experience. Hence history, too, formed a dimension of religious experience and significance and was invested with meaning.[95] In ancient Egypt, at least in the earlier stages of its development, the opposite conviction prevailed.

Just as Ramesses II was able to read the last-minute intervention of the *Ne'arin* (soldiers) as the doing of Amun, so other individuals could interpret events in their personal biographies in terms of divine intervention. On one stela at Assiut, a man thanks the god Upuaut for saving him from a crocodile.⁹⁶ Penitent inscriptions at Deir el-Medina trace illness (usually eye illnesses) to some form of transgression—perjury, theft, slander, or other crimes.⁹⁷ The public avowal of such guilt on stela inscriptions, albeit invariably in an indirect form, was designed to placate the deity. Publication was a therapeutic measure that remedied the fault associated with concealment. If the guilt had been patent, some litigant would long since have arrived on the scene and arraigned the perpetrator before the public courts. The Egyptian expression for the act of publication literally means "proclaiming the manifestations of power,"⁹⁸ and refers both to punitive and to healing or saving interventions. The poem on the Battle of Qadesh also belongs to this genre of proclaiming the manifestations of power. To experience the presence of god was to incur an obligation to publicize that experience. The abundant texts gathered under the heading of personal piety spring from that sense of obligation. But it would be entirely erroneous to regard them merely as a literary genre. The discourse of personal piety stems from a new construction of reality in which time, destiny, and history become intelligible in a religious sense. So what we have here is neither just a new theology of history—in the biblical sense of "history as revelation"—nor just a new belief in destiny that makes happiness or unhappiness dependent on the piety of the individual. Rather, it is both together, time as the dimension of "occurrences" in the broadest sense. This dimension was now explicitly related to the will of the deity. For the Middle Kingdom, the sphere of random occurrences was extraneous to the connection between doing and faring as granted by connective justice, a realm of chaos susceptible only to the power of magic. By being related to god's will, this sphere was salvaged and retrieved for the domain of meaningful time. *Neheh* (cyclical infinitude) and *djet* (unchanging permanence) were joined by "history" as the third aspect of time:

> Your being is the fullness of time [*neheh*],
> your image is permanence [*djet*],
> your *ka* [a double or soul, representing will, planning,
>   conscience] is all that occurs.⁹⁹

This formulation of god's presence in history is found in a hymn to the sun in the tomb of Tjai from the time of Merneptah.¹⁰⁰ But it also figures in texts of different genres, functions, and disseminations and may therefore be regarded as a binding expression of the new image of the world. In Ramesses II's inscription at Luxor we read: "His *ka* is everything that exists."[101] In the Leiden Amun Hymn this idea is extended to a notion of creation by the word: "His *ka* is everything existing as an utterance in his mouth."[102] Ramesses II's marriage stela reads: "What you have commanded is everything that occurs"—that is, "Everything that occurs, occurs at your command."[103]

In the Ramesside theology of history, which traces all that happens to the planning will of god, vestiges remain of Akhenaten's time-creating god in his hymns to the Aten. The Aten was the god not only of light but also of time; both result from his agency. The *Great Hymn* says: "You are life-time itself." But the Aten was conceived of as a cosmic power and not as an ethical authority; he created time but not what happened in it—that was the business of the king. Akhenaten figures as the lord of destiny, exactly like the kings of the Middle Kingdom. In his ethical capacity Akhenaten referred to himself as "he who lives on *ma'at*," an epithet normally reserved for the sun god. After the demise of the Amarna religion, this division of labor, allotting cosmic agency to god and historical, fate-determining action to the king, was revoked; so, too, was the distinction between cosmic and historical time. The time created by Amun encompassed the events—themselves the work of Amun's will—that happened in it.[104]

As lord and planner of events, the Ramesside god stood in the lineage of the royalist religion of the age of Amarna, which in its turn recalled the loyalism of the Middle Kingdom, itself a throwback to the "patrons" of the First Intermediate Period. The king's will was implemented on the spot; he spoke and it happened. "Your will be done" was the typical reaction of courtiers to kingly declarations of intent. "Speak and it shall happen, command and it shall be done, what your *ka* wills is that which shall occur."[105]

The theologization of the notion of kingly will involved a thoroughgoing change in Egyptian thinking about history. By its very nature, the royal will could only direct individual actions: renewal of a temple, erection of obelisks, the making of statues and cult equipment, appointment of officials, the digging of a well, and the like.[106] The Egyptians would never have said that *everything that happens* was a product of royal will, because "everything" includes the entire sphere of contingent misfortune they abhorred as a manifestation of nonbeing. The point was rather that *everything the king wants, happens*. In this miraculous energy that immediately realized his will, the king stood revealed as "a god who commands and executes his will": "I am a god who commands and it is done. Nothing goes awry that comes from my mouth."[107] The king was mirrored by the deity, whose authority was of the same kind. This pattern belongs to the theology of representation; it is not yet the theologization of the role of the king. That stage was reached only when the king no longer represented god but was subservient to him because by its very nature the will of god is directed at the whole, at "everything that happens," and so exceeds anything that the king might will.[108]

The world in god's hand was not necessarily easier to "read." Cyclical time of eternal recurrence became restless change. But the pious individual who had taken god into his heart and whose heart was guided by the will of god could now choose—as Amenemope's formula has it—"to place himself in god's hand" and there find security.[109] Accordingly, in a literary prayer we read:

I lay yesterday and today in Amun's hands
and I was found whole, my plans enduring.
I make for myself a beautiful abode
until my time is fulfilled,
by giving myself wholly to him: he is my mooring post.
How beautiful is [such] a burial, it has no equal!
A patron among men disappears, his plans come to naught,
[but] I gave myself to Amun and I found the good.[110]

As with the crisis of the polytheistic worldview that culminated in Akhenaten's monotheistic revolution, the movement toward personal piety was of enormous political consequence. At the end of the Twentieth Dynasty, a theocracy—a god-state—was established in Thebes ruled over by Amun himself via the medium of the oracle. This shift signaled Egypt's reversion from the model of "representation" to a model of "direct" theocracy, but with the roles reversed. In the original version of direct theocracy, the king reigned as god; now god reigned as king. A text from this period expresses the new theology in unequivocal terms:

Mighty in retribution, mightier is he than Sekhmet,
like a fire in the storm;

high in grace, who provides for him who praises him,
who turns round to heal suffering,
for he looks on men, there is none that he knows not,
and he hearkens to millions of them.
Who can resist your wrath, who can divert the fury of your
  power?[111]

18

RAMESSES II AND THE
BATTLE OF QADESH

The Historical Semantics of War

JUST AS THE NEW SOCIAL CLASS of patrons transformed the cultural semantics of the Old Kingdom and determined the loyalist worldview of the Middle Kingdom, so the new class of military leaders and military aristocrats determined the cultural forms of the New Kingdom, notably the Ramesside Period. In the traditional worldview of the Egyptians up to that point, war had not played a very significant role. The civilized world was equated with Egypt, which had been created by the sun god and where the king ousted *isfet* by means of *ma'at*. War was one of the forms in which the banishment of *isfet* was enacted. For Egypt did not see itself as one realm among others but as the sole realm; beyond Egypt was a zone of chaos whose outer limits defied exploration, inhabited by enemies "who do not conquer but who cannot be conquered." As this zone of chaos could not be integrated into the Egyptian world of order, so its inhabitants could not be conquered, but only shut out. To this end, the "walls of the ruler" were set up, closing Egypt off against the Near East, with the belt of fortresses in Nubia serving the same purpose in the southern reaches of the land.

In this semantic framework, military action could never lead to permanent results. It belonged not to linear time, in which results could be achieved, but to cyclical time, the iterative sphere of the "again and again." Again and again it was necessary to "smite the east" and to deter the south. Such a semantic framework has no place

The Battle of Qadesh

for the opposition of war and peace. War is integral to a linear semantics of "resultative" action. We speak of "war" only in connection with an action that is designed to bring about a lasting condition and that is justifiable only in terms of that result. War is waged either to fend off an aggressor or to conquer foreign territory. In the nonlinear sphere, the iterative, the "again and again," military action takes the form not of warfare but of raids, forays, and sallies. Military raids are the expression of one power's ongoing control over its environment; their goal is not change but the maintenance of the status quo. A state of peace is impossible in such a constellation.

The image for this constant control is the pictogram of "smiting the enemies," earlier encountered in the painted tomb of Hierakonpolis and on the Narmer Palette. In the latter case, the reference may indeed have been to a historical event in linear time. The wars for the unification of the realm were deserving of the name as we have defined it; they aimed at consolidating the territory and establishing

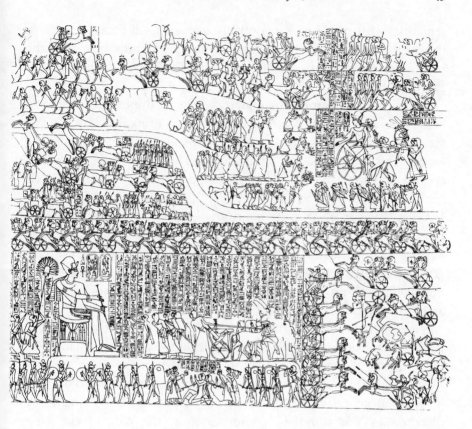

peace. But as early as the ivory tablet of King Den, the caption refers to the "first time of smiting the east" and hence to an event in cyclical time, a ritualized foray.

The historical experience of the wars of liberation against the Hyksos at the beginning of the New Kingdom wrought a radical change in the semantics of war. With a long-term military objective that extended over two generations (Seqenenre and his two sons Kamose and Ahmose) this enterprise was something very different from Egypt's previously sporadic but endless engagement with its foes. The wars against the Hyksos aimed at a result: a victory that was singular and historical. Initially, cultural forms of expression did not keep pace with semantic change. Tuthmosis III, the first Egyptian pharaoh to pursue a systematic war policy in the new sense of the term, had himself represented in the traditional form of "smiting the enemies." The Poetic Stela glorifies him in images that are still entirely attuned to the semantics of control and deterrence, and hence to the semantics of the Middle Kingdom. It was not until Sethos I, who in the early Nineteenth Dynasty explicitly adopted Tuthmosis III as the model for his foreign political activities, that iconographic forms express a semantics of history.

The military campaigns undertaken by Tuthmosis III in almost every year of his reign have often been said to express a ritualistic view of history that accords with traditional Egyptian views of the world. This is not so. The significance of these campaigns was not cyclical and iterative but teleological and resultative. Tuthmosis III could not achieve his goal in one single campaign but only in a series. His aim was peace. And the appropriate generic term for the series of campaigns directed at this objective is war. Peace as the aim of war was synonymous with the transformation of the chaotic, outlying gray belt of enemies, who could be deterred and given a sound beating now and again but not permanently subjugated into a sphere of rule and order. The establishment of a frontier with the other major empires (Mitanni and Hatti) marked the achievement of this aim. Beyond that, war was not waged as a constantly recurring ritual. Quite the contrary: the state of peace was cemented by Tuthmosis IV and Amenophis III by means of treaties and political marriages. This view of political action structured in terms of war/peace and foe/friend dichotomies was a notable innovation on the part of the New Kingdom.

In this new context, the kings took on a role that had not figured in their traditional image of kingship. The political activities of kings like Tuthmosis III, Sethos I, and Ramesses II thus led to considerable internal tensions. Apparently there were circles—presumably among the priesthood—that still adhered to the traditional Egyptocentric worldview, and which either set up rival monarchs like Hatshepsut or influenced the king to change his course. These tensions escalated at the end of the age of Amarna. They found expression in the spectacular scheme of putting a Hittite prince consort on the throne. The failure of this démarche—Zannanza was assassinated on his way to Egypt—brought about the triumph of the opposition forces, the military, which, represented by Horemheb and the first kings of the Nineteenth Dynasty, dictated Egyptian policy from then on. This policy was shaped by the Egyptian-Hittite war that broke out upon the assassination of Zannanza. Only fifty years later was Ramesses II able to terminate the hostilities—and only with very considerable effort.

The Zannanza Affair

OUR ONLY SOURCES for the outbreak of the war are Hittite, among them the *Manly Deeds of Suppululiumas,* as set down by his son Mursilis:

> While my father sojourned in the land of Kargami, he sent Lupakki and Tarhunta-zalma to the land of Amka. They went, attacked the land of Amka, and brought men, cattle [and] sheep back, before the face of my father.
>
> But when the Egyptians heard of the attack on Amka they were struck by fear.
>
> Because in addition their lord Piphururija had died, the queen of Egypt Tahamunzu [wife of the king] sent an ambassador to my father and wrote to him as follows:
>
> "My husband has died and I have no son. The people say you have many sons. If you sent me one of your sons, he could become my husband. Never shall I take one of my servants as husband." When my father heard this he assembled the great ones to confer with them and said: "Never since the ancient days has such a thing occurred!"
>
> He went and sent out Hattu-zitis, the privy councilor, and said: "Go and fetch me reliable news. They might be trying to deceive me. Perhaps they have a prince after all, go and fetch me reliable news."
>
> . . .
>
> The Egyptian envoy, the honorable lord Hanis, came to him. Because my father had instructed Hattu-zitis, when he sent him to Egypt, with the words: "Maybe they have a prince after all; they might be trying to deceive me and not really want one of my sons as king," the Egyptian queen now answered in a letter as follows:
>
> "Why do you say: 'They might be trying to deceive me'? If I had a son, would I be writing to a foreign land in this way which is humiliating for my land and for me? You trust me not and say such a thing. He who was my husband died and I have no sons. Am I perhaps to take one of my servants as a husband? I have written to no other land, I have only written to you. The people say you have many sons. Give me one of your sons and he is my husband and king of Egypt."

[The following is much mutilated. Suppiluliumas is surprised at the urgency with which the Egyptians almost demand one of his sons. He also gives voice to misgivings that the Egyptians might want one of his sons as a hostage, but the Egyptian envoy is able to allay his fears. The text continues:]

> Thus my father preoccupied himself with the question of a son for their sake. And then my father demanded the treaty document "How earlier the weather god took the man from Kurushtama, the Hittite, and brought him to the land of Egypt and made them [the people of Kurushtama] Egyptians; how the weather god concluded a treaty between the land of Egypt and the land of Hatti; how they befriended each other for all eternity; how the tablet was read before them."
>
> Then my father spoke to them as follows: "Since ancient times Egypt and Hattusa have been friends. Now this too has occurred between us. The land of Hatti and the land of Egypt will continue to be friends forever."[112]

In the *Plague Prayers of Mursilis* the same events are recounted from a somewhat different vantage. These are prayers to the Hittite storm god to put an end to a pestilence that has been raging in the land for a number of years and that threatens to wipe out the entire population. The oracles were consulted and pointed to two ancient tablets. One contained offering rites for the river Mala, neglected on account of the plague; the other referred to the Kurushtama treaty.

> The storm god of Hatti brought the people of Kurushtama to Egypt and concluded a treaty with the Hittites concerning them so that they were bound to him by oath. Although both the Hittites and the Egyptians were now bound to the storm god by oath, the Hittites neglected their obligations. They broke their oath to the gods. My father sent troops and chariots to attack the land of Amka, in Egyptian territory. But the Egyptians were afraid and asked straightaway for one of his sons to take over the kingship. But when my father gave them one of his sons, they killed him while they were taking him there. My father gave his anger free rein, set out to war with Egypt, and attacked it. He beat the troops and chariots of the land of Egypt. The storm god of Hatti, my lord, gave my father victory by his counsel; he bested and beat the troops and chariots of the land of Egypt.

But when they brought the captives to Hatti a plague broke out among them and they died.

When they brought the captives to Hatti, these captives brought the plague into the land. Since then the people in the land of Hatti have been dying. When I had found the tablet about Egypt, I had the oracle consulted about it: "These agreements made by the Hittite storm god, that the Egyptians be bound to him by oath like the Hittites, that the deities of Damnassaras were present in the temple, and that the Hittites immediately broke their word—is this perhaps the reason for the anger of the storm god of Hatti, my lord?" Thus was it confirmed.[113]

The plague brought into the country by the Egyptian prisoners raged for twenty years throughout Anatolia and the Near East, and probably in Egypt as well. The Hittites interpreted the plague as a sign of divine wrath, specifically as a punishment for their attack on the Egyptian town of Amka, which had been a breach of treaty. The death of the prince Zannanza exacerbated the conflict, but the plague put an end to military action on both sides for a certain period.

The circles on the Egyptian side responsible for the Zannanza démarche must have been anxious to prevent a war with the Hittites, as well as to salvage, by means of a political marriage, the peace disrupted by the Hittites. The marriage of a royal widow to a foreign prince was wholly outside the bounds of the traditional Egyptian view. The opposition forces that succeeded in thwarting this marriage by the simple expedient of assassination are easy enough to identify; subsequently they took over open control. The leading figure was General Horemheb, who under the young Tutankhamun first assumed the unusual title of regent and successor to the throne. After the death of Tutankhamun and the brief intermezzo of the usurper Ay, Horemheb himself ascended the throne. The full implications of the shift Horemheb stands for only became apparent in the course of time, when Horemheb laid plans for the future line of succession that smacked even more of a coup than did his own accession to the throne.

Horemheb appointed as vizier Paramesse (Paramessu), the commander of the border fortress in Sile. Paramesse was a front officer who also bore the title of ambassador to Asia. Horemheb showered on him a host of other titles: chief priest and military general, as well as the new titles of succession: regent and crown prince.[114] This bestowal of the leadership of the civil administration (vizier), of cults (chief priest), and of the armed forces, and of succession to the throne, all on one man was unparalleled in Egyptian civilization up to that point and indicates that something approximating a state of emergency must have been prevailing. Normally, civil administration, military leadership, and priesthood were strictly separated. Obviously the view taken of the situation following the age of Amarna was a very serious one.

The Military Takes Over

PARAMESSE WAS A TYPICAL REPRESENTATIVE of a new class that regarded itself as the aristocracy of the land, a class of military officers who surely felt greater allegiance to the Asiatic military nobility (the *mari'annu*) than to Egyptian priesthood or officialdom. An important element in the self-image of this class was otherwise alien to the Egyptians: pride in ancestry. This was something new in nonroyal families; more important, pride in nonroyal ancestors was something absolutely unprecedented in royal families. Paramesse's family traced its lineage back to a certain Sethos of centuries previous. Since then, the names (Pa)Ramesses and Sethos had alternated in the family; accordingly, the son of this vizier was called Sethos, and Horemheb likely had this dynamic and highly promising young man in mind when he appointed his father to the highest office in the state. Sethos was thus retrospectively born as successor to the throne, which qualified him for the traditional Egyptian designation of "ruler in the egg." With this appointment of Sethos, Horemheb consolidated the position of the new military elite as the governing power in the country.

This takeover of power by the military leaders in the transition from the Eighteenth to the Nineteenth Dynasty radically transformed Egyptian society and its social semantics, particularly its semantics of war.[115] For W. Helck, Horemheb's rise to power was synonymous with the transformation of Egyptian society into a "military dictatorship" and with "the penetration of the military into all walks of life."[116]

The only group that strictly qualified for the title "military" were the Masters of Horse and the field officers. According to Helck, this group represented the aristocracy in the New Kingdom, especially in the Ramesside Period. Helck's theory must be seen in the context of the debate on the cultural influence of the Indo-Aryan equestrian peoples in the area extending from the Near East to the Aegean. Helck regarded the Hyksos, who introduced horse keeping and the war chariot to Egypt, as Hurrians, that is, as an Indo-European equestrian people, and the *mari'annu* of the Syrian city-states as a war-chariot aristocracy; he suggests further that the introduction of the war chariot brought with it a specifically martial and "heroic" system of values and a stratification of society into aristocracy and nonaristocracy. Though Helck's theories are certainly overstated (the Hyksos were Semites, and the *mari'annu* were not a martial aristocracy that specialized in war chariotry), the archaeological evidence does generally corroborate his view. Traditionally, the military had been closely linked with the organization of building and engineering work and exploratory expeditions. Only in the Ramesside Period does a group of active field officers set itself apart as a rank in its own right, surely an indication that warfare had newly come to be perceived as a significant area of independent political action. That the title "Master of Horse" designated the top military position clearly points to the leading role played by horse keeping and chariot technology.

But the most important indicator of the cultural meaning of war and the social role played by warriors is the conjunction of succession to the throne and military command; the crown prince in the Ramesside Period also bore the title "Great Master of Horse." More clearly than anything else, this conjunction shows that there was indeed a military aristocracy in Egypt, that this phenomenon was restricted to the Ramesside age, and that it was largely made up of the (extended) royal family and battle comrades. The figure that epitomized the typical military aristocrat of the Egyptian stamp was the prince in his war chariot. The fact that in the Ramesside Period the royal family tended to position its members primarily in top posts of active military service shows that this was the sector of society enjoying the greatest social prestige.

The Battle of Qadesh

THE HITTITE WAR had not been brought to a peaceful settlement, but was deferred on account of the plague. The situation was still menacing. Upon his ascension to the throne, Sethos first deemed it necessary, on the domestic front, to placate the gods incensed by the execrable depredations of Akhenaten. A huge program of temple construction was begun. On the external front, Sethos strove to reestablish the empire of Tuthmosis III. The systematic regularity with which Sethos set off on his yearly campaigns followed the model of Tuthmosis III, whom he emulated with such success that many of the vassal princes who had gone over to the Hittites now returned to the Egyptians. The most prominent of these was the Prince of Amurru, a region sorely needed by Egypt for the cedar wood indispensable for shipbuilding. To immortalize his deeds, Sethos developed a new iconographic schema.[117] The king had himself depicted on a chariot, assailing a fortress or fortified city identified by captions. The topographic indications frequently approximated a geographical map. The scene of his return from the Hittite campaign, for instance, shows the entire itinerary complete with fortresses and watering stations. It is the first map in the history of the world. The king clearly thought it essential to include as many concrete indications as possible so as to individualize the event as a unique achievement. This initial attempt to underline historical detail and significance was soon to reach its apogee with the documentation of Ramesses II's feats and setbacks at the Battle of Qadesh.[118]

The turncoat behavior of important Syrian vassal princes prompted the Hittites to retaliate, and this was the situation that faced Sethos I's successor, the youthful Ramesses II, in his fifth regnal year. At this point begins the Egyptian documentation of the Battle of Qadesh. It is probably ancient Egypt's most singular and impressive historiographic enterprise. My discussion focuses on a lengthy literary work, the *Poem*, of which we have two versions on papyrus, various others in temple inscriptions, and a very extensive monumental pictorial composition with text captions, the longest of which supplements the *Poem* in the form of a *Bulletin*. We learn the following:

On the ninth day of the second summer month of his fifth regnal year (that is, in early April of 1274 B.C.E.), Ramesses II set out with his troops and chariots in a northerly direction. In contrast to other Egyptian accounts of military actions, this one does not begin with an indication of the event prompting the actions of His Majesty. Normally, warlike actions were not described as spontaneous undertakings but as reactions to enemy aggression or "rebellion." But in this text there is no mention of any such thing, at least at first. After an uneventful march lasting one month, Ramesses arrived on the ninth day of the third summer month at the city of Shabtuna, immediately south of Qadesh. There two Bedouins who passed themselves off as deserters from the Hittite army were taken captive.

> There came two Shasu, from the Shasu tribefolk,
> to say to His Majesty:
> "It is our brothers who are the tribal chiefs
> of the tribes that are with the Fallen One of Hatti
> who have sent us to His Majesty saying:
> 'We shall become servants of Pharaoh, LPH [Life, Prosperity, and
>   Health][119]
> and we shall separate ourselves from the Ruler of Hatti.' "
> Then said His Majesty to them: "Where are they, your brothers
> who sent you to speak of this matter to His Majesty?"
> Then they said to His Majesty:
> "They are where the despicable Chief of Hatti is,
> for the Fallen One of Hatti is in the land of Aleppo to the North
>   of Tunip [a town in Syria].
> He feared Pharaoh, LPH,
> too much to come southward,
> when he heard that Pharaoh, LPH, was coming northward."
> Now, these two Shasu said these things, and lied to His Majesty.
> For it was the Fallen One of Hatti who had sent them,
> to find out where His Majesty was,
> so as to prevent His Majesty's army from being prepared to fight
> with the Fallen One of Hatti.
> Now, the Fallen One of Hatti had sent the Shasu
> to say these things to His Majesty,
> having come with his troops and chariotry,
> along with all the rulers of every land
> that was in the territory of the land of Hatti,
> and their troops and chariotry, which he had brought with him
>   as allies,
> to fight with His Majesty's army,
> he standing ready and prepared
> behind Old Qadesh—
> but His Majesty did not know they were there.
> The two Shasu who were in the royal presence were interrogated.[120]

Under normal circumstances, the Egyptian army would have halted at Shabtuna, a city on the border of the area allied with Egypt, and reassembled there. Only after careful reconnoitering would they have approached the hostile fortress Qadesh, which was situated in a key position and would have to be taken before they could advance any further northward. The Hittite ruse succeeded. Ramesses continued his march without waiting for the army to reassemble:

> Now, His Majesty was all alone, with just his followers;
> the division of Amun marching behind him,
> the division of Pre crossing the ford
> in the area south of Shabtuna
> at a distance of one *iter* [10.5 km] from where His Majesty was;
> the division of Ptah being to the south of the town of Arnam;
> and the division of Seth [still] marching along the road.
> His Majesty had drawn the first battle line from all the leaders of
>   his army.
> Now they were on the shore in the land of Amurru.[121]

This part of the *Poem* refers to the moment at which Ramesses and his entourage passed to the west of Qadesh. North of the fortress, Ramesses decided to make camp and await the arrival of the Amun division.

> Then came a scout who was in His Majesty's service,
> bringing in two scouts of the Fallen One of Hatti.
> Then said His Majesty to them: "What are you?"
> What they said: "We belong to the Ruler of Hatti,
> he it is who sent us, to see where His Majesty is."
> His Majesty said to them: "Where is he himself, the Ruler of
>   Hatti?
> See, I have heard that he is in the land of Aleppo, to the North
>   of Tunip!"
> They said to His Majesty: "See, the despicable Ruler of Hatti has
>   come,
> along with the many foreign lands that accompany him, whom
>   he has brought with him as allies.
> [There follows a list of tribes from the Dardanoi in the west to
>   the Mitanni in the east, the Keshkesh on the Black Sea to
>   Ugarit, Aleppo, and Qadesh in Syria.]
> They are furnished with infantry and chariotry;
> they are more numerous than the sands of the seashore.
> See, they stand equipped, ready to fight, behind Old Qadesh."[122]

Ramesses assembled his officers and informed them of this new turn. The Egyptians had walked into a trap. Not only was the report of the "deserters" a systematic ruse, but the vassal princes through whose territory the Hittite army had marched, and even the Egyptian garrison commanders, who could hardly have failed to notice the movement of troops, were also involved in this conspiracy. Extreme haste was necessary. The vizier was sent to bring the Ptah division up in forced marches. In the meantime, the Re division had passed through the forest of Labwe and emerged into the plain to the west of Qadesh. At this juncture Muwatallis, the Hittite king, chose to unleash his forces.

> But even as His Majesty sat talking with his high officers,
> the despicable Fallen One of Hatti came with his troops and
>   chariotry,
> and also numerous foreign lands that were accompanying him.
> They crossed the ford south of Qadesh,
> then they entered in amongst His Majesty's troops
> as they marched unawares.
> Then His Majesty's troops and chariots quailed before them,
> on their way north, to where His Majesty was.
> Then the foes from the Fallen One of Hatti surrounded His
>   Majesty's subordinates who were by his side.[123]

The terseness of this account mirrors the swiftness of the chariot attack. The Re division was scattered in perhaps ten minutes, while the camp was surrounded in not more than ten to twenty minutes. The Hittite attack was planned as an ambush, not as an engagement in the field; otherwise Muwatallis would not have left his 37,000 infantry under cover behind Qadesh and restricted the action to the chariotry. His error was to wait so long before launching the attack.

At this point the accounts in the *Poem* and the *Bulletin* change to a different style, marked formally in the *Poem* by the switch to the first person (direct speech by the king) and by the narration of a miraculous turn of events that far transcends any purely military or strategic report. In the *Bulletin,* where the switch to the first person comes only at the end of the account, we read the following:

> Then His Majesty caught sight of them, so he arose quickly.
> Then he raged against them, like his father Montu [Lord of
>   Thebes].

He took up the panoply of war, he girded himself with his coat
    of mail,
he was like Sutekh in his moment of power.
Then he mounted ["Victory-in-Thebes"], his chariot span,
he setting off quickly, being all alone.
His Majesty was strong, and his heart was firm,
none could stand before him.
All his patch blazed with flames,
he burnt up every foreign land with his hot breath.
His eyes became savage when he saw them,
his might flared up like fire against them.
He paid no heed to [even] a million aliens,
he looked upon them as on chaff.
Then His Majesty entered into the hostile ranks of the fallen
    ones of Hatti,
along with the many foreign lands who were with them,
His Majesty being like Sutekh, great in strength,
like Sekhmet in the moment of her fury.
His Majesty slew all the hostile ranks of the despicable Fallen
    One of Hatti,
along with all of his great chiefs and his brothers,
likewise all the rulers of all the foreign lands that came with
    him,
and their troops and chariotry, fallen on their faces, one upon
    another.
His Majesty slaughtered and slew them, fallen on the spot,
as they lay [sprawling] before his horses,
His Majesty being alone, none other with him.
So His Majesty forced the hostile ranks of the fallen ones of
    Hatti to plunge on their faces,
sprawling one upon another,
plunging like crocodiles into the waters of Orontes.
I was after them like a griffon.
I defeated all the foreign lands, being alone,
my troops and my chariotry abandoned me,
none of them stood looking back.
As Re lives for me
and as my father Atum favors me,
regarding every thing of which My Majesty has spoken,
I truly did them, in the presence of my troops and chariotry.[124]

On this account, a miracle must have occurred. At the sight of the enemy, the Egyptian troops fled in confusion. But Ramesses, in his flaring wrath, transformed himself into a fire-spitting dragon that embodied all the warlike deities of the Egyptian pantheon in one— Montu, Seth (Sutekh), Sekhmet—and single-handedly trounced the enemy forces. The enemy experienced his deeds as an awe-inspiring theophany:

> He is no mere man, he that is among us!—
> it's Seth, great of power, Baal in person!
> Not the acts of a mere man are the things that he does,
> they belong to one utterly unique!—
> one who defeats myriads, no troops with him, no chariotry.
> Let's come away, let's flee before him,
> let's seek life for ourselves, that we may breathe air![125]

This outsize elevation of the feats of Ramesses to the plane of the superhuman appears to forgo any attempt at historical individualization and to present Ramesses' victory as a manifestation of timeless superiority. In purely iconic terms, this portrayal of Ramesses at Qadesh corresponds more to the traditional representation of the "smiting of enemies" than to any new approach to battle description. In fact, the linguistic description of the event mirrors the pictorial representation. Ramesses, larger than life and alone in his chariot, shoots his arrow into a horde of enemies who fall over themselves in their confusion and seek salvation by swimming for their lives. The pictorial medium adds to the verbal account a burlesque scene featuring the Prince of Aleppo, who has swallowed so much water that his followers have to stand him on his head.

What we have here is a case of fully intentional hyperbole, most readily noticeable in the numerical exaggerations: millions fled before me, I overcame millions of foreign peoples on my own, my sword arm mowed down hundreds of thousands. This exaggeration is reminiscent of the traditional image of the king:

> He is One and Millions—as nothing are the other thousands of
>   men.[126]

> He who shoots the arrow like Sekhmet
> to fell thousands of those who mistake his power.[127]

Elsewhere, the Qadesh documentation numbers the opposing forces at 37,000 infantry and 2,500 chariots—certainly a very large figure for the period, though not beyond the bounds of credibility. Such exact figures lay claim to the status of factual information. So the sudden move to the sheerly incredible numbers at this juncture is a clear shift of perspective and of genre that coincides with the change to the first person.

The genre that dictates the perspective in which the events are presented can be seen more clearly if we switch from the *Bulletin* to the *Poem*. The *Poem* presents a largely similar account of the proceedings, the most significant difference being four lengthy speeches by the king, of which the first, a supplication to Amun, is the longest and most important. In contrast to the *Bulletin*, this prayer imbues the extraordinary event at Qadesh with a religious dimension. The miracle at Qadesh is worked not by the king but by Amun, who thus changed the course of the battle and reversed the imminent rout of the Egyptians. Whereas in the Old Testament account, Yahweh appears on the field of battle and strikes fear into the hearts of the enemy, Amun contents himself with endowing the king with superhuman powers and letting him experience the presence of god in his solitude. The account of the king's deeds is transformed into one of miraculous rescue—a transformation squarely within the universe of "personal piety." The "miraculous rescue" genre is a paean of praise that publicizes the greatness of god. Normally such praise fulfills a vow made by an individual in dire straits: "I will proclaim your power to the fowl in the sky and the fish in the water...." In the framework of the miraculous rescue genre, the monumental loneliness and abandonment of the king, who has been left in the lurch by his troops and surrounded by 2,500 enemy chariots, reflects the extremity into which he has fallen. In this extremity he sends up the prayer to the deity:

> Indeed, what's up with you, my father Amun?
> Has a father ever ignored his son?
> Now, have I ever done anything without you?
> Do I not go and stop at your word? I have not disobeyed
> a plan that you commanded.
> [...]
> What are they to you, O Amun, these Asiatics despicable and
>   ignorant of god!

Have I not made for you monuments in great multitude,
I have filled your temple with my captures!
I built for you my Memorial Temple, and I assigned to you all
　my property by testament.
[. . .]
Do good to him who counts on you—then people will serve you
　with a will.
I have called on you, O Amun,
while I am amidst multitudes whom I know not.
All the foreign countries have united against me, I being entirely
　alone, no one else with me.

Ramesses' speech is not that of a sinner who interprets his perilous straits as the just punishment of an incensed deity whom he must try to mollify by confessing guilt and promising contrition. Rather, Ramesses is a pious king who points righteously to his obedience and obeisances toward god. His prayer speaks from the same knowledge of being at the mercy of the savior god as we find in the penitent inscriptions at Deir el-Medina. The experience of salvation, of divine intervention, is described with the same expression as in the stelae: "I found that god had come when I called to him. He gave me his hand and I rejoiced."[128] Three times the cue for the personal experience of divine intervention ["I found"] is repeated in the *Poem:*

Amun I found more help ["more effective salvation"] to me than
　millions of troops, hundred-thousands of chariotry.

My heart I found strong, my mind joyful.

I found that the 2,500 chariots in whose midst I was
fell prostrate before my horses.[129]

The description of the predicament, the prayer, and the announcement of the "found" god are all clear indications that the first person singular section of the *Poem* is a variant of the stela formula for personal piety, modified for kingly usage. Ramesses offers a hymn of thanks for rescue from a perilous situation and a paean to the rescuing god, who is feted in contemporaneous hymns in very much the same way:

He is more valuable for him who gives him into his heart,
as the one and only he is by his name stronger than hundreds of
thousands.[130]

This is precisely what Ramesses tells us he experienced at Qadesh, and sets out to document in his account of the battle. The change to the first person singular and the hyperbolic presentation, with its emphasis on the superhuman, is not a throwback to the traditional style of kingly self-representation but a shift to a new form devoted to proclaiming the greatness of god.

There is no cause to doubt that the battle on that day did indeed peak with a turn in the fortunes of the king, and that the youthful Ramesses understood his miraculous rescue as due to the intervention of Amun. What "really" brought about this turn is something that neither the *Bulletin* nor the *Poem* make any reference to. But the pictorial reliefs depict a large formation of Egyptian troops and chariots moving swiftly and in perfect order to the embattled camp. The caption reads:

> The arrival of the *Ne'arin* force of Pharaoh, LPH, from the land of Amurru. They found that the hostile ranks of the fallen ones from Hatti had hemmed in the camp of Pharaoh, LPH, on its west side, while His Majesty sat alone without his army being with him . . . while the army of Amun, where Pharaoh was, had not yet finished pitching camp, and the army of Re along with the army of Ptah were still marching, before their troops [those of the Ptah division] had arrived from the wood of Labwe. The *Ne'arin* force attacked the hostile ranks of the despicable Fallen One of Hatti, who had penetrated the camp of Pharaoh, LPH, and the servants of Pharaoh, LPH, slew them. They let none of them escape, their hearts confident in the great strength of Pharaoh, LPH, their good lord, being around them like a mountain of copper, like a wall of iron forever and ever and always.[131]

Unlike the main body of the army, which had come through the valley of Orontes, the elite corps—referred to with a term taken from the Semitic, *Ne'arin* (literally: "youths")—had proceeded northward along the coast, no doubt to ensure the loyalty of Amurru with a demonstration of pharaonic power. This happy coincidence saved the embattled Ramesses, who, in the semantic categories of the period, described and interpreted the soldiers' arrival as divine intervention. The Hittites, who had entrusted the attack solely to their charioteers and were thus not prepared for an extended pitched battle, were placed under severe pressure by this unforeseen resistance. Their withdrawal turned into disordered flight, during which they incurred heavy losses.

After this success, Ramesses II was still in a serious strategic quandary, however. Two of his four divisions had suffered substantial losses, and across the Orontes was Muwatallis with 37,000 fresh infantry. Laying siege to Qadesh was out of the question. Ramesses' best hope was for withdrawal without further engagement. Negotiations to this end, described by Egyptian texts as a Hittite plea for peace, probably took place the next day. In any event, Ramesses succeeded in bringing about a truce that enabled him to "return home in peace." But nothing now hindered the Hittites from carrying on with their campaign, and they proceeded to devastate the region of Upe (Damascus), then an Egyptian provincial capital, and forced Amurru to return to the Hittite fold.

Thus, despite the miraculous reversal of fortune at Qadesh, the campaign of Year 5 (1274 B.C.E.) was a military failure for the Egyptians. In subsequent years, Ramesses did everything he could to redress the balance. The campaign in Year 8 (1271) brought the conquest of cities in the region of Byblos and Qadesh, and in Year 10 (1269) a second victory stela was set up at Nahr el-Kelb. These campaigns were presumably designed to create favorable starting conditions for peace negotiations. And indeed, following these campaigns, military operations in Syria cease. Egypt then enjoyed an unprecedented sixty-year period of peace, which was consolidated in Year 21 (1258) by an alliance with Hatti and in Year 34 (1245) by Ramesses II's marriage to a Hittite princess.

The Proclamation of the Manifestations of Power

THE TOUCH-AND-GO OUTCOME of the Battle of Qadesh makes it all the more surprising that Ramesses II should have chosen it as the subject of a body of monumental and literary representation unequaled in Egyptian historiography. This documentation is unique first of all for its multiplicity: no fewer than ten different examples have come down to us on temple walls alone! If the Lower Egyptian temples in Memphis and Pi-Ramesse had survived, the number of these testimonies would probably have doubled. In addition, there are two papyri containing the *Poem of the Battle of Qadesh,* one of which (Papyrus Sallier III) carries the date of Year 9 of Ramesses II. No other event was immortalized in so many different forms of Egyptian representational art, monumental and literary. Finally, the sheer size of the Qadesh testimonies is unique. The *Poem* alone is as long as an Egyptian book; the pictorial depiction takes up two tableaux of huge dimensions.

But of greater moment than sheer magnitude are the qualitative aspects of the Qadesh material. The first of these is the new "semiotics of event" informing the pictorial representation. The second is the depiction of Egyptian troops in disarray, an unprecedented departure from the decorum of Egyptian historiographic representation. The third is the religious interpretation of the event.

As far as the first point is concerned, we must once again recall that the pictorial renderings of the battle at Qadesh are the high point of realistic, individualizing historical representation. No other military action in Egyptian history has been handed down to us with a remotely comparable wealth of detail. What is an event? Essentially, it is something that stands out against the backdrop of the normal and predictable by virtue of its unusual nature. Events are exceptions to the rule, and they derive their significance from this exceptional quality. There is thus a certain kinship between "events" and "miracles." A miracle is an event that sets itself apart from the rules embodied in natural laws. On the other hand, there is an operative contrast between "event" and "order." Order is the quintessence of the predictable. Events break with that order. The traditional pictogram of "smiting the enemies" aimed to represent order, the new type of battle picture to represent an event. In the framework of traditional Egyptian order, events were meaningless instances of chaos and destruction. With the Battle of Qadesh, the event becomes the very epitome of the meaningful.

The Qadesh pictures represent the most extreme example of this new direction. Traditional battle scenes depicted the pharaoh in his chariot storming toward a specific locality (usually a fortified city). The Qadesh picture stretches the event over two tableaux, a Camp Scene and a Battle Scene. In these tableaux, the specific locality is not one half of a whole (as was usually the case) with the storming pharaoh as the other half, but forms the organizational principle of the entire depiction; the pharaoh (enthroned or in action) is embedded in the scene. The figures are positioned relative to each other—the *Ne'arin* relieving the camp, the Hittite infantry massed behind Qadesh, the insular situation of the fortress of Qadesh—and projected as if onto a map. Situational reality, the contingency of unique circumstances and occurrences, determines the layout and the coherence of the picture, and the actions of the pharaoh are fully integrated as one element in an all-encompassing scenic panorama.

These unprecedented (and, as it turned out, unique) iconological innovations reflected incipient changes in the Egyptian awareness of history. The historical actions of the pharaoh are no longer seen as performance of a ritual; rather, the king, his allies, his foes are all part of a shifting and unpredictable reality. What lay behind this radical extension of Egyptian means of expression was a new and deeply unsettling experience.

The great importance that Ramesses attributed to the battle of Qadesh is evident in the way in which he had it recorded, documented, and disseminated. The immensity of detail—the formation of the hostile army and the marching order of the Egyptian troops, the tactical ruse and the failure to reconnoiter, the Hittite attack, the Egyptian flight and the timely arrival of the *Ne'arin,* then the intervention of Amun and the miraculous rescue of Ramesses—underlines the uniqueness, significance, and contingency of the event itself.

Events are elements of linear time, not cyclical time. Events divide the flow of time into a before and an after. They are irreversible; they change reality. As actions or deeds, events are resultative. The overwhelming significance of the events at Qadesh lies in the results they engendered. The Qadesh documentation is, from this point of view, paradoxical. The military and political gain of the Battle of Qadesh was negligible; indeed, the battle was more of a setback than an achievement. Amurru and Qadesh were lost to Egypt and the province of Damascus was devastated.

Ramesses II was, as we have seen, eager to represent the Battle of Qadesh as a concrete event that changed the course of history. The king is not represented as enacting a ritual repetition within cyclical time but as performing a deed that changes the world, and which then makes other deeds necessary—but *different* deeds, not repetitions. The result of Ramesses' deed was not victory but peace and the end of hostilities. Ramesses II recognized war as a time-bound and hence terminable condition, and peace as the true consummation of the fighting.

The second point, the failure of the troops, is an integral part of the plot structure. Indeed, the story could not have been told in any other way. There could be no other explanation for the pharaoh's stumbling into an ambush and being left all alone to confront the enemy chariots. But the failure of the troops also had a political significance. For the purposes of the narrative a brief mention of the troops' defection would have sufficed, but the Qadesh *Poem,* in full epic grandeur, has the king harangue his troops twice. The first harangue is an exhortation recalling the fleeing troops:

> Stand firm, be bold-hearted, my troops!
> See my triumph, all on my own,
> with only Amun to be my protector, his hand with me.
> And how cowardly are your hearts, my chariotry!
> It's no use trusting you either!
> Was there not one of you, for whom I did good in my land?
> Did I not arise as lord, when you were poor?
> I caused you to become great men by my beneficence daily,
> [. . .] anyone who requested petitions, "I'll do it," I said to him
>   daily.
> [. . .] Now see, you did a rotten trick, all together as one.
> Not a man of you stood firm to give me his hand as I fought.
> [. . .] .
> The wrong that my troops and chariotry did is greater than can
>   be told.
>
> See: Amun has given me his victory,
> no troops being with me, and no chariotry.
> He has caused every distant land to see my victory by my strong
>   arm,
> being alone, no high officer with me,
> no charioteer.[132]

The other speech of remonstrance bitterly holds up the fecklessness of their actions to the crestfallen troops slinking back home in the evening after forsaking their commander:

> What's wrong with you, my officers,
>   my troops and my chariotry, who do not know how to fight?

Does a man not make himself honored in his city,
at his return, when he has played the hero before his lord?
Fair indeed is fame ["name"] won in battle, over and over,
from of old; a man is respected because of his strong arm.
Have I done no good to [even] one of you,
[for] your abandoning me, alone amidst the strife?
[...]
What will be said in gossip, when it is heard of,
your abandoning me, I being [left] alone, without companion?
And neither high officer, nor chariot-warrior, nor soldier came,
to give me a hand, as I fought.[133]

The *Bulletin* also contains a speech of remonstrance by the king. He does not address the immediate culprits themselves—Ramesses' Asiatic allies and the commanders of his garrisons, who left him in the dark about the movements of the Hittite forces in their territory— but his officers, whom he calls on as witnesses to their treachery:

You see the situation
in which are the garrison-commanders and governors of foreign
    territories, together with the chiefs of the lands of Pharaoh,
    LPH!
[...]
They stand there saying daily to Pharaoh, LPH:
"The despicable Ruler of Hatti is in the land of Aleppo, north of
    Tunip;
having fled before His Majesty when he heard [the report]: 'See,
    Pharaoh has come.' "
But see, I have heard this very hour, from these two spies from
    the Fallen One of Hatti
that the despicable Fallen One from Hatti has come, with the
    numerous foreign countries accompanying him,
with men and chariotry, as many as the sand [of the shore].
See, they stand hidden behind Old Qadesh, and my governors of
    foreign territories
and my chiefs, in whose charge are the lands of Pharaoh, LPH,
    could not tell us they [= Hatti] had arrived![134]

Horrified, the officers confirm the "great crime" committed by the Egyptian commanders and the Asiatic princes in failing to report these circumstances.[135] Failure to report a conspiracy to the king was tantamount to participating in that conspiracy. "The great crime" is also the term used in the *Poem* to describe the failure of the army. This unique documentation of a pharaonic campaign must be at least in part a massive arraignment of the armed forces: Ramesses II is intent upon teaching his army a lesson so as to prevent similar debacles and to instill an unswerving allegiance to the old virtues of bravery and loyalty. Yet, were the walls of the great temples the best place for such an admonition? The chronology of events shows that this so-called instruction took place at a time when foreign policy had undergone a complete volte-face and no war was actually being waged. And here we have the key to the Qadesh puzzle.

Up to now the assumption has been that the images and inscriptions representing the Battle of Qadesh were committed to the temple walls almost immediately after the battle itself. In fact, however, the process was quite drawn out; the final form for the monumental representation was not quickly found, and work continued long after the event. The king's sculptors spent years, possibly decades, translating the significance of the battle into visible terms. Scenes already completed were radically reworked and refashioned to bring out the meaning—Qadesh's uniqueness—even more clearly. Moreover, the subject was taken up over and over again, and depicted in numerous temples and far-flung locations, all the way to the temple at Abu Simbel, built in the second and third decade of Ramesses' reign, long after the Battle of Qadesh. The explanation for these representations of Qadesh is found not in the political situation immediately after the battle but in the changed circumstances that prevailed in the second regnal decade, when Ramesses eschewed further military exploits in favor of a policy of peace and rapprochement.

This far-reaching policy of peace must have been just as unprecedented as the style of the representations of the Battle of Qadesh. Such a policy would hardly have found the support of the military; yet Ramesses had ascended to the throne as a representative of precisely that group. In order to achieve his vision of a "Pax Ramessidica," Ramesses had to distance himself from the military and declare the end of the state of emergency that had justified Horemheb's "military dictatorship." The turnabout he thus aimed at was tantamount to a breach with the military leaders who had installed his dynasty and a reversion to conceptions of pharaonic diplomacy that had been undercut fifty years before by the assassination of Zannanza at the instigation of the successful war party. To underpin this new foreign policy on the domestic front, Ramesses publicly and monumentally pilloried the cowardice of the army before the gates of Qadesh.

Third, the events at Qadesh attained their overwhelming significance for Ramesses within the new semiology of personal piety, according to which history is the immediate expression of the will of god. In the inscription that commemorates his marriage to the Hittite princess, the crowning conclusion of the turn ushered in by Qadesh, Ramesses himself found the most trenchant formula for this new understanding of history: "What you command is everything that happens." Ramesses' meaning is not only that what god commands comes about, but that everything that occurs (including history) *is* the will of god. In this perception, events are no longer a manifestation of the contingency and unpredictability against which god has given men magic. From now on they reflect the will of god.

19

CHANGING THE STRUCTURE
OF THE PAST

Constructing the Past by Breaking with Tradition

TRADITION CARRIES THE PAST within itself but is devoid of any explicit awareness that it does so. To act "according to tradition" means to do something as it has "always" been done. Tradition makes our yesterdays present in a way that masks the fact that they belong to the past. Paradoxical as it may seem, tradition makes the past invisible by negating the difference between yesterday and today and thus ensuring that nothing changes.

The case is entirely different when, after a breach with tradition, conscious efforts are made to appropriate the past to the life of the present. Difference is then not blurred, but starkly delineated. The past is not relegated to the category of "over and done with," but is, on the contrary, elevated to the status of a timeless norm. This normative version of the past is nevertheless perceived as a different time, which may be regarded with retrospective veneration across the breach but cannot be simply continued as a "tradition."

In the Ramesside Period, the Middle Kingdom was elevated to the status of a normative past; it thus introduced into the Egyptian chronotope a new, unprecedented duality. While it is true that the Middle Kingdom itself had looked back to the Old Kingdom across the rift of the First Intermediate Period, it had assimilated this retrospective orientation so completely into its own formal idioms that no manifest difference between old and new remained. The Middle Kingdom did not declare the Old Kingdom the "classical age" but simply took up where the Old Kingdom had left off, thus continuing an existing tradition. The same is true of the Eighteenth Dynasty's relation to the Middle Kingdom. A dual vision of time does not appear until the Ramesside age, when a radical renewal of the formal idiom highlights the difference between old and new.

The culture of the Ramesside Period does not carry the past within itself uncritically but rather elevates the past to the status of an ideal to be lived up to. A normative past does not evolve of its own accord, but is invariably the result of conscious recourse by a later age. It is precisely in this sense that the Ramesside age re-created the Middle Kingdom. The advent of classicism implies a preceding break with tradition, as classicism itself is the product of a configuration of rejection and return.[136] The rift that provoked general awareness of the distance between the two ages and across which the Ramesside age reinvented and reappropriated the tradition of the Middle Kingdom was not the Second Intermediary Period but the age of Amarna. The dividing interval was thus no longer than about twenty years, an astoundingly short period of time and one itself indicative of the radicalism of this revolution.

But though the rift caused by Amarna was brief, it played a part in a process of much longer duration. Over hundreds of years, the increasing discrepancy between the literary language of the Middle Kingdom and the vernacular of the fourteenth and thirteenth centuries B.C.E. had created a distancing effect, whereby the old texts seemed foreign and dissociated from the spoken language. As language change progressed, specialist knowledge was increasingly required to decipher the old texts at all. As long as the written and literary idiom of the New Kingdom adhered to that of the Middle Kingdom, contemporary texts were as different from the vernacular as older texts were. But it was precisely this correspondence between the written languages of the New and Middle Kingdoms that was relinquished in the age of Amarna. From now on, written texts moved very much closer to the everyday vernacular. The Ramesside age extended this innovation and developed a literary idiom of its own, which represented a compromise between written traditions and everyday usage. But in the spirit of restoration, some texts were again being written in the idiom of the Middle Kingdom, now a classical language that had to be learned expressly for the purpose.[137] Thus language change and the break with tradition combined to elevate the Middle Kingdom to its new, classical status.

The Ramesside Renaissance

THE URGE TO START AFRESH that inspired the early Ramesside age is expressed most prominently in the concept of "rebirth," which Sethos I added to his series of names and incorporated into the datings of his first two regnal years. Just as Amenemhet I (who also added "rebirth" to his nomenclature) had seen himself as the founder of the new age that was the Middle Kingdom, so Sethos I saw himself as ushering in a new era. To underpin his new start, it was imperative for him to relegate the age of Amarna, more than twenty-five years previous to his accession, to the rank of a catastrophic "intermediary period."

The concept of "rebirth," so astonishingly close to the French term "renaissance," expresses the determination to repatriate the outraged gods in Egypt by means of a restorative campaign in the building and plastic arts. In Egyptian terminology, images of the gods are not made but "born"; images are not replicas of the divine body but bodies in their own right. Akhenaten's iconoclastic intervention had eliminated this sphere of representation. The declared intention of the Nineteenth Dynasty was to reestablish divine representation at a level of perfection that would equal—indeed, surpass—everything that had gone before.

Alongside its frenetic campaign to put up new buildings, the Ramesside age restored the ancient monuments with a single-mindedness as extreme as that of the Atenist iconoclasts who had torn them down. This loving re-creation of the old soon turned from restoration toward something more like usurpation and appropriation. Countless ancient divine and regal images were rededicated to the name of Ramesses II and brought from all corners of the kingdom to the newly established capital, Pi-Ramesse, in the Delta. Such "recycling" was a new form of return to the past. The most favored targets for this reappropriation were sculptures from the Twelfth Dynasty. This identification of Ramesses II with the kings of the Twelfth Dynasty had a strange sequel. In a much later retrospective view of Egypt's Great Past, Ramesses II, Sesostris III, and Sesostris I merged into a single indistinguishable figure. The "Sesostris" of the late Sesostris romance[138] and the *Aegyptiaca* of Hecataeus of Abdera[139] connect reminiscences of Ramesses II with the canonical memory of the Middle Kingdom. Thus, in the long view, Ramesses II did indeed succeed in achieving identification with Sesostris (both I and III).

Classicism and Carnival

I HAVE ALREADY HAD OCCASION to refer to the wisdom text that proclaims the book to be a more certain form of immortality than the tomb; to ensure one's continuing presence for posterity, literature is a better investment than buildings in stone (see page 68). In the next passage of this same text, its author is revealed as a "classicist":[140]

Become a scribe, take this to heart:
then your name will be equally [immortal].
A book is more valuable than a tombstone with an inscription,
than a stoutly built tomb chamber.
These books function as tomb and pyramid
in the preservation of their names.
For that is assuredly something valuable in the hereafter:
a name in the mouths of men.
A man has passed away, his body has turned to dust,
all his contemporaries have been laid in earth.
But writing ensures that one remembers him
and one mouth passes it on to another.
A scroll is more valuable than a walled house,
than tomb chapels in the West;
it is better than a well-founded castle,
than a memorial stone in the temple.

Is there one here like Hordjedef?
Or another like Imhotep?
Among our contemporaries none is like Neferti
or Khety, the greatest of them.
I mention to you only the names of Ptahemdjehuti and
    Khakheperreseneb.
Is there another like Ptahhotep
or like Kaires?
These wise men who prophesied the future,
what they said has come to pass.
One found it as a saying,
written in their books.
[. . .] Hidden they may be, but their magic extends

to all who read their books.
They are gone, their names [would be long since] forgotten,
but their writings keep their memory alive.[141]

The eight authors mentioned in the text owe their immortality to the
"magic of writing" that "extends to all who read their books." Writing can not only triumph over time, but can press the march of time
into its service. The books have become more important through the
passage of time because what they contain has proven its truth, its
status as a classic. Of the eight names mentioned in the penultimate
stanza, six are familiar to us: Imhotep, Hordjedef, Neferti, Khety,
Khakheperreseneb, and Ptahhotep. Though nothing written by
Imhotep has actually survived, he is variously referred to as having
written an instruction on right living, just like Hordjedef, Khety, and
Ptahhotep, whose works have been transmitted. Neferti and Khakheperreseneb are associated with chaos descriptions or lamentations,
while the two remaining names are associated with one or the other
of these genres. In short, it is wisdom literature that makes an
author immortal. The *Story of Sinuhe* is not found among the classics. Nor is Sinuhe among the names in a much more extensive catalogue of important personalities from the past that was found in a
tomb of the Nineteenth Dynasty in Saqqara.[142] The two lower registers, the only ones to have survived, list thirteen names apiece, the
upper containing names of viziers and high priests of Ptah, the lower
priests of slightly inferior rank, while the two sections are divided by
a horizontal line that contains other names. Of these, four names
reappear from the Papyrus Chester Beatty: Kaires, Imhotep, Khakheperreseneb, and Khety. The fifth is Ipuwer, the "author" of the
Admonitions of Ipuwer, whose appearance confirms that lamentations
and chaos descriptions were also considered "lofty" literature. Apart
from these "authors," the list spans notables from the Old to the
New Kingdom.

The two sources—the manuscript and the tomb relief—point
up the Ramesside Period's fascination with the past in two very different ways. The literary text emphasizes the break with tradition,
while the tomb relief stresses continuity. The papyrus text intimates
that the present does not measure up to the past because there is no
one in the present who can match the greatness of Hordjedef or
Imhotep. The wall relief, by contrast, stresses continuity by extending
the list of outstanding personalities into the present. The one list

reflects the desire for an (unattainable) ideal, the other the desire for continuity.

Like the plastic arts, the literature of the Ramesside Period went its own way and did not seek to emulate the past ideals it canonized. Its subject matter is popular, most of it taken from oral tradition. Some genres—love songs, for instance—have been transmitted only in manuscripts from the Ramesside Period and apparently belonged to sanctioned literary discourse only during that epoch. Above all, the Ramesside Period alone provides some insight into an otherwise completely obscure aspect of Egyptian civilization, which (following Mikhail Bakhtin) I propose to call its "culture of folk humor."[143] Chief among the products of this culture were fabliaux and tales that lived entirely within the oral tradition but for which illustrations now appeared on ostraca.[144] The corresponding texts are known only from manuscripts of a much later period. The images that appear on the ostraca also figure on Ramesside papyri, strung together very much like comic strips.

One of these papyri stands in especially stark contrast to what is usually found on this precious writing material. It is a papyrus in Turin that features a cycle of twelve scenes of a crudely obscene nature.[145] The protagonists are a man and a young woman. The man is depicted with a huge phallus and is quite unequivocally characterized as belonging to the lower orders. His defining features are a high forehead, a starkly delineated profile, a goatee, a slightly protruding belly, and a circumcised penis. Since the Old Kingdom, precisely these features had been used to characterize all members of Egyptian society who lacked the leisure or the means to indulge in personal grooming and body culture.[146]

Egyptian ideas about grooming and beauty, formed in courtly, urban culture, were marked by extreme artifice. Natural hair was removed by means of shaving and depilatories; eyebrows were replaced by cosmetic lines. Wigs were worn and were changed according to office or occasion. Both sexes used face makeup, wore jewelry, and perfumed themselves with unguents. Garments were invariably of radiant white linen and left no scope for the vagaries of personal taste. The physical appearance of Egyptians of high standing was stylized and deindividualized to the greatest possible degree. Such beauty was, of course, reserved for the elite, which was thus set gloriously apart from the plain, unremarkable appearance of the working masses.[147]

From the outset, this distinction was underscored in the pictorial arts. Depictions of the working population—craftsmen, peasants, shepherds—invariably had an element of caricature (or to use Bakhtin's term, of the "carnivalesque") about them. The representation of the "plain" human body not "prepared" for social intercourse by cosmetic arts was in itself a carnivalesque phenomenon. In the literary genre called "satires of the trades," the various vocations were lampooned by highly exaggerated descriptions of the mess, foul stench, exhaustion, and physical deformities they incurred. The aspects of corporeality assiduously denied by the body culture of the elite were foregrounded in these lampoons.[148]

In short, the hero of our story embodies the sphere of "socially unacceptable" physicality, which was marked not only by lack of grooming but also by the hyperbolic exaggeration of physical functions otherwise shamefacedly suppressed. The huge phallus of the man on the Turin papyrus represents the same kind of grotesque exaggeration as is found in the satires depicting the physical effects of work. The young woman, by contrast, embodies the upper echelons' ideals of beauty and as such represents the diametrical opposite of the world the man stands for. Not that she is a high-born lady. She is more likely one of those female musicians, dancers, or attendants frequently present at the festivities of the great to quicken the hearts and senses of the guests—not so much a subject as an object of Egyptian luxury culture. In these scenes, however, she figures largely as a subject; that is, she takes her own pleasure rather than catering to that of others. The comic point of the farcical story resides in its juxtapositions and reversal of roles.

The other images of the Turin papyrus are animal travesties obviously intended to illustrate fables. Such images turn up in their hundreds on the ostraca and papyri of the Ramesside age and depict a world turned topsy-turvy: cat maids waiting on mouse ladies, a mouse pharaoh burning down a fortress defended by cats, a swallow using a ladder to scale a tree in which a hippopotamus is picking figs, and the like. With complete justice, Hedwig Kenner points out that in antiquity "comedy is never harmless . . . but invariably two-sided, comic and threatening at one and the same time."[149] The satirical element of the animal travesties is seen most clearly in their allusions to sacred imagery and in their depictions of a mouse (throughout history a creature standing for the common man) that performs as a statesman or government official—a beadle, prison warder, or judge.

But inversion in itself is not merely comic; it also presses home the point that the established order might look very different. The culture of folk humor draws heavily on the tensions and hopes inevitably generated by the pressures of a strongly segregated and canonized official culture.

In this period, then, a new dimension of aesthetic expression emerged, free of the constraints of official written culture, free of the normative claims of elite literature. This new literature included narratives for entertainment (mythological tales, historical novellas, fairy tales), love songs, and the more specifically carnivalesque genres of the erotic "cartoon-story" and animal fable. It is tempting to classify this realm of writing under the heading "delectation of the heart" (the Egyptian term means "letting the heart forget [its cares]"), typically used in connection with love poetry and drinking verse.[150] In the Ramesside age, the oblivion-generating culture of folk humor, hitherto relegated to the subset of unwritten folklore, was admitted into the written realm of culture for the space of two centuries, where it constituted a "free space" of aesthetic communication.

The development of this free space accompanied the canonization of the school classics. The Ramesside Period originates the idea of an ancient, model literature that could never be equaled, let alone surpassed, and could not be emulated but only copied and learned by rote. Yet the impossibility of taking up where the great classics left off fostered a desire for a "new" literature of humor and entertainment, which now briefly ascended to the rank of "high" art.

20

THE DECLINE OF
THE NEW KINGDOM

T HE END OF THE TWENTIETH DYNASTY (in the decades around 1100 B.C.E.), and with it the end of the New Kingdom, were marked by a renewed collapse of political unity. This decline was caused by an internal disintegration, which was accelerated by the religious movement centering on personal piety and its theology of will. Its root cause was diagnosed by H. Brunner as the "loss of the idea of statehood."[151] But the end of the New Kingdom is also part of a much wider-ranging decline that affected the entire Near Eastern–Mediterranean system of states from the Aegean to the Indus, and gathered momentum during the Bronze Age.

The transition from the Bronze Age to the Iron Age is not merely an issue of formal periodicity, of dividing up ancient history on the basis of changes in weaponry. For this transition has remained ingrained in the cultural memory of the western world as the threshold between one epoch and another. The two bedrock narratives of western civilization—Homer's epics and the Exodus—refer precisely to this transition. Both are set in the thirteenth century B.C.E. and thus cast the anchor of memory into the seabed of a precedent world, far below the disintegrating universe of the Mediterranean and the Near East—the "dark centuries" separating the bright-lit worlds of the late Bronze Age and classical antiquity. Though Egypt did not crumble like the Hittite empire, and indeed survived as a flourishing, creative culture well into late antiquity, the end of the Bronze Age ecumene nonetheless spelled the close of an era that would be referred to later—across the gaping chasm of oblivion represented by the dark centuries—as the primal source of meaning, order, and culture.

Though the disintegration of the New Kingdom was certainly the product of internal political, economic, and intellectual forces, the Egyptian example must also be situated within the general loss of cohesion of the entire Bronze Age world. This collapse was prompted by the great migrations that sped the demise of the Mycenaean world and the Hittite empire: the migrations of the Dorians, of the Sea Peoples, and of the Scythians. Although Egypt was only marginally touched by these movements, and although Ramesses III exaggerated the significance of his defensive battle against the Sea Peoples, Egypt was nevertheless affected by this process of population fluctuation and resettlement. Greatly reinforced by the influx of native Libyans, the mercenaries living in the Delta (most of them recruited from the Sea Peoples and the Libyans) developed into a military aristocracy that was to take over the throne by the Twenty-second Dynasty.

This period is often characterized as one of "foreign rule," but for the Egyptians neither origin nor "race" distinguished the native from the alien; rather, the marker was the attitude demonstrated toward the cultural rules of Egyptian civilization. Not until the incursion of the Assyrians and Persians did the Egyptians encounter "foreigners" in their own sense of the term. Yet, if the seizure of power by the Libyo-Egyptians cannot qualify as foreign rule, it did signify a process of political disintegration, which culminated in the period of "Libyan anarchy." There is, however, no categorical distinction to be made between the incursion of the Libyans—"Meshwesh," in Egypt—and the irruption of the Etruscans in Italy, the Dorians in Greece, the Philistines in Palestine, or the Scythians in Urartu. The consequence of these resettlement processes was a disintegration of political connectivity and a regionalization of the cultures involved, now largely left to their own devices in areas that had suddenly become much smaller.

The new unity arising from this "intermediate" disintegration aimed at a political structure entirely different from that of the Bronze Age world. The unifying idea was no longer that of a "world of states" but of a "world-state." The first empire to pursue this program was the neo-Assyrian. At the height of its power it penetrated as far as Upper Egyptian Thebes. The neo-Babylonian empire inherited the idea but had too little time to advance significantly beyond what the Assyrians achieved before it was itself taken over by the Persians. This process of *translatio imperii* continued through Alexander the Great and the Roman Empire into the Middle Ages and survived until well into the modern age in forms like the Ottoman Empire, the Holy

Roman Empire, and the Czarist Empire. The fact that the Egyptian empire does not figure in this genealogy is a reflection of the breach between the Bronze Age and the Iron Age worlds. The Egyptian idea of statehood that would have fitted in with the succession of empires referred to above had indeed disappeared with the New Kingdom and had no direct connections with the idea of empire that spread from Assyria in the first millennium C.E.

And yet a formula like "loss of the idea of statehood"—Brunner's explanation for disintegration—surely misses the point. After all, the Egyptian state did not end with the decline of the New Kingdom, but lasted for another thousand years and more, until it was incorporated into the Roman Empire. As a civilization, Egypt survived even longer, which would have been inconceivable without an idea of statehood. Indeed, the survival of the state under the unfavorable conditions of successive periods of foreign rule can only have been possible precisely because of a very powerful idea of statehood. Libya, Ethiopia, the Persians, and finally the Macedonian line of the Ptolemies all adopted this idea of statehood and thus legitimized themselves as Egyptian pharaohs. In the age of the Roman emperors, the Egyptian state existed entirely as an idea, not as a reality, but so potent was the idea that Roman emperors were repeatedly able to present themselves as pharaohs.

At this point, let us repeat the thought experiment that I proposed in connection with the end of the Old Kingdom. What image of pharaonic culture would we have if it had disappeared with the New Kingdom? This question is not quite so hypothetical as it was with regard to the Old Kingdom, because many accounts of ancient Egypt do end with the demise of the New Kingdom, as if that were the end of Egyptian civilization altogether.

One argument is indisputable: if Egyptian civilization had ended with the New Kingdom, it could never have become a part of our own tradition. Egyptian civilization found its way into that tradition through two channels: the authors of classical antiquity and the Bible. The former would have had no firsthand experience of Egyptian civilization as a living entity, and would at most have been able to inform us about the ruins, just like the Arab authors of the Middle Ages and European travelers of the modern period. But in fact, the classical authors tell us much more, for they transmit not only an image they based on the tangible traces of Egyptian civilization but also an image passed on by the Egyptians themselves, in the form of both messages and memories of their own culture—in short, the Egyptian self-image of the Late Period. And the image thus transported to western tradition has been a fruitful one indeed.

Again, if Egypt had disappeared in the eleventh century, few traces of pharaonic civilization would have found their way into the Bible. True, the report of the Exodus stems from an authentic account of a sojourn in and departure from Egypt, but those events were experienced not by the Hebrews but by the Hyksos, whose traditions the Hebrews inherited. Israel elevated these transmissions to the rank of a normative past and made them an integral part of its cultural memory only at a time when the Hebrews as a people needed to draw on this past to master their present. That "present," however, could not have predated the first appearance of the prophets. Hence, the literary version of the Joseph legend, the Exodus, and all other biblical references to Egypt are derived from Late Period Egypt, not the Egypt of the Bronze Age, in which the version known to us sets the Exodus. It is precisely this concretization and specification that gives the biblical texts, and the Joseph legend in particular (Genesis 37–50), their unique eloquence and impact.

These are not just idle speculations. They make it clear that our concern with ancient Egypt is not born merely of antiquarian interest but represents a quest for our own remotest past, a past with which we are connected across the centuries by numerous and diverse if frequently covert, links. And we owe our ability to pursue this quest to the fact that Egyptian civilization did not disappear with the New Kingdom.

PART FIVE

Theocracy, Polyarchy, Archaism

Piye's Victory Stela, tympanum
(from N. C. Grimal, La stèle triomphale de Pi('ankh)y au musée
du Caire, *1981, pl. V)*

21

TANIS AND THEBES: THE AGE OF DIVISION

Division of Rule, Concentration of Powers

WITH THE END OF THE NEW KINGDOM began a period of tensions and vicissitudes. This "Third Intermediate Period," as the period between 1080 and 664 B.C.E. has become known, differs in a number of important ways from its two predecessors. For one thing, it lasted over four hundred years, significantly longer than the earlier eras of disorder; for another, the new political models developed in this period functioned smoothly, without the "chaos" experiences that mark the first two Intermediate Periods. Though experiences of upheaval are not entirely absent, they are restricted to the second half of the period, so it makes good sense to distinguish at least two epochs. The first (approximately 1080–820 B.C.E.) is the epoch of Tanis and Thebes and the division into north and south; this age was not without its tensions but it did, in the last resort, enact a relatively equable form of political dualism. The pharaohs ruled in Tanis, while in Thebes Amun was king and the high priests conveyed his will. The second epoch (approximately 820–664 B.C.E.) is the age of Libyan polyarchy, which in its final stage (725–664 B.C.E.) forms part of the Kushite or Ethiopian reign and therefore no longer qualifies as a "genuine" intermediate period. In many of its aspects, the Kushite empire anticipates the Late Period, which began in 663, but four Assyrian invasions prevented it from attaining true political unity. The age of Libyan polyarchy stands out as exceptional in Egyptian cultural memory.

Herodotus calls it a dodecarchy, a rule of twelve: "After the reign of the priest of Hephaestus [Sethos] the Egyptians were made free [from the Assyrians]. But they could never live without a king, so they divided Egypt into twelve districts and set up twelve kings. These kings intermarried, and agreed to be close friends, no one deposing another or seeking to possess more than another" (*Histories*, II.147). From the Twenty-second Dynasty to the Twenty-fourth, Tanis and Thebes were almost matched in influence by Sais (to which Memphis belonged) and Hermopolis. All the kings were more or less closely related by marriage, but that did not prevent them from waging war on one another. The Late Period proper begins with the ascension of Psammetichus I to the throne in 663. The Late Period comprises the Twenty-sixth Dynasty, which ruled from Sais in the western Delta, and the period of Persian domination (525–333 B.C.E.). Its most salient feature is the return to monocracy.

In Thebes, in Year 19 of the reign of Ramesses XI (ca. 1080 B.C.E.), a man by the name of Herihor, whose origins are unknown but who combined the titularies of high priest of Amun, vizier, and general, assumed something approaching royal status by inscribing his name (including the title of high priest) in cartouches, taking for himself the titles of the king, and introducing a new year count. His count, however, began with Year 1 not of his own reign but of an era of "rebirth" *within* the era of the ruling dynasty at Tanis, from which he thus broke away. In themselves, all three moves— introduction of a new year count, assumption of kingship, accumulation of offices—marked a break with tradition. Yet they had little significance beyond that. A short time later, a new order was firmly established, and most of these measures were revoked. They represent nothing more than an exceptional transitional state.

This was the third time in Egyptian history—after Amenemhet (Ammenemes) I (1991 B.C.E.) and Sethos I (1295 B.C.E.)—that a king used the term "rebirth" to proclaim his rule as the beginning of a new age. In Egypt, the interest in continuity was normally greater than the desire for termination and renewal. To start a period of rule by proclaiming it a rebirth was a clear declaration of a breach in continuity. Amenemhet I had used the term to refer to a new start after the First Intermediate Period, Sethos I to the end of the age of Amarna. But Herihor's proclamation of a "rebirth" did not invoke a return to a bygone form of antiquity; rather, it announced a new era that broke decisively with everything that had come before. Accordingly, Egyptian culture in this period manifests a clear break with Ramesside traditions but without any explicit reference back to a particular period or formal idiom. It is indeed striking how little reference this period makes to the past. Thus, though Herihor's era of "rebirth" can hardly claim to be a cultural "renaissance," it certainly qualifies as one of the major turning points and new departures in Egyptian history.[1]

The introduction of a new year count was perhaps the most incisive of all the measures by which Herihor implemented the break with the past and the political system of the Ramessides. Herihor's move makes startlingly clear the meaning of a time calculation based on regnal years. In it, the Egyptian king revealed himself as the sovereign over social time, time as the dimension in which all action, planning, and commemoration occurs. All dates and periodicities, all dues and obligations were dictated by a dimension of time over which he ruled as over an expanse of territory. We might compare this with the *Kol Nidre,* the Jewish prayer for the eve of Yom Kippur that annuls "all oaths and obligations." This prayer is a theocratic form of "clearing the ledgers," which proclaims God, in analogy with the Near Eastern rulers, as the sovereign lord of social time.[2] In the Near East, the advent of a new ruler typically brought with it a new age in which harmony, fertility, and welfare reigned. The new ruler "set justice" by pardoning offenders, revoking obligations, canceling debts, and the like. The king's justice was not so much an act of grace as of restitution, and it is precisely this renewing, time-setting sovereignty that was invested in God by Jewish theocracy.[3] Analogously, Herihor established a new chronology and so declared his break with the time scale ordained by Ramesses XI and with all its correspondent obligations. With this secession, the political relations of the Theban power holder to Ramesses XI, his previous overlord in Tanis, changed from domestic to foreign.[4]

Yet the result was not that the relations of Thebes and Tanis turned hostile; quite the contrary. Not rebellion but a species of "concordat" characterized their political relations.[5] Thus the Twenty-first Dynasty put into practice the epoch-making historical lesson of the New Kingdom: namely, that the ordered world did not come to a grinding halt at the borders of Egypt; rather, there was a dimension superordinate to the Egyptian realm, into which it was in Egypt's best interests to integrate. War was by no means always the most advantageous way of effecting such an integration. The art of foreign policy required finding the ideal form in each specific case. The Egyptians had so perfected this art that in Year 19 of Ramesses XI, the Thebans—and possibly also the Tanites—thought it most to their advantage to master domestic chaos by applying the lessons of foreign policy.

With his proclamation of a new era, Herihor established an external boundary between Thebes and the rest of the world. With his unprecedented accumulation of offices, on the other hand, Herihor did away with internal boundaries. These two moves—differentiation (externally) and concentration (internally)—were mutually reinforcing and equally revolutionary. The previous Egyptian system had rested on a strict severance between kingship on the one hand and the exercise of administrative duties on the other. It was almost unprecedented for a king to be at once vizier, high priest, and military general all rolled into one. Moreover, the king did not merely delegate these functions to some chosen official, for even at the highest levels of officialdom these portfolios were also carefully separated; nor were they usually entrusted to members of the ruling dynasty. An exception was the office of supreme general, which only advanced to the status of a top administrative rank during the New Kingdom and was traditionally exercised in the Ramesside age by the crown prince. The viziers (one each for north and south) and the high priest of Amun and chief of all priests were recruited from other families. Herihor suspended this traditional division of offices. With that gambit, he carved out a new political role for himself, which might be legitimately described as dictator or "tyrant," albeit in a nonevaluative sense of the term. But, unlike later tyrants, he did not legitimize this role "downwards," by means of social measures that might garner broad popular support, but "upward," by means of a radically theocratic exercise of power.

Herihor's accumulation of offices, though reminiscent of Horemheb's earlier foray in this direction, differs in one essential point: Horemheb was not a high priest. Otherwise, the situations in which they found themselves are indeed comparable. As we have seen, Horemheb advanced from head of the armed forces to regent and successor to the throne ("hereditary prince of the whole land") and finally to the kingship.[6] Horemheb's status was also largely comparable to that of a dictator and came about as a result of the general uncertainty that prevailed in the aftermath of the age of Amarna. It is fair to assume that the situation at the end of the New Kingdom was also declared to be a state of emergency that called for correspondingly draconian measures.

It is not difficult to identify the nature of this crisis or the advantages the dictator solution held out. The reign of the Ramessides had crumbled because of their inability to rule over the kingdom—that is, to control and supply it—from Tanis, a location on its periphery. This was a typical crisis of penetration and distribution. The infrastructure crucial to the functioning of a redistributive economy had collapsed: dues no longer reached the state storehouses, and the supplies from those storehouses were insufficient. The circulation of dues and supplies was increasingly inhibited by corrupt officials and local interest groups. Famines, strikes, and lawsuits were the result. No longer able to rely on its officials, the government fell back on "special commissioners," but these (frequently foreign) courtiers with ill-defined powers only compounded the chaos, because they interfered with the work of the regular officials.[7] Together with the infrastructure crumbled the trust, solidarity, and loyalty that had formerly animated Egyptian bureaucracy and without which it could not function. Herihor's solution was to concentrate all powers in one hand, but to restrict them in their range; in other words, to split the country up into manageable territories.

A literary chaos description from this period casts light on the crisis from the point of view of one directly affected. The central character is a man driven out of his home and living abroad. As we have seen, when Sinuhe attempted to flee the grasp of state control, he was forced to cross the national boundary; for him, the experience of things alien only began outside the frontiers of Egypt. In the late New Kingdom, or Third Intermediate Period, leaving one's own town or city already spelled exile in the fullest sense of the word. This drastic change in structures of affiliation and in the political cohesion of the country emerges clearly in *A Tale of Woe* (Papyrus Pushkin 127), which is a literary work masquerading as an actual letter.[8] The first-person narrator is an official close to the throne, with a ship, a wagon, and servants of his own. Deprived of all his property by robbery or revolt, driven out of office, and exiled from his native city, he wanders aimlessly through Egypt. Whenever he manages to make any kind of social contact, it is broken off as soon as his identity becomes known:

> I was always in some city not my own,
> or a town I knew not,
> in the condition of a stranger.
> My old comrades were no more,
> and friends had to be made anew.
> They themselves would be beside me for a while,
> and then move away from me:
> it was because of what I had been that they turned their backs
>   upon my indigence.[9]

The place from which he writes is suffering the reign of terror of a local tyrant, who torments the citizenry with exorbitant taxes and rigged measurement units. In this new Egypt, there is no longer any overarching system of law. Every village mayor rules as he thinks fit:

> The master put me in the wrong with the magistrates, saying:
> "He did a wicked thing to me in my city!"
> His tax had been burdensome to me, more than can be
>   imagined.
> Many have been those crushed by it and seized by him and the
>   staff.
> He caused me to remain deprived of my corn [grain], which
>   others had given to me when he was [gone on] his journey.
> [The people said of his false grain measure]: "How wicked is the
>   carpenter that made it!
> One sack becomes in it a sack and a half."
> By Atum, the Sole One, he did rob them![10]

But the exile's most bitter experience is his sense that he is missed by no one. Thanks to the total disintegration of all social bonds, even a royal official could disappear without attracting anyone's notice. Like the speaker in the *Dispute of a Man with His Ba,* the official sees the tomb as a place offering access to a different community:

> If only there had been a message to comfort my heart when I fell
>   a victim to wrong doing.
> There never was an inquiry after my condition
> in the course of my comings and goings:
> when flesh and bone are abandoned at the desert edge,
> who is going to bury them?
> There was no message to express concern for me.

See! neither the dead nor the living would care for me in my
  sorrows:
What will my sufferings signify a long time hence anyway,
when I am in the realm of the dead and in the sight of the
  horizon-god?[11]

The *Tale of Woe* is a chaos description. It deals with the classic subjects of hunger, violence, arbitrary despotism, local and exorbitant
taxation, collapse of personal relations, isolation and loneliness, disintegration of the social network and of memory, and vain hope for
the intervention of some higher authority, referred to merely as "he."

    At the end of the New Kingdom and in the Third Intermediate
Period, Egypt changed from a territorial state to a pluricentric
agglomeration of small states. The cities were either fortified or else
put up citadels for the citizens to repair to in the face of danger. The
open country no longer provided any safety. El-Hibeh, the site where
this papyrus is said to have been found, was a fortified town that
marked the northern boundary of the Theban god-state. But that state
no longer provided protection from revolt and assault; the local centers had to look out for themselves.

Herihor's measures also suggest a sense of crisis, for they aimed above
all at accomplishing a break with the past, the better to set up a new
system of order. As soon as this order was established, the more
extreme measures were repealed. In Year 7 the new year count was
discontinued. This did not signal a return to the old order, but rather
meant that the new order had established itself firmly enough to allow
the reintroduction of the much more convenient chronology geared
to the regnal years of the dynasty in Tanis, which now no longer
posed a threat to the autonomy of the Theban power holder.

    In the meantime there had been a change in the north similar
to the one in the south, which brought with it the final ratification
of the new order and made temporary emergency measures superfluous. A relatively young man named Smendes (the Greek form given
to his name by Manetho) had ascended the throne in the north. His
origins are just as obscure as those of Herihor, but his relations with
the Theban power holder were so amicable that the suggestion that
he may even have been a son of Herihor is by no means all that far-
fetched.[12] These amicable relations are reported in the *Tale of Wenamun*.[13] Like *A Tale of Woe*, this text masquerades as a nonliterary

genre, this time as an administrative report. The narrative spotlights the historical situation in Year 5 of the Rebirth. Wenamun is sent to Byblos by Herihor to procure timber for the construction of the sacred bark of Amun. Much is made of the authorization for this mission. The real commissioner is the god Amun himself, and the highly satirical point of the story is that, for the Thebans, reference to the divine status of the commissioning party is regarded as completely adequate for the realization of the project. Instead of the usual precious gifts and military escort, Wenamun has to accomplish his mission, as well as he can, with tokens of divine recompense in the form of letters of recommendation and a portable statue of Amun. His first stop is Tanis, where Smendes and Tanutamun, although not yet king and queen, already represent the "foundations Amun has given the north of this land." These two equip him with the bare essentials for his mission; in other words, they play along. The Prince of Byblos, by contrast, is anything but happy with the idea of laying up treasure in heaven and not having any other kind of reward. Wenamun suggests that he give Amun the timber, immortalize his gift on a stela, and request fifty extra years of life from the god in return. The prince's rejoinder is to remind Wenamun that it had been customary to ask—and receive—a certain amount of silver for the wood required for the bark of Amun.

> He called for records from the time of his ancestors and had them read out to me. One thousand *deben* of silver were registered in his documents altogether. [...]
>
> What kind of unsupported mission is this which you are caused to undertake?
>
> I said to him: Wrong! This is not an unsupported mission that I am on. There is not one ship on the river which does not belong to Amun. To him belongs the sea [also]. His is the Lebanon, of which you think: "It belongs to me!" Yes, he, Amun-Re, spoke to Herihor, my lord, who sent me out. And he sent me out with this mighty god [= divine statue]. . . . You say former kings sent silver and gold—if they could have given life and health, they would not have sent such things. [...] But Amun-Re, he is the lord of life and health! And he was the lord of your ancestors. They spent their life making offerings to Amun. You too are a servant of Amun! If you say yes to Amun and carry out his wishes, you shall be healthy, prosperous, and successful

as long as you live, for your entire country and all your people. Desire not anything else for yourself from Amun-Re, the king of the gods![14]

Then Wenamun suggests sending a messenger to Tanis to fetch the necessary payment. The Prince of Byblos agrees, and when the messenger returns, months later, the prince orders the wood to be cut down and stacked on the banks of the river. Wenamun's valedictory proposal to the prince reflects the spirit of the times:

Are you not glad to have for yourself a stela erected on which you can say: "Amun-Re, the king of the gods, sent me his messenger Amun-of-the-Way, together with his human messenger Wenamun, to fetch the wood for the great and noble bark of Amun. I cut it down, I transported it, and I paid for my workers, ships, and crew. I had it taken to Egypt, and for me I requested from Amun another fifty years to be added to my life. Thus it came about"? And when later, in another time, a messenger comes, and he can read, and when he reads your name on the stela, you will receive water in the West according to the ways of the gods that are there.[15]

Opinion is divided as to whether the *Tale of Wenamun* is a literary text or an authentic administrative report. But whatever its genre, the text clearly reflects the intellectual, political, and economic changes that set the new age apart from the New Kingdom; it also shows how fully aware contemporary Egyptians were of those changes. Whether the author took seriously Herihor's symbolic "reimbursement" of the Amun oracle or whether he was lampooning it is unimportant, for he succeeds in illuminating the governmental style of the Twenty-first Dynasty in a most revealing way. In a very badly mutilated inscription, Herihor himself immortalized an oracular dictum in which Amun promised him twenty extra years of life. We have no way of knowing whether or not the Egyptians actually believed in these oracles, by which Herihor attributed to the will of Amun all his political measures, whether grand or trivial. Herihor himself survived the oracular promise only by a matter of months. The *Tale of Wenamun* makes it clear that contemporary Thebans regarded the theocratic governing style of the Twenty-first Dynasty as a curiosity that clearly flouted tradition and that was very difficult if not impossible to make plausible to outsiders like the Prince of Byblos.

Though the new year count was discontinued in Year 7 (probably Herihor's death year), the external separation of spheres of power and the internal concentration of offices remained. Other local dynasts emulated the Theban example and concentrated high priesthood, leadership of the armed forces, and the conduct of civil government in their own persons. Psusennes I, Smendes' successor in Tanis, also styled himself high priest of Amun. Thus the northern and southern kingdoms no longer complemented each other as centers of secular and spiritual rule respectively, but were completely parallel. The principalities that emerged in the second half of the Third Intermediate Period ("Libyan polyarchy") in Herakleopolis, Mendes, Athribis, Sais, and elsewhere were all headed by princes who combined the offices of high priest of the local deity, commander of the armed forces, and chief of administration.[16] This consolidation of power marked the birth of a new form of political organization. Instead of a differentiation of offices under unified supreme rule, a differentiated rule plus accumulation of offices comes to the fore. This new order evolved in the form of amicable foreign policies geared entirely to alliance and supply and hence to as close-knit a foreign political network as possible. The medium or "cement" of this network was kinship, assured either by political marriage or by staffing the most important offices with relatives. Almost all the ruling houses of Egypt were closely linked via kinship or marriage.[17] Instead of the monopoly of power that had formerly defined the Egyptian state as such, systems of alliance emerged, in which the various small states were protected from each other by armed forces of their own. Tax monopoly was replaced by tributes, while the principle of bureaucratic merit, which at least in theory had been the determining factor of officialdom, was replaced by the aristocratic principle of descent.

This "feudalization" of Egyptian bureaucracy was certainly a consequence of the ascent of the Libyans to the top positions in the land. Their tribes were organized in terms of kinship and they imposed this principle on the traditional bureaucratic structures of Egyptian administration. Social position thus became a function of family membership and descent.

Almost all known societies of the ancient and medieval world—Israelite, Greek, Roman, Byzantine—were structured along genealogical lines. The ubiquity of this principle has blinded us to the novel and historically unprecedented nature of the kinship paradigm in ancient Egyptian society. The new genealogical paradigm not only held sway at the level of the ruling houses, but also dictated who held office at the lower levels of local priesthood and administration. Origin and kinship were wholly determinative. Everyone holding office attached great importance to calling himself "son of a same-titled X, himself son of a same-titled X"; each craved as the supreme token of divine grace the handing down of office from son to son, which occasionally led to unbelievably intricate ramifications in family trees and inherited offices across the centuries. The primacy of pedigree grew all the greater as other forms of legitimization and consolidation dissolved. The genealogical "messages" from this period clearly register the disappearance of the traditional parameters that had previously structured and ordered the social sphere. Formerly (at least in theory), expertise acquired in a centrally administered educational system had decided who would perform what office. When this merit system collapsed, descent remained the only criterion to ensure that official positions were not filled arbitrarily or through the manipulation of power. Preferment by genealogy established itself so extensively that Herodotus, writing five hundred years later, had the impression that Egypt was a caste system: "The Egyptians are divided into seven classes: priests, warriors, cowherds, swineherds, merchants, interpreters, and pilots" (*Histories,* II.164).

A thousand years earlier, at the collapse of the Old Kingdom, the patronage principle had taken over, establishing the new social roles of local magnate and client, as well as an attendant ideology of loyalty that influenced later forms of kingship and personal piety. Now the social position, security, and residence of the individual were determined by membership in a lineage of forefathers and predecessors in office, as well as by a relationship to a local deity revered according to the dictates of personal piety. But this time, in striking contrast to the First and Second Intermediate Periods, no voices whatsoever appear to have lamented the collapse of political unity as "chaos." Clearly, no one regarded the political situation as critical or disastrous. The difference over and against the earlier Intermediate Periods was the structure of foreign political connection that integrated the various dynasties and principalities into a common order. The advantages of this new political system must have been so patent that the loss of unity was not experienced as a loss of meaning.

The semantics of social and political action geared to the concept of *ma'at* had faded. Of course the genealogical paradigm was insufficient to fill the vacuum that remained. While genealogy was adequate to the task of forming a new affiliation structure, it was not a normative idea capable of galvanizing new patterns of action. There are scarcely any identifiable indications of a new feudal semantics revolving around concepts such as honor, family name, or lineage. Rather, the central notions of the new cultural semantics came from another source: personal piety and its theology of will. These ideas were obviously easier to realize at a local level and also easier to put into practice within administrative structures of limited scope. For the god of personal piety was the local deity, and the form of personal participation in meaningful religious life was the local festival.

This same process of regionalization and decentralization of Egyptian administration also had a practical side—in fact, the practical aspect was primary. When the central distribution and supply networks of a state break down, local supply systems must take their place. Thus the collapse of centralized government invariably creates an opportunity for local magnates to seize political power and legitimize their territorially restricted but functionally comprehensive sway by guaranteeing the supply of goods. In the Third Intermediate Period this "downward" legitimization was scarcely different from the processes of the First Intermediate Period. It was not mere antiquarian interest in the past that motivated the use of phrases and sometimes even lengthy quotations from the tomb inscriptions of the First Intermediate Period; there was clearly a sense of kinship with the people who had lived fifteen hundred years before. On both the literary and social planes, they were seen as ideals of how to face up to life under comparable circumstances, and so were taken up and incorporated into the mechanisms of self-representation. Oddly enough, the same does not apply to the Twenty-first Dynasty, during which the actual upheaval took place. In the inscriptions from this period all self-representation is subordinated to the radical implementation of the theocratic idea.

The historical dynamic of the Third Intermediate Period is dictated by the oscillation between two political models, the traditional "hypotactic" model of pharaonic rule, with unity at the level of rule and differentiation at the level of administration, and the "paratactic" model introduced by Herihor, with multiplicity at the level of ruler and amalgamation at the level of office. The new model achieved its classical form under the Theban Pinudjem I and the Tanite Psusennes I.

Pinudjem was the high priest of the Twenty-first Dynasty who used the kingly titles most frequently, while Psusennes gave himself the title high priest of Amun. Complete political parataxis was attained; in this case, the model worked particularly well because the rulers were related by marriage (Pinudjem married one of Psusennes' daughters) and pursued a policy of "joint security."[18] The hypotactic and paratactic models dominated the subsequent centuries as alternative political options. Still, we must not imagine this period of more than three hundred years as one of constant fragmentation. Various rulers revived the hypotactic model and were sometimes successful in reestablishing it for a while. Shoshenq I, for instance, the founder of the Twenty-second Dynasty, put an end to the autonomy of the Theban god-state by prohibiting inheritance of the high priesthood and insisting that this office should always be conferred on a son of the ruling king. Thus there are periods of rule that cannot be seriously regarded as "intermediate" and during which an aggressive foreign policy was pursued. Shoshenq I even figures in the Bible, as plunderer of the temple of Jerusalem. But even in periods of strength, it proved impossible to fully reestablish the monopolies on force and taxation that define statehood. On the other hand, the periods when the paratactic model was in the ascendancy were not felt to be chaotic as long as the localization of power was offset by trust-building measures.

Theocracy

THE TERM "THEOCRACY" WAS COINED by Flavius Josephus, with reference to the Jewish idea of the Covenant: the people chooses YHWH as its king, YHWH chooses Israel as his people.[19] Government is exercised representatively by the priesthood, but in close consultation with God, whose will is elicited via oracular inquiry before any important decision is made. As long as the priests did not figure openly as rulers (as was the case with the Hasmoneans), this form of government was a "direct theocracy," in which God rules and the worldly position of ruler remains unoccupied. The priests who ruled de facto saw themselves as servants who received orders from God.

Yet where priests function both as rulers and as representatives of god, it is more accurate to speak of "representative theocracy." In historical reality, the distinctions between direct and representative theocracy are frequently hard to ascertain: de facto rule is invariably bound up with titular rule. But it remains useful to make the distinction at a theoretical level. In its classical form, pharaonic kingship rested on the principle of representative theocracy. The pharaoh represented god as his son, deputy, and image, appearing as ruler, not priest. In his capacity as priest, the pharaoh was represented by others.

As far as the first four Egyptian dynasties are concerned, we may with some justice speak of direct theocracy because there the rule of the pharaoh was understood not as a representation but as an embodiment of god. But the difference between Egyptian and Jewish theocracy could hardly be greater. In Egypt, it is the position of god rather than that of the ruler that remains "unoccupied." The ruler is not an image of god, he *is* god. Even in its classical, representative form, pharaonic kingship never entirely relinquished the idea that the pharaoh, son of god, was also an incarnation of god. The god embodied by the pharaoh, however, was typically demoted to a filial rank: the pharaoh did not embody Amun, Re, or Ptah, but Horus, the son of Osiris, and as such the Son.

In the Amarna Period, Akhenaten consistently wrote the name of his god in cartouches and gave him the title "my father" in the sense of "senior partner in the kingship." This "coregency" model is an intermediate form between direct and representative theocracy. As ruler, the pharaoh did not embody god, but neither did he represent him. God and pharaoh ruled together as father and son. Monotheism was institutionalized as monarchy, and this monarchy was a partnership run by the Aten and Akhenaten together. Akhenaten was correspondingly rigorous in eliminating the priesthood as a representative institution. He acted in person as the priest of his god and did not have himself represented in the execution of this office. De facto, of course, he ruled alone, for there are no indications of techniques for inquiring into the will of the Aten.

The system imposed by Herihor in Thebes comes nearest to the Jewish variety. Though Herihor assumed the title of king, he demoted kingship to a priestly status. He kept his priestly titles and even included the high-priest title as prenomen in his titulary. The title of king was an expression of his standing not vis-à-vis god but vis-à-vis Ramesses XI; it signified his political sovereignty, in the sense of independence from Tanite kingship, not his representative relation to divine power. This important distinction is often blurred in references to the regalia of the Theban high priests. The high priests of the

Twenty-first Dynasty represented the rule of god as servants, not as rulers. This is direct theocracy.

Direct theocracy turned the theology of will into political reality. Ramesses III had already gone a long way in this respect. In his hymns to Amun, he represents himself as a lowly man who has taken god into his heart and serves him faithfully "on his water." His prayers to and dialogues with Amun speak the language of personal piety. On the other hand, in his historical inscriptions this same Ramesses III conveys an almost operatic sense of his own divinity.

Herihor took an entirely different line. Though he adopted certain of the regalia of the Ramesside vision of the king, he relinquished its bombastic aspects. He remained priest, general, and vizier, while leaving ruling authority to Amun. He instituted direct theocracy in order to resolve the cognitive dissonance triggered by Ramesside kingship with its mixture of piety and histrionic self-elevation. Worldview, image of god, and concept of king no longer meshed. The Ramesside paradigm of histrionic divine kingship coupled with the theology of will had, by this time, exhausted itself and run aground on its own paradoxes.

A theology of will requires a procedure for establishing god's intent. To this end, the Egyptian forms of consulting the oracle, already greatly expanded during the Ramesside period, were brought to full perfection. Unlike Mesopotamia, Egypt was not a fundamentally divinatory culture. Only in the New Kingdom do various forms of divination develop. And not until the Ramesside period do we find references to interpretation of dreams, birds' flight, or winds and stars.[20] The oldest, most widespread, and classical form of divining a god's will was to consult oracles, yet there are no traces of oracular consultation in Egypt prior to the New Kingdom. This is less surprising than it may seem, for oracular pronouncements are features of a theology of will that only established itself in the New Kingdom.[21]

The Latin word *oraculum* derives from *os* ("mouth") and is associated with the idea of oral utterance; similarly, the Egyptian technical term for oracle comes from an expression that means "one has spoken." Yet the Egyptian gods did not manifest their will in speech but in the movements of their processional images, which were understood in a figurative sense as "proclamations." In other words, oracles only figured in connection with processions—that is, at religious festivals. The movements of the cult image represented a highly restricted code that largely limited the god to yes or no responses, or at best to selections from various alternatives that were presented in the form of either candidates or written documents. Oracular divination was thus associated with religious festivals in the same way as was personal piety, and likewise developed spontaneously as part and parcel of Egyptian religious festival culture. The festival itself was an enactment of the presence of god, of which the oracular performance was a constituent. Moreover, this enactment took its bearings from the model of the king.[22] The festival was the occasion for the god, as king of his city, to inspect his territory and exercise power over it.

A feature particularly characteristic of the Twenty-first Dynasty was the oracular decree, a written document that guaranteed Amun's protection for certain persons, living and dead. For the living, an oracular decree was a talisman or amulet that warded off all misfortune, including the wrath of other deities. For the dead, an oracular decree functioned as a letter of recommendation to the authorities of the underworld, complete with divine instructions regarding the immunity of the bearer. Both forms of influence on areas beyond human control exceeded the range of action available to the king. Thus the gods ruled not only as kings but also as gods.

Like the royal inscriptions from the Ramesside age, the oracular decrees for the hereafter begin with lengthy eulogies addressed to the ruler, who in this case is not the king but Amun. The style and material of the eulogies are concordant with, or even taken from, the great hymns to Amun. In a Theban decree preserved in a copy from the Twenty-second Dynasty, Amun is celebrated as a primal god and the source of all being; the outward forms of his world-preserving influence are enumerated: sun, moon, Nile inundation. God is the All-Lord from which everything evolved. He encompasses everything, is present in the world in manifold ways, but is at the same time unidentifiable. He is the *ba*—spiritual and immaterial power bodied forth as "world":

This sublime god, the lord of all gods,
Amun-Re, lord of Karnak, first of Thebes,
the august *ba*, who first originated,
the great god who lives on *ma'at*.
The first primal god who brought forth the primal gods,
he from whom every god came forth.
The one god who made himself into millions.
The one and only who created the beings,

who created the world in the beginning.
Mysterious of birth, rich in incarnations, whose origin one does
  not know.

The verses that follow distinguish the self-originating One from
whom everything stems and his manifestation as the sun, first in its
primal rising, then in its daily course:

Sublime image of power that inspires love,
Majestic one, strong in his manifestations,
Lord of sovereignty, mighty in form,
from whose form all form originated.
Who commenced the becoming when there was none beside
  him,
who made the earth bright in the beginning.

Great sun-disk with shining rays,
when he shows himself, every face lives.
Who crosses the heavens without tiring,
morning after morning, whose task is firmly established.
The old man who in the morning rises anew as a youth,
who extends unto the limits of time.
Who runs round the earth and traverses the underworld,
to illuminate both lands for his creatures.

The next stanzas enlarge on the theme of powerful, vigorous world
preservation. "Bull," "ram," and "lion" symbolize the ruling power
exercised by god in his cosmic manifestations as sun, moon, and Nile.
Amun's power over time plays a special role. *Neheh*, cyclical time,
comes already full of his strength. What *neheh* brings is determined
by Amun's will, while his works, brought to fruition in the fullness
of time, endure forever in *djet* time.

Divine god who formed himself,
who created heaven and earth with his heart.
Greatest of the great, mightiest of the mighty,
great one older than the gods.
Bull that rejuvenates itself, with pointed horns,
before whose great name the Two Lands tremble.

The fullness of time comes weighed down with his strength
and extends to the end of perpetual duration.

Great god who commenced all becoming,
who conquered both lands with his strength,
Ram-headed one of sublime form,
more gracious than all gods.
Wild-staring lion, when he raises the two *udjat* eyes [the
    Egyptian symbol for wholeness, integrity],
lord of the flame against his enemies.

Great primal water, that flows forth in its time,
to keep alive that which took form on his potter's disk.
Who crosses the heavens and traverses the underworld
and in the early morning appears at the same place as yesterday.
Lord of strength, of unapproachable majesty,
his rays keep his body concealed.
His right and his left eye
are sun and moon;
heaven and earth are shot through with his beauty.
Vigorous god, who is not sluggardly,
who labors with rising and setting;
men were born of his two divine eyes
and the gods of the utterance of his mouth.
Creator of nourishment, originator of food, who created that
    which is,
eternal one, who spends the years and whose time has no end,
who aging and rejuvenated traverses unending time,
old man who spends his youth.

The second part of this long eulogy is devoted to the regal aspects of
the deity in the narrower sense. God is not only cosmic power but
also a personal, cognizant, omniscient, judging, sentencing, commanding, punishing, and saving god:

Rich in eyes, great in ears,
who leads millions with his rays;
Lord of life, who gives to whom he will,
the whole earth stands under his supervision.
Who commands and it is done, without contradiction,

nothing perishes that he has created.
With sweet name and gracious love,
every face is up early to worship him.
Dreadful in might, great in strength,
every god stands under his fear.
Young bull that drives back the raging,
Strong of arm, who vanquishes his foes.

This god who establishes the land with his counsels
Ba, shining with his two *udjat* eyes;
Ba-like, who incarnates himself in incarnations,
Holy concealed one whom one cannot recognize;
He is the king who creates kings,
who links lands with the commandment he has created.
The gods and goddesses bow down to his power,
because their awe of him is so great.
Who came at the beginning, he has completed the end,
he has established the lands with his counsels.

The revelation of this god is the creation, which reveals him by con-
cealing him. God's presence is by its very nature hidden. The first
stanza of the next section elaborates the idea of the hidden All-Lord
in paradoxes that are the result of centuries of theological labor. The
second (and concluding) stanza again contrasts the cosmic aspect of
god's concealed inner-worldliness with the personalized aspect of his
saving jurisdiction; here, the true ruler-name of the god is written in
cartouches and thus refers to the ruler of Theban theocracy.

Mysterious in incarnations, he whom one cannot know,
who has concealed himself from all gods.
Who withdrew as the sun that cannot be recognized,
who hid himself from what he had created,
flaming torch with great light,
one sees in the midst of his seeing.
One spends the day contemplating him and is never sated with
   the sight of him;
when day comes, all faces pray to him.
Sparkling in manifestations in the midst of the Ennead,
his form is the form of each god.

The Nile comes, the north wind blows upstream
in the inside of this mysterious god.

Who issues commandments for millions of years, whose hand
   trembles not.
With firm-standing oracle and effective commandment, which
   never fails in anything.
Who gives lifetime and doubles the years for him that stands in
   his favor,
He created a wall of iron for him who is on his water,
no misfortune strikes him who treads his path.
Who comes to him that calls,
with a heart inclined to him that worships him,
who extends [his hand] to him who calls his name.
A good protector for him who gives him into his heart,
a succor for ever and ever;
King of Upper and Lower Egypt, Amun-Re, king of the gods,
Lord of heaven and earth,
of the waters and the mountains,
who created the land through his incarnation,
greater is he and more sublime
than all gods of the first primal age.[23]

This final stanza with its direct allusions to god as the ruler of the
god-state vividly demonstrates that Theban theocracy was the institutionalization of personal piety. The ruler titles of Amun are taken
directly from the terminology and the conceptual categories of personal piety.

The parallels between this long text and the *Great Hymn* of
Akhenaten are striking. Both the Theban state and the Amarna state
were theocracies, the former ruled solely by god, the latter representing a coregency in which god was responsible for the preservation of
the cosmos and therefore not concerned to intervene in human affairs
by oracular agency. Both theocracies were based on what was essentially a monotheistic religion, with more emphasis on "mono" in
Amarna, and more on "theistic" in Thebes. The Amarna religion (to
take up Kant's famous distinction) was more "deism" than "theism,"
as the personal aspects were absent from its idea of god. The Theban
religion, by contrast, recognized the other deities, although it saw
them as contained in the one and elevated this one infinitely above

them. Both theocracies attempted the political realization of a truth by renouncing rule over a greater realm: Akhenaten shut himself off from the outside world in the enclosure of his boundary stelae, while Herihor established the Theban god-state as a state within the state.

Against the background of these similarities, the differences show up all the more starkly. The subjects dwelt upon by the Theban text are almost entirely absent at Amarna: primal god, initial emergence, *ba*, immanence, omniscience; ethical authority as judge, ruler, counselor, and commander; rescuer, protector, and patron. The only aspect of god common to both texts is his identification with the sun and the inherent paradox of his omnipresent hiddenness:

> You are far but your rays are on earth.
> You are in their countenance but one cannot recognize your
> course.[24]

This coincidence is no accident. The fascinating idea that god is most remote and concealed in his most overwhelming and all-encompassing presence is already implicit in the new solar theology, which no longer interpreted the circuit of the sun as a "concerted action" by a world of deities but as the solitary, world-preserving action of the One.[25] The Amarna faith was a product of this new solar theology, which by no means disappeared after the failure of the Amarna religion but was elaborated further and integrated into the Amun theology of the Ramesside age.

Another apparent agreement between Amarna and Amun theology is the idea that god "incarnates" himself in the world. In the Amarna hymn we read:

> You create millions of incarnations from yourself, the one;
> towns, villages, field, path and river.[26]

A creation, then, ex deo, not ex nihilo. What is meant here is that the light creates the things of the world by making them visible and thus giving them a form. The incarnations envisaged by the Theban text when it praises god as the *ba* that "incarnates himself in incarnations" are of a different kind. Here God bodies forth as what Plato called the "soul of the world." In the Theban view, Amun was the *ba* of the world. The world was his body, by analogy to an anthropology in which a body is inspirited by a *ba* that leaves it after death but that ideally maintains contact with it in other forms. At Amarna, there is no mention of the concept of *ba;* only in the Ramesside age does *ba* come to express the relation between god and the world.

A further parallel between the religion of Amarna and that of Amun is the relationship between god and individual lifetime. In Amarna we read:

> When you rise, they live;
> when you set, they die.
> You yourself are the time in which and through which one lives.[27]

In Thebes:

> Who gives lifetime and doubles the years for him that stands in
> his favor.

The difference is clear: the god of Amarna creates the time in which all life unfolds by his motion and manifestation as cosmic energy; in contrast, the Theban god creates time by his voluntary decision and allots it to those who stand in his favor. The time he creates is the destiny that comes from god.

But I have been comparing unequal testimonia. The Theban text is not a hymn but an elaborated form of titulary, compiled from Ramesside Amun hymns. The immediate purpose of this titulary was not to glorify god, nor to instruct men on his greatness, but to ensure the performance of the provisions set out in the decree that followed. Every royal decree first of all established the king's authority for issuing provisions and making demands. The Ten Commandments also stand in this tradition, starting with a predication of law-giving authority: "I am YHWH thy God who led thee out of the land of Egypt." The Theban eulogy to Amun is an equivalent kind of preamble, which identifies the ordaining authority as such. The addressee is Osiris, god of the underworld. The provisions relate to the deceased, Neskhons, or to her husband, Pinudjem. Neskhons is to be deified, both her *ba* and her mortal coil. She is to be welcomed in the underworld, where she is to be given food and drink; her *ba* is to be given freedom of movement. Her heart shall remain attached to her still living husband. She is to receive her offerings; the liturgy of the seventy praisings of Re will be performed for her; no misfortune shall befall her; finally, Amun guarantees to provide anything else that may be necessary for her deification. The command that "one shall never destroy her *ba* in the underworld" is a security against the Judgment of the Dead.

The oracular decrees are thus examples of applied theology, in which the desire for an all-encompassing security discovers a world-encompassing, hidden All-Lord. The threats that haunted the people of the New Kingdom and the Third Intermediate Period stemmed in the first place from the gods. In a typical decree, a petitioner sought security from

Sekhmet and her son, from the collapse of a wall and from the thunderbolt, from leprosy, blindness, and the Evil Eye, from the seven stars of the Great Bear and from a falling star, from the Ennead of Upper Egyptian Heliopolis and their taboos, from the books of the beginning of the year and the books of the end of the year, from any death, any illness, any accusation, any evil, any disorder, any failure, any bad word, any hard word, any evil word, any mockery, from the punitive power of Amun, Mut, Khonsu, Amun-in-Luxor, Montu, and Ma'at, from a severe oracle, from the gods that seize one in flight, that track one down in the country and kill one in the town and vice versa, from all gods and goddesses executing punitive justice when they are dissatisfied, from the sublime great one in Heliopolis, from any messenger demon and any vagabond demon, from any illness and fever.[28]

Only an all-encompassing god could give protection from such ubiquitous threats. Magic and personal piety—these were the very spheres attacked by Akhenaten's revolution. Personal piety had been stripped down to its origins in loyalism and transferred onto the king. No personal relations between god and man were possible in Amarna. For individuals, god was only approachable via the king as mediator. The hereafter, elaborately anticipated in the provisions of the oracular decree for Neskhons and Pinudjem, had been struck out of the "world according to Amarna," whose dead lived on in their tombs, temples, and gardens.[29] And above all, magic—the dimension to which the oracular decrees for the living belonged—was banished completely from Amarna.

In Egypt, magic and personal piety were more closely associated than one might assume. Both were domestic forms of religion, and

Bes Pantheos (Saite Period, 7th–6th century B.C.E.)
(from S. Sauneron, Le papyrus magique illustré de Brooklyn, *pl.*
IV, drawing by Aleida Assmann)

each supplemented the other. Magic was ritual for home use.[30] In the temples, priests, who were representatives of the king, performed rituals to ensure the continued functioning of the cosmos and the welfare of the community. Different (though analogous) rites were performed by specialists—notably physicians who were also priests—for private persons. This is the realm of magic, where the context for ritual performance first had to be created. The temple was a holy place; the private home was not. Likewise, while temple rituals were integrated into cyclical, sacred time, the performance of magic spells usually took place ad hoc, in response to an emergency. Different means had to be employed, and thus it is relatively easy to distinguish magic texts from sacred texts. But (except during Amarna) there was no tension whatsoever between temple and domicile.

The oracular decrees prove the point. They connect the spheres of temple, domicile, and tomb, and place them all equally under the protection of the same god. Significantly, magic was essential in transmitting the theology of the hidden All-Lord and even attempted a graphic description of this idea of god, which in its very grotesquerie underlined the indescribability of the one. Thus, a god with seven heads appears in a magic papyrus from a slightly later period:

The Bes with seven heads,
he embodies the *ba*s of Amun-Re . . .
of the lord of heaven, earth, underworld, the waters, and the mountains.
Who keeps his name secret from the gods,
of the giant of millions of cubits,

of the strong one, who made the earth fast on his head,
... from whose nose the air comes forth to give life to all noses,
who rises as the sun to brighten the earth,
from the emanations of whose body the Nile flows to give life to
every mouth.... [31]
Bes is not so much a great god as a monster. The evil-averting grotesquerie of his aspect typifies a god of disguise. In the passage above,
he appears as the mask of the hidden All-Lord. In the same papyrus
he is depicted a second time, now as a "man with nine heads on one
neck, the face of Bes, a ram's head, a falcon head, a crocodile head,
a hippopotamus head, a lion's head, a bull's head, a monkey's head,
and a cat's head."[32]

Magic is an emphatic pointer to the limits of the Egyptian "theology of will" since it depends on fictions of coherence that are simply
incompatible with such a theology, at least in its radical form. Magic
depends upon the notion of an order that can be influenced to the
extent that one is familiar with it. If god's will manifested itself in a
wholly arbitrary and inscrutable way, there would be no place for
magic. So the theology of will is only one side, while the other is a
notion of coherence based on a system of order recognizable as such.
But the idea of the hidden All-Lord is essential for both.

22

LIBYAN POLYARCHY AND
THE STATE OF NAPATA

Libyan Polyarchy

THE END OF THE NEW KINGDOM was marked by Herihor's revolutionary adoption of the title of king and his introduction of a new
chronology. Though his year count was soon revoked, Herihor's
actions established a division of rule that could not be reversed and
that determined the history of the subsequent centuries. The end of
the epoch of division and the beginning of Libyan polyarchy was
marked by a similar move.

In Year 8 of Shoshenq III's reign, Pedubastis, a prince of the
Tanite line, assumed the title of king, introduced a year count of his
own, and ensconced himself in Leontopolis as founder of the Twenty-
third Dynasty. In so doing, he set off a progressive fragmentation that
quickly led to a proliferation of up to twenty ruling houses, some of
them bearing the title of king, some of "count," and some (by far the
most) the alien title of "chief of the Ma," which is an abbreviation
standing for "chief of the Meshwesh," a Libyan tribe. In the Nineteenth Dynasty, Merneptah had waged war on a "chief of the Meshwesh," who were, at that time, enemies of Egypt and a major threat
to the Pax Ramessidica. At the same time, however, there were Meshwesh who served as mercenaries in the Ramesside army and who lived
in military colonies. But in the first centuries of the first millennium,
the Libyans continued to pose a threat, to which the Egyptian cities
responded by setting up fortresses. Thus there were friendly Meshwesh and hostile Meshwesh. The former were fully assimilated into

Egyptian culture but kept their foreign titles and the Libyan emblem of chiefdom, the feather. They were proud of their Libyan origins, even while they saw themselves as descendants of a Ramesside military aristocracy.

Shoshenq I stemmed from a line of "Great Princes of the Meshwesh," who ruled in Herakleopolis under the Twenty-first Dynasty as counts and high priests of Harsaphes. As lords of Egypt, however, they adapted to the pharaonic form of rule and partially suppressed their traditional social structure, a coexistence of clan chiefs of equal rank. This traditional form was not consigned to oblivion, however; the "text" of the pharaonic system of rule was superimposed on it as on a palimpsest. Once this text faded, the underlying layer became visible and reasserted itself. This turn was ushered in by the secession of Prince Pedubastis and came to full fruition under Shoshenq III, a king of doubtful legitimacy, who had ascended the throne of Tanis as successor to his father, Takelot II, ignoring the claims of Crown Prince Osorkon. Osorkon, who held the office of high priest in Thebes, had a very difficult time there because he had been installed by Takelot II in preference to the native pretender (the eponymous grandson of the priest-king Harsiese) and against the will of the Theban families. The unusual cruelty with which Osorkon attempted to impose his will on the Theban opposition led to a ten-year civil war.

All these events emerge from a long inscription by Osorkon in the temple at Karnak. It has the character of a message, as it presents the events of the time with a certain semantic bias.[33] It tells of a Theban revolt against "the protector of the land," of Osorkon's arrival in Thebes, his ceremonial welcome by the priesthood, his festival offering for Amun, and the god's favorable oracular utterance, and it transmits the following address to the prince by the Theban priests:

> You are the valiant protector of all the gods!
> Amun appointed you [as] the eldest son of your progenitor;
> he has chosen you amongst hundreds of thousands in order to
>   carry out what his heart desires throughout.
> Now we are begging you as we are aware of your affection for
>   him.
> Behold, he has brought you [to us] in order to suppress our
>   misery

and put an end to the tempest confronting us;
because this land was drowned,
its laws having perished in the hands of those
who rebelled against their lord and who were his officials.
Each scribe in his temples would obliterate his ordinances
which the lord of the *heden* plant [= Thoth] had put down on
　the book,
and would wreck the sacred rites of the temples, which had
　fallen into plunder;
yet all this was not in the cognizance of the king.

Most of the rest of this address has been destroyed, but surely it ended with a plea to punish the miscreants severely. The prince acceded to this request in a form that is the ritual equivalent of the ancient "smiting the enemies" pictogram:

. . .
Then the prisoners were brought to him at once like a bundle of
　pinioned ones [?].
Then he struck them down for him [Amun], causing them to be
　carried
like goats the night of the feast of the Evening Sacrifice [. . .] of
　the Going Forth of Sothis.
Everyone was burned with fire in the place of [his] crime.

In all Egyptian history there are hardly any parallels for this description of a ritual execution. The nearest equivalent is an inscription of Sesostris I at el-Tod, again with reference to punishment for desecration of the temples. Otherwise we find reference to death by fire only in imprecations. It figures in fantasies of annihilation, not in Egyptian jurisprudence.[34] Thus it is certainly no coincidence that the imprecation genre flourished so strikingly in the inscriptions of this period. A text dating back to more or less the same period reads:

[whoever impairs this foundation . . .]
he shall be given over to destruction by Amun.
[. . .] He will deliver him over to the fire of the king on the day
　of his wrath. His uraeus shall spit fire on their heads, destroy

their bodies, and consume their flesh, so that they be like Apopis on the morning of the new year. . . . [35]

The Osorkon inscription itself also contains such imprecations:

As to the one who will upset this command which I have
  issued,
he shall be subject to the ferocity of Amun-Re,
the flame of Mut shall overcome him when she rages,
and his son shall not succeed him. . . . [36]

The purpose of Osorkon's imprecation is as a deterrent, but it displays above all a lack of a sense of justice and also of self-confidence. Here we are obviously in the presence of chaos from above rather than from below. So it comes as no surprise when later in the inscription civil unrest rears up:

Thereafter in the regnal year 15, fourth month of Shomu, day 25,
[. . .] the sky did not swallow up the moon,
a great convulsion broke out in this land like . . .
. . . children of rebellion, they stirred up civil strife among
  southerners and northerners.
. . . he did not weary of fighting in their midst,
even as Horus following his father.
Years elapsed in which one preyed upon his fellow unimpeded.

This time Osorkon apparently opted for a more conciliatory gesture. With a fleet of ships full of offerings, he set off for Thebes in a triumphal festal procession, organized a huge feast there for Amun, and then addressed a long oracle question to the god, who "readily agreed." But the following sentences, although heavily damaged, indicate that the revolt soon flared up again:

. . . those who rebelled against him.
Not one of the grandees of the interior of this land said, . . .
It so happened that he was there quite alone,
there was not a friend . . .

From a mark on a nilometer (a well-like structure used to measure the water level of the Nile) we learn that Harsiese, Osorkon's adversary, held the office of high priest of Amun in Year 6 of Shoshenq's reign; the rebellion was evidently successful.[37]

But soon there was "good news" from Thebes:

> Behold, he has done what you said [even though] the appointed
> time has not arrived.
> You shall give still more for his service.
> Rely not upon the army; devise not plans of fighting;
> the great name . . .

Inadequate as this text is for a reconstruction of the historical events, it is of major interest for its subjective evaluation of those events. It is one of the few "messages" from this period to fall back on the topoi of the chaos description and place the events within an "intermediate period." Some fifty years later, the Theban god-state was fundamentally reformed in an attempt to put a definitive end to the revival of such unrest. First Osorkon III (just like Osorkon II before him) set up his son Takelot, already the priest-king ruler of Herakleopolis, as high priest in Thebes. But when he later appointed this son coregent (about 755 B.C.E.), the two offices he had possessed remained vacant, which meant that the god-state was without a high priest. Instead, the office of "God's Wife of Amun," which dated back to the New Kingdom and was held by the presumptive queen (in this case Shepenwepet, daughter of Osorkon III), was upgraded to a pontificate. The supreme post in the god-state was now invested in a woman. And since, as consort of Amun, she had to remain virgin, the danger that high-priest dynasties would evolve in Thebes was removed once and for all.

For Thebes, this move had consequences that Osorkon III could hardly have intended: it suspended the paratactic model with its dictatorial amalgamation of offices. Theban families now occupied the civilian and military offices. A woman was henceforth the head of the god-state; her spiritual office of chief priestess ("Divine Adoratrice") and her royal blood (she had to be a princess) assured her of her regalia (cartouche inscription of her name, burial in the temple forecourt, courtly entourage in pharaonic style). Thus Thebes became a capital again, the seat of a quasi-pharaonic court. But at the head of civilian government there was now an "Overseer of Upper Egypt," an administrative official functioning as "Majordomo of the God's Wife of Amun." After an interval of centuries, monumental building resumed. The overseers and majordomos had rock tombs of fantastic dimensions built for themselves in the necropolis of the officials, not only recalling the grand tradition of the New Kingdom but over-shadowing all other private tombs ever erected in Egypt.[38]

The Kingdom of Napata

THE MOST SUCCESSFUL ATTEMPT TO END the Third Interme-diate Period and reestablish a unified Egyptian empire around a mon-umental, immortality-oriented form of kingship originated in Napata, a state that had formed at the extreme southern tip of Kush in the vicinity of the Fourth Cataract. This process was so remarkable that it is worth looking at more closely.

Napata was not the first state to have evolved to the south of Egypt. Both the history of settlement and the rudimentary efforts to set up political organizations like chiefdoms—or even kingdoms—can be traced back to the fourth millennium and initially ran parallel to developments in Egypt. Then, however, the emergent Egyptian state with its new political boundaries, military power, and economic exploitation brought an end to these ambitions. The Nubian tribes reverted to an earlier style of political organization and in the course of the First Dynasty disappeared entirely, at least from the vista of archaeologists. After an interval of several hundred years, a new wave of settlement set in. Inscriptions report that as early as the Sixth Dynasty various tribes in Lower Nubia grouped to form a coalition. Farther south was the country of Yam, which was probably situated in the vicinity of the later kingdom of Napata, in the region of the Fourth Cataract. In archaeological terms, the settlement history of this area begins to take on clear contours in the Middle Kingdom, con-temporaneously with the unification of the tribes in Lower Nubia. But among the finds made in Kerma, the capital of the Upper Nubian state, on the east bank of the Nile, north of the Third Cataract, are stone vessels with the names Pepy I and Pepy II from the Old King-dom and Amenemhet (Ammenemes) I and Sesostris I from the early Middle Kingdom. In its early history, the kingdom of Kerma was perhaps a principality that, like Byblos to the north, oriented itself to Egypt, was presented with the same gifts by the Egyptian court, and supplied Egypt with important commodities—cedar wood in one case, gold and ivory in the other.[39] But that is largely speculation. In the Middle Kingdom, at any rate, Kerma developed into a powerful center, which reached its apogee in the Second Intermediate Period, when Egyptian control over Lower Nubia broke down.

The Hyksos rulers saw in the rulers of Kush their natural allies against the rebellious house of Thebes. Thus the latter's war of liberation was directed at both fronts, the Hyksos in the north and the Kushites in the south. But the consequences of Theban expansion were very different in the two regions. Whereas the north was integrated into a system of foreign alliances that subordinated the local vassal princes to Egyptian supremacy, the south was incorporated into the sphere of Egyptian rule and administered as a crown colony. Accordingly, the south experienced a much more intensive form of Egyptianization than the north, not only politically and economically but above all in religious matters. Temples were erected at centers of communication, where they served not only cultic but also administrative purposes. These cult sites developed an influence that frequently extended well beyond the borders of the region in question. In these Nubian cult centers not only were the "national" god Amun-Re and other major Egyptian deities worshipped, but the ruling Egyptian king was also venerated as a god. (Since the king was also represented as the sole official link between gods and men, there were scenes in which he came up against himself in his dual role of god and priest.) This religious colonization of Nubia was then extended to Upper Nubia, the core territory of Kush. At Gebel Barkal, in the vicinity of the Fourth Cataract, Tuthmosis III erected a temple for Amun as a "branch" cult of the temple at Karnak. Moreover, Gebel Barkal was declared to be something like the primal home of the god from the south, an identification that hinged on the figure of the god Min, with whom Amun of Karnak had long since merged. By equation with Min, Amun now became "Lord of the Nubians, Ruler of Punt," of whom the hymns wax rhapsodic:

> Whose scent the gods love
> when he returns home from Punt,
> rich in fragrances, when he comes down from Nubia,
> beauteous of face, when he comes from God's Land.

Thus, through the cult of Gebel Barkal, Nubia was incorporated not only politically but also religiously into the Egyptian world. No longer was Nubia simply the land of gold and other luxury goods, for which it had always been appreciated and exploited. It now gained religious significance as a holy landscape where the gods were at home. This new significance was fundamental to the events that followed.

The state of Napata thus had two very different pasts to draw on, an older and more properly Nubian one, centered in Kerma, and a younger, Egyptian one, which in the New Kingdom had replaced Kerma with the viceroyalty of Kush and Egyptianized the country with temples and myths. It was the Egyptian past that the Nubian state of Napata appropriated for itself and from which it derived an astonishingly dynamic semantic system. The revival was anything but self-evident, for the cultural sources feeding this new semiology had long since dried up: the cults had disappeared, the temples were in disrepair, the Egyptian priests, scribes, soldiers, and traders had all gone elsewhere. The last viceroy of Kush was the same Panehsy who, at the behest of Ramesses XI, had tried to restore order in Upper Egypt and as such was the final, and ultimately unsuccessful, antagonist of Herihor. With the establishment of the Theban god-state in 1069 B.C.E. and the division of rule in Egypt, the Egyptian presence in Nubia came to an end. There was no continuity between the Egyptian kingdom of Kush and the state of Napata, but a hiatus of several hundred years, which was bound to relegate all Egyptian traditions to complete and utter oblivion. The reversion to these traditions across a gap of centuries was an astonishing and improbable cultural feat that calls for an explanation.*

Napata's beginnings can be traced back no further than 850 B.C.E., that is, two hundred years after the collapse of the New Kingdom. The key site is the city and cemetery of el-Kurru, the first center of the Napata state, some ten miles downriver from Gebel Barkal. The first archaeological traces of rulers of Kurru are a series of tumulus graves reminiscent of the circular tomb sites of the rulers of Kerma. Thus the traces (we have no "messages") identify the beginnings of this dynasty as culturally Nubian. But among the finds from these sites are objects of indisputably Egyptian origin—stone vessels, gold and faïence jewelry, pottery—that point to trade relations with Egypt. The tomb sites of the following generations, however, point to something more fundamental: cultural influence from Egypt. The

---

*My description of the beginnings of the state of Napata owes much to Timothy Kendall, who on the basis of unpublished excavation notes and finds by G. A. Reisner has submitted the most plausible reconstruction of these events.

masonry of the tomb chambers now featured hewn stones; the pottery was illustrated with scenes in the Egyptian style; some finds even have hieroglyphic script. These traces are joined by iconographic and epigraphic messages that indicate the presence of Egyptians and the development of an Egyptian-style mortuary cult for the Nubian rulers. In the next generation of tombs, the process of Egyptianization proceeds rapidly and dramatically. Instead of the Nubian tumulus, the tombs now feature Egyptian pyramids on mastaba-like substructures.

The earlier assumption was that this Egyptianizing influence came from the Amun priests of the temple at Gebel Barkal, who despite being cut off from their homeland continued with their cult through the Third Intermediate Period. But Timothy Kendall has been able to show that this temple had crumbled centuries before. Egyptianization must have come from Egypt itself. But how? Kendall hypothesizes that Theban Amun priests fleeing from a revolt sought refuge with the rulers of Kurru. As we have seen, such a revolt did indeed take place, in Year 11 of Takelot II's reign (about 840 B.C.E.), when the ruler of Tanis set up his son Osorkon as high priest of Amun and thus seriously undermined the independence of the Theban god-state.[40] The uprising was quelled with a great deal of bloodshed, and various priests were executed in the cruelest possible way—reason enough for the priests of Amun to flee to Nubia. In the course of this unrest, the god-state broke off its relations with the Twenty-second Dynasty in Tanis and based its chronology on the regnal years of the Twenty-third Dynasty in Leontopolis. The time frame of the Theban unrest corresponds exactly to the cultural changes in Nubia.

The consequence of this cultural change was that the subsequent generations of the ruling house of Kurru saw themselves as the legitimate inheritors of the throne of Egypt. Their god was Amun of Gebel Barkal, who was equated very closely with the Amun cult of Thebes. The basis for this cultic, theological, and political construction was the great stela of Tuthmosis III in Gebel Barkal, which now regained its intelligibility and revived memories of the sacred standing of Nubia in the New Kingdom.

Whoever the initiators of this cultural change may have been, one thing is certain. The interest in Egypt was not just a vague and more or less spontaneous "throwback" to the Egyptian traditions of the New Kingdom but a conscious reconstruction of semiologies that had been submerged for several hundred years. A number of factors may have been at work here: the influence of Egyptian settlers in the country, the continuing visibility of the temples even in a state of decay, the ongoing trade relations with Egypt, the presence of Kushite mercenaries in Egypt, Egyptian traders, interpreters, and even envoys in Kurru, and, perhaps, an incoming stream of political refugees.

The process of Egyptianization gave the rulers of Kurru a voice with which they have communicated their messages to us across the centuries. The earliest inscriptions were clumsy and the oldest temples modest brick edifices. But that changed very quickly. The first of these rulers was Alara/Arii, who is said to have trusted in Amun and been rewarded with the kingship.[41] Kashta (the "Kushite"), his successor, already bore the full Egyptian royal titulary and instituted a much more ambitious building campaign in purely Egyptian style. The highpoint of this evolution was reached by Piye, his successor. His historical inscriptions are not only in the best Egyptian tradition, but within that tradition represent an apex of historical narrative; they articulate his ambition to put an end to the Third Intermediate Period culturally as well as politically, and to usher in a new age of glory. The Kushite rulers did not rely only on the strength of their armed forces; they attached equal significance to the eloquence of their oratory, the persuasive power of their religious mission, and the glories of their architecture. This time we are in the presence of a genuine renaissance, although it did not reach its full flowering until the reign of the Saites in the Twenty-sixth Dynasty.

The ascent of the house of Kushite rulers to the Twenty-fifth Dynasty took place in stages. The first stage, the establishment of local rule in Kurru, is beyond our ken and can only be deciphered from archaeological traces. The second stage was the claim to Egyptian recognition as an equal-ranking kingdom in the polyarchic context of the Third Intermediate Period. Therewith, the ruling house of Kurru placed itself on a par with the Egyptian dynasties and principalities. The third stage was the bid for pharaonic monocracy in the classical mold. This move called for recourse to the great traditions of the past. The new order with which the Kushite rulers aimed to supplant the polycentric courts of the Third Intermediate Period could be legitimized only as a return to an old and true system, a reversion to the classical form of the division of powers. Spiritual, secular, and military offices were once again placed in different hands. In this the Kushites drew on the measures introduced by Osorkon III

(Twenty-third Dynasty) to put an end once and for all to the civil unrest that had broken out around the office of high priest in Thebes. They had Princess Amenirdis, daughter of Kashta and sister of Piye, adopted by the ruling God's Wife of Amun and Divine Adoratrice, Shepenwepet, daughter of Osorkon III.

Piye's Epic

BEFORE THE KUSHITE DYNASTY restored pharaonic kingship in all its traditional pomp, the polycentric system that had developed in the Third Intermediate Period found a champion in Piye (Piankhy). At the very point at which that system was mortally threatened by Tefnakht, a Libyan prince of the Delta who sought to unify the empire (from the north this time), Piye intervened and restored the balance of political polycentrism by means of military force.

Piye's victory stela, found in Gebel Barkal in 1862 by an Egyptian officer home on leave, reveals the extreme political fragmentation of Egypt at the end of the Third Intermediate Period. But far from being bewailed as "chaos," this fragmentation is conceptualized and codified as a political order in its own right. Thus we have here the exact opposite of the two previous intermediate periods. The tension between polycentric reality and monocratic theory does not express itself in lamentations and chaos descriptions. Rather, we find a positive portrayal of this situation as an accepted, normative order. The victory stela of Piye defends the system of multiple kings, princes, and counts ruling side by side against the aggressor from within, who set out to restore unity.

Piye's interest in conserving the polycentric political order is already apparent from the scene in the lunette of the stela. While this area had always been reserved for cultic, not historical scenes, the lunette of Piye's victory stela presents a graphic depiction of the essence of the political order advocated by Piye: the various kings and princes overcome by Piye venerate him; in return, their titles and claims to rule are confirmed. Only the main adversary, Tefnakht himself, is absent, either because Piye was unwilling to include him in this iconic codification of order or because Tefnakht had not recognized that order of his own free will. In the middle of the lunette, Piye faces right, while Amun, accompanied by Mut (standing), sits behind him on the throne and looks in the same direction. On either side of this group, the power holders of Lower and Middle Egypt are depicted in two registers apiece. The right-hand group is headed in the upper register by the queen and king of Hermopolis, who are foregrounded by their upright posture. In his right hand, the king holds a sistrum; with his left hand he leads a horse. The other eight dignitaries are shown prostrating themselves. In the lower right-hand register, three more "kings" (of Tanis, Leontopolis, and Herakleopolis) are seen kissing the earth. Thus the right-hand group contains only regal personages, identifiable as such by title and cartouche writing as well as by the diadem in the form of the royal cobra (uraeus), the most distinctive symbol of kingship. The upper left-hand register portrays two Ma chiefs, recognizable by the feather each wears, and the lower a non-Ma chief and two more Ma chiefs. None of these figures are represented as "rebels" or "wretched foes"; rather, they sport the full panoply of their status as rulers.

In this way, a political démarche running counter to all traditional ideology was depicted graphically even for those unable to read. The royal titulature and uraeus also signified control of time. Life in Egypt at this time was thus divided up into various "time zones" particular to each king. Far from seeing this temporal multiplicity as symptomatic of chaos and anarchy, Piye affirmed it as a god-given order by codifying it in the picture section of his stela.

The source of Piye's ability to see the various rival principalities and mini-kingdoms as a political order was a new model of himself as "king of kings," which he enlarges on in another text:

> Amun of Napata has appointed me governor of this land,
> as I might say to someone: "Be king," and he is it,
> or: "You will not be king," and he is not.
> Amun of Thebes has appointed me governor of Egypt,
> as I might say to someone: "You are crowned!" and he is
> crowned,
> or: "You are not crowned," and he is not.
> Whoever is protected by me runs no risk of seeing his town
> conquered, at least not if I can help it.
> The gods make a king, men make a king—
> but I am a king made by Amun.[42]

Piye saw himself as a "king of kings" appointed by Amun, with other kings subordinate to him—those other kings having been appointed either by gods or by Piye himself. This model enabled Piye to look down on the chaos of "Libyan polyarchy" as from a great height and to represent it as order.

Still, the inscription on the stela describes a situation of extreme fragmentation, and does so with unusual precision. The lands of the Twenty-second and Twenty-third Dynasties had been successively whittled down to pocket-sized urban territories by appanages and primogenitures. In Middle Egypt, Hermopolis and Herakleopolis were independent kingdoms. The Theban god-state was already under Kushite rule. Within the inscription are two lists that record the protagonists of the Lower Egyptian small-state constellation and specify their titles. One list names the members of the coalition drummed up by Tefnakht to subdue the realm from the north and reestablish central rule. The other list names the princes and power holders who ultimately submitted to Piye. A meticulous distinction is made between three different categories of power holder: kings, Ma chiefs, and counts or other lords who are not Ma chiefs. Contemporary monuments confirm these lists down to the last detail. The precision of the description indicates the significance Piye attached to the status quo. His campaign against Tefnakht was not planned as a revolutionary reshuffle. He rather adopted the ploy of establishing inner political order via foreign policy by annexing (but not integrating) existing areas of rule as vassaldoms to his Kushite-Theban kingdom, whose superordinate status he consolidated. His intention, which he held to be a divine mission, was to preserve existing structures and at the same time to impose a new superordinate structure on them. This new structure, because it was designed not to dissolve the old but rather to protect, strengthen, and preserve it, was politically weak. Piye tried to offset this weakness by means of political semantics. The text he had inscribed on the victory stela at Gebel Barkal was in the first place a publication and externalization of this semantics.

The historical situation in 730–725 B.C.E. so meticulously recorded by the inscription was the background to, but not the occasion of, Piye's action, which was triggered rather by a dynamic that jeopardized the balance of polycentric power. Based in Sais in the western Delta, Tefnakht had built up a significant territory and entered into an alliance with the "kings" of the Twenty-second and Twenty-third Dynasties and their many sublines and Ma chiefdoms. He sallied forth southward, threatening the "kings" of Herakleopolis and Hermopolis, in a bid to set up a new political order under his suzerainty. At this point the story recorded on Piye's stela begins:

> One came to report to His Majesty:
> There is a chief of the west
> who is count and prince of *Ntr*, Tefnakht,
> he is in the nome of harpoons, in the nome of the desert bull,
> in Hapi, in [. . .],
> in Anu, in the house of gold, and in Memphis.
> He has taken possession of all the west,
> from the northern swamps to Lisht,
> and now travels southward with a great army,
> the whole land allied in following him,
> the counts and district governors follow him like dogs.
> No fortress of the southern nomes has closed its walls to him [a
>   list of these follows].
> When he turned to the eastern nomes,
> they too opened their gates to him:
> [another list follows].
> Lo, now he beleaguers Herakleopolis.
> It has coiled itself up like the snake Uroboros
> and lets not those out who want to get out, nor those in who
>   want to enter, and fights every day.
> He has surrounded it on all sides,
> every count knows his bastion,
> every man has been assigned a section
> among the counts and administrators.

The second message comes from the embattled "counts and garrison commanders in their towns." They report that Nimlot in Hermopolis has also come under great pressure and appears to be preparing to surrender to Tefnakht:

> Lo, he has gone to join him
> and has disavowed his loyalty to His Majesty.

Thereupon Piye sent orders to the commander of the troops stationed in Egypt to attack Tefnakht, which indicates that Upper Egypt must already have been firmly in Kushite hands. At the same time he sent an army to Egypt with detailed instructions: battle was to be joined only by day, and only after prior announcement; if the opponent asked for respite he should be given it; if he awaited reinforcements, let them come. It was precisely these reinforcements that Piye set out to campaign against. War was to be declared on them in the following terms:

> [Though] we know not whom we are to address
> when we turn to the army,
> [listen:] prepare the best chariot of your stables,
> order your battle lines!
> Then you will learn that it is the god Amun who has sent us!

Piye attached very great importance to playing by the rules, waging a just war based on a divine mission—in that sense, a *holy* war. In his description of his military action, Piye presents himself not as a conquering warlord possessed of great strategic wisdom, swiftness, unpredictability, and audacity, but as the rightful ruler because of his piety, leniency, mercy, trust in god, missionary zeal, and consistency. While the first part of his speech of instruction centers on the rules of warfare, the second turns to the behavior of the army in Thebes. Thebes appears here as a holy city in which peace must be preserved at all costs. The army is told to lay down its arms, cleanse itself in the waters, and don priestly linen. Military strength is pointless before god:

> No hero has strength without him.
> He makes the weak strong
> so that the many flee before the few
> and one alone vanquishes thousands.

Therefore the soldiers must cleanse themselves, fall prostrate before god, and call to him:

> Show us the way,
> so that we can fight in your shadow.
> The troop you send out will succeed in its attack,
> and before it the multitude will be gripped by terror.

The semantics marshaled by Piye to force recognition of his supreme kingship by the territories of the north is the theocratic semantics of

the Theban state. The measures described were completely unprecedented. Where else in all Egypt is there anything even remotely comparable? A whole army is instructed to cleanse themselves and don
priestly robes before entering the temple and praying to Amun for
succor. Before essaying an appreciation of the text and its importance
as a historical, literary, and cultural document, I will briefly recapit-
ulate the events it narrates.

The army dispatched by Piye marched via Thebes to Herakleopolis, where it encountered a coalition of three kings and five princes
who had thrown in their lot with Tefnakht. Two battles ensued, in the
course of which the forces of the coalition withdrew to Lower Egypt,
while Nimlot escaped to Hermopolis, his seat of government. Then
the Kushite army besieged Hermopolis and reported to the king. Piye,
"enraged like a panther" at the escape of the coalition forces, swore an
oath to set off for Egypt himself, but only after celebrating the festival
of Luxor in Thebes according to the letter of the prescribed procedure, which took no less than three weeks. The army, apprised of His
Majesty's ire, attempted to mollify him with a series of successful
actions: at three points the inscription reads: "They made report to
His Majesty but his heart was not satisfied." After the Theban festivities, Piye set off for the besieged Hermopolis, berated his army, and
intensified the siege until Hermopolis began to "exude the stench of
decomposition." Nimlot, at the end of his tether, first sent envoys,
and finally his queen. Unfortunately, much of the text is lost, but after
a long gap the reports and speeches continue: apparently Nimlot saw
the error of his ways and returned contritely to his vassal status.

The text sets very great store by these speeches, which account
for two-thirds of the entirety. The speeches reveal the inner motivation of the protagonists, illuminate attitudes and stances, interpret
events, and name objectives. The supreme literary quality of the text
stems largely from these speeches, which I shall look at a little later.

The events in and around Hermopolis end with the surrender
of the king, the confiscation of his treasury, an offering of thanks to
Thoth (the god of Hermopolis), and a scene of a very unusual kind
that arouses Piye's wrath for the second time. The text recounts three
such outbreaks of anger, all of which culminate in a ceremonious
oath on the part of the king. What has happened? During an inspection of the stables Piye discovers that some or all of the horses have
died of hunger. Hardly surprising after months of siege. But how does
Piye read this state of affairs?

> True as I live and Re loves me,
> and my nose rejuvenates itself with life:
> this here is worse in my eyes, to let my [!] horses starve,
> than all your other crimes.

Piye takes this occasion to proclaim his divine mission more forcefully than elsewhere in the text:

> Know you not that the shadow of god lies on me?
> He does not let my cause fail.
> If another had done this who knows me not,
> I would not have blamed him for it.
> I am born in the body, created in the divine egg,
> the seed of god is in me.
> As true as his *ka* endures, I act not without him,
> he it is who orders me to do what I do.

The point of this scene is to define Nimlot's guilt in terms of the consequences of the siege. Although he should have known better, he closed his gates to the ruler sent by god and thus bears the blame for all the consequences of the ensuing siege. Whereas a foe would have been acting in self-defense, Nimlot's actions are not merely blameworthy but sinful. As for the significance of horses in this period, it is necessary to know that Kushite kings had themselves buried with their favorite chargers. The most noble gift Osorkon IV could make to the Assyrian king Sargon II was "twelve excellent horses from Egypt, that have not their equal in all the land."

The text goes on to describe three instances in which towns opt for an alternative course: they close their gates but, confronted with an ultimatum, choose to avoid a siege and to surrender. In all three cases, Piye takes a lenient view: he restricts himself to confiscating the treasuries, giving over the storehouses to the Amun temple in Karnak, and organizing an offering of thanks for the respective local gods. In transferring the storehouses to Karnak, Piye reverts to a political practice of the New Kingdom that had led to a huge accumulation of riches in the Theban Amun temple. It is a practice that accords well with Piye's piety and his theocratic idea of statehood.

Piye then proceeds to Memphis with his army and confronts that city with the same ultimatum. But Memphis responds with a slap in the face. It not only closes its gates, but is even impertinent enough to send out a war party made up of a motley band of craftsmen and sailors. Memphis has no prince, as it is already within Tefnakht's sphere of influence. Tefnakht himself makes a brief appearance, exhorting the besieged and then disappearing again on horseback. The siege and capture of Memphis forms the narrative climax of the whole inscription and vividly illustrates the highly idiosyncratic narrative perspective.

The actual military engagements are given fairly short shrift. There are two of them, and the first cannot really qualify as a battle. The army is sent out to gain control of the Memphite fleet, which it accomplishes without bloodshed because the ships are in harbor, unmanned. The second is the capture of Memphis: "Memphis was taken like a cloudburst. Many men were killed, others taken prisoner and brought before His Majesty." The victory over Memphis is described not as the heroic deed of a great general but rather as Piye's almost automatic success as the instrument of divine will. The text dwells much less on the military engagement than on the psychology of the rebellion and the siege, on Piye's demand for recognition, first refused, then enforced (all reflected in speeches), and on the lengthy postlude to the conquest. This postlude encompasses the religious actions of Piye in Memphis, Babylon (Kher-aha), and Heliopolis, and the dispatch of envoys by the potentates of Lower Egypt. The final part of the inscription is devoted to an account of kowtowing surrender by the Delta princes, again in the form of long speeches, and a list of all the power holders who recognize the supreme rule of Piye. Finally, Tefnakht himself sends an offer of peace in another lengthy speech. Piye's mission is thus accomplished.

The text closes with the attempt of the four Delta kings to pay their respects to the Kushite in his palace. But a problem of cultic purity arises: three of the kings have to wait outside while only one, Nimlot, is admitted; it seems that the others are uncircumcised and eat fish, which is "an abomination of the palace." This is the first mention of the purity taboos for which the Egyptians of the Late Period were notorious. Herodotus reports in epic detail on the strict exclusiveness of Egyptian table customs, which allowed no sharing of meals with foreigners. The biblical story of Joseph paints a comparable picture. In Piye's admittance of Nimlot and attendant humiliation of the Delta kings, he represents himself not only as a legitimate ruler but as a "pure," priestly king whose orthodoxy of practice sets him off favorably against the Libyans. Completely new boundaries are drawn with the aid of religious purity prescriptions, which probably originated in the Theban god-state rather than in Kush.

The Piye text is striking above all for its literary quality. Its only real rival among royal inscriptions is the *Poem* on the Battle of Qadesh. But the Piye text is almost twice as long—which needs to be seen in the context of the forms and conventions of Egyptian written culture. Most royal inscriptions are short, no longer than fifty to one hundred verses. The books written on papyrus are naturally more voluminous. But a literary work like the *Story of Sinuhe* runs only to between five hundred and six hundred verses. Ramesses II aimed at a comparable length with the *Poem* on the Battle of Qadesh. His intention was not to present this event in the form of a military report but to publicize and immortalize it as a literary "book." Every genre, then, has a size of its own, a "specific gravity," and we cannot understand an Egyptian text properly unless we read it in the framework of the genre whose conventions it sets out to obey or to flout. The Piye text, notably, consists of about nine hundred verses, and thus exceeds all previous (or future) limits. This length is approximately equivalent to a two-volume work in our literary culture, and clearly indicates the importance Piye granted to his subject.

Piye gives his text the title "decree"; what he had in mind, however, was not merely an unprecedentedly long inscription, but a literary work in inscription form—a book. The text divides into two sections of more or less equal length. The climax of the first part is the capture of Hermopolis, with Nimlot as main adversary; that of the second part the taking of Memphis, with Tefnakht as main adversary. The battles of the first part are preceded by the religious actions in Thebes; those of the second are followed by the sacred actions in Memphis, Babylon, and Heliopolis. The ratio of narrative to direct speech—approximately 2:3—also corresponds to the typical construction of literary narratives.[43] The extreme artifice of this composition bears comparison to a baroque oratorio, with the narrative sections as recitatives and the speeches as arias, together with a number of choruses. In fact, we even have a final, crowning chorus. As in an oratorio, the narrative sections center on the plot, while the speeches illuminate it from within in a lyrical and subjective way. Completely absent from the text are the "eulogistic" sections that normally make up about half of the text in New Kingdom regal inscriptions and that still play an important part in Prince Osorkon's chronicle. In these eulogies, the central factor is not the account of a historical event but the description of essential, timeless features of the king. The Piye text restricts this element to a few verses and allots even those to an opening speech by Piye himself:

> Command uttered by His Majesty:
> "Hear what I have done in excess of the forefathers:
> I am a king, symbol of god,
> living image of Atum,
> who came forth from the womb, designated as ruler,
> so that those feared him who were older than he.
> His father knew, his mother recognized:
> already in the egg he is appointed as ruler.
> The present god whom the gods love,
> son of Re, who acts with his hands,
> Miamana [Beloved of Amun] Piye."

Here already, the epic narrator steps in:

> One came to report to His Majesty . . .

By Egyptian standards, this eulogy is extremely short, an immediate signal that this text will differ from the customary design. Piye figures not as the traditional god-king, the incarnation of a timeless identity, but as the priest-general of the Third Intermediate Period, whose individual identity marks him out as blessed and "divine" by virtue of his piety and energy.

More than in the text's sheer size, its literary character appears in its conscious recourses to the great traditions of Egyptian literature, its use of linguistic, formal, and motivic models, its "classicism."[44] Piye mobilizes the cultural memory of Egypt and legitimizes himself through his "education" at least as much as through piety and military success.[45] The speeches are the high points, and among them the professions of loyalty are especially noteworthy. The speeches by Nimlot, Peftjauawybastet, and especially Tefnakht recall the Ramesside prayers of personal piety with their constitutive elements of hymnic appellation, lament, confession, oath, and eulogy.

Peftjauawybastet addresses Piye as follows:

> [*appellation*] Hail to you, Horus, mighty king,
> bull attacking bulls!
> [*lament*] The nether world seized me,
> I foundered in darkness.
> Give me the light of your countenance!
> I could find no companion on the day of distress,
> no succor on the day of battle
> [*the two preceding verses are quotes from the* Instruction of
>   Amenemhet I]
> except you alone, you mighty king—
> light up the darkness in my face!
> [*oath*] I shall serve you with my property,
> Herakleopolis shall pay taxes to your authority.
> [*eulogy*] You are truly Horakhty, the sovereign of the
>   circumpolar stars,
> as long as he exists, so you exist as king.
> As he is immortal, you are immortal,
> King of Upper and Lower Egypt, Piye, ever-living!

Considerably more extensive is the speech of Tefnakht:

> [*appellation and lament*] Be gracious! I cannot see your face in
>   the days of wrath [or blindness].
> I cannot stand before your searing breath
> and I am chastened by your majesty.
> [*eulogy*] Lo, you are Seth, the First of the South,
> Montu, the strong bull,
> To whatever town you turn your face,
> you will not find me in it, even if I have to flee to the islands of
>   the ocean.
> I fear the power of your wrath
> and say to myself: His flame is hostile to me.
> Is then the heart of Your Majesty not cooled by what you have
>   done to me?
> I am sorely wretched.
> Punish me not according to my sin,
> you who wield the scales and judge with the weightstone.
> Impose triple penitence on me,

but spare the seed that you may harvest it in time,
do not tear up the fruit tree by its roots.
[*oath*] As true as your *ka* endures, the dread of you sits in my
    body,
the fear of you houses in my bones.
[*lament*] I cannot sit in the beerhouse,
and I cannot have the harp played to me.
I eat the bread of hunger
and drink the water of thirst
since the day you heard my name.
Pain sits in my bones,
my head is bald, my clothing dusty,
until "one" placates Neith for me [which only Piye, as a king
    sent by god, can do].
Long is the course you have taken against me, your eyes fixed on
    me.
Will my *ka* be acquitted,
will the servant then be cleansed of his trespasses?

The image of the repentant Tefnakht living on bread and water and
doomed to forgo the diversion of a harp recital is strikingly reminiscent of an anecdote about this ruler related by Plutarch and Diodorus,
who both record that Tefnakht turned his back on high Egyptian
civilization and affected a primitive lifestyle. On a campaign against
the Arabs, the king once had to manage without his usual military
paraphernalia and make do with what was at hand. The simple life,
we are told, so appealed to Tefnakht that he proceeded to curse Menes
as the founder of the Egyptian cultivation of opulence, and even went
so far as to record the curse in the temple of Amun at Karnak.[46] In
the anecdote, Tefnakht voluntarily adopts the frugal existence he
laments in the Piye text. But both sources agree in connecting his
name with unwonted privations.

The importance attached by Piye to his own piety, religious
deeds, and cultic actions, though in line with the traditional presentation of the king as military commander and lord of the cult, goes
a decisive step further, in a direction typical of the Third Intermediate
Period's fusion of military leader and high priest. Although this fusion
has often been deemed a canny ruse designed to provide a military
dictatorship with at least some semblance of legitimacy, Piye's text
illuminates the construction from within and convincingly reveals the

religious aspect of his office to be anything but a mask. Piye performs his official activities as cult lord but also demonstrates the liturgical expertise of a professional priest thoroughly familiar with the cult and anxious to preserve its purity. Breaking the seal, opening the bolt, seeing god, closing the bolt, sealing the seal—these were normally actions commissioned by the king but performed by priests. The king did not intervene in person. But in Heliopolis, Piye obviously does actual priestly service and thus demonstrates—in the sense of a "message"—how he himself saw the union between military leader and priest and how he enacted that view in the historical situation.

Piye's victory epic not only tells of political measures, but was itself a political measure. Indeed, its political benefits may have been greater than any deriving from military successes. The disorder of the Third Intermediate Period sprang to a large extent from the widening gap between the diction of the official inscriptions and a political reality largely divorced from the tenor of political discourse. Piye's text succeeds in capturing this reality, verbalizing it, conceptualizing it, and thus making it susceptible of representation as a system of political order.

23

MEMORY AND RENEWAL:
THE ETHIOPIAN AND SAITE
RENAISSANCE

Historical Outline

PIYE'S SUCCESSFUL CAMPAIGN OF 728 B.C.E. thwarted Tefnakht's bid to reunite Egypt under his aegis. But only a short time later, in 727, Tefnakht assumed royal rank and established the Twenty-fourth Dynasty. He ruled for eight years and was succeeded by his son Bocchoris.

In 716, Piye's brother Shabaka ascended the throne. According to Manetho, with him Libyan polyarchy comes to a definitive end. Shabaka took Bocchoris prisoner and had him burnt alive. He decided against ruling Egypt from distant Napata and made Memphis his capital. His selection of Neferkare as his throne name was a further link with the Old Kingdom and its capital, Memphis, as Neferkare was also the throne name of Pepy II. Shabaka codified his attempts to restore ancient Memphite traditions in a stela, the so-called *Memphite Theology*, which we shall consider in some detail. In Thebes he enlarged the small Eighteenth Dynasty temple at Medinet Habu, which soon became a religious center of the very first importance. In addition, Shabaka erected edifices at Karnak, Edfu, Esna, Dendera, Abydos, Memphis, and Athribis, and also launched a comprehensive program of cultic renewal.

In 702, Shabaka was succeeded by his nephew Shebitku, a son of Piye's, who also took a name from the Old Kingdom—Djedkare—as his throne name; for his Golden Horus name Shebitku even chose Khaemwaset ("Crowned in Thebes"), after the already legendary son of Ramesses II, the patron of all antiquaries and conservationists. He ruled for twelve years and was followed in 690 by his brother Taharqa, who built temples in Nubia (notably Kawa) and decorated them after the manner of Memphite pyramid temples. In Karnak, Taharqa planned the sacred lake in the form in which it is still preserved today. He also continued Shabaka's work on the aforementioned temple at Medinet Habu. His partner, the administrator of the god-state in Thebes, was Mentuemhet, owner of a mortuary palace of staggering dimensions, full of reliefs of unprecedented artistic quality and iconographic richness. Taharqa's rule was characterized by repeated clashes with the Assyrians, whose bid for territorial power had now reached Egypt. In 674 B.C.E. there was fighting at Ashkelon, from which Taharqa emerged victorious. But in 671 the Assyrian Esarhaddon captured Memphis and deported the entire court to Nineveh. In 669, Esarhaddon undertook a further Egyptian campaign but died in the course of it. His successor, Ashurbanipal, continued the war and in his pursuit of Taharqa penetrated as far as the Thebais. The provincial Kushite governors surrendered and were transformed into Assyrian vassal princes. When they broke away from Ashurbanipal shortly after, he undertook the third of his campaigns against Egypt. This time, the Lower Egyptian vassals were deported and executed. Only Necho of Sais (probably a descendant of the Twenty-fourth Dynasty) was spared, and together with his son Psammetichus was designated the Assyrians' agent or chief vassal king in Egypt. Thus the Assyrians, too, played a part in putting an end to Libyan polyarchy (or feudalism) and preparing the way for the Twenty-sixth Dynasty. Egypt was now governed by twenty remaining vassals, called kings in the Assyrian annals, amongst whom was Mentuemhet of Thebes.

In 664 B.C.E. Taharqa died, leaving to his successor, Tantamani, no more than the claim to an Egypt subjected to Assyrian supremacy. Tantamani's resolve to reconquer the territory is documented in a stela that provides a highly impressive testimony of this dynasty's missionary zeal. In it, the young king recounts a dream in which he is visited by two snakes:

> In Year 1 of his coronation as king . . . His Majesty saw a dream by night: two serpents, one upon his right, the other upon his left. Then His Majesty awoke, and he found them not. His Majesty said: "Wherefore has this come to me?" Then they answered him, saying: "Thine is the Southland; take for thyself also the

Northland. The Two Goddesses shine upon thy brow, the land is given to thee, in its length and breadth. No other divides it with thee."[47]

The dream was obviously in the nature of a divine instruction, "salutary for him who takes it to heart but fateful for him who ignores it," as the text says with a learned allusion to the *Instruction of Ptah-hotep*.[48] Tantamani's reconquest of Egypt proceeded much like Piye's pilgrimage from temple to temple, with the same resounding welcome from the priesthood everywhere. Not until Memphis did he encounter any resistance, which was quickly quelled. The leader of the pro-Assyrian forces, Necho I, fell in battle. The Delta princes (the vassals set up by the Assyrians) surrendered to Tantamani, who breaks out in a prayer of thanks to Amun for having made the dream vision come true:

> My lord is with me, this sublime god,
> Amun-Re, lord of Karnak, who resides in Gebel Barkal:
> the great god, beneficent to him who acts for him
> who watches over those he loves,
> who gives strength to him who is on his water;
> he who stands under his counsel cannot commit any violation
> he who is guided by him cannot go astray.[49]

Ashurbanipal's retaliatory attack ended in disaster for the Egyptians. For the first time in its long history, Thebes was conquered, plundered, and reduced to ashes. The shock must have been all the greater as the Kushite ruler Tantamani had set himself up even more decidedly than his predecessors as the envoy of Amun. Perhaps that shock is one of the reasons why this source of political mythodynamics dried up for all time. No future pretenders to the throne would ever again wage war on Amun's behalf. Indeed, the Twenty-sixth Dynasty would discard any notion of "holy war" in favor of a strikingly secular style of self-representation.

The Assyrians changed the political complexion of Egypt. They replaced the twenty vassal kings with their agent, Psammetichus I, putting him in charge of all Egypt on condition that he abstain from rebellion of any kind. Thus at a stroke the Assyrians reestablished unity de jure, leaving it to Psammetichus to rebuild it de facto, which he did with considerable skill. Psammetichus' accession in 663 B.C.E.

signaled the beginning of the Late Period and the return to monocracy. In Year 9, in the first "reunification of the empire" to originate
in the north, he sent his daughter Nitocris to Thebes in a triumphal
procession so that she might be adopted by the God's Wives of Amun,
Shepenwepet II and Amenirdis II. In Thebes, the princess was
received by Mentuemhet, who had somehow contrived to weather the
conflicts between Assyrians and Kushites. Mentuemhet was confirmed
in his offices. But subsequently the "dictatorial" accumulation of
offices was systematically dismantled and cut back to a crisply administered centralist bureaucracy. The office of governor of the south was
uncoupled from that of mayor of Thebes and conferred on the majordomo of the God's Wife of Amun. The people appointed to this office
were from the north. Thus the classic monopolies of the state were
reestablished. The local militias that had sustained the various princedoms of the Third Intermediate Period were now placed back under
the supreme command of the king.[50] This feat was achieved by Psammetichus with the help of a mercenary force made up of Greeks,
Carians, Jews, and other foreigners. In 653, Psammetichus drove the
Assyrian garrisons out of the country and as far back as Ashdod
without any negative consequences for Egypt.

Psammetichus I died in 610. His successor, Necho II, is best
known for his exploits in Palestine. He killed King Josiah of Jerusalem,
who had barred his way near Megiddo (2 Kings 23:29), and substi-
tuted a man of his choice for Josiah's successor, Jehoahaz. Necho II
brought more Greeks into the country, built up a trading fleet with
their aid, and undertook the construction of an immense canal to
link the Red Sea with the Pelusiac branch of the Nile. Psammetichus
II, who came to the throne in 595 B.C.E., ruled for only six years and
was succeeded in 589 by his son Apries (the biblical Hophra). Apries
could not avert the fall of Jerusalem, which precipitated a mutiny in
distant Elephantine. The further course of Apries' rule was punctuated
by conflicts between the Greek mercenaries and the Egyptian army,
which put up a rival king, Amasis. In 570, Amasis defeated Apries'
mercenary forces at Momemphis. Apries himself fell in battle and was
buried in Sais with all ceremonial pomp. Although Amasis led a revolt
against the Greeks, he became the most cosmopolitan and philohel-
lenic king of his dynasty. He died in 526, shortly before the Persians
under Cambyses conquered Egypt in 525.

Discovering and Inventing the Past

THE SEVENTH CENTURY B.C.E. brought about a profound change in the Egyptians' consciousness of history. Starting with the legitimization propaganda of the Kushite rulers and quickly spreading through broad sections of the educated strata in Egypt, an entirely new relationship to the past and, with it, a new construction of cultural time emerged. Egypt developed an awareness of the immense depth of its history, and expressed that awareness in a great variety of artistic and literary forms. Inherited poetic, linguistic, iconic, or architectural forms were no longer simply perpetuated as something normative to which there was no alternative, but were consciously selected from a range of possible options. "Messages" thus acquire a new, reflexive dimension, through which allegiance to the past and to Egypt as a cultural (id)entity is asserted.

As we have seen, in Egypt recourse to models from the past had always been one of the central means of instituting cultural and political renewal after a break with tradition. Whenever the time came to revive a forgotten tradition or festival, to replace a cult image or make a cultic innovation, the archives were studied. Some kings explicitly laud their own archival work; some sayings in the *Book of the Dead* are marked as having been found by one king or another in the course of inspections or restoration work.[51] Examples abound: the kings of the early Twelfth Dynasty emulated the pyramid temples of the Sixth Dynasty, while Hatshepsut modeled her mortuary temple at Deir el-Bahri on that of Mentuhotep II. The texts placed in the burial chamber of Sesostrisankh, an official during the reign of Sesostris I (twentieth century B.C.E.), were very closely modeled on Unas' Pyramid Texts, while Hatshepsut drew on texts from the Twelfth Dynasty in her coronation inscription. Likewise, the marked inclination of the Twenty-second Dynasty to emulate the artistic style of the age of Amenophis III is an attempt to take up a tradition that dates from before the Ramesside age.

A clear distinction must be made, however, between this kind of conscious renewal across a break and instances of unbroken tradition, such as the uninterrupted use of the same texts in the cult. An impressive example of such liturgical continuity is a papyrus collection of cult recitations from the early Ptolemaic period (320–200 B.C.E.). An introductory note designates this collection as a copy of a manuscript from the age of Amenophis III (ca. 1400–1360 B.C.E.).[52] We might normally regard this historical reverence as a manipulation of the truth, a legend designed to bestow upon the text the authority of high old age—but study of the texts shows that the reference is an understatement and the collection is a great deal older even than it claims to be. Indeed, this very same combination of texts is also to be found on coffins of the early second millennium B.C.E., while the individual texts already appear in pyramids dating from the Sixth Dynasty (2400 B.C.E.). The transmission is astonishingly seamless. What we have here is a written liturgy carefully preserved across two thousand years and repeatedly rehearsed in the cult in exactly the same wording. Both forms—recourse to ancient models across time, and continuing use of the same texts and models—were present within Egyptian culture from the outset.

In the Ramesside age, a clear structure of center and periphery in literary tradition emerged, as well as the canonization of a group of classical authors selected as basic texts for instruction in schools.[53] In this period, one of the high priests of Ptah in Memphis was a son of Ramesses II called Khaemwaset, who qualifies as the first known antiquarian and conservationist in human history.[54] Numerous monuments at Giza and Saqqara bear evidence of recovery by him. Alongside his office as high priest, this prince must have been an indefatigable and extremely thorough restorer of ancient Memphis. He was clearly fascinated by the period in which Memphis was the capital of the land, a period that had survived in the form of countless imposing monuments, notably the three pyramids of the Fourth Dynasty, an epoch of the Old Kingdom dating back over a thousand years. For Khaemwaset, this epoch appeared as an ancient heritage of classical and unchallengeable greatness, a testimony to a normative past to be preserved at all costs as the epitome and exemplar of all things great, successful, and valid. Five hundred years after Khaemwaset, his personal fascination had turned into an essential element of the Egyptian zeitgeist.[55]

And yet, the historical consciousness of the Twenty-fifth and Twenty-sixth Dynasties, though dependent upon various traditional forms of reference to the past, was wholly different again, both qualitatively and quantitatively. References to the past now took place on a scale that was completely unprecedented in Egyptian history and that certainly merits being called a renaissance. Much more comprehensively than in the Ramesside age, Egypt now discovered its own antiquity and elevated it to the rank of a normative past. Almost the entire literate upper stratum—above all, the kings themselves—now began to emulate Prince Khaemwaset by visiting and copying the monuments of their forefathers. This wholesale return to the models of the past was tantamount to a cultural revolution, and it spread into every aspect of Egyptian life. It now became customary to give oneself a "beautiful name," reminiscent of names from the Old Kingdom, and to have oneself portrayed in the style and raiment of that age. Inscriptions on tombs and coffins were modeled on ancient Pyramid Texts, and written in a much purer Middle Egyptian than was used in the Kushite era. The copies were so stylistically accurate that individual blocks torn out of context were occasionally dated to the Fifth Dynasty[56] or the age of Amenophis III before the original locations were established.[57] In some cases there is still controversy as to whether particular items are from the Twelfth Dynasty or the Twenty-sixth.

The minute care expended on copying the style of the past in the artistic ateliers was also evident in the scriptoria of the temple libraries. There, during the Saite age, the foundations were laid for a tradition of philology that was later to come to full fruition in Alexandria. The various versions of the *Book of the Dead* were pored over with an exhaustive concern for authenticity, which extended not only to the original wording of the spells but also and above all to their order and completeness. Until the Saite Period, the papyri containing the *Book of the Dead* had been highly individual in form, choosing selectively from the total stock of spells and recomposing them into sequences as dictated by specific requirements. Now the scribes set about establishing a definitive edition, collating various manuscripts and recording variants in a clear process of canonization.[58] The Pyramid Texts stemming from this period are also of astounding quality. In those instances where they deviate from the Old Kingdom versions, the proposed revisions are invariably valuable amendments designed to keep the meaning of the text transparent.

In the eclecticism of its cultural forms, the Saite Period seems almost theatrical. One cannot quite escape the impression that enacting the past was more important than shaping the present. In a sense, what we have here is an adumbration of the "Egyptomania" of later ages, but in which the Egyptians themselves participated. If we take "Egyptomania" to mean enthusiasm for the formal idioms of Egyptian civilization donned like a costume by later ages, the Saite Period certainly displays elements of this kind of masquerade. Yet it is also true that the traditions invoked were not arbitrarily chosen, but were invariably the authoritative sources for a particular genre, topic, or location. The biographical inscriptions quote models not from the New or Old Kingdom but from the First Intermediate Period. Cultural identification was not with the bureaucratic ethos of the Old Kingdom, the loyalism of the Middle Kingdom, or the courtly society of the New Kingdom, but with the principle of the "patron," the self-made, self-accountable magnate who keeps his piece of the territory alive and well in times of hardship and crisis.

The conventional assessment of the Ethiopian-Saite renaissance is aptly summarized by the following remark: "The genuine root of archaism is the confusion of mythic primordiality with historical past. Egypt was alive as long as it harked back to its primal mythic foundations. The historical past, though it had the apparent advantage of being accessible to inquiry and recovery, was no substitute for the vitality and normative strength of the mythic tradition. All that the quest for authenticity revealed was outward forms, not living spirit."[59]

Nothing, however, could be further from a true appreciation of the historical significance this cultural revolution held for Egypt. In no sense are we dealing here with "confusion," but rather with a discovery of the historical past, which did not in any way signify a loss of the mythic dimension. Quite the contrary. Probably no epoch was so mythopoetically creative as the Late Period. A mentality now arises in Egypt that links the consciousness of an immense, documented (and thus historical) past with the presence of the gods, thereby anchoring all these historically real institutions, made venerable by their enormous age, in the foundations of a mythic prehistory.[60]

Egypt was not alone in this breakthrough of historical awareness. Other peoples of the ancient world went through a very similar process around the same time, exhibiting a variety of approaches to the restoration of their historical pasts. In Israel, the Exodus traditions formed the nucleus of a normative past and a comprehensive recapitulation of history. In Greece, Homer's texts were disseminated and advanced to the status of fundamental texts. Both of these cases present the codification of a past that was some five hundred years old. In Assyria, a comprehensive collection and philological edition of the entire literary tradition took place, leading to the conception of a "national library," an idea emulated by Pisistratus in Athens, and eventually leading to the library in Alexandria. The restoration of the "past," in the sense of a normative cultural idea, is anything but a sign of cultural decline. If there is "confusion" here at all, it is the product of literal-minded historicism, and that is something Egyptologists, and not Egypt, have to answer for.

In its quest for a normative past, Egypt could hardly have been in a more different situation from Israel, Greece, and Mesopotamia. The testimonies of the past were there, overwhelmingly immediate, visible, and accessible. There was no need for a codification of legendary memories. The peculiar conservatism of hieroglyphic script and the thoroughness of Egyptian school education kept the knowledge of the classical language and its seminal texts alive. These factors, together with the ongoing usage of archaic texts in cult, ensured that the monuments of the past were not only visible but also readable. All that was needed was an interest in receiving these messages; and it is precisely this interest that distinguishes the Ethiopian and Saite Period.

In the Saite age, the art of the past became the model to be copied to the fullest degree of perfection. The art of this period and of later epochs was not only archaizing, but more rule-governed, one might even say ritualized, than all earlier art. The pictographic nature of Egyptian art, its predilection for graphic formulae grounded in hieroglyphic script, asserted itself now as never before. Both aspects— the reference back to a Great Past and the increased normativity of artistic expression—shine through in Plato's famous account of Egyptian art. In his *Laws,* he suggests that in their temples the Egyptians had formulated the models or standard types (the Greek word is *schemata*) recognized and codified for all time as "good":

Long ago, apparently, they [the Egyptians] realized the truth of the principle we are putting forward only now, that the movements and the tunes which the children of the state are to practice in their rehearsals must be good ones. They compiled a list of them according to style, and displayed it in the temples. Painters and everyone else who represent movement of the body of any kind were restricted to these forms; modification and innovation outside this traditional framework were prohibited, and are prohibited even today, both in this field and in the arts in general. If you examine their art on the spot, you will find that ten thousand years ago (and I am not speaking loosely; I mean literally ten thousand), paintings and reliefs were produced that are no better and no worse than those of today, because the same artistic rules were applied in making them.[61]

This account gives us an inkling of the way the Egyptians themselves saw their own Late Period artistic practice and communicated this view to outsiders. Through the refractions of Plato's specific interests, we gain some insight into the way the Egyptians themselves may have conceived of the phenomenon of artistic canonization and fixation. Important first of all is the figure ten thousand, an exaggerated assessment also found in Herodotus, as is the notion that in this colossal stretch of time nothing had changed, that the Egyptians had succeeded in halting all development. Equally significant is the idea of a canonization of artistic idioms: add nothing, take nothing away, change nothing. By calling a halt to development, one maintains contact with original knowledge. The third important aspect of Plato's excursus is the centrality of the "art of the muses" in the Egyptian education system. Though Plato's account is naturally marked by his own ideas on education, it does underline the generally prescriptive character of art as a cultural grammar, a metatext of right forms and instruction, especially once we translate it away from the school sphere and into that of religious cult.

A glance at the countless so-called sculpture models—examples exist in all major museums—suffices to confirm Plato's claim that the Egyptians adhered to "schemata" and strict rules. The schemata he is referring to are certainly not the well-known rules of proportion that transform three-dimensional reality into two-dimensional representation.[62] What interests Plato is the perpetuation of a model in the sense of a foundational or iconic grammar of "well-formed" movements, attitudes, positions—in short, behavior. Plato transposes this "model" aspect from the artistic to the educational plane. But in the sphere of art, the sculpture models show what an orientation to models or "schemata" really means.

The aristocratic or elitist element of such "living in the past" is unmistakable. In his *Joseph* novels, Thomas Mann brilliantly foregrounds the social implications of cultural memory, showing how "living in citations" and adhering to behavioral models from the past could produce and intensify personal dignity.[63] In this sense, the archaism of the Late Period articulates an aristocratic cultural awareness in which the upper strata set themselves apart not only from the lower echelons of their own people but also as representatives of Egyptian civilization over and against Assyrians, Greeks, Jews, and Persians.[64]

In its cultivation of forgotten traditions, the Saite Period created a completely new formal idiom and generated the characteristic late-Egyptian identity of calmly assured, age-old cultural wisdom. The Egyptians of this period lived in the awareness that they were the inheritors of an immense past. They studied the archives, compiled king-lists and family trees, and knew the historical location of the astounding monuments of the past. They lived in a mnemonic dimension encompassing thousands of years, preserved in overwhelming array before their very eyes by pyramids and mastabas, sphinxes, obelisks, and stelae, all of which were illuminated down to the last chronological and historical detail in annals and lists, inscriptions and images. If it is true that the past is not simply present but has to be brought forth by retroactive reference, then we can say that no other period in Egyptian history had a past of such richness.

Shabaka's Memphite Manifesto

THE FIRST AND MOST IMPORTANT INSTANCE of such reference to the past dates from the age of King Shabaka. The text is known as the *Memphite Theology,* and its theme is the glorification of the city of Memphis. The political program of the Ethiopian kings of the Twenty-fifth Dynasty included the restoration of Memphis not only architecturally but also intellectually and religiously. Memphis was to be the capital of an Egypt that saw itself as the rebirth of the Old Kingdom. The decision in favor of Memphis was in itself an act of renovation, a reawakening of the ancient past. The text in question is an inscription on a basalt block that claims to be the rendering of an ancient papyrus inscription. In the title, Shabaka explains what prompted this rewriting:

His Majesty had this book written anew in the house of his father Ptah. His Majesty had found it as a work of his ancestors, worm-eaten, and one did not know it from beginning to end. So His Majesty had it rewritten so that it is more beautiful than it was before.

The stone was exhibited in the British Museum as early as 1805. A century elapsed before the meaning of the inscription began to be deciphered, and a number of formidable riddles remain to this day. Not only is the text extremely difficult, but the block itself, which was used as a millstone, is much defaced, so much that the entire central section of the inscription has been lost. The most important problem, the dating, has yet to be resolved. Earlier, controversy centered on the question of whether it came from the First/Second or from the Fifth/Sixth Dynasty.[65] More recently, convincing evidence has been adduced suggesting that part if not all of the work dates from the Twenty-fifth Dynasty.[66] The margin of error is thus no less than twenty-five hundred years. Yet, whatever the share of the Twenty-fifth Dynasty in the actual composition of this work, there is no doubt about the productive engagement with the text in that period. Earlier, I quoted parts of the *Memphite Theology* as instances of the mythological commemoration of the unification of the empire. I draw on it here as a testimony to the strong and novel relationship to the past instituted by the Kushites. To me, both readings of the text seem appropriate. The work has a great deal to tell us about the remembered past, and about the "present" in which such memory gained significance—that is, the needs and conditions that prompted the quest for and invention of the past.

The subject of the text is Memphis, its mythic and political significance as the location where creation emerged from the primal waters and as the seminal locus of pharaonic kingship. An understanding of the *Memphite Theology* requires that we bear in mind the close connection between the Egyptian ideas of creation and of rule. The oldest Egyptian document subscribing to the cosmology of Heliopolis describes the creator-god Atum ("the Universe") as both unfolding in the world and creating it. In parallel to this process, at once transitive and intransitive, rulership emerges, being handed down from one generation of gods to the next until in the fifth generation Horus inherits rule and henceforth incarnates himself in every ruling pharaoh as god of historical kingship. Egyptian cosmogonies are at the same time invariably "cratogonies," combining an account of the birth of the world with a report on the emergence of rule.

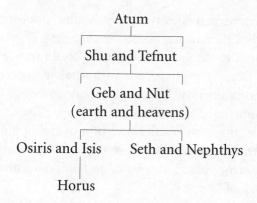

The *Memphite Theology* supplements this family tree in a highly significant way:

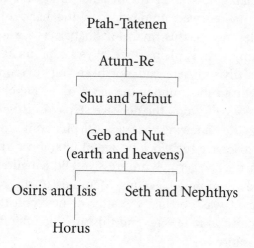

The *Memphite Theology* both builds on the source from Heliopolis and seeks to outdo it. Thus scholars have attempted to date the text to a period in which Heliopolis and Memphis might have vied for supremacy as the primal locus of creation and rule. From this perspective, the Late Period would hardly qualify. Here we would expect rivalry among Tanis, Thebes, Memphis, and possibly also Bubastis. This train of thought prompted Kurt Sethe to reconstruct a prehistoric "kingdom of Heliopolis" succeeded by an early historical "kingdom of Memphis," while others located the text in the Fifth/Sixth Dynasty, the first flowering of the Heliopolitan sun cult. But this line of argument misses the point. Quite independently of historical and political considerations, the theogony of Heliopolis, from the Old Kingdom to the systems of the Greco-Roman temples, played the role of a "Great Tradition," an authoritative, interregional, pan-Egyptian cosmo-cratogony. Every local cosmogony was bound to take its bearings from this universally valid theology. The tension between the unassailable, universally valid tradition of Heliopolis and the various "minor" traditions of religious centers such as Thebes, Memphis, Elephantine, Hermopolis, Esna, Edfu, and Sais determined the entire religious history of Egypt.

The *Memphite Theology* begins by proclaiming Ptah-Tatenen the primordial deity, self-created creator of the gods, and ruler over the unified kingdom as king of Lower and Upper Egypt. Omitting any mention of the following generations in the cosmo-cratogonic process, the text jumps to the legal dispute between Horus and Seth, a myth that explains how, after the original unity, the division of the kingdom and its renewed unification in the hand of Horus came about. The relevance of this myth for Shabaka, who was confronted by a divided kingdom, is plain to see. Piye's exploits had, if anything, reinforced this division. He had not been out to reunify Egypt but to thwart a reunification under the aegis of Tefnakht. It was Piye's brother, Shabaka, who took the decisive steps toward ending the Libyan polyarchy and renewing the classical pharaonic monocracy. His objective was to revive the glorious age of pharaonic kingship, visibly represented in the staggeringly impressive Old Kingdom monuments in and around Memphis. Elevating Memphis to the royal capital of a reunified Egypt was not just a matter of new construction; it was also a feat of cultural renewal—and this provided the impetus for the ensuing renaissance.

Following the foundation of Memphis as the residence of Horus, the crowned ruler of reunified Egypt, the text describes the burial of Osiris and with it the origins of the Memphite Giza-Saqqara necropolis:

That is the place [where the beautiful burial] of Osiris in the
    house of Sokaris
[was prepared] . . . Nephthys and Isis in Busiris,
for Osiris had drowned in his water.
Isis and Nephthys looked out, they saw him, and grabbed him.
Horus commanded Isis and Nephthys:

take hold of him, prevent him from drowning.
Horus to Isis and Nephthys. To be spoken: Hurry, grab him . . .
Isis and Nephthys to Osiris. To be spoken: We have come to
   grab you . . .
they turned their heads at the right time.
And so they brought him to the shore.
He entered into the secret gates
in the holiness of the lords of eternity
in the wake of him who rises in the land of light,
on the paths of Re in the "Great Throne" [Memphis].
He entered the palace,
he joined the gods,
Tatenen, Ptah, lord of the years.
And so Osiris arrived in the earth in the royal fortress
on the north side of this land where he had arrived.
But his son Horus appeared as king of Upper Egypt,
appeared as king of Lower Egypt
in the embrace of his father Osiris
together with the gods who were before him and behind him.[67]

This passage claims the tomb of Osiris for Memphis, whereas the Great Tradition locates it at Abydos. The proliferation of sacred locations was unproblematic in the Late Period. Every temple celebrating the "Osiris mysteries" contained an Osirian tomb. In the New Kingdom, the Memphite Sokar festival, which celebrated the annual death, mummification, burial, and resurrection of Sokar-Osiris, developed into a religious festival observed all over Egypt and attained the status of a Great Tradition. Abydos was the "Mecca" for pilgrims, but the Memphite Sokar cult was also celebrated in Thebes and finally in all other major cult centers, where it became a festival dedicated to the burial of Osiris. The passage cited above cannot be any older than the New Kingdom, a dating supported by such motifs as the "holiness of the lords of eternity" and by the interpretation of the tomb as the nocturnal "path" of the sun, an idea central to the royal tombs of the New Kingdom.[68]

The next verses revolve around the "royal fortress" and the reconciliation between Horus and Seth. Though fragmentary, they do show the central status of "Memphis." After a major gap, the second section begins, devoted to the relation between Ptah and Atum, the origin of the cosmo-cratogonic genealogy. This Memphite creation story is one of the very few Egyptian texts dealing with the subject of creation in a narrative form.

The gods that originated from Ptah/became Ptah:[69]

Ptah on the Great Throne	[...]
Ptah Nun	The father who [begat] Atum
Ptah Naunet	The mother who bore Atum
Ptah-Wer	That is heart and tongue of the Ennead
[...]	[...] everything ... who bore the gods
[...]	[...] who bore the gods
[...]	[...]
[...]	[... Nefer]tem at the nose of Re, day by day.

originated through the heart as symbol of Atum,
originated through the tongue as a symbol of Atum,
being great and powerful.[70]

This unfortunately very fragmentary text deals with the origin of the Ogdoad, the eight deities who in Hermopolitan theology personify eight aspects of the preexistent primordial condition, from Ptah, who thus figures as the transcendent unity preceding and underlying preexistence. The conscious ambivalence of the term *ḫpr m*, which can mean either "originate from" or "turn into," is also found in a Ramesside hymn to Amun-Re:

The Eight were your first manifestation
that you perfect these to a unity.[71]
Your body was concealed among the primal ancients,
because you kept yourself concealed as Amun at the head of the
    gods.[72]

Amun "develops" into the Ogdoad, and "perfects" them into a unity, the relation of Eight to One being conceived of both as an unfolding and as a contraction.

But Ptah transferred [his strength]
to the gods and their *kas*

by means of this heart through which Horus originated from
  Ptah,
by means of this tongue through which Thoth originated from
  Ptah.

It came to pass that heart and tongue gained power over all
  other parts
on the basis of the teaching that it [the heart] is in every body
  and it [the tongue] in every mouth
of all gods, humans,
animals, insects, and all living things,
the heart thinking and the tongue commanding whatever they
  desire.

In the guise of tongue and heart, a portion of Ptah's original creative
power remains in all living things that have come forth from him.
An anthropological discourse now begins:

His Ennead stood before him
as teeth, that is the seed of Atum,
and as lips, that is the hands of Atum.
Verily, the Ennead of Atum originated
through his seed and through his fingers.
But the Ennead is in truth teeth and lips
in this mouth of him who thought up the names of all things,
from whom Shu and Tefnut came forth, he who created the
  Ennead.

This section of the *Theology* has always been interpreted as a
polemical engagement with Heliopolis. However, it seems to me
much more convincing to read it as a commentary, in which the
ancient, supraregionally valid teachings are specifically related to
Memphis. The "seed" and "hands" of Amun, by which in an act of
self-begetting he brought forth Shu and Tefnut, are interpreted as
"teeth" and "lips," forming the frame for the tongue that creates
everything by naming it:

That the eyes see, the ears hear,
and the nose breathes air is in order to make report to the heart.

This it is that makes all knowledge originate.
The tongue it is that repeats what is thought by the heart.

The process of creation is here conceived in bodily terms. "Phallus" and "hand"—the traditional physical symbols of creativity—are represented as "teeth" and "lips." The genuinely creative organs are heart and tongue. As the Egyptians made no strict distinction between "body" and mind/spirit, knowledge and language are also understood as bodily phenomena. Knowledge originates in the heart on the basis of the perceptions reported to it. The knowledge formed in the heart is communicated by the tongue.

And thus were all gods born,
that is Atum and his Ennead.
But all divine speech [hieroglyphs] originated
from that which was thought up by the heart and commanded
    by the tongue.
And thus were all *kas* created and the *hemuset* determined,
which bring forth all food and all offering meats by this word,
[the word invented by the heart and commanded by the tongue].
[And thus is *ma'at* given to him] who does what is loved,
[and *isfet* to him] who does what is hated.
And thus is life given to the peaceable
and death given to the criminal.
And thus were all trades created and all arts,
the action of the arms and the walking of the legs,
the movement of all limbs in accordance with the instruction
of these words that were thought up by the heart and uttered by
    the tongue and provide for all things.

Thus it was that Ptah was called "He who created all things and
    caused the gods to originate,"
for he is Tatenen who formed the gods,
from whom all offering meats and food came forth,
all offerings to the gods and all perfect things.
Thus it was found and recognized
that his power is greater than that of all other gods.

And so Ptah was well pleased after he had created all things
and all hieroglyphs,
after he had formed the gods,

after he had created their towns
and founded their nomes,
after he had endowed their offering cakes
and established their chapels,
after he had created their bodies [= cult images] in their
    likeness, such that they were content.
And thus the gods entered their bodies
of every kind of wood and mineral,
all kinds of clay and all other things that grow on him
from whom they originated.
And thus assembled around him all gods and their *kas*,
content and united with the lord of the Two Lands.

This is the most elaborate Egyptian account of creation by the Word, and it differs from the biblical account in two ways. The first is the role of the heart, that is, the planned conception of creation—an idea absent from the Bible. The second is the role of script, the hieroglyphs, mentioned on two occasions. These two points are closely related. For what the heart thinks up are not the names of things but their "concepts" and their "forms." Hieroglyphic script is a rendering of the forms and relates to the concepts by way of those forms. The tongue vocalizes the concepts "thought up" by the heart and given outward and visible form by hieroglyphic script:

But all hieroglyphs originated
from that which was thought up [conceived of] by the heart and
    commanded by the tongue.

Ptah is the god of artists and craftsmen, the one who endows things with their "design," their immutable form, depicted by the written signs. Thus Thoth, the god of the "tongue," is also the god of hieroglyphic script. He is able to transform the thoughts of the heart into spoken and written language. Creation is an act of articulation—conceptually, iconically, phonetically. The written signs originate at the same time as the things they stand for and the names they bear:

And so Ptah was well pleased after he had created all things
and all hieroglyphs.

The totality of creation is encompassed in the term "all things and all hieroglyphs." If the distinction between a sphere of original Forms

(Ideas) and a world of infinitely reproduced Images is a principle of Plato's philosophy, then the Egyptian division of creation expresses a primal, pretheoretical Platonism. The hieroglyphs are the Forms of the things that constitute the totality of the real world. Egyptian "hieroglyphic" thinking presents a relation between thing and written sign similar to that between thing and concept in Greek philosophy. When Ptah conceives of the Ideas of things, he at the same time invents the script that Thoth has only to record, in the same way that, taking the form of the tongue, Thoth utters the thoughts of the heart. Thus an onomasticon, a list of words arranged not alphabetically but in an order reflecting the structure of reality, is described as a catalogue of "all things that exist: what Ptah created, what Thoth copied down."[73] Thoth, the god of script, only has to find, not invent, what is inherent in the structure of things. In his *Mysteries of the Egyptians*, the Neoplatonist Iamblichus perceptively identifies the latent Platonism of hieroglyphic thinking in his interpretation of Egyptian script as an imitation of divine "demiurgy": "For they [the Egyptians], endeavoring to represent the productive principle of the universe and the creative function of the gods, exhibit certain images as symbols of mystic, occult and invisible conceptions, in a similar manner as Nature (the productive principle), in her peculiar way, makes a likeness of invisible principles through symbols in visible forms."[74]

The collaboration between Ptah, who creates all things, and Thoth, who records them, is reminiscent of the collaboration between God and Adam in Paradise. God creates living things and "Adam gave names to all cattle, and to the fowl of the air, and to every beast of the field" (Genesis 2:20). Adam's act of naming and Thoth's act of recording fulfill the same function of linking things and words. And as this is creation by the Word, Adam and Thoth both "read" from the created things what they then utter or record.

Where do these considerations take us? It is evident to me that Shabaka's inscription combines various source texts. Some of the dramatic passages of the *Memphite Theology* may date back as far as the Middle or Old Kingdom, but the section on the creation of the world cannot be any older than the Ramesside age. The history of these ideas can be traced very exactly in the hundreds of hymns that have come down to us. Before the New Kingdom, everything coming forth from words did so through wordplay, without any serious intention.

Language figured as one "excretion" of the creator, alongside many others. Not until the Eighteenth Dynasty does the idea of intentional creation by the word emerge. There, however, it is restricted to the creation of the gods: the gods come forth from the mouth, that is, from the words of the creator. Only in the Nineteenth Dynasty does evidence appear for the idea that the entire world originates from the divine word. In the Memphite texts, the heart of the creator, as the organ of mental conception, plays the central role.[75] But these texts make hardly any mention of hieroglyphic script. This element is peculiar to the text we are looking at; and at the same time it is its most "modern" feature. This understanding of hieroglyphic script can only have emerged at a time when hieroglyphs had acquired the status of a purely sacral medium: in the Late Period. The assessment of hieroglyphic script as a sacred, priestly script in which only sacral texts are written and into which only priests are initiated first appears in the work of Greek authors. Though usually dismissed as a misconception, this idea faithfully reflected the image that Egyptian priests had of their script systems, one that they were eager to communicate to the Greeks. Indeed, not until the Late Period did hieroglyphic script develop into a kind of "thing-script" whose repertory of signs was coextensive with the totality of things in the world.

The linguistic archaism of the Late Period springs from the same ideological motives as its artistic counterpart. And again, a Greek text interprets this archaism in a way that corresponds very closely, in both concept and wording, to Plato's theory of art. In his *Mysteries of the Egyptians,* Iamblichus connects the Egyptian imperative (or prohibition) "Thou shalt not change anything" to language and religious texts. The specific reference is to the preeminence of ancient tongues like Babylonian and Egyptian as holy languages:

> For the gods have made known that of the Sacred Nations, like the Egyptians and likewise the Assyrians, the entire dialect is suitable for sacred places. Hence, we believe that we ought to address our communications in speech native to the gods; and because such a mode of speaking is primitive and ancient . . . we have always preserved the law of the tradition till time present inviolate. . . . And it is necessary with the ancient prayers, as with the sacred places of asylum, to preserve them inviolate and in

the same manner, neither taking anything from them nor adding anything to them from any other source.

The Greeks, Iamblichus continues, are besotted with novelty: "They have no ballast in them and they do not preserve what they received from anybody. But the foreign priests are steadfast in their customs and continue firmly with the same words, for which reason, making use of the words grateful to them, they are themselves beloved of the gods. Nevertheless, to change them in any way is not lawful for any human being."[76]

The idea of a "sacred language" corresponds to the Egyptian term "words of god" (divine speech), which covers both hieroglyphic script and the specific form of Middle Egyptian written in that script. The cultivation of the ancient texts, the unswerving adherence to the same cult liturgies for century upon century, and the equally rigid conformity to the original graphic form of hieroglyphic script all accord well with Iamblichus' argument that the fundamental idea was one of sacral communication with the gods, that care in the preservation of the form was dictated by the fear that the sacred texts might otherwise become "unreadable" for the gods.

The Shabaka text is a monument of cultural renewal that is at its most forward-looking in its recourse to the most ancient retrievable models. The ideational world of the *Memphite Theology* shaped the theological systems of the Late Period temples; the "trinity" of thought, word, and written sign became the basis of a priestly theory of hieroglyphs that determined the western view of hieroglyphic script all the way to Champollion.

The *Memphite Theology* must be seen in the context of a comprehensive program of religious renewal aimed at nothing less than the restoration of the holiness of the land and its sacred centers. The traces and reflections of this reform are best studied in Thebes itself. There the Kushite rulers set about building with alacrity, and the construction program was itself bound up with the reorganization of Theban religious festivals. The development of Thebes into a sacred landscape is most clearly evident in the Theban necropolis. The valley of Deir el-Bahri was first elevated to a sacred location by Mentuhotep II, who had his mortuary temple built there. In the Eighteenth Dynasty, Queen Hatshepsut took up this tradition by closely modeling her mortuary temple on the five-hundred-year-old predecessor and expanding a Hathor sanctuary situated between the two into a temple in its own right. This Hathor sanctuary now became the destination of the newly conceived Festival of the Valley procession. The old processional route was renovated, and the mortuary palaces of the Twenty-fifth and Twenty-sixth Dynasties were built in alignment with this route. The Asasif valley for the processional route, and Deir el-Bahri as the destination of the festive procession, thus became sacred sites of the first importance. In Thebes, as in Memphis, we see the traces of a renewal and reinvention of traditions that are bound up with the sacred nature of a given site. In Memphis, these traditions concerned the cosmogonies of the Ramesside Ptah theology and the ancient role of Memphis as "the scales of the Two Lands" in the dispute between Horus and Seth and as the first capital of the country. The theologies and festivals of the sacred sites were renewed in a bid to revive their religious aura. But in contrast to the New Kingdom and the Third Intermediate Period, the aim of renewal was not so much the accumulation of riches through donations to the temples as the accumulation of "holiness," of religious meaning.

The most important medium of resanctification was the religious festival, wherein space and time, geography and chronology entered into a remarkable synthesis. The key text codifying festival culture for the Late Period was the *Book of Traversing Eternity,* which probably dates from the Saite Period.[77] It is a liturgy for the dead, a cultic recitation addressed to the dead person and wishing him participation in thirty-nine Theban, thirty-nine Abydenian, and seventy-eight (that is, two times thirty-nine) Memphite and other festivals. As such, it is a veritable festival calendar. It is not, as has frequently been thought, a guide to the afterworld, but to this world—more specifically, to its sacred dates and sites. The Egyptians of the Late Period no longer sought divine presence in the afterworld but rather in the religious centers of the land and, above all, of their own towns. And so, after an interval of centuries, monumental tombs started springing up again. With their tombs, the Egyptians remained present in their towns and held communion with succeeding generations as fellow citizens. In the inscriptions on these tombs, the idea of the town as the locus of a social membership that transcends death plays a significant role.[78] The festival of the local god was the most important occasion for visiting the tombs, for the congress of the living and the dead. Thus the local deity was regarded (as a late piece of wisdom literature has it) as "he by whose command are the life and death of the people."[79]

What we have here is an attempt not so much to secularize the belief in the hereafter, but to sacralize the here and now. The town becomes a sacred place, the land of Egypt a holy land—indeed, the "holiest of lands"—to the degree to which it becomes the focus of Egyptian hopes for the afterlife. In late Egyptian thinking, all Egypt transmutes into a *templum mundi*.

Taharqa's Annus Mirabilis

THE STELA DATING FROM YEAR 6 of Taharqa's reign is one of the most impressive royal inscriptions of the pharaonic tradition, distinguished for the vigor of its mythic imagination. The events of Year 6 (an exceptionally high Nile inundation, a deluge in Nubia, the king's accession to the throne after six years of coregency with Shebitku, the visit of the queen mother to Egypt) are described in detail and given a religious and mythological interpretation. The text begins with a general survey of the king's virtues and the benefits they have conferred:

His Majesty was one beloved of god,
he spent day and night
seeking good works for the gods,
rebuilding temples that had crumbled,
restoring their images as they were,
building their storehouses and equipping their offering tables,
bringing them offerings of all things
and making them offering tables of electrum and silver.
The heart of His Majesty was now content
doing good works for them day by day.
The land was bounteous in his time
as it had been at the time of the All-Lord.
Everyone slept until bright morning,
no one said "If only I had!"
Ma'at was introduced throughout the lands,
isfet was nailed to the floor.

The inscription's praise may sound formulaic, but I know of no other text that so clearly and explicitly links the king's role as restorer of the cults to the myth of the Golden Age. The piety of the king bestows blessings on the land, and these blessings are interpreted as a return to the primal condition, when the creator himself ruled over creation. History is consciously desired and experienced as a return.

Miracles occurred in the time of His Majesty
in Year 6 of his coronation
such as had not been seen since the time of the ancestors,
because his father Amun-Re loved him so dearly.

His Majesty asked for a flood
from his father Amun-Re, lord of Karnak,
to prevent drought in his time.
And everything came about
that was uttered by the lips of His Majesty, on the spot.

There came the time of the rains, and the Nile rose
in all places day by day.
It rose for many days by a cubit, day by day.
It overflowed its banks to the mountains of Upper Egypt
and flooded the hills of Lower Egypt.
The land lay sluggish in the primal waters;
one could not distinguish land from river.
It rose to a height of 21 cubits, 1 handbreadth, 2½ fingers at the
    quay of Thebes.
Then His Majesty called for the annals of the forefathers,
to read of the floods of their time, and nothing comparable was
    found in them.

The nilometer marks at the quay of Thebes have been preserved, and they do indeed record the highest water level known in all antiquity. Some decades earlier, under Osorkon III, there had been a somewhat less serious inundation that caused major havoc and was regarded as a disaster. The king had besought Amun to avert the flood.

The next "miracle" has a causal connection with the first but is given a section to itself:

But the heavens rained in Nubia
so that the mountains sparkled from end to end.
Everyone in Nubia had an abundance of all things;
Egypt was in fine festivity.

They praised god for His Majesty's sake.
His Majesty was overjoyed
at what his father, Amun, had done for him
and had offerings made to all gods—bulls and birds, bread and
   beer,
in the fullness of joy at what his father had done for him.

At this point in the account, Taharqa inserts a reflective, summarizing passage:

And so His Majesty said: My father, Amun-Re of Karnak,
has performed four beautiful miracles for me in one single year,
in Year 6 of my appearance as king,
such as have not been seen since the time of the ancestors.
The flood came like a cattle thief
and flooded this whole land.
No record was there of any such thing since time immemorial,
no one said: I have heard something like this from my father.
It [=the flood] made the entire harvest good for me,
for it killed the rats and snakes therein
and prevented the locusts from devouring it
and the south wind from reaping it.
I brought into the countless barns,
Upper Egyptian and Lower Egyptian grain
and all grain that grows on the earth.

As we have so far encountered only two miracles, the flood and the rains (unless the extermination of pests and the absence of hot southerly winds count as miracles in their own right), the other two miracles must be hidden away in the following narrative, which recounts events of a quite different nature:

But I had come from Nubia together with the brothers of the
   king.
His Majesty had demanded that I should be with him
because he preferred me to all his brothers and children
and I was distinguished before all of them by him.
The hearts of the notables turned to me,
and love of me filled the hearts of all people.
I received the crown in Memphis

after the falcon had flown away to heaven.
My father, Amun, had commanded me
to put all lands and all foreign lands under the soles of my feet:
in the south as far as Retehu-Qebet,
in the north as far as Qebeh Hor [in the sense of "ultima
    Thule"],
in the east as far as the rising of the sun,
in the west as far as its setting.

[But she was abiding] in Nubia, the sister of the king, sweet of
    love,
the Queen Mother Abala, she lives.
But I had gone away from her as a youth of twenty,
when I went to Lower Egypt to His Majesty.
She voyaged downstream to see me after long years.
She found me on the throne of Horus
after I had received the crowns of Re,
after the two crown serpents had united on my head
and all gods protected my body.
She rejoiced beyond all measure when she saw the beauty of His
    Majesty,
as when Isis beheld her son Horus,
appearing on the throne of his father, Osiris,
after having been a boy
in the nest at Khemmis.
Thereupon Upper and Lower Egypt and all foreign lands
bowed their heads before this Queen Mother.
They were in festivity beyond all measure,
their old together with their young,
and sang to this Queen Mother a song of rejoicing:

Isis, she has conceived Horus,
as the Queen Mother has united with her son.
O King of Upper and Lower Egypt, Taharqa, who lives eternal
    among the gods,
you will endure, living for ever
by that which your father Amun commands to your keeping,
the active god who loves those who love him
and knows those who keep faith with him,
who wills that your mother unite with you in peace

to contemplate your beauty, that he has created for you.
You live and are healthy,
as Horus lives for his mother, Isis,
enduring, on the throne of Horus,
for ever and ever.

What astonishes in this text is that such an event—the journey of a queen mother to Lower Egypt, and the meeting between mother and son after many years—should have been eternalized on a stela. Even more astounding is the interpretation of this meeting in the light of the Horus-Isis myth. The celebration of this reunion as a mythic event immediately calls to mind Thomas Mann's conception of a "life lived in myth" or "in quotations," the "following in the footprints of the past" that informs contemporary action and present events with meaning and splendor because one experiences them as the reenactment of primal mythical forms and norms. Mann's juxtaposition of Jacob's "ceremoniousness" and Joseph's ludic, eclectic attitude to mythology is a fruitful way to understand the difference between the Twenty-fifth and Twenty-sixth Dynasties' relation to the past and that of their precursors. Naturally the Kushites trod more self-consciously in the tracks of mythology than had their Egyptian predecessors, because the myths were less self-evident, less "second nature" to them. They first had to appropriate the Egyptian "primal forms and norms" for themselves. The Saites, for their part, had to restore Egyptian tradition and culture after what was generally felt to be a traumatic break. The history of ideas is a history of reception. And yet it makes a crucial difference whether a people simply carries on in a tradition or consciously and explicitly links itself with traditions of past times; such was the situation of the Twenty-fifth and Twenty-sixth Dynasties.

The Cult of the Past

THE ARCHAISM OF THIS AGE, with its changed view of history and its novel construction of cultural time, also generated new forms of religious life: festivities and rites that related to time in a highly marked way, to time unfolded into past, present, and future. We see this change most clearly in a festal custom that became prominent in this period, if it was not, indeed, actually invented in the Twenty-fifth and Twenty-sixth Dynasties: I am referring to the cult of the "ancestor gods."

The ancestor gods were dead gods, and as such received a veritable mortuary cult. They embodied the depth of time, the incipient awareness of which developed during this epoch. They were gods of the past, or more precisely of what came before the past, the truly and everlastingly completed past, the mythic primordial age that brought forth the foundations for the present. The celebrants of the cult of the ancestor gods were aware of being separated from that past, and their awareness expressed itself in cultic acts of remembrance for the dead.

The Theban version of this cult was the Decade Festival. The god Amun-in-Luxor—a statue carried by priests—crossed the Nile every ten days from Luxor to Medinet Habu to bring a libation for the ancestor gods. The destination of this procession was not the mortuary temple of Ramesses III but the small Eighteenth Dynasty temple that he appended as an annex to his own huge temple site. In the Twenty-fifth Dynasty, the relative stature of the two temples reverses. By means of constant addition and conversion, the small temple gradually took on huge dimensions and soon became the most significant cult center on the western side. The Divine Adoratrices had their tombs built in its temple court. The Egyptian name of the site, Djamut (Coptic: Djeme), became the name of the whole region, transcribed by the Greeks as "Thebai."

Amun-in-Luxor performed this mortuary cult as the embodiment of a filial role normally associated with the king. In the Late Period the figure of the one god, Amun, split into three generations. The state-god of Karnak was joined by the deceased primal form Amun-Kematef, the preexistent primeval god, "who has completed his time," and by the filial form of Amun-in-Luxor. This trinity had a demonstrably temporal character. Kematef was the god of the accomplished past, Amun-in-Luxor the god of the periodically self-renewing present. In the classical system of Egyptian religion, the latter role would have belonged to the king, who embodied the self-rejuvenating, constantly recurring presence of the divine. But the new distinction between a father form and a son form of the divine essentially transposed certain central functions of the classical concept of the king into the world of the gods.

Though the king still bore his divine titles, he now only played the role of a god—a god who would be there even without him, a god whom the king no longer incarnated. The roles formerly distributed between gods and king were now allotted completely to the world of the gods, and the king could only participate by identifying with the god who had taken over his role.

The paradigmatic shift of religious meaning from political theology to the temple cult is evident in the transformed figure of Amun. In the New Kingdom, the temple of Luxor and the annual Luxor feast were the site and the occasion for the cultic affirmation of the king as son of god. Luxor was the place where the king was symbolically begotten by Amun and recognized as his son. This begetting and recognition were ritually performed in connection with the coronation and repeated every year.[80] Naturally, Amun had played the part of the father in this festival play about the birth of the god-king. But now he was invested in the role of son as well and enacted it in a separate festival that took him to the western side of Thebes every ten days to perform the mortuary offerings to his deceased divine ancestors.

This festival, too, had an analogy in the New Kingdom: the Festival of the Valley, which was closely connected to the Luxor feast. In the Luxor feast the king celebrated his filiality vis-à-vis the god Amun; in the Festival of the Valley he celebrated his filiality vis-à-vis his dynastic forebears. In the Luxor festivity the king proceeded to Luxor in the company of Amun, Mut, and Khonsu of Karnak to have his divine filiality affirmed in the temple of Amun; in the Festival of the Valley he proceeded in the same company from Karnak to the mortuary temples of his ancestors, on the western side of Thebes, to assure himself of their blessings as the legitimate son of his bodily ancestors.

From now on, this complex festival culture connecting heaven, the earth, and the world of the dead was a preserve of the gods. The symbolism of rule was replaced by a symbolism of time. Dead, living, and future gods communicated on a cultic plane and thus kept the world in motion.

In the Greco-Roman Period, this model, developed by the Twenty-fifth and Twenty-sixth Dynasties in Thebes, became part of every major temple site. Now each center had not only its "Medinet Habu" but also its "Luxor temple," a cultic site of the dead ancestor gods combined with a "birth house," the festive scene of the annual rebirth of the filial form of god.

PART SIX

Egypt under the Persians and Greeks

Reproduction from the Tomb of Petosiris
Dachla (Greco-Roman Period)
(from J. Osing et al., Denkmäler der Oase Dachla, *Mainz, 1982,*
pl. 27)

24

HISTORICAL OUTLINE

In 525 B.C.E. Cambyses conquered Egypt. Throughout the fifth century, Egypt remained a satrapy of the Persian empire under the rule of Darius I, Xerxes, Artaxerxes I, and Darius II. The Persians had an entirely different style of ruling from the Assyrians, whose policy had been to obligate the local power holders as vassals. Where such power holders did not exist, the Assyrians "invented" chiefs who acted as middlemen within the administrative system. Thus the leaders of the Libyan military aristocracy became the partners of the Assyrians, and Mentuemhet and other Middle and Upper Egyptian officials were made equivalent to them in station. Though the Twenty-sixth Dynasty rulers contrived to transform the feudal structure of the Assyrians into a bureaucratic system, they were unable to entirely expunge either the Libyan principalities or their memory. The feudal structure lived on as a "subtext," ultimately resurfacing in the fourth century B.C.E. The Persians themselves might also have formed an alliance with this military elite; but they chose, instead, a different elite: the priesthood. By that choice, the Persians accepted the cultic/ideological role of pharaonic kingship with all its titles.[1] To legitimize themselves in Egyptian eyes, they assumed the filial role vis-à-vis the gods, engaging in unremitting activity on their behalf: temples were built, expanded, and renovated, cult images created, priestly positions multiplied, offering tables furnished with meats, festivals organized, oracles questioned and obeyed, and sacred animals looked after, buried, and enthroned. And all this activity had to be published and eternalized via inscriptions. If a pharaoh played his role well, it made little difference whether he was Libyan, Persian, or Macedonian; trouble set in only if one of them played his role badly. This was precisely the criticism leveled at Cambyses.

As we shall see, there must have been an element of truth to Cambyses' bad reputation, though a fair amount of it can probably be attributed to later legends forming at the time when the Persians began neglecting their religious duties.[2] Xerxes and Artaxerxes I, for example, never set foot in Egypt, leaving government to the satraps. Only at this juncture was Persian rule experienced as alien rule, with the upshot that it was shaken off, albeit briefly. The years 460–455 B.C.E. thus witnessed an anti-Persian revolt organized by Inaros and Amyrtaeus, two descendants of Libyan dynasties in league with the Athenians. The anti-Persian stories recorded by Herodotus date from this period. Herodotus accuses Cambyses of slaying the Apis bull, but a stela and a sarcophagus from Cambyses' sixth regnal year clearly document the proper ritual burial of the sacred animal. Moreover, Cambyses' successor Darius I built the great Amun temple at the oasis of el-Khargeh; its decorations present the earliest instance of a theological compendium. In these matters, Cambyses and Darius drew on the advice and assistance of a highly placed Egyptian who instructed them in their pharaonic dignities and duties.

The statue of the physician Udjahorresnet in the Vatican collection at Rome was probably one of the pieces brought back from Egypt by the emperor Hadrian. In its inscriptions, Udjahorresnet reports on his career.[3]

> The Great King of All Foreign Lands, Cambyses, came to Egypt,
> the foreigners of all foreign lands being with him.
> In its entirety did he gain mastery of this land, they setting
> themselves down therein.
> He was the Great Ruler of Egypt and the Great King of All
> Foreign Lands,
> His Majesty handing over to me the office of Chief Physician,
> having caused me to be beside him as Companion and
> Controller of the Palace,
> when I had made his royal titulary, in his throne name of
> "Descendant of Re."
> And I caused him to know the greatness of Sais, which is the
> seat of Neith, the great, the god's mother who gave birth to
> Re,

and who was the initiator of birth after there had been no birth,
and the lore about the meaning of the temple of Neith:
it is heaven in all its aspects;
and the lore of the meaning of the houses of the Red Crown
and all gods and goddesses that are in them,
and the lore of the meaning of the Resnet and Mehnet sanctuary,
    the temple of Re and the temple of Amun:
the secret it is of all gods.
[...]
I made a petition to His Majesty Cambyses,
concerning all those foreigners who had settled down in the
    temple of Neith,
that they should be driven thence and that the temple of Neith
    should be in all its splendor as it was aforetime.
And His Majesty commanded that all the foreigners who had
    settled in the temple of Neith,
and that all their houses and all their superfluities [or
    abominations] which were in this temple should be thrown
    down,
and that all their own baggage should be carried for them
    outside the wall of this temple.
And His Majesty commanded that the temple of Neith should be
    cleansed
and all its people placed in it, together with the priesthood of the
    temple.
And His Majesty commanded that the revenues should be given
    to Neith the great, the god's mother,
and to the great gods who are in Sais, as they were aforetime.
And His Majesty commanded that all their festivals and all their
    processions should be made, as they were aforetime.
And His Majesty did this because I caused His Majesty to know
    the greatness of Sais.
It is the city of all the gods, they resting on their thrones in it
    eternally.
[...]
The King of Upper and Lower Egypt, Cambyses, came to Sais.
He proceeded to the temple of Neith,
and prostrated himself before Her Majesty as deeply as any king
    has done.
He ordered a great offering of all good things

for Neith the great, the god's mother, and for the great gods of
Sais.

[...]

His majesty did all good deeds in the temple of Neith.

He ordered libations for the lord of eternity in the temple of
Neith,

as all earlier kings had done.

But His Majesty did this because I had caused him to know how
every king has to do all good deeds in this temple, because of
the meaning of this temple as the seat of all the gods who
remain in it forever.

[...]

I ordained the divine offering for Neith the great, the god's
mother, by the command of His Majesty for all time.

I put up monuments for Neith, the Lady of Sais, with all things,
as a faithful servant does for his lord.

I am a man who is good for his city:

I saved its people from the great storm when it sprang up in all
the land, the like of which had never been in this land.

I have protected the weak from the strong,

I saved the fearful when their case came up,

I did them good deeds at the time when it was necessary to act
for them.

[...]

I am one honored by his father and praised by his mother, held
in the hearts of his brothers. I set them up in priestly office
and gave them good arable land at the behest of His Majesty
for all time. I organized a beautiful burial for those who had
no burial, ensured the livelihood of all their children, secured
all their houses, and did them all the good deeds a father does
for his son, when the storm broke out in this nome in the
midst of the very great storm that reigned in all the land.

[...]

King Darius, may he live for ever, commanded me to return to
Egypt, while His Majesty was in Elam when he was Great King
of All Foreign Lands, in order to restore the office of the
House of Life [...] after the ruin. The foreigners brought me
from land to land and caused me to reach Egypt, as the Lord
of the Two Lands had commanded. In accordance with that
which His Majesty had commanded did I act, having provided

them with all their students, who were the sons of men of quality, without there being children of people of low rank among them. Under the direction of every scholar did I place them, [well versed] in all their works. With all their beautiful things did I equip them, and with all their requirements as indicated in the writings, as it had been before. The reason why His Majesty did this was because he knew the usefulness of this craft for causing the sick to live, and in order to cause the names of all the gods, their temples, their offerings, and the conduct of their festivals to endure for ever.

This text complements the testimony of the Bible with regard to the Persian treatment of subjected peoples. Just as Cyrus let the deported Jews go back home and Ezra (equipped with the Persian title "Scribe of the Laws of the Heavenly God") was sent to Jerusalem to ensure that the traditional laws—the Torah—were enforced, so the Persians in Egypt strove to rule the country in collaboration with the Egyptian elite and in accordance with the prevailing semantic systems and laws. Udjahorresnet is an exact parallel to Ezra, who was his junior by almost a hundred years.

Darius was the first and last Persian king to build an Egyptian temple or indeed to undertake any sacred building work in Egypt at all. After the Egyptian uprising following the Battle of Marathon, quelled by Xerxes in 484 B.C.E., and above all after the rebellion of Inaros and Amyrtaeus, the Persian attitude toward Egypt underwent a sudden change. Egyptian names disappeared from all higher ranks in the military and administration, both spheres now openly displaying the face of an occupying power. The massive influx of Persian, Phoenician, Jewish, and Babylonian mercenaries and settlers led to the emergence of a middle and upper class from which the Egyptians themselves felt largely excluded. Only in the lower echelons of local administration do we find any Egyptian names.

Toward the end of the fifth century B.C.E., the grandson of Amyrtaeus declared himself king, with no opposition from Artaxerxes II, and formed the Twenty-eighth Dynasty all on his own. His successor, Nepherites I, came from Mendes in the middle of the Delta and founded the Twenty-ninth Dynasty. Nepherites' son Muthis ruled for only a few months before the throne was usurped by Psammuthis, ousted in his turn shortly after by Achoris. After a brief period of rule by Achoris' son, Nepherites II, Nectanebo I ascended the throne as first king of the Thirtieth Dynasty. Achoris had already undertaken a building and renovation program, which was then continued on a huge scale by the kings of the Thirtieth Dynasty: Nectanebo I, Tachos, and Nectanebo II. Most of the great Ptolemaic building projects, aimed at the systematic renewal of the Egyptian cults, are a continuation of work commenced or completed in the Thirtieth Dynasty. In 343 B.C.E. Artaxerxes III reconquered Egypt. For ten years the Persians were lords of Egypt again, until they were finally defeated by Alexander the Great.

The tumultuous history of the last Egyptian dynasties had the effect of reviving the feudal structure of the Libyan principalities of the Delta. Amyrtaeus, Nepherites, and Nectanebo were descendants of the ruling dynasties of Sais, Mendes, and perhaps other locations in the Delta. Alongside these, the principality of Herakleopolis was still in existence, its lineage extending back to the age of the Twenty-first Dynasty. It was this city that would become the "Zion" of Egyptian messianism in the fourth century B.C.E, and it was there that Egyptians looked for the advent of a king who would finally put an end to the hated alien rule exercised by the Persians and the Greeks.

With Alexander the Great's triumph over the Persians, Egypt also fell to the Greeks. Immediately after the Battle of Issos, and before continuing his campaigns farther east, Alexander hurried to assume the Egyptian mantle. His arrival in Egypt either was organized in the most meticulous conformity with traditional Egyptian semiologies or was portrayed that way by the Egyptians, who saw in him the long-desired bringer of salvation. In the coming of Alexander, expectation, experience, and memory intersect. Immediate experience is colored by expectation, subsequent memory even more so, with many contingent or inconvenient facts simply ignored in the process. According to the version transmitted to us, Alexander's first move was to repair to the oracle of Ammon ("Ammon" is the Greek form of Amun) at the oasis of Siwa, and have himself confirmed as son of Zeus-Ammon—a royal election oracle fully in line with the theology of will and the style of the Theban god-state. With this act he presented himself to the Egyptians as a god-sent savior-king, reviving the messianism abandoned in the Twenty-sixth Dynasty. From the very outset, then, he established the mold within which the Macedonians legitimized themselves as rulers in Egypt; that is, as divinely appointed bearers of salvation, who were sent to put an end to the disastrous rule of the Persians. Accordingly, the Macedonians blackened the memory of Persian rule, just as the kings of the Twelfth Dynasty had demonized the memory of the First Intermediate Period. The Persians had carried off the divine images; the Macedonians, by contrast, would do all they could to get them back. The Persians had destroyed the temples; the Macedonians would make superhuman efforts to reconstruct all the temples and build new ones. The Persians had killed sacred animals; the Macedonians would be especially meticulous about observing the animal cult. This Macedonian vilification of Persia was especially well received by the Egyptians because Egyptians and Greeks had been traditional allies against the Persians for centuries. But as the image of the Persians receded in Egyptian memory and experience, the potential of these large and public actions on the part of the Macedonians as a source of orientation and meaning was bound to fade.

The special interest of this final phase of pharaonic history is its dramatic (not to say melodramatic) character. As the Ptolemaic dynasty was at pains to act in accordance with the alien customs, expectations, and systems of meaning it encountered, it had a somewhat theatrical character from the outset. The Ptolemaic court must have presented the curious spectacle of an Egyptian drama played by Greek actors in Egyptian costume. If it is true, as I have suggested, that the Saite Period with its "costumed" archaism presents the first instance of Egyptomania (enacted by Egyptians themselves), then the same is doubly true for the Ptolemaic period. The institution of consanguineous marriage, for example, conformed to Egyptian custom with a degree of strictness unequaled in prior Egyptian history.

After the death of Alexander in 323, Ptolemy I first governed Egypt as a satrap under the nominal reign of Alexander's successors Philip Arrhidaeus (Alexander's mentally incompetent brother) and Alexander IV (his minor son). Not until 304 did Ptolemy I have himself crowned pharaoh and set up Alexandria-ad-Aegyptum as his capital. Alexander, a pupil of Aristotle, and Ptolemy I, himself a historian who had written an account of Alexander the Great, laid the cultural foundations for the museum set up by Ptolemy II, which contained the famous Library of Alexandria. The foremost teaching and research center of its time, this institution also functioned as an academy for the education of princes. Among the philosophers, historians, and other scholars and intellectuals whom Ptolemy I attracted to his court was Hecataeus of Abdera, whose ambitious history of Egypt shows the full intensity of the Greek engagement with Egyptian culture, and served as guide and instruction for Ptolemy and his princes.

The Ptolemies went to immense trouble to be good pharaohs. They studied Egyptian traditions to find out what was expected of a good king and then did everything they could to live up to that standard. These efforts manifested themselves most notably in four areas.

In their building program, the Ptolemies took up and put into practice the vast project of national renewal previously envisaged by Nectanebo I and Nectanebo II. The Ptolemies placed the construction of temples at the head of the list of pharaonic obligations, a decision of major cultural consequence. In the period of Alexander the Great, when the Greeks were welcomed enthusiastically as liberators from Persian rule, there had been some experiments in the direction of hellenizing Egyptian art. But these experiments bore little fruit. The temple reliefs of the Ptolemaic age are closely modeled on those of the Thirtieth Dynasty; they thus stand as the sole example of resistance to Hellenism in all Mediterranean and Near/Middle Eastern artistic traditions (as far as Gandara in northern India!). This resistance does not indicate "nationalist" opposition to the Macedonian regime but rather a deliberate decision on the part of the Ptolemies to demonstrate their political and cultural independence from the confederation of *diadochoi,* Alexander's successors.

In terms of cult practice, specifically animal cults, the Ptolemies also referred to earlier traditions and extended them. Up to the threshold of the Ptolemaic era, animal cults had been a secondary phenomenon rather than the vital nerve center of Egyptian religion. Secondary phenomena can be indispensable, of course, and as early as the New Kingdom animal cults were already an integral feature of Egyptian religion. But the Ptolemies placed the animal cult at the very inmost heart of Egyptian religion. Every cult now had a triangular base:

cosmic/solar manifestation
(Re form)
e.g., Apis-Osiris

living incarnation   transfigured immortalization
(animal form)   (mummy as Osiris figure)
e.g., Apis bull   e.g., Osiris-Apis

Because the kings also saw themselves as living incarnations of the supreme deity, they occupied the same theological category as the sacred animals. Perhaps this explains their consuming interest in the animal cult. In any case, the connections between animal cult and royal cult were now very close.[4]

The cult images in the temple were another area of concern. The first four Ptolemaic kings had themselves specifically lauded for hunting down and bringing back the divine images removed by the Persians; they thus cast themselves as the inheritors of the late Egyptian role of the savior-king.

These three religious fields of kingly activity—temple construction, animal cult, divine images—are matched and mirrored by three major motifs omnipresent in anti-Persian propaganda: destruction of the temples, killing of the sacred animals, abduction of the divine images. In the fourth area, by contrast, the Ptolemies made vigorous efforts to bring about a religious, cultural, and political synthesis between Egyptian and Greek traditions. In this regard, their most important move was the creation of a new god, Sarapis, who united within himself not only the Egyptian gods Osiris, Apis (Ptah), Amun, and Re, but was also identical with the supreme figures of other religions, notably Zeus. The cult policies of the first two Ptolemies established Sarapis and Isis as deities of such stature that their cults spread throughout the Mediterranean region. Although Egypt itself took hardly any part in this new, international form of Egyptian religion, the cults of Sarapis and Isis dictated the prevalent image of Egyptian religion entertained outside Egypt until well into the nineteenth century.

The Ptolemies spared no effort to rule the country in accordance with Egyptian ideas and practices. They instituted the annual priestly synod to discuss and adopt important political decisions.[5] They also issued the "philanthropa" decrees, in which they presented themselves as law-abiding kings in the ancient Near-Eastern sense, as protectors of the weak and saviors of the poor. The notion of royal legal sovereignty extended not only to the promulgation of laws but also to their revocation. The philanthropa decrees were acts of renunciation—amnesties, tax relief, debt waivers. Up to the Battle of Raphia in 217 B.C.E., the Ptolemies' policies successfully fostered Egyptian integration. Then came the Egyptian uprisings and the collapse of the consensus held dear by the Ptolemies.

The uprisings began in Lower Egypt, orchestrated by Egyptian soldiers from the victorious army at Raphia and by rebels from underprivileged strata. In 206 B.C.E., the rebels set up a counterkingdom in Thebes under their leader, Horwennefer. He was followed by Ankhwennefer, who ruled until 186. At the priestly synod of Alexandria, Ptolemy V had Ankhwennefer declared an enemy of the gods, but finally pardoned him; likewise, a philanthropa decree of 185 promised amnesty to all who had fled the country. In 131, when a struggle for the throne among Ptolemy VIII, Euergetes II, and Cleopatra II plunged the country into civil war, an Egyptian named Harsiese arrived on the scene as counterking in Thebes. Though soon driven out of Thebes, he managed to hold out briefly as pharaoh in the fortress of el-Hiba. Further uprisings ensued, but without any new ascensions to the throne. In 165 one Dionysios Petosarapis essayed a rebellion that found considerable favor with the Egyptian population. In 164 rebels in Faiyum stormed the Ammonion of Myeris near Crocodilopolis. At the same time unrest broke out in Thebaid, which long remained a hotbed of unrest: it was the scene of major rebellions in 88, 63, and 55 B.C.E. In 29 the Thebans rose up against what was now the Roman government.

At the heart of all these uprisings were the high taxes imposed to pay for various expensive wars. The consequence was a large-scale exodus from the countryside, which left extensive areas of arable land to dry out and encouraged the emergence of an urban proletariat that was all too receptive to calls for rebellion against the government. In the Roman period, though not in the Ptolemaic age, Greeks paid less tax than indigenous Egyptians.[6] This ethnic distinction further exacerbated hatred of the Greeks and stimulated political messianism.

25

THE *DEMOTIC CHRONICLE* AND THE POLITICAL MESSIANISM OF THE LATE PERIOD

Alexander the Great and the Egyptian Myth of the Savior-King

THE TRADITIONAL CONCEPT of royalty in the Egyptian state proclaimed that the king was the son of the supreme god, begotten by him, and sent to earth to bring justice to men and build temples for the gods. As long as this chain of mutual obligation remained unbroken, the welfare of the land and the blessings of the gods were assured. But if it snapped, the result was cognitive dissonance and chaos. The status quo no longer corresponded to the salvational order of things, and hopes were placed in the advent of a savior-king. As we have seen, when Alexander the Great arrived in Egypt, he went to the oracle of Ammon (Amun) at the oasis of Siwa and had himself confirmed as the son of god. It was an act of supreme political acumen, permitting him to assume the role of the savior-king. Alexander reactivated the political mythodynamics of divine filiation, which saw in the legitimate ruler not only a genealogical descendant of the supreme god but the son of his flesh, begotten in a mythical union with the queen.[7] Later there were even stories (perhaps disseminated by Alexander himself) to the effect that Amun had come to Alexander's mother, Olympia, in the shape not of Philip II but of Nectanebo II: Alexander was thus linked to the last king of the last legitimate Egyptian line. According to traditional Egyptian ideology, which Alexander was so eager to revitalize, a legitimate pharaoh needed two fathers: a divine one (Amun) and a real one—a reigning king, who himself fulfilled these conditions. This myth of legitimacy also reappeared in an inverted, burlesque form as a comic folk narrative. In this version, Nectanebo, driven out of Egypt by the Persians and accepted into the Macedonian court incognito as a magician, sleeps with Olympia in the guise of Amun.[8] In both versions, serious and comic, the narrative reintroduced the ancient Egyptian king myth to the Macedonian court and connected Alexander with three different fathers: Amun (divine father), Philip II (legitimate father), Nectanebo II (physical father).

After visiting the oracle of Ammon, Alexander had himself crowned in Memphis and then journeyed to Thebes to have his divine descent confirmed by Amun in his Theban form and to renew the cult of the royal *ka* in the temple of Luxor (the curled horns of the ram of Luxor became a distinctive element in Alexander's iconography). Even more than his visit to Siwa, Alexander's journey to Thebes made reference to the past, reviving notions that had already largely faded in the Saite Period. Before Alexander's advent, the divine descent of the pharaoh had mostly lost its political significance. In the Late Period, the reigning king was no longer brought anew into the world each year; his role was now ascribed to the child-god of the temple triad.[9] With his appearance in Egypt, Alexander repoliticized the ritual and thus contrived to have himself perceived not as a conqueror but as a liberator. This was the start of a new semiology, with which the Ptolemies legitimized themselves in Egypt.

Deuteronomism and Messianism: *The* Demotic Chronicle

THE CLEAREST TESTIMONY of Late Period Egyptian messianism is a text in demotic script recapitulating the history of the Twenty-eighth, Twenty-ninth, and Thirtieth Dynasties in the form of an oracular commentary. On its recto, Papyrus 215 of the Bibliothèque Nationale in Paris displays a text known as the *Demotic Chronicle*.[10] The text on the verso deals with (among other things) Darius' codification of all laws in force up to Year 44 of Amasis.[11] The very earliest scholars working on the *Chronicle* were struck by the similarities to the "deuteronomistic" view of history, which makes success and failure depend on the attitude of king and people toward the law. (This pattern is particularly prominent in historiographic books such as Kings 1 and 2 that belong to the same tradition as Deuteronomy.)

The resemblances are indeed astounding.[12] In both Deuteronomy and the *Chronicle,* a history ending in disaster is recounted: in the Judaic text, the Babylonian conquest of 587 B.C.E.; in the *Chronicle,* the Persian conquest of 343 B.C.E. In both cases the catastrophe is blamed on the kings' failings. And in both cases, the kings are measured against the "law"—and found wanting—according to the shared formula: King X strayed from the law; he was punished for his sins; his sins were visited on his son.

In the *Demotic Chronicle,* the rulers who follow the "Medes" (Persians) are singled out for censure and occasional praise:

> The fourth ruler who came after the Medes [...]
> "He was not!"
> That is to say, he was not on the path of god.
> He was not long allowed to be ruler.[13]

Here, as in the biblical Book of Kings, the good rulers are the exception. One such is described thus:

> The second ruler who came after the Medes,
> that was Pharaoh Nepherites:
> because he did what he did conscientiously,
> his son was allowed to succeed him.[14]

> The fifth ruler who came after the Medes,
> that is to say "Hakoris," the lord of the diadems:
> his time of rule was allowed to run to its term
> because he was beneficent to the temples.[15]

But later we hear of the same ruler:

> He was toppled because he forsook the law
> and did not concern himself about his fellowmen.[16]

The good ruler is rewarded with a long term of office, and his son is allowed to succeed him on the throne. Bad rulers reign only briefly, and their throne is taken over by a usurper.

Of Nectanebo II, who lost the throne to the Persians, we are told:

Apis, Apis, Apis—
that is to say: Ptah, Phre, Harsiesis,
who are the lords of the office of ruler.
You forgot them when you sought to amass riches.
His fortune lies in the threefold. For Apis means the gods he
    named above.
Apis is Ptah.
Apis is Phre.
Apis is Harsiesis.[17]

In this text, Apis figures as *ter-unus*, the triune god in whom merge
Ptah, Re, and Horus, the first gods of the kingdom.[18] This oracle is
typical of the syncretism of late antiquity, proclaiming the identity of
different supreme gods in a superordinate one god:

The one is Zeus, is Hades, is Helios, is Dionysos.
One god in all gods.[19]

The one Zeus, the one Hades, the one Helios is Sarapis.[20]

This deuteronomistic evaluation of the kings in terms of their attitude
to the law and their adherence to the path of god is revolutionary for
the traditional Egyptian image of the king. Equally radical is the
future-oriented messianism that informs the prophecies from Herakleopolis about the advent of a savior-king:

Oracle: *The goddess Emhoyet, she comes,*
she brings him from Heliopolis to her apron.
Commentary: That is to say: Emhoyet, who is the uraeus snake,
she brings him from Herakleopolis, being satisfied,
to her apron in the king's palace.
It is Harsaphes who commands the ruler who shall be.
In other words: It is a man from Herakleopolis who will rule
    after the foreigners [and] Ionians.

Take the joy, prophet of Harsaphes!
That is to say: the prophet of Harsaphes rejoices after the
    Ionians.
For a ruler has come in Herakleopolis.
May he open the kilns!

I have given him cattle!
That is to say: the ruler-to-be
opens [the gates] of the temples
and has offerings made [again] to the gods.
Hail, hail, O Son of the Month!
Beautiful, beautiful is Herakleopolis!
That is to say: Much that is good will be vouchsafed to
    Herakleopolis in the designated period.[21]

The "deuteronomism" and "messianism" of the texts are systemati-cally connected. The experience of bad kings, who are chastised with the rod of the "law," determines the image of the good king, of whom it is said: "He will not forsake the law."[22] The first and prime salva-tional deed performed by the good king is the opening of the temple and the bringing of divine offerings, which had been, from as early as the Fifth Dynasty, the traditional role of the pharaoh. But this role was now magnified by the traumatic experience of plundered and destroyed temples, divine images dragged off elsewhere, forsaken cults, forgotten rites and festivals. This trauma was to dominate the late Egyptian mentality.

The Oracle of the Lamb

THE MESSIANISM THAT SUFFUSES the *Demotic Chronicle* also speaks from another demotic text of this period preserved on an early Roman papyrus: the *Oracle of the Lamb*. The text tells of a scribe living in the age of Bocchoris (the last king of the Twenty-fourth Dynasty) who finds a book describing the events of the future. The "Lamb" (possibly a variant form of the ram-god Harsaphes of Herak-leopolis, the "Zion" of Egyptian messianism) confirms for the scribe that what the book says is true. The content of the book is a chaos description in the classical style:

... And it will come to pass in that same time that the rich man
    will be a poor man.
... No one will tell the truth ...
... removing the White Crown from Egypt. When one seeks it,
    one will not find it. ...
Manifold horrors will take place in Egypt.

The fowl of the air and [the fish of the sea] will eat their blood
   and their flesh,
and the wise will cast [their children] into the water
. . .
Woe upon Egypt! [It weeps] for the manifold curses that will
   befall it.
Heliopolis weeps because the east has become too . . .
Bubastis weeps. Nilopolis weeps,
because the streets of Sebennytos have been made into a vineyard
and because the mooring post of Mendes has become a bundle
   of palm leaves and persea twigs.
The great priests of Upoke weep.
Memphis weeps, the city of Apis.
Thebes weeps, the city of Amun.
Letopolis weeps, the city of Shu.
Fear conceives suffering.
The Lamb consummated all curses on them.
Thereupon Psinyris said to him:
When will this happen without our having seen it before?
Thereupon it [the Lamb] said: When I am a uraeus at the head
   of the Pharaoh, then [these events] will happen. But after nine
   hundred years have passed I shall rule over Egypt, and it will
   come to pass that the Mede who turned his face toward Egypt
   will go back to the foreign lands and his outlying places.
   Wrong will be confounded. Law and the judgment will return
   to Egypt. Retribution will be taken on them [the Medes] for
   the chapels of the gods of Egypt, and on Nineveh, the nome
   of the Assyrian. And it will further come to pass that the
   Egyptians will surge into the land of Syria and rule over its
   nomes and find the chapels of the gods of Egypt. The good
   fortune that will happen to Egypt is beyond words. He who is
   hated of god will fare ill, and he who is pleasing to god, to
   him god will be pleasing when he is buried. The barren
   woman shall rejoice and she who has a child shall rejoice for
   the good things that will happen to Egypt. The small number
   of people who shall be in Egypt shall say: Were but my father
   and grandfather here in the good times that are to come.[23]

Herodotus also reports on a prophecy to Bocchoris (whom he con-
fuses with the Fourth Dynasty King Mycerinos): as punishment for
the sins of his forefathers his lifetime will be restricted to only six

more years, which will be followed by one hundred fifty years of foreign rule.²⁴ And various Ptolemaic rulers emphasized in official inscriptions that they had restored to Egypt the stolen images of the gods, thereby linking their rule to popular messianic beliefs and establishing their reign as the promised age of salvation.²⁵

The prophecy for the future savior-king is that he will rule for fifty-five years:

> . . . he of two years, who is not our [crowned one].
> He of the fifty-five [years is] our crowned one.²⁶

The Potter's Oracle

THE FIGURE OF FIFTY-FIVE also appears in the *Potter's Oracle*, another political prophecy, which has been transmitted in Greek.²⁷ In the *Oracle*, a king, identifiable as Amenophis III, visits Hermopolis, where he encounters a potter whose wheel has been shattered and whose wares have been confiscated. The potter interprets his misfortune as a sign of future disaster: a time will come when the "girdle-bearers" will rule over Egypt: they worship Typhon (= Seth) and will destroy the Egyptian temples; law and order will disappear from the land, siblings and spouses will wage war on each other, and internecine strife will dominate the land. As in the *Prophecies of Neferti*, two thousand years earlier, all nature is drawn into the general misery:

> The Nile will be low, the earth barren,
> the sun will darken, because it does not want to see the
>   misfortune in Egypt.
> The winds will wreak harm on the earth.

Later, however, the "girdle-bearers" will "fall from the tree of Egypt like autumn leaves" and the divine images will return. The sun god himself will send a savior-king, who will be enthroned by Isis and reign for fifty-five years. The land will thrive, the Nile risings will be high, summer and winter will follow a regular rhythm, the winds will be mild, and the sun will shine, exposing all wrongdoing and turning over miscreants to justice.

The names of Amenophis III and Bocchoris are also associated with a cycle of legends that revolves around the same theme: the sufferings of Egypt at the hands of the foreigners, and the interlopers' ultimate expulsion. Like the oracles, these texts reveal a new historical awareness: from the vantage point of a calamitous present, both past and future gain a new significance; and as political hopes increasingly attach to a vision of the future in which Egypt will regain its greatness, the past becomes the cradle of that greatness and the source of its visible remnants.

Deuteronomism, Messianism, Apocalypse

BOTH THE "DEUTERONOMISM" of the *Demotic Chronicle* and the "messianism" of the *Potter's Oracle* are typical responses to historical experiences of disaster—primarily the Assyrian invasions of the first half of the seventh century B.C.E.; to a lesser extent the reign of the first Persian kings and the Ptolemies.

Deuteronomism is a response to the experience of failure, of catastrophe; messianism is a reaction to oppression. Deuteronomism in this general sense is tantamount to constructing and understanding history in terms of guilt or blame. Disastrous events are seen as the consequences of moral transgressions. Such an interpretation requires a standard of rightness and goodness by which to measure the deeds of the kings. In the classical age, the king himself was the measure, and it was hardly conceivable (and certainly never explicitly stated) that he might fail to meet that measure. In Babylon, by contrast, the code of princely behavior held up an ideal mirror to rulers, who could then only be measured in terms of that ideal.[28] Under the impact of the disaster of 587 B.C.E., deuteronomism, and the historiography that derives from it, takes the dissociation of the king and the law (as the gauge of what is right) a stage further. In Egypt, this kind of thinking was fueled not only by the historical experiences of disaster but also by Darius I's codification of the law, which required that the law be written down and hence objectified as independent of the will of any one particular king. The king no longer personified the law, but espoused it as something he was bound to obey. Though the text on the verso of the *Demotic Chronicle* does not explicitly say that this law was connected to any idea of a divine legislative will, traditional Egyptian belief nevertheless anchored the law in the will of god, notably the sun god. The sun god was the *fidei defensor* in a broad and general sense, and was undoubtedly seen as performing this function specifically in support of Darius' new codification as well. Any king who strayed from the codified path would "be punished."[29]

Messianism—the anticipation of the advent of a savior-king sent by god to drive out foreigners, punish wrongdoing, reestablish justice on earth, and bring peace and plenty, happiness, and the divine presence—is a well-known and widespread response to political oppression.[30] Particular to the Late Period messianism of Egypt was its access to a long literary tradition of political propaganda. The role of savior-king, bringer of justice, and guarantor of peace and plenty was part of the traditional image of the king and was explicitly expressed by each ruler in his inscriptions, most especially in times of crisis or uncertain legitimacy.

There was no shortage of "dark ages" in Egyptian history, but again and again kings appeared who lightened the darkness and reestablished nearness to god. The ancient texts depicted the worst horrors as emanating from ages without kings, and painted lurid pictures of the dread consequences of anarchy and interregnum. Chaos came from below, from human failings and rebellion, while salvation came from the king. The only exception was Tutankhamun, who was challenged by a revolution from above; but the tradition of repression was so strong that even he did not permit himself to name any names. The overriding dogma remained: chaos came from below, order from the king.

For the Egyptians of the Late Period, however, the horror vision was chaos from above, in the form of rulers heedless of the law. The Egyptians no longer viewed the king as the living embodiment of divine power, a living "token" of the god Horus. The function of bodying forth the divine had been assumed by the sacred animals.[31] As for the rest, the priests had long since taken matters into their own hands. With their daily rituals, they ensured that the offering tables of the gods were never empty and the drink offerings flowed copiously. With the recitation of sayings against Seth and Apopis, they warded off any possibility of civil war or invasion by foreign foes. They performed the Osirian ceremonies and saw to it that the laws remained in force and people abided by them. Their principal duty was scrupulous compliance with the divine regulations and unswerving service to the gods. The king's sole responsibility was to provide the material basis for the priests' service by means of temple construction and the provision of offerings.

Longing for the Golden Age

IN THE CLASSICAL EGYPTIAN TRADITION, the state offset the effects of the cleavage that ran through the "riven world." Every king claimed that his reign was the return of a kind of Golden Age. "The land was flooded in his time," says Taharqa, "as it was in the time of the All-Lord."[32] This ideology of consummated eschatology was also propagated by the Ptolemies.[33] The question is to what extent it conformed to the Egyptian view of the world at the time. Significantly, the temple texts of this era testify to a fundamentally altered attitude. Only now, as never before, do the descriptions of the primordial era become conspicuously nostalgic, plaints for an unrecoverable past:

> Ma'at had come out of heaven in their [the primal gods'] time
>   and united herself with the earthly ones.
> The land was flooded, the bodies were filled.
> There was no year of hunger in either land.
> The walls did not cave in, the thorn did not yet prick
> in the age of the ancestor gods.[34]

The ancestor gods are those deceased gods whose worship in mortuary cults assumed ever greater importance in the Late Period.[35] In this theology, the remoteness into which the gods had retreated with the elevation of the firmament (a remoteness that is bridged by cult, at least symbolically) was transferred from the spatial to the temporal dimension. The mortuary cult of the gods' ancestors maintained the present's link with the primal age.

In the Late Period, the belief that it was possible to cross the temporal and spatial distances into which the gods had retreated attained almost dogmatic status, and the cult dedicated to this mediation became so fervid that the original underlying idea of the remoteness of the divine was transformed into its exact opposite: a belief in the close proximity of the gods, with Egypt figuring as "dwelling of the gods," "temple of the world," "holiest of lands."[36] This view of Egypt sprang from premonitions of the imminent end of the cults and their symbolic reconciliation of past and present, there and here, and from fear that this time the severance between gods and men would be so absolute that no myths or rites could ever bridge it. A text known as the *Asclepius Apocalypse* from the early Christian period paints a bleak picture of the irrevocable decline of the (Egyptian) world:

> And yet there will come a time when it will be seen that the piety and unremitting devotion with which the Egyptians have worshipped the gods was futile and that all sacred addresses to the gods will be vain and fruitless. For the deity will ascend once more from the earth to the heavens and forsake Egypt. This land, once the seat of religion, will then be bereft of divine presence. Foreigners will inhabit this land, and not only will the old cults be neglected, but religion, piety, and the cult of the gods will be actively prohibited by law. Of the Egyptian religion only fables will remain and inscribed stones. [. . .] In those days the people will be weary of life and will cease to revere and venerate the cosmos. This Whole, so good that there never was, is, nor will be anything better, will be in danger of disappearing for good; the people will regard it as a burden and revile it. They will no longer love this world, this incomparable work of god, this glorious edifice, fashioned from an infinite variety of forms, instrument of the divine will, pouring its favor unstintingly into its work, where in harmonious variety everything worthy of worship, praise, and love shows itself as one and all. Darkness will be preferred to light, death to life. No one will raise his eyes to heaven. The pious will be taken for madmen, the godless for wise, the evil for good. [. . .]
>
> The gods will turn away from men—O painful separation!— and only the evil demons will remain, mingling with men and driving their wretched victims by force into all kinds of crime, into war, robbery, fraud, and everything hateful to the nature of the soul.
>
> Then will the earth no longer be solid and the sea no longer navigable, the heavens will not hold the stars in their orbits, nor will the stars keep to their course in the firmament. Every divine voice will necessarily fall silent. The fruits of the earth will rot, the soil will become barren, the very air will be oppressive and heavy. And these things will hold sway in the senescent world: absence of religion, of order, and of understanding.[37]

In this description, the disintegration of the world, its loss of form and inhabitability, is not the consequence of a political collapse but of a religious decision, a conversion. Men will forsake the old religion, rooted in worship of the cosmos, and turn to a new religion that regards the cosmos as a burden to be reviled. Observation of cult practice will be terminated and prohibited; no longer will worship sustain the gods and welcome them on earth. As a result, the gods will leave the earth, and the earth, no longer ritually maintained, will fly out of joint. The senescence of the world is nigh. Augustine understood this text as referring to Christianity's triumphant advent, and he read it as an avowal of capitulation by an inferior heathen culture sensing its own imminent demise.[38] Yet these images and their dark forebodings of the End of Time have their roots deep in Egyptian culture. An apocalypse conceived of as an environmental disaster is reminiscent of the daily sayings recited against the god Seth, which also seek to fend off a danger that is likewise represented as eco-doom. The meaning of Egyptian religion lay in sustaining the cosmos by means of offerings, communion, and veneration, "with a pious heart, unremitting devotion, and sacred address"; the world has need of such unremitting devotion if it is to be a fit habitation for humankind.

26

THE CULTURAL CONSTRUCTION OF OTHERNESS: TRAUMA AND PHOBIA

The Demonization of Seth

THE KUSHITES HAD PLACED THE MYTH of the legal dispute between Horus and Seth over the "Eye," symbol of the double crown of Egypt, at the heart of their policy of religious renovation. In elevating Memphis to the status of coronation city and capital, they revived a tradition that extended back to the origins of the state and the initial unification of the kingdom In this myth, Seth stands for everything that contrasts with Horus' kingship: brute force, physical strength, and anarchy. These disruptive forces are not, however, marginalized and "cast out," but tamed and integrated. So, too, the tenor of the *Memphite Theology* is not demonization but reconciliation.

In the age of the Saites and Persians, the myth of Horus and Seth was taken up and rewritten. The framework of the legal dispute was retained: Seth is arraigned and found guilty; he is punished, and the lament of his cities is described in terms of a political defeat.

Su wails, *Wns* is in mourning,
Grieving plaints are [heard] throughout Oxyrhynchos.
The oases Khargeh and Dakhla cry out their woe,
misfortune roams through their centers.
Kynopolis keens, for its lord is not in it.
Hypselis is a barren place, Ombos torn down,
their houses destroyed, all their inhabitants annihilated.
Their lord is no more, who planned rebellion is no more,
for he has fallen into captivity.[39]

Seth now appears in the guise of a foreign ruler who has been defeated and driven out. No mention is made of reconciliation and integration. Seth girds himself for a new invasion, thus compounding his former crimes. With his allies he returns to Egypt and wreaks the most devastating havoc in the temples. Isis is again forced to accuse him before the sun god:

> O Re-Horakhty, Sole Lord, whose like is not,
> who gives commands, whose word is complied with,
> whose judgment one cannot escape:
> Remember what you ordained when the decrees were created!
> Therein you gave guidance, that is to say: steps for men,
> cult regulations for the gods,
> instructions for the king in his palace [...]
> Behold, Seth, the rebel, has come on his way,
> he has turned once more to Egypt,
> to plunder with his hand.
> He is in the course of appropriating the land by force,
> in keeping with the way he behaved before
> when he destroyed the holy sites,
> when he tore down their chapels,
> when he made uproar in the temples.
> He has inflicted suffering, he has repeated injury,
> he has made unrest rise up anew.
> He has brought suffering to the sanctuary,
> he has planned rebellion in Memphis.
> Behold, he penetrates into the Serapeum,
> he has brought injury to the house of Opet.
> He has hewn wood in Iusaas,
> he has caught fish in Lake Moeris.
> He has hunted game, he has caught fowl,
> in the temple precinct of the First of the Houses.
> He has set foot [in the Pure House],
> he has made uproar to the Ennead.
> He has planned battle, he has roared
> to the gods of Menset.
> He has inflicted new suffering
> on the banks of This.
> He has made uproar in Mendes/Busiris;
> the city and nome of Busiris/Mendes are in sore distress.

He has approached the House of Bas;
he has done violence in its walls.
He has taken wood from the Sais of Neith;
he has done bad deeds in the embalming house.
He has made unrest arise anew in the Imhet cave
and strife in Kher-Aha.
He has brought what Atum abhors into the temple of the
 Ennead.
He has devised contumely and made uproar
in the temple of Amun-Wer in the Imhet cave.
He has bethought himself of battle; he has set fire
in the temple of the eastern Bas.
He has neared Saft el-Henna, he has entered the walled quarter,
he has done sacrilege to the holy Nebes tree
—when it greens, the earth greens—
He has neared that sacred chamber of Iusas
with the acacia, which contains death and life.
He has planned to eat the Mafdet [the sacred panther]
before the countenance of Mut and Bastet.
Behold, he has eaten the Abdu fish [a sacred fish]
at the places of the *ba* of the east.
He has set foot on the land near Khefthernebes
before the countenance of Re in heaven.
He has fed of the sacred ram
in the temple of Amun the great.
He has laid hands on the *Mnhp* plant
before the countenance of the ram of Mendes.
He has organized a massacre of the people in Busiris
before the countenance of Wennefer, the Justified.
He has fed of the Abdu fish
and eaten of the *Ꜥdw* fish
in the great hall of Heliopolis.
He has cut off supply, he has stolen the offerings
from the palace of the Sole Lord, whose like is not,
[so that wailing reigns in his two houses to all gods,
and the rites are not performed at the established times].
He has caught the hawk and the *itn* fish
before the countenance of Shu and Tefnut.
Behold, he has bound the Apis bull
before the countenance of him who made all that is.

He has let the milk of Sekhat-Hor dry away,
he has thrown down the *htmt* cow, the mother of god.
He has cut off supply on the lake of the *Tm* trees,
he let the lake of the *htmt* cow dry up.
He has planned to stand up as a robber,
he has sought to elevate himself.
Suffering reigns in the place where he abides.
Destruction is in what you [Re-Horakhty] have commanded.
[. . .]⁴⁰

Seth has become an Asiatic conqueror toppling the legitimate Egyptian king, Horus, and wreaking his murderous and lawless brutality on the temples and their gods. Seth is the very quintessence of religious sacrilege. He eats sacred animals, violates the taboos, cancels the supply of offerings. His objective is the destruction of the very cults that keep the universe in motion. If Seth achieves his objective, a catastrophe of cosmic dimensions will follow:

O fall back in the attack,
that the sun be not darkened on the sandbank of the Lake of the
    Two Knives,
that the heavens not swallow the moon at the *Mspr* festival in
    Heliopolis,
that the tortoise not drink the Nile empty and the waters dry
    out,
that a flame not emerge in the midst of the ocean and one flame
    be consumed by the other,
that the upstream and downstream voyaging of the sun be not
    known,
so rich in ways when crossing the heavens,
that the two heavens not turn at once
and heaven unite with the earth,
that the ark be not opened in Heliopolis
and its contents revealed,
that the garment be not loosened in Memphis,
and the arm of "such-and-such" [a name too holy to be uttered,
    possibly "Osiris"] be espied,
that the lamp go not out in the night of evil,
at that time that we hope will never occur,
that the sea not become sweet

and its waters drunk dry,
that the four sayings be not known in Heliopolis
and the heavens fall down when they hear them,
that the divine dwelling in the midst of *špt-ptrtj* not take on a
    bloody hue,
and the court in this land be not[41] hindered,
[the dwelling] in which the All-Lord sits, that god of whom there
    is no second,
in which they are judged,
that the hole in Pharbaitos be not laid free and the heaven
    opposite it be airless [?],
that the seal of Anubis be not removed
and the clay of Ptah broken,
that the bushes that serve as a hiding place be not cut away,
to drive out him who has concealed himself in it,
so that no uproar arise
and there be no one to march against the mouth-opener in
    Babylon,
that the donkey not frighten the cat,
nor she expose her rear end to him,
that the crocodile not pounce on the swimmer
in the estuary of the *'ntj* waters.[42]

This global environmental disaster is triggered by the profanation of
sanctuaries and the disclosure of cult mysteries; in short, by the vio-
lation of those boundaries that were the guardians of the sacred: taboo
and secrecy.[43]

Reinforcing Cultural Boundaries

JUST AS IN TIMES OF POLITICAL INSECURITY the Egyptian
towns girded themselves with walls and became citadels, so under
foreign rule Egyptian culture surrounded itself with symbolic walls
and protective zones. This defensive policy was clearly a response to
the experiences of the Persian and Ptolemaic periods. An exact parallel
is found in Judaea, where Jewish culture surrounded itself with the
symbolic wall of the law against the Persian and Hellenistic threat to
its cultural identity. The *Letter by Aristeas* from the second century
B.C.E. makes eloquent use of these fortification metaphors:

The lawgiver, armed by god with profound wisdom, surrounded us with impenetrable palisades and walls of bronze, in order that we shun all contact with any other people, remaining pure in body and soul and free from deceptive ideas, and that we worship God, who alone is God, who alone is mighty and powerful, in contrast to the created world. [...] So that we should not besmirch ourselves with anything and not be spoiled by contact with the bad, he surrounded us on all sides with purity instructions, commandments on eating and drinking, touching, hearing, and seeing.[44]

Mary Douglas has interpreted this stance as typical of an "enclave culture," which immures itself within a wall of ritual purity taboos, the better to withstand the pressure for conformity from outside.[45] In Egypt, the symbolic fortifications are "abhorrence, taboo" (purity/ impurity) and "secrecy" (knowledge/betrayal of knowledge). These boundaries provide a context for the fantastic but probably not totally inaccurate statements made by Herodotus about the purity commandments observed by the Egyptians in their contact with the Greeks and probably with all foreigners. No Egyptian would touch a knife or cooking utensil that had previously been used by a Greek, nor eat the meat of an animal slaughtered with a Greek knife. Nor could any Egyptian ever bring himself to kiss a Greek on the mouth.[46] Though both categories of distinction and self-segregation (abhorrence and secrecy, impurity and betrayal) had a long history in Egypt, their traditional function had been to divide sacred from profane, not indigenous from alien. Taboos were valid for the priests, not for Egyptians in general. Priests had to prepare themselves for sacred duties by strict purity and abstinence rules; analogously—within the category of secrecy—priests were subjected to arcane discipline, which was designed to preserve the sacred rites from profanation, not necessarily by foreigners but by the uninitiated.

You shall not recite this in the presence
of any other person except your own self.
[...]
This document is truly secret.
The profane shall not look on it,
in no place and at no time.[47]

Sacred be the place in the highest measure,
not seen, not heard by anyone
except a chief lector-priest and a *sem* priest [one of the titles of
the high priest].[48]

In the Late Period, the concept "profane" underwent a change, as did
the meaning of taboos and secrecy. The sacred objects and rites were
protected not so much from the impure and the uninitiated but from
the foreigner. Foreigners symbolized the ultimate in impurity and
noninitiation and also stood for the threat posed by Seth, the sacri-
legious will to destruction, desecration, and plunder—the vandalistic,
iconoclastic impulse. Late Period cult texts also occasionally articulate
the rule forbidding foreigners entry to the sanctuary and attendance
at the secret rites. Foreigners are explicitly denied access to the crypts
of the Hathor temple in Dendera:

The hidden place of the mighty in the Sistrum House,
in the event that the destroyers invade Egypt:
The Asiatics enter not there,
the Bedouins harm it not,
the profane go not around within it.
Whoever recites a spell [?] against it,
may the milk of Sekhmet be in his body.

The place whose secret is concealed,
in the event that the Asiatics penetrate into the fortress:
The Phoenicians approach it not,
the Aegeans enter it not,
the sand treaders go not around within it.
Let no magician perform his rites there.
Its gates open not to the unauthorized.[49]

In a book of rituals from the Late Period, the House of Life, with its
fourfold function of library, scriptorium, school for the priests, and
sanctuary, is referred to thus:

It shall be very, very well concealed.
No one shall know it, no one see it
except the disk of the sun, that looks into its secret.[50]
Those officiating . . . shall enter in silence, their bodies covered,

so as to be protected against sudden death.
The Asiatic must not enter, he must see nothing.[51]

This secrecy commandment was especially typical of the Greek and
Latin texts circulating under the collective name of *Corpus Hermeti-*
cum, a collection of treatises believed to have been written by Hermes
Trismegistus, a sage of primordial times, but shown by Isaac Casau-
bon in 1614 to be a work of late antiquity. Hermeticism was, from its
origin, bound up with notions of the strictest secrecy and esotericism.
One of the texts actually contains a passage forbidding translation
into Greek (although the text handed down to us is itself in Greek):

> Leave this text untranslated, so that these secrets remain hidden
> from the Greeks and their irreverent, feeble, and orotund speech
> does not undermine the dignity and vigor of our language and
> the energy of the names. For the discourse of the Greeks, though
> outwardly impressive, is empty, and their philosophy is nothing
> but verbose noise. We by contrast, we employ not words but
> sounds full of energy.[52]

The Egyptians' attitude toward foreigners had nothing to do with
racism or nationalism; rather, it reflected their concern that foreigners
might act in a blasphemous way toward the gods, who, offended,
might then turn away from Egypt.[53]

The Egyptians' fear that other religions might undermine their
own was unfounded, as far as the Greeks were concerned. The Greeks
acted on the belief that the gods were supranational and intercultural.
Herodotus even opined that the Greeks had adopted most of their
deities from the Egyptians. At all events, in matters of religion, there
were no fundamental differences between the peoples. Even if the
Egyptians did everything exactly the other way around from everyone
else, their gods were the same as those worshipped by others, and
thus their names could easily be translated from one language into
another. The Greeks had no difficulty in recognizing their gods in the
Egyptian deities. Such open-mindedness was not limited to an intellectual like Herodotus, but was also apparent in the ease with which
the Ptolemies hellenized Egyptian place names. Their method was to
add the suffix "polis" to the Greek translation of the respective local
deity: Heliopolis, Hermopolis, Diospolis, Apollinopolis, Aphroditop-
olis, Letopolis, Herakleopolis, and so on, quite as if they were dealing
with cities of Helios, Hermes, Zeus, Apollo, Aphrodite, Leto, Herakles.

This translation of divine names and the underlying conviction that the gods were intercultural was by no means a specifically Greek position, but was fully in line with ancient Near Eastern polytheism. Two- and three-language lists of divine names dating back as far as the third millennium have come down to us from the Sumerians, including the three-column list called *anu ša ameli*.[54] The first column records the Sumerian names, the second their Akkadian counterparts, the third the function or specialty of the deity in question. The method that underlies the translation requires that a name refer not only to a particular figure (like any other proper name) but also to a specific task or area for which the deity in question is responsible; this common denominator then permits the pairing of deities from different religions. Translating these names meant being aware of the divine specialties, and this knowledge is the specific achievement of Near Eastern polytheism. In creating conceptual definitions of the gods, polytheism provided a foundation or "interface" for translation between cultures. In this framework, the religion of another people was the least alien thing about them.

Persian religious practice was fundamentally different. The Zoro-astrianism of the Achaemenids categorically ruled out any kind of translatability between its own religious world and the Egyptian pantheon. For political reasons, other religions might be tolerated or even encouraged, but any cross-cultural connection on the religious plane was unthinkable. Thus specifically religious confrontations such as those imputed to Seth may have taken place under Persian rule: destruction of temples and cultic images, killing and consumption of sacred animals. The Greek and Egyptian complaints about these desecrations may have been only in part tendentious. Very different is the case of Jedaniah, the leader of the Jewish military colony in Elephantine, who writes to the Persian governor that though Cambyses destroyed all the Egyptian temples, he spared the Jewish Yahu temple in Elephantine.[55] How are we to understand this letter? It can hardly be an accusation. Rather, it is an appeal to a kind of religious solidarity between Persians and Jews against the Egyptians. This Persian-Jewish solidarity indicates that a conflictual front had emerged in the sphere of religiosity. On the Egyptian side the counterreaction took the form of the hate rituals against the god Seth.

But the Egyptian response does not appear to have ended there. In the same letter to the Persian governor, Jedaniah requests formal permission to rebuild the Yahu temple destroyed three years earlier by Egyptian soldiers at the command of the Persian governor

Vidranga. The letter suggests that the priests of the ram god Khnum at Elephantine made use of the temporary absence of the satrap Arsames/Arsham to bribe Vidranga into committing this atrocity. In the meantime, and much to the gratification of the Jewish community, Vidranga and all the other culprits had been executed, but the temple had not been rebuilt and the community had spent the last three years mourning and fasting.

The source of the Khnum priests' rancor against the Jews and the Yahu temple can be elicited from other documents. The memorandum granting permission for the rebuilding of the temple makes specific reference to a cereal offering and to incense. Not mentioned (and therefore prohibited) is the practice of burnt offerings, in which sacrificial animals are immolated on the altar. In another document explicit mention is made of "sheep, oxen, goats [. . .] not being used for holocaust offerings, only incense and cereal."[56] It is now generally agreed that the burnt offering of the paschal lamb was the bone of contention. The Khnum priests, whose temple and animal necropolis were in the immediate vicinity of the Yahu temple, must have taken offense at the sheep sacrifices of the Jews. What happened at Elephantine is precisely what Moses predicted would happen in response to the pharaoh's demand that the Jews celebrate the sacrificial feast in Egypt and not in the desert: "It is not meet so to do; for we shall sacrifice the abomination of the Egyptians to the Lord our God: lo, we shall sacrifice the abomination of the Egyptians before their eyes, and will they not stone us?" (Exodus 8:26).

The Myth of the Lepers

IN GREEK SOURCES, the god Seth, stylized into the archenemy by the hate rituals, is linked with the Jews. In chapter 31 of his *De Iside et Osiride,* Plutarch quotes a source that calls Seth the tribal father of the Jews. After being driven out of Egypt, Seth fled for seven days and then, once safe, begot his sons Hierosolyma and Juda. As we have seen, the figure of Seth personifies Egyptian fears of the deadly power of the desert, of the destructive fury of the Asiatic invaders, and of the religious enemy who slaughters sacred animals and tramples over all the religious mysteries. A demotic prophecy from the Roman period interprets incidences of disaster and disorder as manifestations of Seth.[57] This text also links the figure of Seth with the Jews. Isis appears as the adversary of Seth and the Jews, who are designated as "lawbreakers driven out of Egypt at the command of Isis." "Attack the Jews," the text continues, "for godless men will plunder your temples" and "your greatest temple will be sand for the horses." The fear of the "foreigners [who] will inhabit this land" and who "will not only neglect the old cults but actively prohibit them" (as the *Asclepius Apocalypse* has it) crystallized not around the Greeks and Romans as representatives of political force but around the Jews as adherents of an alien religion.

This representation of the Jews is a variation on the "myth of the lepers," which we have already encountered in the memorialization of the Amarna Period. Here we are concerned less with the original impetus for the formation of the legend than with the historical conditions in which it gained currency and meaning in Hellenistic Egypt. Only Manetho's version contains clear reminiscences of the Amarna experience; all other versions of the legend refer unequivocally to the Jews. The oldest rendering of the story is found in Hecataeus of Abdera, whose version avoids (almost) all the anti-Judaic allusions so typical of later forms.[58] In Hecataeus, a plague is raging in Egypt, from which the Egyptians conclude that the gods are incensed at the large number of foreigners living in Egypt with their alien cults and customs. The Egyptians resolve to banish the foreigners. Hecataeus makes no mention of the foreigners' place of origin or of how they got to Egypt in the first place. The exiles establish colonies in Greece and Palestine, the former led by Danaos and Kadmos, the others by Moses, the founder and lawgiver of the Jerusalem colony. Moses puts a ban on images of the gods "because no god has a human form; heaven alone, which encompasses the earth, be lord and god of all."[59]

While Manetho set the "myth of the lepers" in the reign of Amenophis III, Lysimachos, an Alexandrian historian who probably lived in the second century B.C.E., recounts a version in which a famine prompts the king Bocchoris to appeal to the oracle.[60] (As we have seen, Amenophis III and Bocchoris are the two kings traditionally bound up with prophecies in the Late Period traditions, Amenophis with the *Potter's Oracle* and Bocchoris with the *Oracle of the Lamb*.) Bocchoris is ordered to cleanse the temple of the "impure and impious," a reference to Jews afflicted with leprosy and other ailments who sought refuge in the temple. He thereupon commands that the lepers be drowned and the others banished into the wilderness. Thus, as with Hecataeus, a state of emergency, in this case a famine, initiates events. But there is also a link with Manetho: the foreigners banished from the land are carriers of a contagious disease. They assemble around "one called Moses," who leads them out of the country and commands them to be "benevolent to none and destroy all temples and altars."[61] The multiple variants of the story are characteristic manifestations of an oral tradition, in which each version takes up and modifies formulaic elements, such as persons (Amenophis, Bocchoris) and narrative motifs (hardship, recourse to the oracle or a soothsayer, expulsion of the impure/impious).

With Apion, whom Flavius Josephus set out to refute, Moses is an Egyptian from Heliopolis who led the Jews out of Egypt. Once in Jerusalem, "he maintained his allegiance to the mores of his country and set up hypaithral [uncovered] prayer houses in various parts of the city, all facing east, because that way lay Heliopolis. Instead of the obelisks he put up pillars with models of a ship underneath them. The shadow cast by the statue on this basin described a circle analogous to the circuit of the sun in the heavens."[62] Apion's version is the only one from which the motif of the alien religion is absent.

The Egyptian Apion was the curator of the museum in Alexandria in the first half of the first century C.E. His successor in office was Chaeremon, probably also an Egyptian, who later went to Rome as tutor to Emperor Nero.[63] Chaeremon's rendering of the story is especially close to the demotic prophecy in which Isis calls for the expulsion of the Jews. Isis appears to King Amenophis in a dream and upbraids him for failing to restore a temple that had been destroyed in times of war. The priestly scribe Phritibantes (the "chief of the temple") advises him to mollify the goddess by purging Egypt of the lepers. King Amenophis herds 250,000 lepers together and drives them out of the land. Their leaders are Moses and Joseph, whose Egyptian names are Tisithen and Peteseph. In Pelusium they are joined by 380,000 exiles denied the right of emigration by Amenophis. Together the two groups conquer Egypt. The king is forced to flee to Nubia; later, his son and successor Ramesses drives the "Jews" out, to Syria, and reconquers Egypt.

Tacitus, in his *Histories,* presents a conflation of various different versions of the Exodus myth.[64] Egypt is stricken by a plague that leaves its victims with physical deformities. King Bocchoris consults the oracle and learns that he must "purge" the land and banish this race because they are hateful to the gods. Moses assumes leadership of the

Jews in their exile, leads them to Palestine, and founds Jerusalem. To establish his influence once and for all, Moses gives the people a new religion contrary to all other religions: "The Jews regard as profane all that we hold sacred; on the other hand, they permit all we abhor." In their temple the Jews consecrate the statue of a donkey and sacrifice a ram to it, "apparently in derision of Ammon"; they also sacrifice a bull "because the Egyptians worship Apis." Tacitus' version represents the apogee of myth formation by opposition. All the rites of one side are represented as the blasphemous inversion of what is sacred to the other.

Pompeius Trogus, a historian writing at the beginning of the first century B.C.E., gives a very detailed report of the Exodus, combining the biblical version with the Egyptian myth.[65] In Trogus' version, Moses is the son of Joseph. The Egyptians, afflicted by leprosy and other ills, are warned by the oracle to drive him out of Egypt together with other lepers. In his flight, Moses abducts the sacred utensils of the Egyptians, who set off in pursuit but are forced to turn back by a storm. Moses arrives in Palestine after a seven-day journey on foot and decrees that the seventh day be a holy day. Mindful that they had been driven out of Egypt for fear of contagion, Moses forbids the Jews any contact with foreigners; this prohibition gradually develops into a religious taboo.

This entire mythology dramatizes the idea of religious sacrilege. Manetho's rebellion of the lepers is in the first instance an attack on the gods, whose cult is prohibited and whose dietary taboos are systematically violated. Amenophis' first concern is to salvage the divine images and the sacred animals. The atrocities of the vandal rebels, adherents of an invisible god and an invisible religion, are directed at the temples, cultic images, and sacred animals—the outward, visible signs of the traditional world of the gods. The Egyptian versions are notable for their almost phobic concern with purity and their meticulous care for the cultic images and the sacred animals. This phobia is triggered by a trauma that corresponds exactly to the graphic prophecies of the Potter and the Lamb, as well as to the depredations of Egypt imputed to the Persians in the legends assembled by Herodotus: destruction of the temples and cultic images, desecration of the mysteries, killing of the sacred animals.

While Manetho's version of this story revolves around traditional material that dates back to the age of Amarna and even to the Hyksos, the other versions under discussion here make clear reference to the Jews, and some of them present explicit parallels to the biblical Exodus story. In the biblical account, the emergency is a dual one: first the travail of the enslaved children of Israel, who cry out to God in their extremity, and then the invidious position of the Egyptians, afflicted by plagues until they free the Israelites. The exodus itself has a dual form, appearing both as a mass release and a military pursuit. Finally, the colony motif also has a double form, first as the settlement of the children of Israel in Goshen, and then as the foundation of a people following the revelation of the Law on Mount Sinai and its proclamation by Moses.

The biblical version is an exact counterpart to the Egyptian version. In the latter, the Jews are presented as lepers by the Egyptians, while in the Bible the Egyptians are portrayed as torturers and slave drivers. Both versions are steeped in phobic abhorrence. The Exodus myth with its Jewish Egyptophobia portrays the Egyptians as tyrants, oppressors, magicians, and idol worshippers, while the Egyptian Judeophobia of the myth of the lepers portrays these foreigners as taboo violators, temple desecrators, blasphemers, atheists, and misanthropes. (But as I hope to have made clear, this is a variant of the Egyptians' Asiatic trauma, and not some more specific kind of anti-Semitism.)

The myth of the lepers epitomizes the constellation of mutual cultural abhorrence. Idolatry and iconoclasm are dialectically interrelated. One side sees ultimate sacrilege and radical evil in a religion deluded by creatures and images and unable to address the Creator directly. The other identifies the most heinous of sins in a religion that destroys the images and violates the taboos, thus cutting off all contact with the world of the gods and their benevolence—the fruitfulness of the land, justice among men, the very fabric and organization of the world. The Golden Calf in the biblical legend corresponds to the slaughter of the sacred animals in the Egyptian version. The symmetry is perfect. The abhorrence of idolatry stems from the desire for redemption from the world, the abhorrence of iconoclasm from the desire to keep the world in functioning order. In the history of Jewish exegesis of the Bible, recognition of this relationship has never been lost. Invariably, the Law has been seen as the inversion of idolatry, most impressively by the great, if not orthodox, philosopher Rabbi Moses ben Maimon (Maimonides, 1135–1204) in his *Guide for the Perplexed.*

All the motifs of this story—fear of the other religion as a negation and destruction of one's own faith; the suspicion of a conspiracy among its adherents, foreign political foes, and lepers—reappear fifteen hundred years later in France. Chronicles dating from the year 1321 report that all the lepers in France were rounded up and killed because they had attempted to eradicate Christianity by poisoning the fountains and wells and thus to seize rule for themselves. Some versions suggest that "the Jews" had conspired with the lepers, but the majority tell a more complex story, in which the author of the conspiracy between the Jews and the lepers was the Islamic king of Granada. Unable to destroy the Christians by force of arms, he resorted to this subterfuge, offering the Jews a huge sum of money to implement it. The Jews made use of the lepers as the instrument of their foul plot.[66]

When bubonic plague broke out in France twenty-five years later, the general fear soon found expression in massacres of Jews. Again there was common belief in a conspiracy and an attempt to poison the wells. Since the lepers had already been killed, only the Jews remained as scapegoats for the disaster.[67] What is the explanation for this continuity? Carlo Ginzburg suggests that the medieval dissemination of Flavius Josephus' tractate *Contra Apionem* brought the Egyptian myth to the western world and facilitated the association of Jews and lepers, together with such traditional anti-Semitic clichés as ritual murder and the cult of the donkey.[68] The story does figure, though, in Tacitus' *Histories* and was taken up by Christian historians such as Orosius. Undoubtedly there were other more universal anthropological and psychohistorical factors at work as well. In comparable circumstances, parallel forms of mass hysteria and scapegoat-seeking will emerge spontaneously in different societies. And yet it cannot be denied that a significant number of elements in western anti-Semitism can only be explained as the survival of an Egyptian semiology that dates back to the age of the Persians and the Ptolemies.[69]

Rituals of Expulsion and Presentification

CONDITIONED AS WE ARE by the biblical idea of redemption, we find the iconoclastic impulse comprehensible. By contrast, we find it very difficult to understand the Egyptian veneration of images, what the Bible demonizes as "idolatry."

The Papyrus Jumilhac, a Thirtieth Dynasty manuscript containing a codification of priestly knowledge, describes the connection between cultic practice and "cosmic maintenance" that dominated late Egyptian mentality:

When few offering breads are on their altars,
then the same happens in the whole country
and meager will be the sustenance of the living.
When the libations at this place are interrupted,
then the flooding of the Nile will be meager at its source hole
and the mouth of the tortoise sealed.
A year of famine reigns in all the land;
there are neither fruits of the tree ["tree of life"] nor vegetables.
If one neglects the Osiris ceremonies
at their time in this place . . .
then the land will be bereft of its laws,
the lowly will flee their lords,
and there will be no commands for the many . . .
If one does not behead the foe one has in front of one,
the foe of wax, of papyrus or of wood, according to the rules of
    the ritual,
then the foreigners will rise up against Egypt
and civil war and unrest will arise in all the land.
One will not heed the king in his palace
and the land will be bereft of his protection.[70]

Cultic practice sustains the world, in its natural aspect as fertility and abundance, in its social aspect as vertical solidarity, and in its political aspect as external and internal peace through pharaonic authority. In the riven world, cosmogonic energies are no longer manifest in an exclusively positive and creative way. To sustain life, it is necessary to declare war on chaos. Hence the course of the sun is accompanied on earth by ritual actions with a double meaning: praising the sun god and combating Apopis. As Amenemope proclaims in his teachings, "One acclaims the uraeus snake and spits on Apopis."[71] The sun god is the object of love, delight, rapturous admiration, while Apopis is the target of hatred, abhorrence, and rampant destructiveness.

One hate ritual against Apopis has come down to us. A text of unusual length (fifty-two pages of autographed hieroglyphics), it contains a veritable orgy of violent fantasies leveled not at an earthly political foe but at a wax effigy of the cosmic foe, which is subjected to every imaginable indignity and aggression before finally being destroyed by fire.[72] The first saying is recited so as "to spit on Apopis," the second "to take the harpoon to strike Apopis," the third "to bind Apopis," the fourth "to take the knife to pierce Apopis," the fifth "to set fire to Apopis," the sixth "to throw Apopis to the flames," and so on. This endless tirade of hatred hurled at the cosmic foe was designed for recitation "every hour of the morning, noontide, evening, and night, at high festivals, and if necessary during storms, cloud formation, or thunder, when the eastern sky turned red, or when bad weather was in the offing." Thus the enemy of the sun was kept at bay and the circuit of the sun sustained.

The text hinges on the parallelism between cosmos and kingship. What Pharaoh does to the foes of the sun is likewise done to the foes of Pharaoh. "Come to Pharaoh, Re: fell his foes as he felled Apopis and punished the miscreant for you";[73] "Behold, Pharaoh drives out all your enemies for you, Re: drive out all his enemies among the living and the dead."[74] All the gods' warlike action against Apopis is also directed at the foes of the pharaoh. Horus uses his iron harpoon to smash the heads of the enemies of Re as well as the heads of the enemies of the pharaoh;[75] the slaughterers take their knives to cut down the enemies of Re and also the enemies of the pharaoh.[76] Clearly, this destruction ritual was thought conducive not only to cosmic but also to political welfare, sustaining the rule of the pharaoh along with the course of the sun; hence the fear that internal and external foes might gain the ascendancy if, even once, the wax effigy of the Apopis dragon was not given the full treatment.

This kind of symbolic violence played an immense part in Egyptian cultic practice and became more and more dominant as awareness grew of the land's peril.[77] With the increasing demonization of Seth, the political dimension of the "foe" became increasingly prominent. In the course of time, Seth gradually became known as "the Mede" and thus equated with the hated Persians. The symbolic violence acted out in the temple rituals helped Late Period Egyptians come to terms with the experience of foreign rule, to resolve the cognitive dissonance caused by the presence of a foreigner on the pharaonic throne. In name, the rites were performed on behalf of the Ptolemaic king sitting on the throne. But occasionally at least, the Egyptian priests probably had no major difficulty in extending the blanket term "foes" to the Greeks and including them in the scope of the hatred and abhorrence that these rites modeled and enacted.

The hate rituals were not an invention of the Ptolemaic age. The anxieties suffusing late-Egyptian views of the world had a long history.

Typical of the Late Period, however, was the idea that connective justice could be assured by means of cultic ritual. Our sources so far—the rites, the political prophecies, the legends of the banishment of the lepers—all reflect a phobic, almost compulsive fixation on cult: what the Bible calls "idolatry." Yet the biblical texts on idolatry display exactly the same attitude. The Book of Deuteronomy, in the imprecation of chapter 28, paints a wildly horrific picture of what will happen if Israel is unfaithful to the covenant, whose supreme commandment is complete abstention from any kind of idolatry. Over the Israelite image of the world and history, as over its Egyptian counterpart, hovers the dread nexus of infidelity and catastrophe. The story of the Golden Calf dramatized to the Jews the precise meaning of infidelity. At that moment, the world was indeed at stake.

The Golden Calf is the same Apis bull of which the *Demotic Chronicle* says:

Apis, Apis, Apis—
that is to say: Ptah, Phre, Harsiesis,
who are the lords of the office of ruler.

As astounding as are the parallels between the *Demotic Chronicle* and the biblical reading of history, the differences in this confrontation between idolatry and iconoclasm are no less remarkable. Egyptian revolts broke out when cultic practice was endangered by official neglect. In Judaea, revolts took place for exactly the opposite reason, when rulers like Antiochus IV Epiphanes attempted to enforce alien cultic customs. As early as Deuteronomy, the characteristic failure of the kings to observe the law and adhere to God's ways consisted in too much religion rather than too little—that is, in the introduction of alien cults. What "displeases" Yahweh is not the curtailment of his offerings and festivals but the introduction of "heathen" customs and the recidivism symbolized by the Golden Calf. Israel's phobia was the worship of false gods, Egypt's the neglect of the gods.

It is a misinterpretation, albeit a frequent one, that these Egyptian anxieties were nothing more than the projected fears of a parasitic priestly caste worried about the loss of offerings. Naturally there must have been small-minded priests supremely concerned with maintaining the offering funds that furnished their livelihood. But the semiologies informing Egyptian cult practice must be sought elsewhere. Why did the Egyptians believe that the only way they could contact the gods was by way of images and sacred animals?

The Egyptians thought the gods to be remote and hidden. But there were two ways in which they manifested themselves on earth: inhabitation and incarnation. In classical Egyptian religion, incarnation was largely realized by the pharaoh. The god Horus embodied himself in the king as the last link in the dynasty of gods unfolding into human history. Inhabitation was realized by the divine images, which were prominently foregrounded by the Egyptians. The Egyptian texts that theorize cult practice present the daily inhabitation of the gods in their images as a unification of *ba* and image, with the *ba* descending from heaven and entering the cult likeness in the temple. For example, the *ba* form of the god of Edfu is the winged sun disk called Apy. "Once Apy has arrived in the heavens on each day to see his image in his sanctuary, he sets himself down on a statue. He unites with his [relief] images and his heart is content in his chapel."[78] "The splendid Apy is radiant in the mountains of the East so that he can be one with his image in Edfu."[79] "Your *ba* in heaven unites with his image so that the one unites with its counterpart."[80]

A convenient label for late Egyptian theology might indeed be "theology of inhabitation." Underlying this theology is the idea that language and ritual can persuade the remote and hidden powers of the heavens, the underworld, the past, and the future to inhabit the here-and-now of the temple. But unceasing application and unremitting effort are necessary. The temple is the locus of advent and conjunction, where the concept of "habitation" is dramatized. Every morning the god "comes down," "beholds," and "enters" his dwelling, then "unites" with his images; every night he "goes to rest" and "sleeps" in his temple.[81] The temple, though never bereft of the god's presence, is at the same time the place of his never-ending advent. The temple's towers are antennae and landing bases, so to speak, to which the god "comes" in the form of falcon and phoenix.[82] But the entire temple and the rites performed in it are a single permanent entity designed to prevent the influx of divine presence from ever being interrupted.

Under the conditions of foreign domination, the idea of incarnation, on the other hand, was transposed from the king to the sacred animals. The god of Edfu embodied himself in a sacred animal recognizable as such by the priest because of its form and coloring. In this incarnation, the god forfeited the omnipotence celebrated in his hymns; he thus exposed himself to the hazards of this world, from which he then had to be protected by the performance of extremely precise and powerful rites. The same rites that protected the incarnate god also preserved the king and the land from misfortune, since the god, by virtue of his incarnation, united his destiny with that of the country. By incarnation in the sacred animals and inhabitation in the sacred rites and images, the divine engaged in a very profound contact with the human world, not to redeem it, but to sustain it. The influx of divine presence takes the form of an energy that animates the statues and becomes flesh in the sacred animals.

This world-sustaining energy is generated by "connectivity." In the arrangement of its chambers with their ubiquitous and all-embracing writing and imagery, and in the rites performed on its premises, the temple guaranteed the connection of all separate things. A relational, connective magic was wrought through words, images, sacred acts, and architecture—the full range of symbolic forms in all their cultural materializations.

One brief Greek text from Edfu presents an intensely cogent and trenchant articulation of the connective principle: "With power, O king, with power, O falcon, with swift chargers, O sun god, let the flame run its course!" In this short passage, the cult of the sacred animal, the political rule of the king, and the cosmic energy of the sun's circuit are harnessed into a triangle of salvational power.

The temple was the locus of connective practice, and its medium was language. The texts covering its walls were not only renderings of the cultic recitations that resounded within its precincts; they also described the temple and elucidated the theology behind it. In the *First Book of Kings,* the Bible tells of the construction and consecration of Solomon's temple, and reconstructions of that temple have frequently been attempted on the basis of the description. In Edfu and other Egyptian temples of the Greco-Roman Period, we have much more extensive and detailed descriptions to compare with architectural reality. But there is something else that these texts have to tell us. The temple and all that went on within it were nothing other than the precise implementation of language, specifically written language. In layout, decoration, and ritual practice the temple corresponded with minute accuracy to the holy writings, which were referred to with a very strange and characteristic expression: "*ba*s of Re," probably best rendered as "solar energy." The sacred writings codified the world-sustaining power of the circuit of the sun, the temple translated it into earthly practice, and the texts carved on the walls communicated it in a way that remains accessible to us across the interval of thousands of years and the chasms of cultural otherness.

27

RE-MEMBERING OSIRIS

Re-Membering Osiris

PERHAPS THE MOST IMPRESSIVE EGYPTIAN RESPONSE to the experience of foreign rule was the transformation that the ancient rituals of the Osirian mysteries underwent in the temples of the Greco-Roman Period. It is also a very striking instance of the connection between historical experience and the cultural construction of meaning.

The ceremonies centered on the ritual reconstitution, embalming, and mummification of the dismembered body of the god Osiris, who was murdered by his brother Seth. We do not know whether the transformation of these rituals predated the Greco-Roman Period. The earliest extant sources for their late form date from the Ptolemaic Period. The rites celebrated in the month of Khoiak are the most important all-Egyptian ritual of the Late Period and were performed in all the temples throughout the land. The rites revolved around the creation of an effigy of Osiris in the shape of a corn mummy and its ritual burial. A golden casket was filled with vegetable mold and grains of barley, which were left to grow for eight days. This ritual symbolized the embalming and mummification of Osiris' dead body. The crucial aspect is the restoration of unity, the transformation of dismembered remains into an integral whole. The process of reunification was symbolically enacted by a procession of priests carrying canopic jars. These were lidded vessels used throughout Egyptian civilization to hold the entrails of mummified bodies. The procession is described at length in an inscription dated from the first century B.C.E. that appears in the Osiris chapel, which is located on the roof of the Temple of Hathor at Dendera. Forty-two priests take part in the procession, personifying the forty-two nomes of the land. Attended by the major deities, each bears a canopic vase holding one of the scattered remnants of Osiris' mangled corpse. The body of Osiris is then ritually reassembled from these parts. The canopic jars probably also contained an offering of Nile water. The accompanying texts make repeated mention of the outflowings of Osiris; in the Late Period, Osiris was associated more and more closely with the Nile and its inundations. The spells recited during the ritual interpret the gift of water in two ways: at one level, they refer to the specific part of Osiris' body in the vase as the contribution of the respective nome to the "re-membering" of the god; at another level, they interpret the body parts as representations of the nomes or nome capitals, so that the ritual restoration of Osiris' physical and spiritual integrity also symbolizes the reunification of the entire land. The words spoken by the king, who accompanies the procession, clearly express this equation of Osiris *redivivus* and the totality of the land of Egypt:

> I bring you the capitals of the nomes: they are your limbs, they
>   are your *ka,* which is with you.
> I bring you your name, your *ba,* your shadow, your form, your
>   image, and the towns of your nomes.
> I bring you the main gods of Lower Egypt joined together.
> All are the members of your body; they are united.

The embalming ritual is applied to the entire kingdom of Egypt, to heal its disintegration, to unite, inspirit, and renew it. The festal period begins with the discovery and the embalming of the forty-two scattered parts of the murdered Osiris; they are reassembled from the forty-two nomes of the country, ritually reunited, and revived. The rituals end with the burial of Osiris and the accession to the throne by Horus, his son and avenger. The festival has its roots in the cult of the dead, the embalming ritual. Not until the Late Period did it acquire a political meaning.

On the one hand, the ritual emphasizes diversity. The forty-two nomes and nome capitals are carefully distinguished and listed with all their specific local features. At this level, the ritual is the expression of an extreme regionalism that conceives of each nome as a cosmos in its own right. In the temples of the Ptolemaic period this liturgical geography played a crucial role, providing the central element around which the knowledge of the sacred traditions was codified. Egypt appears as a canon of forty-two "bodies" of knowledge, each forming an entire library of essential sacred books. Excerpts from this canon are present in all the temples. Each temple is a cosmos in its own right; but in the form of extensive processional images taken from this canon, each temple also represents the totality of Egypt and ritually celebrates that totality in the form of the Khoiak mysteries. Diversity is emphasized so that it can be reunited—embalmed—in a ritual form. The Egyptians equated the dismembered body of Osiris with the multiplicity of the nomes, in order to celebrate the wholeness and integrity of the land in a ritual of reconstitution. The motive was concern for the continuing existence of Egyptian civilization in the face of a crisis that was interpreted and ritually enacted as a disintegrating force.

In the Greco-Roman Period the integrity of Egyptian civilization as a coherent system of meaning was increasingly threatened by disintegration and cultural amnesia. Seth, the murderer of Osiris and the mutilator of his corpse, was also the Asiatic, the foreigner. Prior to the Late Period these two aspects of Seth had existed side by side; now they intermeshed. Seth's murderous assault took on a new political meaning. It stood for the constant danger by which Egypt felt threatened. And the source of that danger was invariably located in the north. The great victory festival of Horus of Edfu enacts the myth as an incursion from the north by Seth that is repulsed from the south by Horus. The topic of invasion from the north also plays a central role in other Late Period mythologies. The political and sacramental interpretation of these myths in the rituals and festivals of the period articulates a pan-Egyptian response to Persian, Greek, and Roman rule. The Khoiak rituals seek to avert the demise of Egyptian culture, not only by uniting the forty-two nomes in analogy to the reconstitution of Osiris' torn limbs, but also by compiling lists and liturgies to preserve the immense fund of cultural knowledge that had accumulated in and around those nomes.

Priesthood as a Way of Life

AT THE END OF THE NEW KINGDOM, the first priestly dwellings appeared in the temple at Karnak, and during the Third Intermediate

Period the custom of priests actually living inside the temple precincts gradually established itself. The temple walls now encompassed not only the performance of a cult but also a specific form of human cohabitation. But the difference between this way of life and the lives of other Egyptians was not only a matter of enclosure within temple walls; rather, it centered on specific rules for the conduct of life—the so-called Egyptian Torah. The priests were bound by rules that combined ritual purity instructions with moral maxims. These rules were inscribed on the passageways through which the priests entered the temple every day, and were part of a much more comprehensive fund of knowledge guarded and administered by the priests. In written form, this knowledge was enshrined in a small library of books that codified the entire treasury of relevant knowledge.

Clement of Alexandria has left us a description of such a library.[83] He speaks of forty-two "absolutely essential" books that formed the central core of any temple library, and were attributed to Thoth-Hermes himself. The priests were the repositories of this knowledge. Thus they were not required to know all the books, but to concentrate on specific subjects in accordance with their rank and office. Clement invites us to imagine a priestly procession, with the participants emerging from the sacred building in a hierarchical sequence that mirrors the structure of their library. First comes the singer, carrying a musical emblem. He will have memorized two books of Hermes, one containing hymns to the gods and the other a biography of the reigning king. Next comes the astrologer, carrying a palm branch and an astrological symbol. He will have mastered the four astrological books of Hermes, dealing with darkness, the planets, the encounters and appearances of sun and moon, and the rising of the dekan stars. He is followed by the scribe, who wears a quill and carries the instruments of his craft. He will have learned the ten hieroglyphic books that address cosmography and geography, the constellations of the sun, moon, and five planets, the soil of Egypt and the nature of the Nile, the construction of the temples, the land allocated to the temples, and the objects used in the temples. The stolist comes next. His area of expertise includes the ten books dealing with education, cults, and sacrifices. Last comes the prophet,[84] bearing a *situla* and water, followed by attendants who carry a ceremonial plate piled with bread. The prophet will know the ten hieratic books, which concern the laws, the gods, and priestly education.

Up to this point the list is arranged in ascending order. The prophet has the highest rank, the stolist the next highest, the scribe the third highest, and so on. According to Clement there were also six medical books, on the anatomy of the body, on illnesses, on bodily organs, on drugs, on eye ailments, and on women's ailments.

The book catalogues that have come down to us from the temple libraries of Edfu and el-Tod confirm Clement's account.[85] The tendency toward self-segregation and canonization is clearly visible throughout these sources, not least in the sacred number 42, which corresponds to the number of nomes in Egypt, just as in the Hebrew Bible the sacred numbers 22 and 24 correspond to the number of letters in the Hebrew and Aramaic alphabets respectively. A canon has no place for randomness in its form and structure. The 42 nomes and the 22/24 letters are symbols of the Whole, formulas for all that is. The canon, as the realization of such cosmic formulae, represents the universe in book form. The canon of the 42 books reflects the idea of Egypt with its 42 nomes in the same way as the "canopic procession" of the 42 nomes in the ritual of Re-Membering Osiris.

(The Hebrew Bible also displays all the features of a core library of "essential" working knowledge. It is in fact much more of a library than a book. In its final canonical form, it limits itself to three departments: Torah, Prophets, and Writings, in descending order of normativity. True, the libraries of Qumran and Tebtunis are thought to have contained some one thousand scrolls, a huge figure indeed; but in terms of content, the character of a working library, as opposed to a collection library, is again readily apparent.)

"Textual communities" is the term Brian Stock has used for the heretic movements of the Middle Ages that derived their justification for unorthodox procedures from a body of literature intended for their use alone.[86] Many of the features Stock identifies as typical of the movements of the eleventh and twelfth centuries C.E. are present in the Qumran community and in numerous similar groupings, such as the Orphics, Pythagoreans, Gnostics, early Christians, Hermeticists, and the like.[87] Distinguishing characteristics of textual communities are on the one hand an identity-forming corpus of writings, on the other a structure of authority and leadership that derives from formal interpretative competence. Philological and political competence collapse into one. Leadership is invested in those who have the profoundest knowledge and the most convincing interpretation of the texts.

Is the Late Period Egyptian priesthood such a textual community? Probably only in part. First, the factor of dissidence is entirely absent. The priests were not a sect; they were not setting themselves apart from a "mainstream" culture, but were the core representatives of official religion. Their marked need for self-segregation had other motives. They avoided contact with foreigners and the impure, led strictly cloistered and regimented lives, and devoted all their time to worship, meditation, and cultivation of the scriptures. For those reasons alone, they were bound to steer clear of the profane business of the world. In addition—and perhaps even more crucial—the priests of the Late Period saw themselves as Egypt's social and intellectual elite. In the Greek period, there was no longer any form of officialdom equal to the priesthood in rank, with the result that the priests came to be seen as the indigenous elite. Every elite needs to parade the signs of its distinction. One typical way of foregrounding such distinction is to affect a sophisticated lifestyle, which is then elevated to the level of a fine art extremely difficult to master. Indeed, the only guarantee of mastery is birth into the right circle; such is the principle underlying all forms of aristocracy. In Egypt, the distinguishing fine art had a specifically written form: knowledge of the books, command of script, virtuosity in the handiwork of Thoth. In this respect, the priestly confraternity did indeed resemble a textual community. Yet it is also crucial (and this is the second distinction over and against textual communities in the narrower sense) that the priests saw their most important function not as the cultivation of written traditions or the interpretation of sacred texts but the performance of religious rites. The texts were nothing other than the indispensable source for the correct performance of the rites. The canonic texts contained either the recitations and ritual instructions or the necessary basic information concerning the layout and decoration of temples, astronomy, kingship, legislation, right and wrong, proper living, and so on. That central caveat aside, the Egyptian temples of the Late Period did indeed house an alternative community with a way of life characterized by asceticism and contemplation.

A central feature of the elitism of the Egyptian priests in the Greco-Roman era was the stylization of hieroglyphic script into a species of cryptography. At that time the priests were using no fewer than four different writing systems: demotic and Greek for everyday purposes, and hieroglyphic and hieratic for religious purposes,[88] such as the inscription of temples and stone monuments and the copying and writing of temple literature. Hieroglyphic script was used for inscriptions, as before, and hieratic for books. At this late stage of Egyptian civilization, both forms of script were learned only by priests. Ordinary scribes were conversant with demotic, some with Greek. Hieroglyphic and hieratic script had attained the status of purely religious writing, without any everyday communicative function; its sole purpose was to preserve priestly tradition and aestheticize its representation. The intent of this arcane cryptification of script was not so much to mystify as to enhance visibility. Viktor Shklovski has called the aesthetic techniques of enhancing visibility "alienation," the goal of which is to heighten awareness and to prevent staleness of perception. Habit, says Shklovski, makes "life drift on into nothingness. Automatization devours everything, clothes, furniture, women, fear of war."[89] The function of art is to "alienate" the objects of everyday reality so that they resist automatic perception. The gaze is arrested, orientation is difficult, automatic perception is replaced by conscious, laborious, complicated decipherment.

Egyptian cryptography has been interpreted in terms of this kind of formal alienation. The enigmatic surface of the script is a reading stimulus. It arrests the gaze of the beholder, thus preventing it from gliding effortlessly from the surface of the script to the voice "behind" it, and from the voice to the meaning. Egyptian cryptography endeavors to tangle the gaze in the "thicket of signs"; reading becomes difficult, though not impossible.[90] The fundamental principle that informs all enigmatic modes of writing is deconventionalization. Either conventional signs are invested with an unconventional meaning, or new signs are invented to replace the conventional ones. These potentialities reside in the fundamental openness of the hieroglyphic system, an openness that is itself a function of the iconic nature of hieroglyphic signs. Accordingly, cryptography was possible only with hieroglyphic script, not with the cursive script that was derived from it. Hieroglyphs had a dual function: they stood for linguistic units on the phonemic or the semantic plane,[91] and at the same time, like pictorial art, they iconically represented existing things.[92] The process of conventionalization entails the discontinuing of representation on this second (iconic) plane. The sign comes to stand for a specific referent, regardless of whether the "original" referent is still iconically recognizable as such. The sign must now only stand out distinctively and discretely from the other signs in the system. Almost all originally iconic scripts have shed their iconicity in the course of their development. To recognize an "a" (as a grapheme or phoneme) it is not necessary to recognize in it the bull's head it once signified.

The development of hieroglyphs was very different. They retained their function as images even after they had become script characters. Their graphic quality, forfeited in the course of conventionalization, could be reanimated at any time. Moreover, all things representable as images could be used as script characters, which then could graphically represent the referent or its initial consonants. Or, via metaphor and metonymy, a hieroglyph might represent a concept not amenable to graphic representation.

"Ordinary" cryptography follows the rules of normal writing. Only at a second glance do we realize that the signs are unusual, enigmatic. But there is another kind of cryptography. This kind gives the initial impression of being a pictorial scene, in which the written characters look like figures in a tableau. Only when we look more closely do we realize that the figures conceal a script. Inscriptions in scenic or figural cryptography are normally found in temples, while inscriptions in mock-scriptural cryptography are usually encountered on private monuments. But the boundaries between the two forms are fluid. Figural cryptographies display a multiplicity of nonscenic elements, and script cryptographies may contain little pictorial scenes. These we may call script games, by analogy to word games. The effect of these images as visual puns hinges largely on their potential for signifying different things. Indeed, cryptography in general has a markedly ludic quality. But a special degree of polysemy is achieved when a sign functions in two entirely different semantic systems—that is, both as a script character and as a pictorial figure. A similar kind of polysemy characterizes arabesque or ornamentalized Arabic script, which functions both as part of a decorative structure and as script. In Egyptian calligraphy, the equivalent to the Arab-Islamic ornament is the figural composition.

By its very nature, hieroglyphic script invites oscillation between image and text; again, the boundaries of each are fluid. This fluidity is seldom found in sculpture in the round (although there are examples of script games in this form) and not at all in cursive script. But it is very much present in paintings, reliefs, and hieroglyphics. The Egyptian language makes no conceptual distinction among these three, referring to them indiscriminately as "script," and the same artists worked in all three media. Accordingly, in Egypt the distinction between the written sign and the iconic sign was always very much more permeable than in cultures with alphabetic script.

Egyptian cryptography belongs squarely in the aesthetic and

ludic sphere, and as such is an element of leisure culture. Impressive testimony of such productive play is found in the inscriptions of Senenmut, an official of Queen Hatshepsut's, who boasts of having invented two new cryptograms:

> Signs I have created as an invention of my heart,
> as something done in the fields [= occupation of leisure] not
>   found in the writings of the forefathers.[93]

The express, if metaphorical, mention of leisure foregrounds the playful character of this form of cryptography. Its province was an aesthetic sphere, set apart from the administrative or cultic functions of script. But for all its ludic aspects, Egyptian cryptography was anything but an idle amusement. For the Egyptians, the hieroglyphs were not arbitrary signs, but sprang from the nature of what they stood for and rested on an essential kinship between the sign itself and what it represented. Aleida Assmann has termed this principle "direct signification."[94] Assonances and graphic references, wordplay and script games all reflected the things of the world and their interconnections. The ludic handling of signs pointed up kinships and connections that lay in the nature of things and not merely in the signs. As such, it is a form of etymo*graphy* based on faith in the revelatory character of script, rather as etymo*logy* in Kabbalistic philosophy and the thinking of Heidegger rests on faith in the revelatory character of language. In Egypt, wordplay and script games were sacred forms of ludic activity, indicators of hidden connections and the cosmic coherence of the universe.

There are isolated instances of purposely enigmatic hieroglyphic inscriptions dating back as far as the Old Kingdom (second half of the third millennium B.C.E.).[95] They are somewhat more frequent in the Middle Kingdom (first quarter of the second millennium B.C.E.[96] and again in the New Kingdom (second half of the second millennium B.C.E.).[97] But before the Late Period, such inscriptions still remained extremely rare. Then, suddenly, in the period of the conquest of Egypt by Alexander the Great, the boundaries between normal script and cryptography vanished. Cryptographic principles invaded the whole system of hieroglyphic writing.[98] The result was that the repertory of signs grew immensely, swelling to at least ten times its original size. Almost every religious center developed its own script system.[99] The difficulty of deciphering script grew proportionately, and there is little doubt that the Egyptians themselves considered it a secret code accessible only to the initiated.

The priestly theory that underlies hieroglyphic script in cryptographic form has come down to us in Horapollo's tractate on hieroglyphics. This Greek text from late antiquity is usually relegated to the category of "fruitful" misunderstandings because it has itself been misunderstood as a description of "the" Egyptian script system. In fact Horapollo describes a variant, and quite patently that variant is the script that Porphyry calls symbolic. Porphyry and Clement of Alexandria distinguish three kinds of script. Porphyry calls these epistolic, hieroglyphic, and symbolic; Clement epistolic, priestly, and hieroglyphic. Clement's triad clearly refers to demotic, hieratic, and hieroglyphic script. But Porphyry does not appear to count the hieratic as a script in its own right, making instead a distinction within hieroglyphic between normal script and cryptography. If we collapse the two descriptions we obtain the following schema:

1. epistolic ("letter script") = demotic
2. priestly   = hieratic
3. hieroglyphic   = hieroglyphic
4. symbolic   = cryptographic

Horapollo's description refers to "symbolic" script. Conventional (phonetic) meanings need not detain us here. The interesting quest is for the links with reality that are identifiable behind the "script games." Thus it is not especially interesting that the word for "to open" is written with the symbol for a rabbit because the word for "rabbit" has the same consonants. It is much more interesting that a rabbit never closes its eyes even in sleep and is for that reason a quintessentially suitable symbol of "being open." All of Horapollo's descriptions of signs work along these "symbolic" lines. Odd as his interpretations may seem, they are indicative of the thought processes of Egyptian priests in the Late Period. The demotic *Myth of the Solar Eye* contains a passage that might have been written by Horapollo himself: "If one wants to write the word 'honey,' one draws a picture of Nut with a reed in her hand,"[100] and "if one wants to write the word 'year,' one draws the picture of a vulture because it causes the months to be."[101] The more fully the script signs are laden with such symbolic knowledge, the better they can fulfill their task as depositories of cultural memory.

The priests themselves believed that their signs were images of the words of creation as conceived and uttered by Ptah and recorded by Thoth. In Iamblichus' *Mysteries of the Egyptians* (quoted earlier in support of the Platonism of the *Memphite Theology*), the symbolic script of the Egyptians is interpreted as an imitation of divine "demiurgy."[102] Iamblichus perfectly expresses the principle of "direct signification" that underlies the cryptography of the late temple inscriptions.

But there is more. Though infinite in its ambitions, and refined to the point of the highest virtuosity, the Late Period hieroglyphic writing system was just one aspect of an art that itself only developed in this period: temple decoration. At some point between the sixth and fourth century B.C.E., Egypt set about codifying and inscribing upon its temple walls the entire corpus of cultic knowledge. The oldest temple decorated in this way was erected at the el-Khargeh oasis in the reign of Darius I.[103] The system of temple decoration was itself an integral part of this crucial body of knowledge. Among the forty-two "absolutely essential" books in any temple library, Clement of Alexandria also lists books about the art of temple decoration.[104] The writing system is only a part of this larger "grammar of the temple," which in its turn is only a part of the immense edifice of knowledge enshrined in the forty-two books. Without the rites translating this knowledge into action, the whole system would be mere theory, for it is the rites themselves that keep the world in working order.

This specifically Egyptian view is the foundation of the Greeks' mythical vision of hieroglyphs. The mistake of the Greeks was not that they interpreted hieroglyphic script as a secret code rather than a normal writing system. The Egyptians had in fact transformed it into a secret code and so described it to the Greeks. The real misunderstanding of the Greeks was to have failed to identify the aesthetic significance of cryptography as calligraphy. The question then arises whether their misunderstanding might not also have been encouraged by the Egyptian priests. It surely cannot be pure chance that the systematic complication of hieroglyphic script coincided with the Greek invasion and Ptolemaic foreign rule. The crucial difference between this alien yoke and the preceding periods under the Persians and Assyrians was the massive influx of Greek immigrants, which led to the emergence of a new upper class in Egypt as the old elite and other "natives" found themselves politically ousted. In this new demographic context, the elite had a heightened need for self-definition. The point was not to make the script indecipherable for the lower orders; they had never been able to read hieroglyphic inscriptions. Rather, the priests sought to heighten command of the script to the level of virtuosity, and transform command of written knowledge into a secret science. This intensification of the complexity—and corresponding intensification of the significance—of the knowledge administered by the priestly elite was their means to compensate for the loss of political significance and to preserve the social distance between themselves and the illiterate masses.[105]

Exclusiveness and aestheticization are not irreconcilable opposites; on the contrary, they are closely connected. Every aristocracy responds to social and political challenges by raising its formal standards and thus achieving both greater exclusiveness and additional visibility. An elite can have no more effective way of setting itself apart from the lower strata of society than by enhancing its own conspicuousness, elegance, and formal sophistication.[106] The Egyptians chose script and secrecy as their route to prominence. The more conspicuous they made the knowledge they possessed, the greater was the mystery enshrined within it. Plutarch writes: "They place sphinxes appositely before their temples, intimating that their teaching about the gods holds a mysterious wisdom."[107] For the Greeks the intriguing, apotropaic, and enigmatic figure of the sphinx symbolized the aesthetic, elitist, and enigmatic aspects of Egyptian religion.

CONCLUSION

Egypt as Trace, Message, and Memory

A ROUND 320 C.E. a Greek historian by the name of Hecataeus traveled to Alexandria, the capital of the Ptolemaic kingdom, to codify for Ptolemy I a historical past for the newly founded Egyptian state and thus to create a basis for a Hellenistic-Egyptian pharaohship. Hecataeus' four-volume work was also designed to edify and instruct Ptolemy I by providing him with a model of enlightened monarchy. In line with the ecumenical spirit of Hellenism, Hecataeus set about dismantling the cultural boundaries that had emerged in Egypt as a response to the Persian and Assyrian empires. The gist of his argument was that the cultures of the world were interrelated, and that Egypt was the source of them all. It was from Egypt that conquerors and colonizers had set out to the ends of the earth. Greece itself owed its origins to immigrants from Egypt.

Ptolemy I was doubtless delighted with this historical construct. After all, it was nothing other than the proclamation of the cultural supremacy of his territory over all other areas of the Hellenistic world, and it provided him with the legitimization that comes from a return to origins. But above all, Hecataeus made an invaluable contribution to the construction of cultural continuity. He urged the Ptolemies to see themselves as the inheritors and bearers forward of this most ancient culture; to this end Egypt, in all its extraordinary temporal length, had to be made comprehensible to them. The Ptolemies needed to be aware of what they had been called upon to perpetuate. The Hellenistic project was not a bid to hellenize the east but to find forms of expression in which indigenous traditions could be made transparent and translatable. Hellenism provided local traditions with a common idiom that allowed for a newly sophisticated and flexible mode of self-expression. "Greek was the language of communication and tradition. In other words, it served as a vehicle."[1] Hellenism set out not so much to overlay different peoples and cultures, religions and traditions with a uniform varnish of Greek culture as to provide them with a "flexible medium of cultural and religious forms of expression." The culture of late antiquity owes at least as much to the eastern civilizations as to the Greek legacy, and the linguistic, intellectual, mythological, and iconic forms imported from Greece were not an antithesis or even an alternative to local traditions. They simply gave those traditions a new voice.

The Egyptians seized on this opportunity with alacrity. Only one generation after Hecataeus, the Egyptian priest Manetho wrote a history of Egypt that availed itself not only of all accessible Egyptian sources but also of the new medium of Greek historiography. Greek discourse on Egypt thus gained an entirely new dimension. Unlike Hecataeus and Herodotus, Manetho was not an outsider looking in, but a native exponent of Egyptian self-representation. Manetho's history, particularly the king-list, made the Egyptian chronotope transparent to the Greeks. For the Greeks, Egypt had always been the civilization with the longest memory; it now became measurable and fathomable.

Without Hellenism, such an encounter between Egypt and Europe by means of a common cultural form of expression would have been impossible. Thus Hellenism was a decisive cultural phase for Egypt; through historiography, philosophy, theology, and magic, the influence of Egypt on late antiquity was as great as the influence of Hellenism on Egypt. Late antiquity also marked Egypt's entry into the cultural memory of Europe.

If the Egyptian encounter with Hellenism was particularly fertile, the confrontation with Christianity could not have been more devastating. The demise of Egyptian civilization as a semantic universe was a direct result of the advent of the redemptive religions. To the very end the unshakable convictions that informed Egyptian theology—especially in its Greek forms of hermeticism, Neoplatonism, and alchemy—were that man is at home in the world, that human participation is essential to the divine scheme of sustaining the world, and that the unending task of reconciling the human and the divine is the true source of worldly coherence and continuity. The longing to be redeemed from this world instead of being piously incorporated into it was completely alien to Egyptian thought.

The only explanation that suggests itself for the swift success of the redemptive religions of Christianity and gnosis in Egypt is a sociological one. The world as the home of men and contentment with civilization were and are semiologies of the elite. By contrast, Christianity and gnosis were able to offer new and fascinating meanings to those classes that felt increasingly excluded by the priestly, elitist culture of Hellenic Egypt.

When the knowledge of hieroglyphic writing disappeared in the late fourth century, the messages from pharaonic Egypt fell silent. Only with the deciphering of the Egyptian hieroglyphs by Champollion in 1822 did Egypt again become "readable." Of course, there were still the traces and the memories, and these were so numerous and so impressive that Egypt never truly lapsed into oblivion. To a greater or lesser degree, it remained present in the cultural awareness of all later civilizations, with the relative exception of the Arab world.[2]

No real attention has been paid to the significance of the image of Egypt enshrined in the cultural memory of western civilization. Siegfried Morenz's overview *Die Begegnung Europas mit Ägypten,* that is, "Europe's encounter with Egypt," is a never-ending source of wonder for the quality of its scholarship and the breadth of its coverage. But Morenz's fixation on Herder's ideal of "understanding civilizations on their own terms" leads him to ignore the aspect of memory.[3] Cultural memory does not merely "encounter" the past, but carries the past within itself. Not only does cultural memory address, interrogate, and research the past, but it is also haunted by the past.

This crucial aspect of cultural memory is seen most clearly in the history of the so-called reception of Egypt. Egypt's presence in the cultural memory of the west has always had a mythical quality, which has perhaps been dismissed too smugly as mere "Egyptomania." Of course there have been genuine encounters with Egypt, as with other countries, China, for example, or Mexico. Moreover, it is wholly reasonable to record the history of such encounters and to assess them according to the criterion of "understanding a civilization on its own terms." But Egypt is an exception in that these encounters play a very minor role in comparison to the influence that the memorial legacies of Egypt exerted on Europe's self-image.

Like Israel and Greece, Egypt is a part of the past that the west rightly regards as its own.

The European memorialization of Egypt is quite different from its memorialization of other exotic cultures. Edward Said glosses over this difference when he attributes Europe's interest in Egypt to the paradigm of "orientalism," an interest in another culture determined by colonial aims and designed to further the exploitation of that culture.[4] For Said, Napoleon's expedition to Egypt, with its joint economic, scientific, and military objectives, is the "primal scene" of orientalism. But like Morenz, Said trains a harsh and piercing light on an event that was anything but typical. Of course Egyptology partakes of orientalism, and modern Egyptology still too often assumes a rather patronizing or ironical tone about the sources it is investigating. But my concern here is not with modern Egyptology, which in regard to cultural memory has more often been an organ of oblivion than of recall. In its approach to the sources, almost nothing remains of that memorial image that left so strong an imprint on western culture up to the time of Hegel.

As Vassilis Lambropoulos reminds us, European identity rests on two foundations that exist in a state of mutual tension and opposition: Athens and Jerusalem, Hellas and Israel, Hellenism and Hebraism.[5] Yet this is not the whole story. Both Greece and Israel themselves take their bearings from Egypt, and each in so distinctive a way that their all but mutually exclusive images of that civilization must be taken into account whenever we speak of western historical awareness.

Moreover, Egypt's continuing presence took the form not only of memories but also of traces, huge monuments dotted over all the face of the land, from the pyramids of Giza and Saqqara to the temples of the Greco-Roman Period. Yet for the travelers gazing at them in wonder, those monuments remained obstinately mute, more like mysteries than messages. The loss of the ability to decipher the hieroglyphs did not completely bar access to the systems of meaning that gave rise to the monuments, though that assertion is a pet tenet of modern Egyptology, which believes that the decipherment of hieroglyphic writing led to a complete rediscovery of ancient Egyptian civilization. This view conveniently neglects the fact that ancient Egypt had been a cynosure of European cultural curiosity for centuries and that it was from this very interest that Egyptology itself came forth. That preoccupation with Egypt was by no means provoked solely by the mystery of the mute traces, but was based on an abundance of biblical and classical texts that described Egypt as a living culture and remained very much alive within the European cultural canon. These texts fall into four main traditions.

The biblical tradition paints a largely negative picture of Egypt. Politically, Egypt figures as a repressive system, in religious terms as the land of idolatry, magic, mortuary cults, and superstition. By contrast, the Greek and Roman tradition is largely positive, not to say adulatory. Politically and economically, Egypt appears as a land of wise legislation, ruled by sage, law-abiding monarchs, and of almost miraculous fertility, which enabled the population to devote themselves at a very early stage to the sciences, to the arts, and above all to adoration of the gods. Egypt appears here as remarkably devout and erudite. The Egyptians were the first to recognize the nature of the gods, to establish religious cults, and teach them to others.

The patristic tradition is a kind of halfway house between the biblical and classical traditions. Among the patristic writers, Clement is particularly notable for his attempt to create a balanced image of Egypt and to reconcile the wildly diverging positions of the biblical and classical traditions.

The Neoplatonic, hermetic, gnostic, and alchemistic traditions were at least in part sustained by Egyptian priests (albeit making use of the Greek language) and were thus more in the nature of messages and testimonies than external descriptions of Egyptian civilization.

In the Renaissance all these traditions—and especially those of our fourth category—coalesced in an intensive preoccupation with things Egyptian. Newly discovered manuscripts were hailed as the rediscovery of Egyptian wisdom, among them the book by Horapollo found in 1419 on the island of Andros.[6] Horapollo was thought to be the key to the mystery of hieroglyphic writing. Together with the contemporaneously discovered Ammianus Marcellinus and his obelisk translations, Horapollo's book was the first instance of a systematic scientific and artistic engagement with ancient Egypt and hence an incipient form of Egyptology. Hieroglyphs, considered a primal language that drew upon a scriptural order "written into" nature and translated it into a human system of signs, enjoyed a particularly high degree of interest.

The humanistic engagement with the biblical tradition also sparked a scholarly interest in Egypt. Indeed, the work of the humanist

Hebraists[7] was much more decisive for the Egyptomania of the eighteenth century and for the inception of modern Egyptology than the discourses on hieroglyphics and hermeticism, which by the late seventeenth century had already begun to fade from view. Since this tradition has been largely ignored, I will treat this phase in the rediscovery and reinvention of Egypt in a little more detail.[8]

The Hebraists took an interest in Egypt as part of their endeavor to understand biblical texts and their historical context. Amongst this company was the indefatigable Athanasius Kircher, and most notably, John Spencer, whose three-volume work on the ritual laws of the Hebrews was the first systematic religious-historical engagement with ancient Egypt on the basis of a critical analysis of biblical, patristic, heathen/classical, and Jewish literature.[9] This late-seventeenth-century approach to ancient Egypt, stimulated by a concern with the history and theory of religion, explored the relation between natural and revealed religion and hence the significance of Egypt for Moses' doctrine of revelation. Prompted by the biblical verse "And Moses was learned in all the wisdom of the Egyptians, and was mighty in words and in deeds" (Acts 7:22), the Hebraists raised questions about the influence of Moses' Egyptian schooling on his later lawgiving. Spencer was primarily interested in the Egyptian rites that formed the backdrop for Moses' ritual laws. Others placed the question of Moses' theological instruction or initiation in the foreground. That ancient Egyptian religion was a mystery religion was held to be axiomatic. The negative image of Egypt (idolatry, animal cultism, magic, superstition) was attributed to Egyptian popular religion, while the positive image was traced back to the religion of the initiates, imagined as a form of monotheism. Indeed, the concepts of monotheism and polytheism were themselves coined in the seventeenth century, in the context of this discourse.

Spencer set out to prove that practically all the laws, rites, and institutions introduced by Moses were borrowed from Egypt. Though he clearly went too far in his assertions, he nonetheless made visible an astounding range of ancient Egyptian cultural and religious practices thanks to the biblical, patristic, and rabbinical sources he collected for the purpose. Ralph Cudworth, Regius Professor of Hebrew in Cambridge and Spencer's friend, supplemented Spencer's image of Egyptian rituals with a reconstruction of ancient Egyptian theology that was to have an extraordinary impact on the eighteenth century. Cudworth set out to refute atheism by showing that all religions (including atheism itself) presuppose the idea of a Supreme Being, which by virtue of being common to all must in fact be accepted as true. In this connection, the Egyptians were especially significant because they were held to be the oldest civilization and as such nearest to the truth.

In the eighteenth century, William Warburton's nine-volume *The Divine Legation of Moses*[10] developed the arguments of Cudworth and Spencer. Warburton characterized the arcane theology of Egyptian mystery religion as the veneration of the One, the anonymous Supreme Being, an approach that reveals the influence of Spinoza's *natura naturans*. Years before, in a brief and elegantly written tractate, *Origines Iudaicae,* John Toland had portrayed Moses as an enlightened Egyptian priest, a nome prince of Goshen initiated into the Egyptian mysteries, attaining as such to a "Spinozian" view of the deity.[11] Toland's Moses emigrated with the Hebrew settlers of his province in order to realize his vision of the true religion—an interpretation that anticipated to a surprising degree the theories of Sigmund Freud, whose book *Moses and Monotheism* (1939) represents, together with Thomas Mann's *Joseph* novels, the last and most impressive contribution to the discourse on Egypt that takes its bearings from the Bible.

Toland's theories were also highly instrumental in the emergence of Freemasonry, which originated in London around 1700 and made the "Spinozian" version of Egyptian mystery religion central to its own system of mysteries. Among the abundant Masonic literature on Egypt is the tractate *On the Mysteries of the Ancient Egyptians,* by Ignaz von Born, master of the Viennese lodge to which Mozart and Haydn belonged.[12] A second and vastly more significant tractate is *The Hebrew Mysteries or the Oldest Religious Freemasonry* (1788), by Brother Decius (the well-known philosopher Karl Leonhard Reinhold writing under his secret Illuminati name), who also belonged to von Born's lodge.[13] Von Born's tractate inspired Mozart and Schikaneder's opera *The Magic Flute* (1791), while Reinhold's work had an impact on Schiller's ballad "The Veiled Image at Sais" (1795) and his essay *The Legation of Moses* (1790). Von Born and Reinhold agreed on the idea of an original form of monotheism based not on revelation but on reason. Both had read Warburton's account of Egyptian mystery religion, and Reinhold had also studied Spencer's ideas on the Egyptian origins of Moses' ritual laws.

Without mentioning Spinoza, Reinhold's reconstruction of the

Egyptian mysteries essentially equates God with Nature. Reinhold traces the divine names of Jehovah and Isis to the same concept of an all-encompassing being. According to Exodus 3:14, "Jehovah" (translated in the King James version as I AM THAT I AM) means "I am the being one," and an inscription at Sais passed down by Plutarch and Proclus proclaims Isis as "all that was, is, and shall be." The addition "no mortal has raised my veil" was generally interpreted as a reference to the concept of "natural mysteries" (*secreta naturae*), much aired at the time. The image of Isis veiled or unveiling was a popular motif on the frontispieces of works on natural history; the goddess was generally equated with Nature.[14]

Moses, then, had translated into Hebrew the idea of God that he had attained in the last stage of his initiation. And the God of Moses was none other than the all-encompassing, all-creating, and all-preserving Being whose veil cannot be raised. Reinhold was not the only one to associate Egyptian religion with the teachings of Spinoza. In his book *L'Egypte ancienne* (1762), P. A. d'Origny defended Egyptian religion against the stricture of atheism or materialism, calling on Spinoza to help make the point:

> If it is sufficient to make a chimera of the deity in order not to be an atheist, then the Egyptians were no atheists, venerating as they did nature in general and more especially in the form of their seven great immortal gods, not to mention numerous earthly and animal gods; but if on the other hand all those are to be considered atheists who, like Spinoza, only recognize Nature or the force of Nature operative in all beings as a deity, then the Egyptians in general certainly qualify.[15]

Interpreted in this way, Egyptian religion became a precursor of the hotly debated religious ideas that were espoused by the champions of the Enlightenment and later elevated to the level of a state religion by the French Revolution. Egyptian religion—not the people's but the initiates'—was conceived as a religion of Reason and Nature. With no recourse to revelation and guided by reason alone, the Egyptians had arrived at the same notion of the deity as Spinoza and Moses (properly understood); the Egyptian achievement thus furnished the strongest argument against revealed religion's exclusive claim to the truth. The Egyptians had kept their religion secret because only the most formidable minds were able to sustain its truth. The Freemasons, in particular, had a great deal of sympathy for this idea; as rediscoverers of that truth, they too had to constitute themselves as a secret society. The image of Egypt—the initiates anticipating Spinoza's boldest visions; the priests at once entertaining and intimidating the population with demons in animal shape, deified kings, and pompous ceremonies—was a mirror that the society of the ancien régime held up to itself.

Such an image of Egypt was by no means the preserve of occult traditions and secret societies. We find it in Voltaire's description of Egyptian rites, while Schiller's essay on the legation of Moses spread the image throughout the European intellectual world. On his desk, framed under glass, Beethoven had a sheet of paper on which he had copied three sentences from Schiller's essay to remind himself constantly of this most elevated expression of the divine:

I am what is.

I am all that is, that was, that shall be; no mortal has ever lifted my veil.

He alone is of himself, and to this One all things owe their being.[16]

These lines, accepted as ancient Egyptian wisdom in the late eighteenth and early nineteenth century, expressed a creed of tolerance and consensus that embraced all religions and philosophical persuasions.

This is not, of course, to suggest that such an enlightened image of Egypt completely did away with the mixture of distaste and astonishment provoked by the sacred crocodiles! The eighteenth century's image of Egypt was a highly ambivalent affair, and this very ambivalence was by no means the least significant reason for the fascination Egypt aroused. The revulsion that tempered the admiration of Egyptian civilization was partly intellectual, partly aesthetic. Intellectual distaste was provoked by a religion that made the truth the exclusive and jealously guarded preserve of a small number of initiates. Not all shared the approval of this exclusivity displayed by the Freemasons, the Illuminati, the Rosicrucians, and other secret societies, who were convinced that in this world the truth could survive only by being shrouded in mystery. Critics charged that the secretiveness of the priests served not the truth itself but the self-appointed guardians of the truth and the state institutions they upheld; the notion of a "dual doctrine" (one for the priests, the other for the people) was enough to support the assumption of a *trahison des clercs*. The Egyptian priesthood was pressed into service as a mirror held up to the churches of their age by such anticlerical minds as Fontenelle, Diderot, Voltaire, and Rousseau.[17]

In the course of the eighteenth century the existing discourses that kept the memory of Egypt alive were joined by another, dedicated to the traces. Up to this point, the art and architecture of Egypt had played an astonishingly subordinate role, although here again Athanasius Kircher is a notable exception; his systematic collection of all Egyptian relics extant in Rome laid the foundations for the Vatican collection. Travelogues about Egypt had typically made no attempt at a careful description of the monuments. But from the mid-eighteenth century on, not only did historians, theologians, philosophers, philologists, and artists turn their attention to Egypt, but so did the "antiquarians."

Surprisingly, ancient Egypt was the last civilization to be caught up in this new enthusiasm. Not until Richard Pococke and Frederik Ludwig Norden did travelogues provide descriptions and illustrations adequate to the requirements of antiquarianism.[18] These were joined by volumes containing illustrations of Egyptian art, such as those by Bernard de Montfaucon[19] and above all by the Comte de Caylus.[20] Only then did Egyptology expand to include the systematic establishment, collection, and study of the traces. Egyptian civilization thus became visible not only intellectually but also in the literal sense of the word, and it was this new visibility that led to the "Egyptomania" and the "Egyptian Revival" of late-eighteenth-century and nineteenth-century art and architecture.[21] The most thoroughgoing antiquarian enterprise took place in the framework of Napoleon's expedition to Egypt (1798), the results of which were published between 1809 and 1828 in the twenty-six sumptuously illustrated volumes of the *Description de l'Egypte*.[22]

This work is customarily referred to as the starting point of modern Egyptology. In fact, modern Egyptology is essentially nothing other than the triumph of antiquarianism over the image of Egypt that had been operative for so long in the cultural memory of the west. The fascination with hieroglyphics, the "deistic" quest for a natural religion—both were now jettisoned as a huge misunderstanding. Attention turned to the monuments themselves and to the sources suddenly restored to eloquence by François Champollion's deciphering of the hieroglyphs in 1822. The only surviving link between the eighteenth-century image of Egypt and modern Egyptology was the quest for Egyptian monotheism, whether esoteric or primal. This went on until 1971, when Erik Hornung's devastating and justified critique demolished those last vestiges of the eighteenth century's dream vision of Egypt.[23]

The difference between the image of Egypt informing premodern and modern Egyptology rests first on the rejection of the biblical, Greek, Latin, and other testimonies on ancient Egyptian culture, whose value as sources was greatly diminished by the discovery of an abundance of Egyptian testimonies, and second on an interpretative abstinence that had already distinguished the antiquarianism of the sixteenth to eighteenth century and was elevated to a principle by the positivism of the nineteenth and twentieth centuries. Today we know infinitely more about Egypt than did the experts of the eighteenth century. But we are also infinitely less sure of what to do with that knowledge. Only gradually are endeavors emerging to supplement the antiquarian preoccupation with traces (the merits of which are beyond question) with an attempt to enter into a dialogue with the newly readable messages of ancient Egyptian culture and thus to reestablish them as an integral part of our cultural memory.

ABBREVIATIONS

AHAW *Abhandlungen der Heidelberger Akademie der Wissenschaften*
AOH *Acta Orientalia Academiae Scientiarum Hungaricae*
APAW *Abhandlungen der Preußischen Akademie der Wissenschaften*
ASAE *Annales du Service des Antiquités Égyptiennes*
ÄA Ägyptologische Abhandlungen
ÄAT Ägypten und Altes Testament
ÄgFo Ägyptologische Forschungen
ÄHG Jan Assmann, *Ägyptische Hymnen und Gebete* (Zurich, 1975)
BASP *Bulletin of the American Society of Papyrology*
BiblAeg Bibliotheca Aegyptiaca
BIFAO *Bulletin de l'Institut Français d'Archéologie Orientale*
BiOr *Bibliotheca Orientalis, Leiden*
BSFE *Bulletin de la Société Française d'Égyptologie*
BZAW *Beihefte Zeitschrift für die Alttestamentliche Wissenschaft*
CdE *Chronique d'Égypte*
CGC *Catologue Général Cairo*
CT A. de Buck, *The Egyptian Coffin Texts*, 7 vols. (Chicago, 1935–61)
GM *Göttinger Miszellen*
GOF *Göttinger Orientforschungen*
HÄB Hildesheimer ägyptologische Beiträge
JAOS *Journal of the American Oriental Society*
JEA *Journal of Egyptian Archaeology*
JNES *Journal of Near Eastern Studies*
JSSEA *Journal of the Society for the Study of Egyptian Antiquities* (Toronto)

KÄT   *Kleine Ägyptische Texte,* Wiesbaden

KRI   Kenneth A. Kitchen, *Ramesside Inscriptions,* 7 vols. (Oxford, 1968 ff.)

KRI II   Kenneth A. Kitchen, *Ramesside Inscriptions. Historical and Biographical,* II (Oxford, 1979)

LÄ   W. Helck, E. Otto (later W. Westendorf), *Lexikon der Ägyptologie,* 6 vols. (Wiesbaden, 1972–87)

LL   Jan Assmann, *Liturgische Lieder an den Sonnengott* (Berlin, 1969)

MÄS   *Münchner Ägyptologische Studien*

MDIK   *Mitteilungen des Deutschen Archäologischen Instituts Abt. Kairo*

MIFAO *Mémoires de l'Institut Français d'Archéologie Orientale du Caire*

NGAW *Nachrichten der Göttinger Akademie der Wissenschaften*

OBO   Orbis Biblicus et Orientalis, Fribourg-Göttingen

OLZ   *Orientalistische Literatur-Zeitung*

OMRO Oudheidkundige Mededelingen van het Rijksmuseum van Oudheiden te Leiden

PT   Kurt Sethe, *Die altägyptischen Pyramidentexte,* 4 vols. (Leipzig, 1908–1922)

RAC   *Reallexikon für Antike und Christentum*

RdE   *Revue d'Égyptologie*

SAGA   *Studien zur Altägyptischen Geschichte und Archäologie*

SAK   *Studien zur Altägyptischen Kultur*

SPAW   *Sitzungsberichte der Preußischen Akademie der Wissenschaften*

SSAW   *Sitzungsberichte der Sächsischen Akademie der Wissenschaften*

STG   Jan Assmann, *Sonnenhymnen in thebanischen Gräbern* (Mainz, 1983)

TUAT   *Texte aus der Umwelt des Alten Testaments*

UGAÄ   *Untersuchungen zur Geschichte und Altertumskunde Ägytens*

Urk I   Kurt Sethe, *Urkunden des Alten Reichs,* 2nd ed. (Leipzig, 1933)

Urk IV Kurt Sethe, *Urkunden der 18. Dynastie,* reprint of the 2nd ed., (Berlin/Graz, 1961)

Urk VI Siegfried Schott, *Urkunden mythologischen Inhalts* (Leipzig, 1930)

YES   *Yale Egyptological Studies*

ZÄS   *Zeitschrift für ägyptische Sprache und Altertumskunde*

ZDMG *Zeitschrift der Deutschen Morgenländischen Gesellschaft*

ZPE   *Zeitschrift für Papyrologie und Epigraphik*

NOTES

1. Jakob Burckhardt, *Über das Studium der Geschichte,* "Weltgeschichtliche Betrachtungen," ed. Peter Ganz (Munich, 1982), 149. See also *Weltgeschichtliche Betrachtungen,* ed. J. Oeri (Berlin/Stuttgart, 1905), 23; Kröner edition, ed. Rudolf Marx (Stuttgart, 1978), 24.

INTRODUCTION
The Meaningful Form of History

1. Ignaz von Born, "Über die Mysterien der Aegyptier," in *Journal für Freymaurer* 1 (1784): 24.
2. Von Born, "Über die Mysterien," 18–19; he cites Marcus Aurelius, *Ad me ipsum* 10.10.
3. For this concept of meaning, see esp. N. Luhmann, "Sinn als Grundbegriff der Soziologie," in J. Habermas and N. Luhmann, *Theorie der Gesellschaft oder Sozialtechnologie* (Frankfurt, 1971), 25–100.
4. Jakob Burckhardt, *Die Kunst der Betrachtung. Aufsätze und Vorträge zur Bildenden Kunst,* ed. Henning Ritter (Cologne, 1984), 175. Burckhardt's concept of cultural history and the aims of archaeology in general belong to a tradition of antiquarianism whose counterposition to history has been highlighted in a brilliant essay by Arnaldo Momigliano, "Ancient History and the Antiquarian," in *Journal of the Warburg and Courtauld Institutes* 13 (1950): 285–314. I am grateful to Carlo Ginzburg for drawing my attention to this essay.

5. H. White, *Metahistory: The Historical Imagination in Nineteenth-Century Europe* (Baltimore and London, 1973); see also id., *The Content of the Form: Narrative Discourse and Historical Representation* (Baltimore and London, 1987); id., *Tropics of Discourse: Essays in Cultural Criticism* (Baltimore and London, 1985).

6. J. Huizinga, "A Definition of History," in H. J. Paton, R. Klibanski, eds., *History and Philosophy: Essays Presented to E. Cassirer* (Oxford, 1936), 1–10, esp., 9.

7. On Bakhtin and his notion of "chronotope," see J. Bender, D. E. Wellbery, eds., *Chronotypes: The Construction of Time* (Stanford, Calif.: 1991).

8. See J. Assmann, "Zeit der Erneuerung, Zeit der Rechenschaft: Mythos und Geschichte in früheren Kulturen," in J. Huber, A. M. Müller, eds., *"Kultur" und "Gemeinsinn", Interventionen 3* (Basle/Frankfurt, 1994), 171–94.

9. *De Civitate Dei*, XII, 14. See W. Kemp, *Christliche Kunst, ihre Anfänge, ihre Strukturen* (Munich, 1994), 75–79.

10. A. Kemp, *The Estrangement of the Past: A Study in the Origins of Modern Consciousness* (New York/Oxford, 1991), esp. chap. 1: "Foundations of the Medieval Past," 3–34.

11. K. Pomian, *L'Ordre du temps* (Paris, 1984), 39–40.

12. C. Lévi-Strauss, *Das wilde Denken* (Frankfurt, 1973), 270. See also id., *Strukturale Anthropologie* (Frankfurt, 1960), 39.

13. H. Nowotny, *Eigenzeit: Entstehung und Strukturierung eines Zeitgefühls* (Frankfurt, 1989); W. Kaempfer, *Die Zeit und die Uhren* (Frankfurt, 1992). The most radical approach with regard to the concept of time is taken by the ethnologist Maurice Bloch in "The Past and the Present in the Present," in *Ritual, History and Power: Selected Papers in Anthropology*, London School of Economics, Monographs on Social Anthropology No. 58 (London, 1989), 1–18. I owe this reference to Thomas Levin (Princeton) and Gadi Algazi (Tel Aviv). Bloch proceeds on the assumption that every culture has concepts of linear and cyclical time. He interprets these as profane and sacred time. Linear time is the time in which everyday activity takes place and is largely similar across cultural boundaries. Cyclical concepts of time, by contrast, are centered in various forms of ritual and ceremonial communication, and thus display marked differences from one culture to another. By identifying linearity with profane time and cyclicality with sacred time, Bloch of course turns Augustine's concept of time on its head.

14. Cf. esp. M. Bloch, op. cit.

15. This is the objection leveled by Thomas Mann at Oswald Spengler's cultural morphology.

16. For more detail on the following, see J. Assmann, *Zeit und Ewigkeit im alten Ägypten* (Heidelberg, 1975).

17. Wolfhart Westendorf has made some especially telling comments on the spatial associations of *djet:* "Raum und Zeit als Entsprechung der beiden Ewigkeiten," in *Fontes atque Pontes; Festgabe Hellmut Brunner* (Wiesbaden, 1983), 422–35. In this essay, Westendorf contends that *neheh* and *djet* are for all intents and purposes the Egyptian equivalents of "time" and "space," respectively. And indeed W. Kaempfer himself writes: "What we call *space* is nothing other than the *realization* of time, and what we call *time* is pure *potentiality*" (Kaempfer, *Die Zeit und die Uhren* [Frankfurt, 1991], 18).

18. For the Egyptian annals and king-lists, see the excellent study by D. B. Redford, *Pharaonic King-Lists, Annals and Day Books: A Contribution to the Study of the Egyptian Sense of History* (Mississauga, 1986).

19. See J. Z. Smith in Bender and Wellbery, *Chronotypes,* 67.

20. Essential reading on this whole issue is Redford, *Pharaonic King-Lists.*

21. A. K. Grayson, "Histories and Historians in the Ancient Near East," in *Orientalia* 49 (1980): 140–94; id., *Assyrian and Babylonian Chronicles.* Texts from Cuneiform Sources 5 (Locust Valley, Penna., 1970); J.-J. Glassner, *Chroniques mésopotamiennes* (Paris, 1993).

PART ONE
The Predynastic Period and the Old Kingdom

1. A good overview of the history of research on Egyptian prehistory and early history is provided by M. A. Hoffman, *Egypt Before the Pharaohs: Prehistoric Foundations of Egyptian Civilization,* 2nd ed. (Austin, 1991). It has an extensive bibliography.

2. "[Your babble,] there is no one conversant with foreign tongues who could explain it. It is like the conversation of an inhabitant of the Delta with a man from Elephantine": Papyrus Anastasi I 28, 6. See H. W. Fischer-Elfert, *Die Satirische Streitschrift des Papyrus Anastasi I: Über-setzung und Kommentar,* Äg Abh. 44 (Wiesbaden, 1986), 238, 242 (q).

3. W. Helck, *Politische Gegensätze im alten Ägypten,* HÄB 23 (Hildesheim, 1986): 7.

4. W. Kaiser was the first to demonstrate this, in a series of pioneering articles. The most recent is "Zur Entstehung," *MDIK* 46 (1990), esp. 287–99.

5. W. Kaiser, "Zur Südausdehnung der vorgeschichtlichen Deltakulturen und zur frühen Entwicklung Oberägyptens," *MDIK* 39 (1985): 85–86. See also J. Seeher, "Gedanken zur Rolle Unterägyptens bei der Heraus-bildung des Pharaonenreichs," *MDIK* 47 (1991), 313ff.

6. This is the view taken by C. Köhler in her Heidelberg Ph.D. dissertation,

Tell el Fara'in-Buto: Die Keramik der Schichten III–VI. Untersuchungen zur Töpfereiproduktion einer frühen Siedlung des Nildeltas (1993); see also her "The State of Research on Late Predynastic Egypt: New Evidence for the Development of the Pharaonic State?" *GM* 147 (1995): 79–92.

7. H. Case and J. C. Payne, "Tomb 100: The Decorated Tomb at Hieraconpolis," *JEA* 48 (1962): 5–18.

8. E. Winter, "Wer steht hinter Narmer?" in *Zwischen den beiden Ewigkeiten. Festschrift Gertrud Thausing* (Vienna, no year given), 279–90.

9. See J. Vercoutter, *L'Égypte et la vallée du Nil I, Des origines à la fin de l'Ancien Empire* (Paris, 1992), 240.

10. See Helck in *LÄ* IV: 652–54.

11. H. Junker, *Die politische Lehre von Memphis,* Abh. der Preußischen Akademie der Wissenschaften Jg. 1941 phil.-hist. Kl. Nr. 6 (Berlin, 1941), 23–36.

12. H. A. Schlögl, *Der Gott Tatenen,* OBO 29 (Fribourg, 1980). The case for the Twenty-fifth Dynasty is urged by F. Junge, "Zur Fehldatierung des sog. Denkmals memphitischer Theologie, oder: Der Beitrag der ägyptischen Theologie zur Geistesgeschichte der Spätzeit," *MDIK* 29 (1973), 195ff.

13. H. te Velde, *Seth, God of Confusion,* Probleme der Ägyptologie 6 (Leiden, 1967).

14. Kurt Sethe, *Urk* I, reprint of the 2nd ed. (Berlin and Graz, 1961), 366, 4–5.

15. Papyrus Cairo 86637 xv, 9–10; see also Papyrus ChB VII rto 8.4. Translation after C. Leist, *Tagewählerei. Das Buch ḥȝt nḥḥ phwj dt und verwandte Texte* (Wiesbaden, 1994), text vol., 142–43.

16. On this and the following, see esp. E. Martin-Pardey, *Untersuchungen zur ägyptischen Provinzialverwaltung bis zum Ende des alten Reichs* (Hildesheim, 1976); id., "Die Verwaltung im Alten Reich," *BiOr* 46 (1968), 533–52; N. Strudwick, *The Administration of Egypt in the Old Kingdom* (London, 1985).

17. W. Helck, *Thinitenzeit* (Wiesbaden, 1987); E. Martin-Pardey, *Provinzialverwaltung;* H. G. Fischer, *Denderah in the Third Millennium B.C.* (New York, 1968).

18. See W. Schenkel, *Die Bewässerungsrevolution im Alten Ägypten* (Mainz, 1978).

19. The Abusir papyri from the mortuary temple of King Neferirkare-Kakai (2470 B.C.E.) convey an impression of the sophistication of the bureaucratic written culture of the period. The entries were tabulated and split up into lines and columns by means of horizontal and vertical strokes. The lines were mostly equivalent to days, with a red line after each tenday period marking the end of a "week." The columns listed commodities, supply sources, persons, and other variables. See P. Posener-Kriéger,

Les Archives du temple funéraire de Néferirkarê-Kakai, 2 vols. (Cairo, 1976).

20. J. Baines, *Fecundity Figures. Egyptian Personification and the Iconology of a Genre* (Warminster, Eng., 1985) assembles related phenomena under the heading "decorum," thus indicating the normative (canonical) character of this culture.

21. On this point, cf. R. Müller-Wollermann, *Krisenfaktoren im ägyptischen Staat des ausgehenden Alten Reichs* (Tübingen, 1986).

22. On the Egyptian economy, see R. Müller-Wollermann, "Warenaustausch im Ägypten des Alten Reichs," in *Journal of the Economic and Social History of the Orient* 28 (1985): 121–68; J. Janssen, "Gift-Giving in Ancient Egypt as an Economic Feature," *JEA* 68 (1982): 253–58, and more generally K. Polanyi, C. M. Arensberg, H. W. Pearson, eds., *Trade and Market in the Early Empires* (Glencoe, Ill., 1957); and K. Polanyi, *Primitive, Archaic and Modern Economies* (New York, 1968), and *Ökonomie und Gesellschaft* (Frankfurt, 1979).

23. The following draws largely on S. J. Seidlmayer, *Gräberfelder aus dem Übergang vom Alten zum Mittleren Reich,* SAGA I (Heidelberg, 1990).

24. K. Sethe, *Urk* I, 2nd ed., 118–19.

25. E. Martin-Pardey contends that not one of these lineages was able to hold out beyond the Sixth Dynasty and into the First Intermediate Period. Thus it is by no means established that the new patrons emerged from the ranks of the nomarchs. An entirely different stratum of society may have come into its own here; see *Provinzialverwaltung,* 150–52.

26. On the Egyptian corvée system, also known as "leiturgical" administration (from Gr. *leitourgia,* "public service"), see M. Weber, "Agrargeschichte des Altertums," in *Handwörterbuch der Staatswissenschaften,* 3rd ed. (Jena, 1909), 80–90 (though Weber greatly overrates the significance of irrigation farming).

27. D. Wildung, *Imhotep und Amenhotep. Gottwerdung im alten Ägypten,* MÄS 36 (Munich, 1977).

28. K. Sethe, *Urkunden des Alten Reichs* (in *Urk* I), 7.

29. P. Montet, "Le rituel de la fondation des temples égyptiens," in *Kêmi* 17 (1964), 79.

30. Berlin Papyrus 3029, ed. A. de Buck, *The Building Inscription of the Berlin Leather Roll,* Studia Aegyptiaca I (Analecta Orientalia 17), 48–57; more recent studies: H. Goedicke, "The Berlin Leather Roll," in *Fs Mus Berlin* (Berlin, 1975), 87–104; J. Osing, "Zu zwei literarischen Werken des Mittleren Reichs," in *The Heritage of Egypt* (Festschrift Iversen) (Copenhagen, 1992), 101–119, esp. 109–119.

31. On the pyramids, see esp. R. Stadelmann's two books: *Die ägyptischen Pyramiden: Vom Ziegelbau zum Weltwunder* (Mainz, 1985) and *Die großen Pyramiden von Giza* (Graz, 1990).

32. See C. Kaufmann, "Stil und Kanon: Zum Stilbegriff in der Ethnologie der Kunst—Versuch einer Standortbestimmung," *Ethnologia Helvetica* 16 (1992): 31–89.

33. See A. and J. Assmann, eds., *Kanon und Zensur* (Munich, 1987); J. Assmann, *Das kulturelle Gedächtnis* (Munich, 1992), chap. 2.

34. Hecataeus of Abdera, in Diodorus, *Bibl. Hist.* I 51. But Hecataeus was more than a traveler. He came to Alexandria in 320 B.C.E. and stayed for fifteen years.

35. Theban Tomb 131, southern wing, eastern text strip. See E. Dziobek, *Denkmäler des Vezirs User-Armun* (Heidelberg, 1998), 78–80.

36. An allusion to the famous maxim from the *Instruction of Hordjedef* also quoted in the *Instruction for King Merikare:*

    Furnish your house of the West sumptuously
    and make excellent your seat in the necropolis.

    See H. Brunner, *Altägyptische Weisheit: Lehren für das Leben* (Zurich, 1988), 102, verses 11–12, also 430; Die Lehre für Merikare, ibid., 153, verses 301–302, and esp. Die Lehre des Ani, ibid., 202, verses 89–109.

37. See J. Assmann, *Zeit und Ewigkeit,* 15ff.

38. Theban Tomb 50, see Schott, *Liebeslieder,* 137 no. 101, verses 17–18.

39. Papyrus Chester Beatty IV, vso. 2.5ff. See H. te Velde, "Commemoration in Ancient Egypt," in *Visible Religion* I (Leiden, 1982), 135–53, esp. 143–44.

40. See M. Weber, *Beiträge zur Kenntnis des Schrift- und Buchwesens der alten Ägypter* (Ph.D. diss., Cologne, 1969).

41. *Urk* I, 221–23; A. Roccati, *La Littérature historique sous l'ancien Empire Égyptienne* (Paris, 1982), 222; M. Lichtheim, *Ancient Egyptian Autobiographies Chiefly of the Middle Kingdom,* OBO 84 (1988), 19.

42. W. Schenkel, *Memphis—Herakleopolis—Theben: Die epigraphischen Zeugnisse der 7.–11. Dyn. ÄA* 12 (Wiesbaden, 1965), 108–109.

43. Anu of Assiut, after D. Franke, *Das Heiligtum des Heqa-ib auf Elephantine, Geschichte eines Provinzheiligtums im Mittleren Reich,* SAGA 9, 1994, 22 with n. 72.

44. See my book, *Ma'at, Gerechtigkeit und Unsterblichkeit im alten Ägypten* (Munich, 1990), and pp. 70 of the present work.

45. C. Kaufmann, "*Stil und Kanon,*" 49.

46. See also my book *Stein und Zeit,* chap. 1: "Gebrauch und Gedächtnis. Die zwei Kulturen des pharaonischen Ägypten," 16–31.

PART TWO
The First Intermediate Period

1. S. Seidlmayer, *Gräberfelder* (I, n. 62), 403.
2. Excellently compiled and translated by W. Schenkel in *Memphis—Herakleopolis—Theben. Die epigraphischen Zeugnisse der 7.–11. Dynastie Ägyptens* (ÄA 12, 1965, cited hereafter as *MHT*).
3. Schenkel, *MHT* No. 37; J. Vandier, *Mo'alla* (Cairo, 1940).
4. Khuy is not the predecessor in office but the founder of the dynasty, after whom the second nome was called House of Khuy. Cf. the stela of *Merer, MHT* No. 42.
5. See the restoration account by Intef, son of *Mjjt, MHT* No. 377: "I found the chapel of Prince *Nhtj* the Magnificent destroyed. Its walls were old, all its statues broken, there was indeed no one left who remembered him. Thereupon it was restored; its foundations were extended, its statuary work refashioned; doors of stone were made for it in that they were built anew, so that his place would be more high-ranking than that of the other venerables. . . ."
6. Precisely the same views and the same life feeling returned in the New Kingdom and determined the relation between god and man.
7. W. Schenkel, "Nie kam Mißgeschick über mich," *ZÄS* 91 (1964): 137–38.
8. See my article "Inscriptional Violence and the Art of Cursing," in *Stanford Literary Review* (spring 1992): 43–65.
9. Cf. CG 20 007.4; *Urk* I, 151.3; Dendereh pl. 11 and 13; cf. *Urk* I 144.16; BM 1164.3, 1671.1.
10. See my *Ma'at* (I, n. 91), 97–99.
11. Schenkel, *Bewässerungsrevolution*, 30–31.
12. London UC 14333 ed. Goedicke, *JEA* 48, 25ff., 26 line 6–7.
13. Text passages: *MHT* No. 28 and No. 104.
14. (*Urk* I 199.2, 200, 17) in the form: "I saved the weak from the hand of him who was stronger than he, as far as it was in my power." On "vertical solidarity," see my *Ma'at*, passim.
15. J.M.A. Janssen, *De traditioneele egyptische autobiografie vóór het Nieuwe Rijk* (Leiden, 1947), I, 72–73, Bh1–15.
16. E.g., W. Barta, "Die erste Zwischenzeit im Spiegel der pessimistischen Literatur," in *Jahrbuch Ex Oriente Lux* 24 (1974/75): 50–61.
17. G. Björkman, "Egyptology and Historical Method," *Orientalia Suecana* 13 (1964): 9–33; E. Hornung, *Geschichte als Fest: Zwei Vorträge zum Geschichtsbild der frühen Menschheit* (Darmstadt, 1966), 27; W. Schenkel, "Repères chronologiques de l'histoire redactionnelle des Coffin Texts," in W. Westendorf, ed., *Göttinger Totenbuchstudien: Beiträge zum 17.*

Kapitel. GOF IV.3, 1975, 29–31; M. Lichtheim, *Ancient Egyptian Literature* I (Berkeley, 1973), 134–35, 139, 149–50; F. Junge, "Die Welt der Klagen," in *Fragen an die altägyptische Literatur* (Gedenkschrift E. Otto), (Wiesbaden, 1975), 275–84.

18. M. Halbwachs, *Les Cadres sociaux de la mémoire* (Paris, 1925); and *La mémoire collective* (Paris, 1950). See also my book *Das kulturelle Gedächtnis: Schrift, Erinnerung und politische Identität in frühen Hochkulturen* (Munich, 1972), chap. 1.

19. On this point, see David Frankfurter, *Elijah in Upper Egypt: The Apocalypse of Elijah and Early Christianity* (Minneapolis, 1993), esp. chap. 7: "*Chaosbeschreibung*: The Literary and Ideological Background of the Apocalypse of Elijah," 159–94, and chap. 8: "*Vaticinia sine Eventibus*: The Use of Egyptian *Chaosbeschreibung* Tradition in the Apocalypse of Elijah," 195–238.

20. W. K. Simpson, ed., *The Literature of Ancient Egypt* (New Haven, 1972), fig. 6; J. Assmann, *Stein und Zeit*, 307.

21. B. Brecht, *Der kaukasische Kreidekreis*, Edition Suhrkamp 31 (Frankfurt, 1964), 119–20. See S. Wenig, "Bertolt Brecht und das alte Ägypten," in *ZÄS* 96 (1969): 63–66.

22. A. Erman, *Die Literatur der Ägypter* (Leipzig, 1923), 130–48; the passages cited are on pp. 133, 135–37, 139, 141. For a more recent translation, see M. Lichtheim, *Ancient Egyptian Literature* I, 149–63.

23. S. Luria, "Die Ersten werden die Letzten sein," in *Klio* XXII (N.F.IV) (1929): 405–31.

24. P. Seibert, *Die Charakteristik: Untersuchungen zu einer altägyptischen Sprechsitte und ihren Ausprägungen in Folklore und Literatur*, ÄA 17 (Wiesbaden, 1967), 20–24. W. Schenkel, "Sonst-Jetzt. Variationen eines literarischen Formelements," in *Die Welt des Orients* 15, 1984 (Festschrift H. Brunner), 51–61.

25. Papyrus Leiden I 344, 10, 13–11,4. A. H. Gardiner, *The Admonitions of an Egyptian Sage* (Leipzig, 1909), 75–76.

PART THREE
The Middle Kingdom

1. See K. Burke, *A Rhetoric of Motives* (Berkeley, 1969); J. Assmann, *Stein und Zeit*, 252ff.; C. Eyre, "The Semna Stelae: Quotation, Genre, and Functions of Literature," in *Studies in Egyptology* (Festschrift M. Lichtheim) (Jerusalem, 1990), 134–65.

2. "Instruction for King Merikare," ed. Helck, *Die Lehre für König Merikare* (Wiesbaden, 1977), 17–18; Assmann, *Stein und Zeit*, 252.

3. *Römischer Katholizismus und Politische Form*, 2nd ed. (Munich, 1925), 23.

4. For the history of the Thirteenth and Seventeenth Dynasties, which ruled without interruption in Upper Egypt while the Fourteenth, Fifteenth, and Sixteenth Dynasties were reigning in Lower Egypt, see D. Franke, *Das Heiligtum des Heqa-ib auf Elephantine: Geschichte eines Provinzheiligtums*, SAGA 9 (Heidelberg, 1964), 62–89.

5. G. Posener, *Littérature et politique dans l'Égypte de la xii.e dynastie* (Paris, 1956).

6. H. Brunner, "Die Lehre vom Königserbe im Mittleren Reich," in *Ägyptologische Studien* (Festschrift Grapow) (Berlin, 1955), 4–11.

7. On the role and diction of propaganda in the Egyptian state, see E. Blumenthal, *Untersuchungen zum Königtum des Mittleren Reichs I. Die Phraseologie* (Berlin, 1970), and N. C. Grimal, *Les Termes de la propagande royale égyptienne de la xix.e dynastie à la conquête d'Alexandre* (Paris, 1986).

8. See A. Schlott, *Schrift und Schreiber im Alten Ägypten* (Munich, 1989).

9. See my *Das kulturelle Gedächtnis: Schrift, Erinnerung und politische Identität in frühen Hochkulturen* (Munich, 1992), 48–85.

10. See the chapter "Schrift, Tod und Identität" in my *Stein und Zeit*, 169–99; R. B. Parkinson, *Voices from Ancient Egypt: An Anthology of Middle Kingdom Writings* (London, 1991).

11. J. Assmann, "Der literarische Text im alten Ägypten," in *OLZ* 69 (1974): 117–26. See also A. Loprieno, *Topos und Mimesis: Zum Ausländer in der ägyptischen Literatur*, ÄA 48 (Wiesbaden, 1988); "The Sign of Literature in the Shipwrecked Sailor," in *Religion und Philosophie im Alten Ägypten* (Louvain, 1991), 209–218; "Defining Egyptian Literature: Ancient Texts and Modern Literary Theory," in *JAOS* 1992.

12. See H. Brunner, *Altägyptische Erziehung* (Wiesbaden, 1957); id., "Die 'Weisen' und ihre 'Lehren' und 'Prophezeiungen' in altägyptischer Sicht," in *ZÄS* 93 (1966): 29–35. On the similar circumstances in ancient Israel, see R. H. Whybray, *The Intellectual Tradition in the Old Testament*, BZAW 135 (Berlin, 1974); F. W. Golka, "Die israelitische Weisheitsschule," in *Vetus Testamentum* 33 (1983): 257–70; B. Lang, "Klugheit als Ethos und Weisheit als Beruf: Die Lebenslehre im Alten Testament," in A. Assmann, ed., *Weisheit* (Munich, 1991), 177–92; G. Theißen, "Weisheit als Mittel sozialer Abgrenzung und Öffnung: Beobachtung zur sozialen Funktion frühjüdischer und urchristlicher Weisheit," in ibid., 193–204. On Mesopotamia, see A. Sjöberg, "The Old Babylonian Eduba," in *Assyriological Studies* 20 (1975): 159–79.

13. The phrase is from T. Luckmann, *The Invisible Religion: The Problem of Religion in Modern Society* (New York, 1967).

14. H. Brunner, "Die 'Weisen', ihre 'Lehren' und 'Prophezeiungen' in altägyptischer Sicht," *ZÄS* 93 (1966): 29–35. But the litterati were also officials serving the state. In Egypt, as opposed to China and Greece, there

was no "autonomous intelligentsia," no critical voice with a legitimacy of its own over and against the state. The educated elite and the powerholding elite were one and the same.

15. See A. Assmann, "Was ist Weisheit," in A. Assmann, *Weisheit,* 15–44.

16. See J. Assmann, *Das kulturelle Gedachtnis,* 20–21.

17. P. Seibert, *Die Charakteristik: Zu einer altägyptischen Sprechsitte und ihren Ausprägungen in Folklore und Literatur,* ÄA 17 (Wiesbaden, 1967).

18. See "Das Bild des Vaters im alten Ägypten," in my *Stein und Zeit,* 96–137.

19. See "Schrift, Tod und Identität," in my *Stein und Zeit,* 169–99; R. B. Parkinson, *Voices from Ancient Egypt.*

20. Cf. my book *Ma'at: Gerechtigkeit und Unsterblichkeit im Alten Ägypten* (Munich, 1990). The concept of *iustitia connectiva* is coined in analogy to the Latin term *iustitia correctiva.* It is not itself an original term but a concept of theoretical metalanguage. See *Ma'at,* chaps. 3 and 9; *Das kulturelle Gedächtnis,* 232ff.

21. W. Helck, in *Historisch-Biographische Texte der 2. Zwischenzeit,* No. 32, 29. I. Shirun-Grumach, *Offenbarung, Orakel und Königsnovelle,* ÄAT 24 (Wiesbaden, 1993), 126–27, proposes a different translation: "A reward is that which [I] have done for that which [he] has done; it is *ma'at* in the heart of the god." But it is surely more likely that god "rewards" the king rather than vice versa. My assumption here is that in conclusion Neferhotep is formulating the general principle underlying the actions he has been describing. Both god and king find the reward for their actions in the principle of "do as you would be done by" (or *ma'at*). On *mtn.wt* ("wage" or "ration"), see P. Lacau and H. Chevrier, *Une Chapelle blanche de Sésostris Ier,* vol. II (Cairo, 1969), pl. 41 (scène 29): Speech of Amun-Re. "I have given Sesostris all life, duration and rule. His wage/his ration consists in all life and expanse [joy] of heart from me."

22. Papyrus Berlin 3024, 115–16, ed. Adolf Erman, *Das Gespräch eines Lebensmüden mit seiner Seele* (Berlin, 1896). Among numerous more recent translations, see *Gesänge vom Nil,* by Erik Hornung (Zurich, 1990), 115.

23. Bauer B 2, 109–110; Assmann, *Ma'at,* 60.

24. Bauer B 1, 109–110; F. Vogelsang, *Kommentar zu den Klagen des Bauern,* Unters. z. Gesch. u. Altertumsk. ÄA (Leipzig, 1913), 100.

25. Literally: "climb down (to us)."

26. Bauer B 2, 105–108.

27. *mdd:* a carpenter's term meaning "joining" (by tongue and groove).

28. Merikare P 123; see E. Otto, "Ägyptische Gedanken zur menschlichen Verantwortung," in *Die Welt des Orients* 3.1 (1964): 19–26, esp. 24; G. Fecht, *Der Vorwurf an Gott in den Mahnworten des Ipuwer* (Heidelberg, 1972), 131.

29. "Verhandlungen des 6. Rheinischen Landtags. Dritter Artikel. Debatten über das Holzdiebstahlgesetz. Von einem Rheinländer" (Rheinische Zeitung No. 298, 25.10.1842. Beiblatt) in Karl Marx/Friedrich Engels, *Gesamtausgabe*, Erste Abteilung, vol. I (Berlin, 1975), 222. In this article, Marx takes the view that the state must not be an instrument for the realization of private interests. I am grateful to Gadi Algazi (Tel Aviv) for drawing my attention to this quotation and am also indebted to Wolf Daniel Hartwich for further information.

30. F. Nietzsche, *On the Genealogy of Morals*, Second Essay: " 'Guilt,' 'Bad Conscience,' and the Like," trans. W. Kaufmann and R. J. Hollingdale (New York, 1989), 58.

31. Ibid., 59.

32. Ibid., 60–61.

33. On the phrase "laws of *ma'at*," see A. B. Lloyd, *Historia* 31, 43.

34. K. A. Wittfogel, *Die orientalische Despotie: Eine vergleichende Untersuchung totaler Macht* (Frankfurt/Berlin/Vienna, 1977; orig. 1957).

35. E. Brunner-Traut, *Frühformen des Erkennens: am Beispiel Altägyptens* (Darmstadt, 1990), 82ff.

36. Id., "Wohltätigkeit und Armenfürsorge im Alten Ägypten," in G. K. Schäfer, T. Strohm, eds., *Diakonie—biblische Grundlagen und Orientierungen*, Veröffentlichungen des Diakoniewissenschaftlichen Instituts der Universität Heidelberg 2 (Heidelberg, 1990), 23–43 (citation: p. 25).

37. "Wohltätigkeit," 26.

38. H. Kelsen, Nature and Society: A Sociological Inquiry (Chicago, 1943).

39. J. Assmann, *Ma'at*, 60ff.

40. Metternich Stela M 50, C. E. Sander-Hansen, *Die Texte der Metternichstele, Analecta Aegyptiaca* VII (Copenhagen, 1956), 35–36, 41; A. Klasen, *A Magical Statue Base (Socle Behague) in the Museum of Antiquities at Leiden*, Oudheidkundige Mededelingen ut het Rijksmuseum van Oudheden te Leiden N. R. XXXIII (Leiden, 1952) 10, 52; H. Sternberg, "Die Metternichstele," in O. Kaiser, ed., *Texte aus der Umwelt des Alten Testaments* (TUAT), Vol. II.3, Rituale und Beschwörungen II (Gütersloh, 1988), 376.

41. S. Schott, *Urkunden mythologischen Inhalts* (Leipzig, 1929) (cited in the following as *Urk* VI), 7.15–16.

42. Papyrus Chester Beatty III, rto., 11,2–3.

43. For a detailed treatment, see my article "Die Geschichte des Herzens im alten Ägypten," in J. Assmann and T. Sundermeier, eds., *Die Erfindung des inneren Menschen* (Gütersloh, 1993), 81–112.

44. G. Posener, *L'Enseignement loyaliste: Sagesse égyptienne du Moyen Empire* (Geneva, 1976).

45. Ibid., 58–63.2 (text), 19–20. Posener refers to K. Sethe, *Urkunden der 18. Dynastie* (reprint Graz, 1961) (referred to hereinafter as *Urk* IV), 20:

"May he [Re] give that the *h3tj*-hearts bring him worship and the *jb*-hearts praise him in the bodies."

46. Cf. M. Lichtheim, *Ancient Egyptian Autobiographies Chiefly of the Middle Kingdom*, OBO 84 (Fribourg, 1988).

47. On this formulaic phrase, see J.M.A. Janssen, *De traditioneele egyptische autobiografie vóór het Nieuwe Rijk* (Leiden, 1947), 195; Leiden V 4 = Sethe, *Lesestücke zum Gebrauch im akademischen Unterricht* (reprint, Darmstadt, 1959), 72.15; A. Hermann, *Die Stelen der thebanischen Felsgräber der 18. Dyn.*, ÄgFo II (Glückstadt, 1940), 23*, 53*, 57*.

48. CG 20543, from Dendera. See W. Schenkel, *Memphis—Herakleopolis—Theben*, 114; M. Lichtheim, *Autobiographies*, 43–44.

49. Stela London BM 142 ed. *KRI* III, 218–19.

50. Papyrus BM 10470 col. 4. See my *Ma'at*, 149.

51. *Urk* IV, 974.

52. *ÄHG* No. 226.

53. H. W. Fischer-Elfet, *Die Lehre eines Mannes für seinen Sohn* (Wiesbaden, 1999).

54. *Urk* IV, 965–66.

55. A paradigmatic instance of this attitude is the report of Sabni, who in the inscriptions on his tomb lauds himself for having at great personal risk brought back the corpse of his father, Mekhu, from foreign parts and buried it in Egyptian soil (*Urk* I 134, 13–14; 135, 14–15). See also A. Roccati, *La Littérature historique sous l'ancien empire égyptien* (Paris, 1982), 205, 217–18.

56. *ÄHG* No. 227. The latest edition is by R. Koch, *Die Erzählung des Sinuhe*, BiblAeg. XVII (Brussels, 1990), 80–81.

57. *Urk* IV, 20.9–17.

58. J. Assmann, "Weisheit, Loyalismus und Frömmigkeit," in E. Hornung and O. Keel, eds., *Studien zu altägyptischen Lebenslehren*, OBO 28 (Fribourg, 1979), 1–72; "Die loyalistische Lehre des Echnaton," in *Studien zur Altägyptischen Kultur* 8 (1980): 1–32.

59. N. Luhmann, "Rechtszwang und politische Gewalt," in *Ausdifferenzierung des Rechts: Beiträge zur Rechtssoziologie und Rechtstheorie*, 154–72.

60. See F. Junge, "Die Welt der Klagen," in *Fragen an die altägyptische Literatur*, Gedenkschrift E. Otto (Wiesbaden, 1977), 275–84; J. Assmann, "Weisheit, Schrift und Literatur im Alten Ägypten," in A. Assmann, ed., *Weisheit* (Munich, 1991), 475–500, esp. 485ff.

61. On the following see A. and J. Assmann, "Kultur und Konflikt: Aspekte einer Theorie des unkommunikativen Handelns," in J. Assmann, D. Harth, eds., *Kultur und Konflikt* (Frankfurt, 1990), 11–48, esp. 17–31; J. Assmann, *Ma'at*, chap. 7.

62. *Ipuwer*, 12.13–14, ed. A. H. Gardiner, *The Admonitions of an Egyptian Sage* (Leipzig, 1909; reprint, Hildesheim, 1969), 84; G. Fecht, *Der Vor-*

wurf an Gott in den Mahnworten des Ipuwer, Abh. der Heidelberger Akademie der Wissenschaften (Heidelberg, 1972), 110.

63. *Urk* IV, 1091.3; G. Fecht, *Der Vorwurf an Gott,* 70–71.

64. A. H. Gardiner, *The Admonitions of an Egyptian Sage,* 78–79; G. Fecht, *Vorwurf,* 54ff.

65. See my *Ma'at,* 177–84.

66. G. Posener, *L'Enseignement loyaliste: sagesse égyptienne du Moyen Empire* (Geneva, 1976), § 3 pp. 22–23, 72–73.

67. On this point, see J. Assmann, *Re und Amun: Die Krise des polytheistischen Weltbilds im Ägypten der 18.–20. Dynastie,* OBO 51 (Fribourg, 1983), 264ff.; "State and Religion in the New Kingdom," in W. K. Simpson, ed., *Religion and Philosophy in Ancient Egypt* (New Haven, 1989), 55–88, esp. 72ff.; and *Ma'at,* 252–72.

68. Cf. K. Sethe, *Dramatische Texte zu altägyptischen Mysterien spielen,* Untersuchungen zur Geschichte und Altertumskunde Ägypteus 10 (Leipzig, 1928), 64–5.

69. Posener, *L'Enseignement loyaliste,* 90–91, § 5, 26–29.

70. A. Volten, *Zwei Altägyptische Politische Schriften: Die Lehre für König Merikare und die Lehre des Königs Amenemhet* (Analecta Aegyptiaca IV) (Copenhagen, 1945), 22–27, papyri 47–59.

71. A. M. Blackman, *The Story of King Kheops and the Magicians* (London, 1988), 10.

72. A. de Buck, in *JEA* 23 (1937): 152–64; H. Goedicke, in *JEA* 49 (1963): 71–92.

73. On the symbolism of fire and sword, see E. Hornung, *Altägyptische Höllenvorstellungen,* Abh. Sächs. ADW Leipzig 59.3 (Berlin, 1968).

74. See my book *Der König als Sonnenpriester* (Glückstadt, 1970), 22, 35, 58–65; *Ma'at,* 205–212.

75. Since the first publication by K. Sethe [*Die Ächtung feindlicher Fürsten: Völker und Dinge auf altägyptischen Tongefäßscherben,* APAW (Berlin, 1926), p. 5], there has been general agreement that this must have taken place in the context of the ritual "breaking of the red pots." Cf. J. v. Dijk, "Zerbrechen der roten Töpfe," in *LÄ* VI (1986): 1389–96.

76. See G. Posener in *Syria* 43: 277–87; A. M. Abu Bakr, J. Osing, "Ächtungstexte aus dem Alten Reich," *MDIK* 29 (1973): 97–133; J. Osing, "Ächtungstexte aus dem Alten Reich (II)," *MDIK* 32 (1976): 133–85. On wood figurines from Abusir and Giza, see G. Posener, *Cinq figurines d'envoûtement* (Cairo, 1987), 2, nn. 1 and 2.

77. Posener, *Cinq figurines,* 3, with nn. 3 and 4.

78. See my *Ägyptische Hymnen und Gebete* (Zurich, 1975), No. 233, verses 56–79; text: *Urk* IV, 610–24.

79. E. Hornung, *Altägyptische Höllenvorstellungen,* Abh. Sächs. ADW Leipzig 59.3 (Berlin, 1968), 19 and pl. IIIb.

80. See my "Inscriptional Violence and the Art of Cursing: A Study of

Performative Writing," in *Stanford Literature Review* (Spring 1992): 43–65. For an anthology of Mesopotamian imprecations, see F. Pomponio, *Formule di maledizione della Mesopotamia preclassica* (Brescia, 1990).

81. *Zwei altägyptische politische Schriften,* ed. Volten, Analecta Aegyptiaca IV (Copenhagen, 1945), 47–49, plates 91–94. See also P. Seibert, *Die Charakteristik: Untersuchungen zu einer ägyptischen Sprechsitte und ihren Ausprägungen in Folklore und Literatur,* ÄA 17 (Wiesbaden, 1967), 90–94.

82. Stelae Berlin 14753 and 1157, ed. K. Sethe, *Ägyptische Lesestücke* (reprint, Darmstadt, 1959), 83–85; J. Assmann, *Stein und Zeit,* 255–56.

83. *Merikare* papyrus 97–98, ed. Volten, 50–51; Seibert, *Charakteristik,* 95–98.

84. My thanks to Jean Ziegler for pointing out this passage to me.

85. A. de Buck, *The Egyptian Coffin Texts,* vol. VII (Chicago, 1961), 463f–64c; W. Schenkel, "Soziale Gleichheit und soziale Ungleichheit und die altägyptische Religion," in G. Kehrer, ed., *Vor Gott sind alle gleich: Soziale Gleichheit, soziale Ungleichheit und die Religionen* (Düsseldorf, 1983), 26–41; J. Assmann, *Ma'at,* 215ff.

86. I deal briefly with the parallels in the political theories of T. Hobbes and C. Schmitt in *Ma'at,* 215ff., and in *Politische Theologie zwischen Ägypten und Israel,* Schriften der C. F. von Siemens-Stiftung, Reihe Themen (Munich, 2nd ed., 1995).

87. *Merikare* papyrus 61f., after Schenkel, "Soziale Gleichheit," 36.

88. R. O. Faulkner, "The Installation of the Vizier," in *JEA* 41 (1955): 18–26; cf. fig. 2, lines 2–3 (text), 22 center (translation).

89. *CT* VII, 466e–67d. See also Ps. 35:10: "[Thou] deliverest the poor from him that is too strong for him, yea, the poor and needy from him that spoileth him" (see also verses 23–24). Similar in Papyrus Cairo 50838 IV, 5 = *ÄHG* No. 87 C 71–72. See also J. Assmann, *Re und Amun,* 176; Papyrus Leiden I 344 vso. V.2, ed. J. Zandee, *Der Amunshymnus des Pap. Leiden I 344 vso.* (Leiden, 1992), 387: "Who saves the weak from the violent, who raises the child that has no parents."

90. *Urk* IV, 1092.14; Faulkner, *JEA* 41, fig. 2, bottom, p. 23, top.

91. For more detail on this see my *Ma'at,* 213ff, 251–52. We find an exact corollary in the ancient Indian, where the natural condition is referred to as matsyanyaya, the "law of the fishes" (big fish eat little fish). See R. Lingat, *The Classical Law of India* (New Delhi/Berkeley, 1973), 207–208; L. Dumont, *Gesellschaft in Indien: Die Soziologie des Kastenwesens (Homo Hierarchicus)* (Vienna, 1976), 351.

92. See my *Stein und Zeit,* 259–87, and "Weisheit, Schrift und Literatur," 485–87.

93. This subject dominates the *Dispute of a Man with His Ba,* which refers

not at all to state and kingship. A detailed discussion of this work follows below.

94. S. Schott, *Mythe und Mythenbildungen im Alten Ägypten*, UGAÄ 15 (Leipzig, 1943), 33ff.

95. On this point, see E. Blumenthal, "Die Reinheit der Grabschänder," in U. Verhoeven and E. Graefe, eds., *Religion und Philosophie im Alten Ägypten* (Louvain, 1991), 47–56.

96. On this point, see S. N. Morschauser, *Threat Formulae in Ancient Egypt* (Baltimore, 1987); H. Willems, *JEA* 76 (1990): 27–54; J. Assmann, *JEA* 78 (1992): 149–62.

97. See M. Lichtheim, *Ancient Egyptian Autobiographies*; J. Assmann, *Ma'at*, chaps. 4 and 5.

98. E.g., *Urk* I, 77.7, 79.14. Cf. 79.8 (Henqu, Eighth Dynasty).

99. E.g., *CT* I 159c, 160h, 161k, 162d, 163–64a, 164c, etc.

100. *CT*, spell 571 "for building a house in the middle of the water." The locality referred to is obviously in the next world.

101. J. Assmann, *Ma'at*, 109–113.

102. On this see J. Spiegel, *Die Idee vom Totengericht in der ägyptischen Religion* (Glückstadt, 1935); J. Yoyotte, "Le jugement des morts dans l'Égypte ancienne," in *Sources Orientales* IV (Paris, 1961); S.G.F. Brandon, *The Judgment of the Dead: An Historical and Comparative Study of the Idea of a Post-mortem Judgment in the Major Religions* (London, 1967); J. Vergote, "Immortalité conditionnée de l'âme ou survie inconditionnelle dans l'Égypte ancienne," in A. Théodoridès, P. Nasater, J. Ries, eds., *Vie et survie dans les civilisations orientales* (Louvain, 1993), 65–74; M. Lichtheim, *Ma'at in Egyptian Autobiographies and Related Studies*, OBO (Freiburg, 1992); J. G. Griffiths, *The Divine Verdict: A Study of Divine Judgement in the Ancient Religions* (Leiden, 1991).

103. *Merikare* papyrus 136–37. For a more recent study of Egyptian magic, see R. K. Ritner, *The Mechanics of Ancient Egyptian Magical Practice* (Chicago, 1993). On the passage from *Merikare* see ibid., 20.

104. On the weighing of the heart, see my article "Zur Geschichte des Herzens im alten Ägypten," in J. Assmann and T. Sundermeier, eds., *Die Erfindung des inneren Menschen*, 81–113, esp. 96–100.

105. Turin Stela 156, ed. Varille, in *BIFAO* 54 (1954): 129–35.

106. *Merikare* papyrus 53–57. See J. F. Quack, *Studien zur Lehre fur Merikare*, GOF 23 (Wiesbaden, 192), 34–35.

107. "Diodor über das Totengericht der Ägypter," *ZÄS* 120 (1993): 71–84.

108. Diodorus, *Bibl. hist.* I, 91–93. See Merkelbach, op. cit., 78.

109. J.-B. Bossuet, *Discourse on Universal History*, trans. E. Forster (Chicago, 1976), 308–309; and [Jean Terrasson], *Séthos, histoire ou vie, tirée des monuments, anecdotes de l'ancienne Égypte* (Paris, 1731; rev. ed., 1761).

The account of the judgment of the dead for Queen Nephté is in the first volume, pp. 38–48.

110. V. Herrmann, *Die Motivation des Helfens in der altägyptischen Religion und in der urchristlichen Religion: Ein Vergleich anhand von Totenbuch Kap. 25, Texten der idealen Selbstbiographie und Mt. 25, 31–46.* Degree thesis submitted to the Diakoniewissenschaftliches Institut, University of Heidelberg, winter semester 1990/91.

111. J. Taubes, in K. H. Bohrer, *Mythos und Moderne,* 461. See also (and esp.) H. Cohen, *Die Religion der Vernunft nach den Quellen des Judentums,* 214ff.: "Yehezkel differs from the social prophets in his discovery of sin as the sin of the individual."

112. Ezekiel 18:3–4. See Taubes, op. cit., 462. On this and for a comparison with the Egyptian Judgment of the Dead see my *Maʿat,* chap. 5.

113. See *Maʿat,* chap. 5.

114. See E. Hornung, *Das Totenbuch der Ägypter* (Zurich/Munich, 1979), 240.

115. *CT* I, spell 23.

116. Cantata No. 52 by J. S. Bach, recitative and aria (text anon.).

117. Song III, cf. R. Hari, *La Tombe thébaine du père divin Neferhotep (TT 50)* (Geneva, 1985), IV. See my article "Fest des Augenblicks—Verheißung der Dauer. Die Kontroverse der ägyptischen Harfnerlieder" in *Fragen an die altägyptische Literatur,* Gedenkschrift für Eberhard Otto (Wiesbaden, 1977), 69; E. Hornung, "Altägyptische Wurzeln der Isismysterien," in *Hommages à Jean Leclant,* vol. 3: *Études isiaques* (Cairo, 1994), 287–94, esp. 289.

118. The text has "That I may drive away my sorrow to him."

119. Khakheperreseneb, tablet BM 5645, vso. 1, ed. Gardiner, *The Admonitions of an Egyptian Sage* (Leipzig, 1909), 105.

120. Neferti, 20. I am citing the text of the Papyrus Petersburg 116B, after W. Helck.

121. On the literary form and rhetorical argumentation structure of the *Dispute* see the brilliant study by O. Renaud, *Le Dialogue du désespéré avec son âme: une interprétation littéraire,* Cahiers de la Société d'Égyptologie I (Geneva, 1991).

122. The political philosopher Eric Voegelin (to name only one example) has devoted an important essay to this text: "Immortality: Experience and Symbol" (The Ingersoll Lecture 1965, Harvard University School) in *The Harvard Theological Review* 60 (1967): 235–79.

123. Crucial to the *ba* is its potential freedom from the "I." This independence of the *ba* was more or less completely overlooked by L. V. Zabkar in his much quoted standard work on the *ba: A Study of the Ba Concept in Ancient Egyptian Texts* (Chicago, 1968).

124. Bauer B2 113–15, ed. R. B. Parkinson, *The Tale of the Eloquent Peasant* (Oxford, 1991), 47.

125. "On the day of misfortune" reappears in line 15: "he attacks me on the day of misfortune." The reference is to the day of death and the Judgment of the Dead.

126. Papyrus Berlin 3024, 23–27; Barta 13, 21.

127. On this point see O. Renaud, *Le Dialogue du désespéré*, 55–56, who emphasizes the antagonistic aspect of this passage.

128. *Admonitions of Ipuwer,* after Lichtheim, *Ancient Egyptian Literature* I, 153.

129. This is the view taken by O. Renaud, *Le Dialogue du désespéré,* 49–50, who proposes a purely psychological interpretation.

130. *Book of the Dead,* chap. 30B, ed. E.A.W. Budge, *The Egyptian Book of the Dead,* vol. I, 130 (London, 1910).

131. See *Amenemope* 16, 20–21: "Be not timid toward him, bow not your head, nor cast down your eyes."

132. Papyrus Berlin 3024, 103–130; H. Goedicke, *The Report About the Dispute of a Man with His Ba,* Papyrus Berlin 3024 (Baltimore, 1970), 155–72; W. Barta, *Das Gespräch eines Mannes mit seinem Ba (Papyrus Berlin 3024)* (Berlin, 1969), 16–18, 26–27.

133. Papyrus Berlin 3024, 142–47; Barta, op. cit., 18, 28, 47; Goedicke, op. cit., 178–82.

134. Papyrus Moscow 127, 3, 9–13; R. A. Caminos, *A Tale of Woe* (Oxford, 1977), 40–43.

135. The example of the Fifth Dynasty is particularly apparent in architecture. The mortuary temple of the Sesostris I pyramid is an almost exact replica of a pyramid temple from the Fifth Dynasty. See D. Arnold, *The Pyramid of Senwosret I* (New York, 1988).

136. E. Hornung, *Der ägyptische Mythos von der Himmelskuh: eine Ätiologie des Unvollkommenen,* OBO 46 (1982); H. Beinlich, *Das Buch vom Fayum: zum religiösen Eigenverständnis einer ägyptischen Landschaft* (Wiesbaden, 1991), 314–19.

137. *CT* I, 332–24.

138. Papyrus Nu, pBM 10477, col. 24, after Budge, *Book of the Dead,* 269 (my translation).

139. See H. Brunner, "Seth und Apophis—Gegengötter im ägyptischen Pantheon?" in *Saeculum* 34 (1983): 226–34.

140. *Buch von Fayum,* 300–301.

PART FOUR

The New Kingdom

1. See S. Schott, *Zum Krönungstag der Königin Hatschepsut,* NGAW 1955.5; E. Blumenthal, "Die erste Koregenz der 12. Dynastie," *ZÄS* 110 (1983):

113–20; C. Eyre, "The Semna Stelae: Quotation, Genre and Functions of Literature," in *Studies in Egyptology* (Festschrift for M. Lichtheim) (Jerusalem, 1990), 134–65, esp. 145–46.

2. On this point, see D. Franke, *Das Heiligtum des Heqa-ib auf Elephantine: Geschichte eines Provinzheiligtums im Mittleren Reich, SAGA* 9 (1994).

3. *ÄHG* No. 87.

4. See P. Artzi, "Ideas and Practices of International Co-existence in the 3rd mill. BCE," in *Bar Ilan Studies in History* 2 (1984): 25–39, and "The Birth of the Middle East," in *Proceedings of the 5th World Congress of Jewish Studies* (Jerusalem, 1969), 120–24.

5. See E. Hornung, "Politische Planung und Realität im alten Ägypten," in *Saeculum* 22 (1971): 48–58. Hornung takes the program for "expanding of the frontiers" discernible in the inscriptions of the New Kingdom and generalizes it into the idea of the "expansion of all existing things," substantiating this with reference to phenomena such as the duration of festivals, the number of carrying rods on the processional bark, and the number of rooms in the royal tomb.

6. W. Helck, *Historisch-Biographische Texte der Zweiten Zwischenzeit*, No. 119; K. Sa-Moon, *Divine War in the Old Testament and in the Ancient Near East* (Berlin/New York, 1989), 89, 99; I. Shirun-Grumach, *Offenbarung, Orakel und Königsnovelle, ÄAT* 24 (Wiesbaden, 1993), 123 with n. 3.

7. Sa-Moon, *Divine War*, T. v.d. Way, *Göttergericht und "heiliger Krieg" im alten Ägypten, SAGA* 4 (1992).

8. The concept is probably taken from the political philosopher Eric Voegelin, who expounds it in *Israel and Revolution*, the first volume of his monumental opus *Order and History* (Baton Rouge, 1956). Voegelin in his turn draws on Henri Frankfort, who gave his book *Kingship and the Gods* the subtitle *The Integration of Society into Nature* (Chicago, 1948). Both Voegelin and Frankfort are, in turn, indebted to Hans Kelsen, the Viennese public law scholar who, like Voegelin, emigrated to the United States, and whose book *Nature and Society: A Sociological Inquiry* was published in Chicago in 1943.

9. An exception is astrological divination, which also takes regular processes and recurring events as the basis for its interpretations and forecasts.

10. E. Voegelin, *Order and History*, vol. 4: *The Ecumenic Age* (Baton Rouge, 1974), 73.

11. Papyrus Chester Beatty IV rto. XI, 8–10 = *ÄHG* No. 195, 275–81; see A. de Buck, "De godsdienstige opvatting van den slaap in het Oude Egypte," *Mededelingen Ex Oriente Lux* (1939).

12. J. Assmann, *Liturgische Lieder* (1969), 154–57, 162.

13. Sir Thomas Browne, *Religio Medici*, 8th (11th) ed. (London, 1682), I, 16.

14. See my article "Solar Discourse: Ancient Egyptian Ways of World-Reading," in *Deutsche Vierteljahresschrift für Literaturwissenschaft und Geistesgeschichte* 68 (1994): 107–122.
15. Stela of Ramesses IV in Abydos, ed. Kitchen, *Ramesside Inscriptions* VI, 24.9–10.
16. Medinet Habu VI, pl. 422–23. See J. Assmann, *Der König als Sonnenpriester*, 68.
17. G. Balandier, *Le Désordre: éloge du mouvement* (Paris, 1988), 31, formulated with reference to China.
18. From a cult-theological tractate on the "king as sun priest," ed. J. Assmann, *Der König als Sonnenpriester*.
19. See E. Hornung, "Altägyptische Wurzeln der Isismysterien," in *Hommages à J. Leclant* III (Cairo, 1994), 287–93.
20. *ÄHG* No. 90, 7.
21. On the Amarna religion, see Erik Hornung, *Echnaton: die Religion des Lichts* (Zurich, 1995), trans. D. Lorton, *Akhenaten and the Religion of Light* (Ithaca, 2001). Hornung's interpretation of the Amarna religion and my own largely accord. On the history and religion of the age of Amarna, see also D. B. Redford, *Akhenaten, the Heretic King* (Princeton, 1984); H. A. Schlögl, *Echnaton—Tutanchamun: Fakten und Texte*, 2nd ed. (Wiesbaden, 1985); C. Aldred, *Akhenaten, King of Egypt* (London, 1988); J. Assmann, "Akhanyati's Theology of Light and Time," in *Proceedings of the Israel Academy of Sciences and Humanities*, VII 4 (Jerusalem, 1992), 143–76; *Moses the Egyptian*, 168–92.
22. J. H. Breasted, *Ancient Records of Egypt* (Chicago, 1906).
23. Sigmund Freud, *Moses and Monotheism* (London, 1939).
24. On the history of the discovery of the Amarna religion, see E. Hornung, "The Rediscovery of Akhenaten and His Place in Religion," in *Journal of the American Research Center in Egypt* XXIX (1992): 43–49; *Echnaton*, 9–27.
25. K. A. Kitchen, *Ramesside Inscriptions* III, 433.12.
26. See J. P. Allen, "The Natural Philosophy of Akhenaten," in W. K. Simpson, ed., *Religion and Philosophy in Ancient Egypt*, YES 3 (New Haven, 1989), 89–101.
27. The destruction extended southward as far as Kawa, Soleb, and Faras in Nubia. See R. Hari, "La Religion amarnienne et la tradition polythéiste," in *Studien zur Sprache und Religion Ägyptens* (Festschrift for W. Westendorf) (Wiesbaden, 1984), 1039–1055.
28. On this point, see B. van de Walle, in E. Hornung, O. Keel, eds., *Studien zu ägyptischen Lebenslehren*, OBO 28 (Freiburg, 1979), 353–62; J. Assmann, "Die Loyalistische Lehre Echnatons," *SAK* 8 (1980): 1–32.
29. We owe the first edition of this text to U. Bouriant, *Mission archéologique française au Caire* I (Cairo, 1884), 2–5, also in U. Bouriant, G.

Legrain, G. Jéquier, *Monuments du culte d'Atonou* I (Cairo, 1903), pl. xvi and p. 30; the standard edition is that of N. de Garis Davies, *The Rock Tombs of El-Amarna* VI (London, 1908), pl. xxvii, xli, pp. 29–31. Among the first translators and commentators was J. H. Breasted, *De Hymnis in Solem sub rege Amenophide IV conceptis* (Berlin, 1904).

30. On the motif of different irrigation conditions as an aspect of the well-organized world, see also the first part of Psalm 104. The motif of the "Nile in the sky" also figures in other Egyptian hymns: see *ÄHG* No. 127B, 45–46; No. 195, 166; No. 143, 46, 100ff. (cf. p. 590 ad loc.); No. 144C, 39; No. 214, 9–32 (*Book of the Dead*, chap. 183); No. 242, 7–8; cf. A. P. Zivie (1983), "Regen," in *Lexikon der Ägyptologie* V, 201–206, esp. 202, 204.

31. M. Sandman, *Texts from the Time of Akhenaten*, BiblAeg VIII (1938), 95.17–18. See J. Assmann, *Zeit und Ewigkeit im Alten Ägypten: Ein Beitrag zur Geschichte der Ewigkeit* (Heidelberg, 1975), 55.

32. Sandman, 95.16–17.

33. Sandman, 14.13–16, 15.1–3.

34. See also my books *Re und Amun*, chap. 2, and *Ma'at*, chap. 6.

35. On the typical connections between "light" and "justice" in ancient Oriental thought, see B. Janowski, *Rettungsgewißheit und Epiphanie des Heils: Das Motiv der Hilfe Gottes "am Morgen" im Alten Orient und im Alten Testament*, vol. I: *Alter Orient* (Neukirchen, 1989).

36. Papyrus Cairo 58038, IV, 1–5; see J. Assmann, *Re und Amun*, 76ff.

37. *Der Eine und die Vielen*, 239.

38. N. Abraham, M. Torok, *L'Écorce et le noyau* (Paris, 1978).

39. *Moses the Egyptian: The Memory of Egypt in Western Monotheism* (Cambridge, Mass., 1997).

40. *ÄHG* No. 147.

41. *Urk* IV, 2025ff.

42. See my book *Stein und Zeit*, 268 with n. 41; 274 with n. 69; 279.

43. On this point, see H. Goedicke, "The Canaanite Illness," *SAK* 11 (1984): 91–105.

44. *KRI* I, 111, 1–2.

45. *ÄHG* 190, 20–25.

46. This episode is reminiscent of the *Potter's Oracle*, in which Amenophis III also figures as a protagonist. Cf. L. Kakosy, *Acta Or.* 19 (1966): 345; L. Koenen, *ZPE* 2 (1968), 178ff.; J.W.B. Barns, *Orientalia* 46 (1977): 31ff.; Redford, *Pharaonic King-Lists*, 284–86.

47. For this interpretation, see E. Meyer, *Ägyptische Chronologie* (Berlin, 1904, 92–95, and *Geschichte des Altertums* (repr. Darmstadt, 1953), vol. II.1, 420–26; D. B. Redford, "The Hyksos Invasion in History and Tradition," *Orientalia* 39 (1970): 1–51, and *Pharaonic King-Lists*, 276–96; R. Krauss, *Das Ende der Amarnazeit*, HÄB 7 (Hildesheim, 1978), 204ff.;

D. B. Redford, *Egypt, Canaan, and Israel in Ancient Times* (Princeton, 1992), 408–422; J. Assmann, *Monotheismus und Kosmotheismus,* Sitzungsberichte der Heidelberger Akademie der Wissenschaften (Heidelberg, 1993).

48. See R. Weill, *La Fin du Moyen Empire égyptien: étude sur les monuments et l'histoire de la période comprise entre la XIIe et la XVIIIe dynastie* (Paris, 1918), 22–145; Thomas Schneider, "Ausländer in Ägypten während des Mittleren Reiches und der Hyksoszeit I," *Die Ausländischen Könige,* ÄAT, 42, 1998.

49. See A. Funkenstein, *Perceptions of Jewish History* (Berkeley, 1993); and— of course—Flavius Josephus himself.

50. See J. G. Gager, *The Origins of Anti-Semitism* (New York/Oxford, 1983): J. L. Daniel, "Anti-Semitism in the Hellenistic Period," *Journal of Biblical Literature* 98 (1979): 45–65; A. Kasher, *The Jews in Hellenistic and Roman Egypt: The Struggle for Equal Rights* (Tübingen, 1985); and esp. Peter Schaefer, *Judeophobia: The Attitude Toward the Jews in the Ancient World* (Cambridge, Mass., 1997).

51. Papyrus Sallier I, 1.2–3, ed. Gardiner, *Late Egyptian Stories,* 85; H. Goedicke, *The Quarrel of Apophis and Seqenenre* (San Antonio, 1986), 10–11.

52. See A. Erman, *Gedenksteine aus der thebanischen Gräberstadt, SPAW* 1911; B. Gunn, "The Religion of the Poor in Ancient Egypt," *JEA* 3 (1916), 81–94; H. Brunner, "Die religiöse Wertung der Armut im alten Ägypten," *Saeculum* 12 (1961), 319–44; G. Fecht, *Literarische Zeugnisse zur "Persönlichen Frömmigkeit" in Ägypten,* AHAW 1965; G. Posener, "La piété personnelle avant l'âge amarnien," *RdE* 27 (1975), 195–210. See also the literature listed by H. Brunner, "Persönliche Frömmigkeit," *LÄ* IV, 951–63, and J. Baines, "Practical Religion and Piety," *JEA* 73 (1987): 79–98; J. Baines, "Society, Morality, and Religious Practice," in B. E. Schafer, ed., *Religion in Ancient Egypt* (London, 1991), 123–200.

53. I refer to the cult of a deified nomarch of the Sixth Dynasty, observed above all by the nomarchs of the Twelfth Dynasty. In their predecessor, they saw both a role model and a kind of pioneering hero who deserved credit for establishing the office to which they had acceded. See D. Franke, *Das Heiligtum des Heqa-ib auf Elephantine: Geschichte eines Provinzheiligtums im Mittleren Reich,* SAGA 9 (Heidelberg, 1994), esp. 142–46.

54. A. H. Bomann, *The Private Chapel in Ancient Egypt: A Study of the Chapels in the Workmen's Village at el-Amarna with Special Reference to Deir el Medina and Other Sites* (London/New York, 1991). These cult sites belonged to individual families.

55. A. I. Sadek, *Popular Religion in Ancient Egypt,* HÄB 27 (Hildesheim, 1987).

56. Amenemope 21.5–6; Grumach, *Untersuchungen,* 134.

57. Amenemope XX.3–6; Grumach, *Untersuchungen,* 124–28.

58. *ÄHG* 75.23–24.

59. Ostracon Cairo 12217 rto., ed. G. Posener, in *RdE* 27 (1975), 206–209.

60. Papyrus Berlin 3056, vii, 6 etc.; see *LL,* 248.

61. *LL,* 250–62, contains a large number of such songs.

62. See my book *The Search for God in Ancient Egypt* (Ithaca, 2001), 20.

63. Papyrus Insinger 28,4; M. Lichtheim, *Ancient Egyptian Literature,* vol. III (Berkeley, 1980), 207, and *Egyptian Wisdom Literature in the International Context: A Study of Demotic Instructions,* OBO 52 (Fribourg, 1983), 162–63.

64. Papyrus Chester Beatty IV rto. 8,6–7. See also 7,4: "Your reward is a fine burial for the singer who praises you so that he may emerge in this world as perfect *ba* to praise the lord of the gods."

65. CGC 42 231. K. Jansen-Winkeln, *Ägyptische Biographien der 22. und 23. Dynastie* (Wiesbaden, 1985), vol. I, 194ff.; vol. II, 543.

66. TT 409: *ÄHG* No. 173, 25–26.

67. Hymn of Ramesses III to Amun-Re: *ÄHG* No. 196, 47–48.

68. *ÄHG* 83.6–7 = *STG* No. 13, TT 11.

69. See H. Brunner, "Die religiöse Wertung der Armut," n. 62.

70. See G. Posener, "Amon juge du pauvre," in *Beiträge zur ägyptischen Bauforschung* 12, Festschrift for H. Ricke (Wiesbaden, 1971), 59–63; Assmann, *Egyptian Solar Religion,* 201ff.

71. E.g., *ÄHG* 173.12–13, 42–43, 62–63, 102ff.; 177, 5–11.

72. First highlighted by S. Morenz, *Die Heraufkunft des transzendenten Gottes in Ägypten,* SSAW 109.2 (Berlin, 1964), 109–112.

73. See Amenemope 22.8 and 23.11.

74. See Vernus, in *RdE* 30 (1978): 115–46.

75. *ÄHG* No. 173. O. Kaiser, ed., *Texte aus der Umwelt des Alten Testaments* (TUAT), vol. II.6, Lieder und Gebete II (Gütersloh, 1991), 879–82.

76. See F. Junge, "Sprachstufen und Sprachgeschichte," *Zeitschrift der Deutschen Morgenländischen Gesellschaft,* Supplement VI (1985): 17–34.

77. On the concept of the "connection between doing and faring," see K. Koch, ed., *Um das Prinzip der Vergeltung in Religion und Recht des Alten Testaments* (Darmstadt, 1972); id., J. Roloff, "Tat-Ergehen-Zusammenhang," in *Reclams Bibellexikon* (Stuttgart, 1987), 493–94; id., K. Koch *Spuren des hebräischen Denkens: Beiträge zur alttestamentlichen Theologie: Gesammelte Aufsätze* 1, ed. B. Janowski and M. Krause (Neukirchen-Vluyn, 1991).

78. *Merikare* papyrus 136–37. See J. F. Quack, *Studien zur Lehre für Merikare* (Wiesbaden, 1992), 78–79.

79. 343 Dévaud. See 345 after the London Ms. L$_2$ from the Eighteenth Dynasty, which at this point has the most comprehensible text: "None knows his condition so that he could plan the morrow." In this version,

the homily is also found in the Papyrus Ramesseum I B1, 6 (cf. Barns, *Five Ramesseum Papyri*, 6) and is hence classified as a proverb by Gunn in *JEA* 12, 283. His translation is "There's no one who knows his luck when he plans the morrow." Brunner also refers to the passage in Papyrus Ramesseum I, A1, 18: "This earthly life, one knows not what happens in it."

80. Kagemni II.2.

81. *Eloquent Peasant* B1, 183–84.

82. W. K. Simpson, in *JEA* 52 (1966): 39–52; G. Fecht, in *MDIK* 24 (1969), 113.

83. Abd el Mohsen Bakir, *Egyptian Epistolography*, 77 and 91.

84. On *jjt* see S. Morenz, "Die Bedeutungsentwicklung von *jjt*, 'Das, was kommt' zu 'Unheil' und 'Unrecht'," in *Religion und Geschichte des alten Ägypten* (Weimar, 1975), 343–59.

85. Berlin 24195; similarly, Vienna 5103: "Re arises to observe him who acts; he pays back the deed to him who performs it." See also H. de Meulenaere, "Réflexions sur une maxime," in *Studien zur Sprache und Religion des alten Ägypten* (Festschrift for W. Westendorf) (Göttingen, 1984), 555–59.

86. Cairo CG 22054; see P. Vernus, "La Rétribution des actions: à propos d'une maxime," in *GM* 84 (1985): 71–79.

87. On the concept of "intervention," see B. Albrektson, *History and the Gods: An Essay on the Idea of Historical Events as Divine Manifestations in the Ancient Near East and in Israel* (Lund, Sweden, 1967); with reference to Egypt, see J. F. Borghouts, "Divine Intervention in Ancient Egypt and Its Manifestation," in R. J. Demarée and J. J. Janssen, *Gleanings from Deir el-Medina* (Leiden, 1982), 1–70.

88. I. Shirun-Grumach, *Offenbarung, Orakel und Königsnovelle*, ÄAT 24 (Wiesbaden, 1993), 124–28, discusses the "finding" motif as one of "receiving revelation" (126); but the passages she cites do not revolve around finding God but around finding hitherto concealed objects such as scripts or wells. Using the term "find" to refer to God and his coming appears to be a motif characteristic of personal piety. God also figures as an object of "finding" on Tuthmosis IV's Dream Stela: "That he found this glorious god was by speaking with his own mouth [as] a father speaks to his son" (*Urk* IV, 1542; Shirun-Grumach, 142).

89. Graffito of Pawah in the tomb of Pairi TT 139, ed. Gardiner; see *ÄHG* No. 147.

90. Berlin Stela 20377, *ÄHG* No. 148, 39–40. See also *ÄHG* No. 173, 23–24; 175,7; 179,9–10.

91. Turin Stela 1539+1694, *ÄHG* No. 149, 23.

92. Battle of Qadesh, *Poem* 122–23, *KRI* II, 42,f.

93. On this point, see E. Hornung, *Geschichte als Fest: Zwei Vorträge zum Geschichtsbild der frühen Menschheit* (Darmstadt, 1966), and "Zum altägyptischen Geschichtsbewußtsein," in *Archäologie und Geschichtsbewußtsein: Kolloquien zur allgemeinen und vergleichenden Archäologie* 3 (Munich, 1982), 13–30.

94. In this connection, A. Gehlen speaks of *"Hintergrundserfüllung"* ("background fulfillment"): *Urmensch und Spätkultur* (Bonn, 1956), 56–61.

95. J. Bottéro, "Symptomes, signes, écritures," in J.-P. Vernant, ed., *Divination et rationalité* (Paris, 1974), 70–198.

96. H. Brunner, "Eine Dankstele an Upuaut," in *Das hörende Herz*, OBO 80 (Fribourg, 1988), 173–88.

97. See the texts in *ÄHG* Nos. 147–71.

98. J. F. Borghouts, "Divine Intervention in Ancient Egypt and Its Manifestation," in R. J. Demarée and J. J. Janssen, *Gleanings from Deir el-Medina*, n. 99; J. Assmann, "Aretalogien," *LÄ* I, 425. Shirun-Grumach dates the proclaiming of the manifestations of power back to the Eleventh Dynasty but is unable to adduce textual evidence of the formula; see *Offenbarung*, 43–45.

99. Hymn to the sun in the tomb of Tjai (TT 23) from the age of Merneptah; cf. *ÄHG* 98; *STG* No. 17 18–23 with 23, n. (y). See also the text of Kiki above, p. 235.

100. Cf. *ÄHG* 98; *STG* No. 17 18–23, with 23, n. (y).

101. See *KRI* II, 346.8.

102. Papyrus Leiden I 350, V, 17.

103. *KRI* II, 249.10.

104. On this point, cf. my *Zeit und Ewigkeit im alten Ägypten.*

105. *Urk* IV 96, 14–16. See Shirun-Grumach, *Offenbarung*, 114.

106. Renewal of a temple: Coptos Stela of Rahotep, Shirun-Grumach, *Offenbarung*, 118–19; erection of an obelisk: Hatshepsut Obelisk, *Urk* IV, 363, 2–15 Shirun-Grumach, *Offenbarung*, 117; statues and cult equipment: *Urk* IV 96, 10–16, Stela of Tuthmosis I from Abydos, Shirun-Grumach, *Offenbarung*, 114; appointment of officials: *Urk* IV, 1386, 13–14, Shirun-Grumach, *Offenbarung*, 115; a well: Kubban Stela of Ramesses II, *KRI* II, 356.

107. *Urk* IV, 1074,9, Shirun-Grumach, *Offenbarung*, 115.

108. *Urk* IV, 351,5–6, Shirun-Grumach, *Offenbarung*, 114.

109. See as an early instance the great wooden seated figure of another Amenemope, from the age of Sethos I (in Berlin, 6910), where the inscription on the back begins: "How beautiful it is to sit in the hand of Amun," and closes: "May he grant a beautiful old age in which I am whole in his hand" (*Äg. Inschr.* II, 68–71; *KRI*, 387–88; *ÄHG* No. 169; *STG* No. 206).

110. *ÄHG* No. 186.

111. Hymn on the Banishment Stela, Louvre C 256, ed. v. Beckerath, *RdE* 20 (1968): 7–36.

112. On these events, see R. Krauss, *Das Ende der Amarnazeit* (Hildesheim, 1979); D. Sürenhagen, *Paritätische Staatsverträge aus hethitischer Sicht* (Pavia, 1985).

113. A. Goetze, in J. B. Pritchard, ed., *Ancient Near Eastern Texts Relating to the Old Testament,* 2nd ed. (Princeton, 1955), 395.

114. See D. Polz, "Die Särge des (Pa-)Ramessu," *MDIK* 42 (1986), 145–66.

115. I am drawing here on A. Gnirs, *Militär und Staat: Eine soziologische Untersuchung zur späten 18. Dynastie und zur Ramessidenzeit* (Heidelberg, 1996).

116. W. Helck, *Der Einfluß der Militärführer in der 18. ägyptischen Dynastie,* UGAÄ 14 (reprint, Hildesheim, 1964), 87.

117. See R. O. Faulkner, "The Wars of Sethos I," *JEA* 33 (1947), 34ff.; W. Murnane, *The Road to Kadesh: A Historical Interpretation of the Battle Reliefs of King Sety I at Karnak* (Chicago, 1985).

118. See A. H. Gardiner, *The Kadesh-Inscriptions of Ramesses II* (Oxford, 1960); H. Goedicke, ed., *Perspectives on the Battle of Kadesh* (Baltimore, 1985); T. v. d. Way, *Die Textüberlieferung Ramses' II zur Qades-Schlacht: Analyse und Struktur,* HÄB 22 (1984). Text edition: *KRI* II. (1979), 2ff., on which the translation quoted is based; the line numbers given refer to the original. G. Fecht, "Das Poème über die Qades-Schlacht," *SAK* 11 (1984), 282–333; id., "Ramses II. und die Schlacht bei Qadesch (Qidsa)," *Göttinger Miszellen* 80 (1984): 23–53.

119. "Life, Prosperity, Health," is frequently written in abbreviated form in the Egyptian.

120. *Bulletin,* 8–28, *KRI* II, 103–108.

121. *Poem,* 56–64, *KRI* II, 21–24; Fecht, *SAK* 11, 289.

122. *Bulletin,* 33–51, *KRI* II, 109–112.

123. *Bulletin,* 75–83, *KRI* II, 117–119.

124. *Bulletin,* 84–110, *KRI* II, 119–129.

125. *Poem,* 158–62, *KRI* II, 53. Fecht, *SAK* 11, 299.

126. *ÄHG* 230, 2.

127. *ÄHG* 228, 13–14.

128. *Poem,* 123–24.

129. Ibid., 117, 128, and 132.

130. *ÄHG* 194, 21–22.

131. *KRI* II, 131–33.

132. *Poem,* 169–99.

133. Ibid., 253–66.

134. *Bulletin,* 54–67.

135. Thus Fecht, *GM* 80, 47–48.

136. On this point see A. and J. Assmann, *Kanon und Zensur* (Munich, 1987), 15–19.

137. See F. Junge, "Sprachstufen und Sprachgeschichte," *ZDMG* Suppl. VI (Wiesbaden, 1985), 17–34.

138. A. B. Lloyd, "Nationalist Propaganda in Ptolemaic Egypt," *Historia* 31 (1982), 33–55. See also K. Sethe, *Sesostris*, UGAÄ II; M. Malaise, "Sésostris, pharaon de légende et d'histoire," *CdE* 41 (1966): 244–72.

139. O. Murray, "Hecataeus of Abdera and Pharaonic Kingship," *JEA* 56 (1970), 141–71, esp. 161–64.

140. For more detail on the following, see my articles "Gibt es eine Klassik in der ägyptischen Literaturgeschichte?" in *XXII. Deutscher Orientalistentag*, Suppl. *ZDMG* (1985), 35–52, and "Die Entdeckung der Vergangenheit: Innovation und Restauration in der ägyptischen Literaturgeschichte," in H. U. Gumbrecht and U. Link-Heer, eds., *Epochenschwellen und Epochenstrukturen im Diskurs der Literatur- und Sprachhistorie* (Frankfurt, 1985), 484–99 (= *Stein und Zeit*, 303–313).

141. Papyrus Chester Beatty IV rto. 2.5–3.11; D. Wildung, *Imhotep und Amenhotep: Gottwerdung im Alten Ägypten*, MÄS 36 (Munich, 1977), 25–27.

142. D. Wildung, *Imhotep und Amenhotep*, 28–29.

143. M. Bakhtin, *Rabelais and His World*, trans. H. Iswolsky (Indiana University Press, 1988); and *Literatur und Karneval: Zur Romantheorie und Lachkultur* (Frankfurt/Berlin/Vienna, 1985).

144. E. Brunner-Traut, *Altägyptische Tiergeschichte und Fabel: Gestalt und Strahlkraft* (Darmstadt, 1984).

145. Papyrus Turin Cat. 2031, ed. J. A. Omlin, *Der Papyrus 55001 und seine satirisch-erotischen Zeichnungen und Inschriften* (Turin, 1973).

146. K. R. Weeks, *The Anatomical Knowledge of the Ancient Egyptians and the Representation of the Human Figure in Egyptian Art*, Ph.D. dissertation (Yale, 1970).

147. See my article "Ikonographie der Schönheit im alten Ägypten," in T. Stemmler, ed., *Schöne Frauen—schöne Männer: Literarische Schönheitsbeschreibungen* (Mannheim, 1988), 13–32; C. Müller, "Körperpflege," in *LÄ* III (1979), 668–70; H. Sourouzian, "Schönheitsideal," in *LÄ* V (1984), 674–76; E. Zoffili, *Kleidung und Schmuck im alten Ägypten* (Frankfurt/Berlin, 1992).

148. P. Seibert, *Die Charakteristik: Untersuchungen zu einer altägyptischen Sprechsitte und ihren Ausprägungen in Folklore und Literatur*, ÄA 17 (Wiesbaden, 1967).

149. H. Kenner, *Das Phänomen der verkehrten Welt in der griechisch-romanischen Antike* (Klagenfurt, 1970), 57.

150. See M. V. Fox, "The Entertainment Song Genre in Egyptian Literature," in *Scripta Hierosolymitana* 28, Egyptological Studies (Jerusalem, 1982), 268–316, and *The Song of Songs and the Ancient Egyptian Love Song* (Madison, Wisc., 1985), 244–47.

151. H. Brunner, "Die religiöse Antwort auf die Korruption in Ägypten," in *Das Hörende Herz*, 103–109, esp. 106.

1. For important literature on this period, see esp. E. Meyer, *Gottesstaat, Militärherrschaft und Ständewesen in Ägypten (Zur Geschichte der 21. und 22. Dynastie)*; SPAW (Berlin, 1928); H. Kees, *Herihor und die Errichtung des thebanischen Gottesstaates*, NGAW (1936); and *Die Hohenpriester des Amun von Karnak von Herihor bis zum Ende der Äthiopienzeit* (Leiden, 1964); K. A. Kitchen, *The Third Intermediate Period in Egypt (100–650 B.C.)* (Warminster, Eng., 1973); M. Römer, *Gottes- und Priesterherrschaft in Ägypten am Ende des Neuen Reichs: Ein religionsgeschichtliches Phänomen und seine sozialen Grundlagen*, ÄAT 21 (Wiesbaden, 1994).

2. See my study *Politische Theologie zwischen Israel und Ägypten*, C. F. v. Siemens-Stiftung, Reihe Themen 52 (Munich, 1992).

3. The Mesopotomian discharge decrees at the beginning of a new reign correspond in Egypt to the proclamations of pardon on the occasion of *sed* festivals, as preserved from the reign of Amenophis III in Soleb and Osorkon II in Bubastis (an exact replica of the Soleb inscription). See Kitchen, *Third Intermediate Period*, 321.

4. See D. O'Connor, in B. G. Trigger, B. J. Kemp. D. O'Connor, and A. B. Lloyd, *Ancient Egypt: A Social History* (Cambridge, 1983), 239.

5. This is the expression used by D. O'Connor in his excellent study of the political conditions prevailing in the Twenty-first Dynasty, in ibid., *Ancient Egypt*, 232.

6. For a comparison of Herihor and Horemheb, see M. Römer, *Gottes- und Priesterherrschaft*, 38.

7. On the *chronique scandaleuse* of the late Ramesside period, see P. Vernus, *Affaires et scandales sous les Ramsès: la crise des valeurs dans l'Égypte du Nouvel Empire* (Paris, 1993).

8. R. A. Caminos, *A Tale of Woe* (Oxford, 1977).

9. Papyrus Moscow 127, 3, 7–9, ed. Caminos, *A Tale of Woe*, 38–40, pl. 8. On the distrust encountered by the lonely wanderer, Caminos refers to the remarks by W. Ward, *Orientalia* 31 (1962), 405–406.

10. Papyrus Moscow 127, 4, 13–15.

11. Papyrus Moscow 127, 3, 8–13. Caminos, 40–43.

12. Wente, *JNES* 26, 174.

13. Papyrus Pushkin 120, ed. V. Golenishchev, *Papyrus hiératique de la collection W. Golénischeff contenant la description du voyage de l'Égyptien Ounou-Amon en Phénicie*, Recueil des Travaux 21 (1899): 74–102. H. Goedicke, *The Report of Wenamun* (Baltimore, 1975).

14. Wenamun 2, 8–34.

15. Wenamun 2, 54–60

16. J. Yoyotte, "Les Principautés du Delta au temps de l'anarchie libyenne," *Mélanges Maspero,* I:4 (Cairo, 1961), 121–81.

17. See the family trees in Trigger, et al., *Ancient Egypt,* 236–37.

18. Both rulers were notable for the number of fortresses they built. These were not, however, an indication of any strife between them; rather, they were protection against a common threat, presumably surprise attacks by the Libyans.

19. *Contra Apionem* 2,157–98. See H. Cancik, "Theokratie und Priesterherrschaft. Die mosaische Verfassung bei Flavius Josephus, c. Apionem 2, 157–198," in *Theokratie,* J. Taubes, ed. (Munich, 1987), 65–77.

20. The Ramesside papyrus Chester Beatty III is a manual of dream interpretation. See S. Sauneron, "Les songes et leur interprétation dans l'Égypte ancienne," in *Sources Orientales* 2 (1959). For bird divination, see H. Brunner, "Vogelschau in Ägypten," *GM* 25 (1977), 45–46; for interpretation of wind and stars, see H. Brunner, "Zeichendeutung aus Sternen und Winden in Ägypten," in *Festschrift Ellinger* (1973), reprinted in *Das Hörende Herz* (1988), 224–29.

21. See J. Černý, "Egyptian Oracles," in R. A. Parker, *A Saite Oracle Papyrus from Thebes in the Brooklyn Museum (Papyrus Brooklyn 47,218,3)* (Providence, R. I., 1962), 35.

22. See esp. ibid., 36, fig. 8, comparing and contrasting a sedan chair procession of Horemheb with a bark procession of Amun.

23. The 5 verses "He created. . . . calls his name" are only found in the Pinudjem version (Papyrus Cairo 58033).

24. *ÄHG* No. 92, 25–26; see Zandee, *Der Amunshymnus des Pap. Leiden I 344 verso,* 129 n. 273; 735 n. 219.

25. See the text in Theban Tomb 57 (Khaemhet) from the reign of Amenophis III, *STG* No. 76: "You cross the heavens daily, in whose countenance you are though your progress is hidden."

26. *ÄHG* No. 92, 115–17.

27. M. Sandman, *Texts from the Time of Akhenaten,* BiblAeg VIII (1938), 95.17–18. See above, p. 220.

28. I.E.S. Edwards, *Hieratic Papyri in the British Museum,* 4th ser.: *Oracular Amuletic Decrees of the Late New Kingdom,* 2 vols. (London, 1960), I, 2–7.

29. See Hornung, "Zur Struktur des ägyptischen Jenseitsglaubens," *ZÄS* 119 (1992): 124–30.

30. This corresponds very largely to Durkheim's definition of magic in *Die elementaren Formen des religiösen Lebens* (Frankfurt, 1969), 69ff. Religion is invariably group-oriented and welds its adherents together as "members of the same moral body," whereas magic only establishes discrete, "random and transient," relations, similar to those between doctor and patient.

31. S. Sauneron, *Le Papyrus magique illustré de Brooklyn [Brooklyn Museum 47.218.156]* (New York, 1970), 23 pl. IV, fig. 3.

32. Ibid., 18, pl. II, fig. 2.

33. R. A. Caminos, *The Chonicle of Prince Osorkon,* Anal. Or. 37. (Rome, 1958).

34. See my article "When Justice Fails: Jurisdiction and Imprecation in Ancient Egypt and the Near East," *JEA* 78 (1992): 149–62.

35. Decree for Amenophis, son of Hapu. See *JEA* 78, 156.

36. Caminos, *Chronicle of Prince Osorkon,* 71.

37. Ibid., 111.

38. D. Eigner, *Die monumentalen Grabbauten der Spätzeit in der thebanischen Nekropole,* Denkschriften der Österreichischen Akademie der Wissenschaften VIII (Vienna, 1984).

39. Kemp, in Trigger et al., *Egypt: A Social History,* 130–31.

40. T. Kendall, "The Origin of the Napatan State: El-Kurru and the Evidence for the Royal Ancestors," *Meroitica* 16. See also the brilliant monograph by L. Török, *The Birth of an Ancient African Kingdom: Kush and Her Myth of the State in the First Millennium B.C.,* Univ. Lille III (Lille, 1995) and id., *The Kingdom of Kush: Handbook of the Napatan-Meroitic Civilization* (Leiden, 1997).

41. Macadam, *The Temples of Kawa,* 76–81, pls. 32–34. In this inscription Alara-Arii does not yet call himself "king" but only "son of Amun." Though he does not bear crown or uraeus, he does write his name in cartouches.

42. N. Grimal, *Les Termes de la propagande royale égyptienne de la XIX.e dynastie à la conquête d'Alexandre* (Paris, 1986), 217–18.

43. Cf. F. Hintze, *Untersuchungen zu Stil und Sprache neuägyptischer Erzählungen* (Berlin, 1950).

44. See N. Grimal, "Bibliothèques et propagande royale à l'époque éthiopienne," in *Livre du centenaire, MIFAO* 104 (Cairo, 1980), 37–48.

45. This demonstration of classical literary education is another feature reminiscent of the ideology of the neo-Assyrian court. See P. Machinist, "The Assyrians and Their Babylonian Problem," in *Jahrbuch des Wissenschaftskollegs zu Berlin* 1984/85 (Berlin, 1985): 353–64.

46. Plutarch, *De Iside,* chap. 8; Diodorus, Bibl. Hist I.45; J. Yoyotte, *Kêmi* 21 (1971): 40–42.

47. Dream Stela, ed. N. Grimal, *Quatre Stèles napatéennes au Musée du Caire* (Cairo, 1981), 6–7; id., *A History of Ancient Egypt,* trans. I. Shaw (Oxford, 1992), 351.

48. See H. Brunner, "Zitate aus Lebenslehren," in E. Hornung, O. Keel, eds., *Studien zu altägyptischen Lebenslehren,* OBO 28 (Fribourg, 1979), 105–171.

49. Grimal, *Quatre Stèles,* 15.

50. There were, however, repeated later instances of armed units supporting uprisings against the Persians and also against indigenous rulers. See D. O'Connor in Trigger, et al., *Egypt: A Social History,* 249.

51. Chap. 64, for example, is supposed to have been found by Prince Hor-djedef in Hermopolis and presented to King Mycerinos. Several texts claim to have been found and/or written in the reign of King Den. See J. Osing, "Alte Schriften," in *LÄ* I (1972): 149–54; Redford, *King-Lists*, 151 n. 109.

52. G. Möller, *Über die in einem späthieratischen Papyrus des Berliner Museums enthaltenen Pyramidentexte* (Berlin, 1900).

53. See pp. 275f.

54. F. Gomaà, *Chaemwese, Sohn Ramses' II., Hohepriester von Memphis, ÄA* 27 (Wiesbaden, 1973).

55. On the significance of Memphis in the Late Period as a founder city of Egypt, see J. Bergman, *Ich bin Isis: Studien zum memphitischen Hintergrund der griechischen Isisaretologien* (Uppsala, 1968), esp. 44–66.

56. P. Der Manuelian, "A Fragment of Relief from the Tomb of Montuem-hat attributed to the Fifth Dynasty," *JSSEA* 12 (1982): 185–88.

57. E. Staehelin, "Zu einem ägyptischen Reliefkopf in Riggisberg," *Antike Kunst* 12 (Berne, 1969): 88–90.

58. U. Verhoeven–van Elsbergen, *Untersuchungen zur späthieratischen Buchschrift*, Habilitationsschrift (Cologne, 1994), 15–18.

59. H. Brunner, "Zum Verständnis der archaisierenden Tendenzen in der Spätzeit," *Saeculum* 21 (1970): 161.

60. Eric Voegelin has called this form of thought "historiogenesis": *Order and History*, vol IV: *The Ecumenic Age* (Baton Rouge/London, 1974), 59–113.

61. Plato, *The Laws*, trans. T. J. Saunders (Harmondsworth, 1970), 91; see also my book *Das kulturelle Gedächtnis*, 171–74, 190–94.

62. Thus W. Davis, "Plato on Egyptian Art," *JEA* 65 (1979): 121–27.

63. See my article "Zitathaftes Leben: Thomas Mann und die Phänomenologie der kulturellen Erinnerung," in *Thomas Mann Jahrbuch* 6 (1993): 133–58.

64. A similar view is taken by S. Neureiter, "Eine neue Interpretation des Archaismus," *SAK* 21 (1994): 221–54.

65. Early period: K. Sethe, *Dramatische Texte zu altägyptischen Mysterienspielen*, UGAÄ 10 (Leipzig, 1928); high Old Kingdom: H. Junker, *Die Götterlehre von Memphis*, Sitzungsberichte der Preußischen Akademie der Wissenschaften 1939, No. 23 (Berlin, 1940), and *Die politische Lehre von Memphis*, 1941, No. 6 (Berlin, 1941).

66. F. Junge, "Zur Fehldatierung des sog. Denkmals Memphitischer Theologie, oder: Der Beitrag der ägyptischen Theologie zur Geistesgeschichte der Spätzeit," *MDIK* 29 (1973), 195ff.; H. A. Schlögl, *Der Gott Tatenen, nach Texten und Bildern des Neuen Reichs*, OBO 29 (Fribourg, 1980).

67. Junker, *Politische Lehre* 36–38. My translation follows Junker's restoration of the text and also (largely) his rendering of it.

68. E. Hornung, "Auf den Spuren der Sonne. Gang durch ein ägyptisches

Königsgrab," *Eranos Jahrbuch* (1981): 431–75. H. Brunner, "Die Unter-
weltsbücher in den ägyptischen Königsgräbern," in G. Stephenson, ed.,
Leben und Tod in den Religionen: Symbol und Wirklichkeit (Darmstadt,
1980), 215–28.

69. With this translation I revert to Gardiner and Erman, who in my view
were completely correct in their reading of this phrase.

70. The first act of creation that this refers back to is the creation of the
world of the gods. The customary translation, "great and mighty is
Ptah," is ungrammatical and semantically vague.

71. See F. Junge, "Wirklichkeit und Abbild: Zum innerägyptischen Synkretis-
mus und zur Weltsicht der Hymnen des Neuen Reichs," in G. Wießner,
ed., *Synkretismusforschung, Theorie und Praxis* (Wiesbaden, 1978), 87–108,
105 with n. 59. In Amun, the Eight become One; cf. Papyrus Berlin 13603
in S. Sauneron, J. Yoyotte, "La naissance du monde selon l'Égypte
ancienne," in *Sources Orientales* I (Paris, 1959): 17–91, 58 doc. 15.

72. Papyrus Leiden I 350 III 22–27; J. Zandee, *De hymnen aan Amon van
Papyrus Leiden* I 350, OMRO 28 (Leiden, 1947), 63–66; *ÄHG* No. 135;
Re und Amun, 222–23.

73. A. H. Gardiner, *Ancient Egyptian Onomastica*, vol. I (Oxford, 1947), I.

74. Iamblichus, *De Mysteriis*, trans. A. Wilder (London, 1911), VII. 1.

75. See my book *Re und Amun*, 220–21, 238–41.

76. *De Mysteriis*, VII. 4–5.

77. New edition by F. R. Herbin, *Le Livre de parcourir l'éternité*, OLZ 58
(Louvain, 1994).

78. See E. Otto, *Die biographischen Inschriften der ägyptischen Spätzeit* (Leiden, 1954), 87–94.

79. Papyrus Insinger 28,4; M. Lichtheim, *Ancient Egyptian Literature* III
(1980), 207, and *Egyptian Wisdom Literature in the International Context:
A Study of Demotic Instructions*, OBO 52 (Fribourg, 1983), 162–63.

80. See L. Bell, "Luxor Temple and the Cult of the Royal Ka," *JNES* 44
(1985): 251–94.

PART SIX
Egypt under the Persians and Greeks

1. G. Posener, *La Première domination perse en Égypte* (Cairo, 1936), 7, 12,
170; K.M.T. Atkinson, "The Legitimacy of Cambyses and Darius as
Kings of Egypt," *JAOS* 76 (1956): 167ff.

2. On the Egyptian view of Persian rule, see also G. Burkard, "Literarische
Tradition und historische Realität," *ZÄS* 121 (1994): 93–106.

3. See A. B. Lloyd, "The Inscription of Udjahorresnet, a Collaborator's
Testament," *JEA* 68 (1982): 166–80; G. Godron, "Notes sur l'histoire de

la médecine et l'occupation perse en Égypte," in *Hommages Daumas* (Montpellier, 1986), 285–97; T. Holm-Rasmussen, "Collaboration in Early Achaemenid Egypt," in *Studies in Ancient History and Numismatics* (Aarhus, 1988), 29–38; G. Burkard, "Literarische Tradition," *ZÄS* 121, 97–99. On the tomb of Udjahorresnet, see M. Verner, *BIFAO* 89 (1989): 283–90. The version given here follows Lloyd's translation in part.

4. See D. Kessler, *Die heiligen Tiere und der König: Teil I: Beiträge zu Organisation, Kult und Theologie der spätzeitlichen Tierfriedhöfe*, ÄAT 16 (Wiesbaden, 1989).

5. W. Huß, "Die in ptolemäischer Zeit verfaßten Synodal-Dekrete der ägyptischen Priester," *ZPE* 88 (1991): 189–208, and "Gedanken zum Thema 'Staat' und 'Kirche' im ptolemäischen Ägypten," in *Hellenistische Studien*, Gedenkschrift für H. Bengtson (Munich, 1991), 55–60.

6. Cf. K. Goudriaan, *Ethnicity in Ptolemaic Egypt* (Amsterdam, 1988); J. Mélèze-Modrzejewski, "Le statut des Hellènes dans l'Égypte lagide," *Revue des Études Grecques* 96 (1983): 241–68.

7. H. Brunner, *Die Geburt des Gottkönigs: Studien zur Überlieferung eines altägyptischen Mythos*, ÄA 10 (Wiesbaden, 1964); E. Brunner-Traut, "Pharao und Jesus als Söhne Gottes," in *Gelebte Mythen*, 3rd ed. (Darmstadt, 1988), 31–59; Joachim Kügler, *Pharao und Christus?* Bonner Biblische Beiträge 113 (Bodenheim, 1997).

8. On Pseudo-Callisthenes' Alexander romance, see E.A.W. Budge, *The History of Alexander the Great* (Cambridge, 1889); R. Merkelbach, *Die Quellen des griechischen Alexanderromans* (Munich, 1977), 77–88; L. Koenen, "The Dream of Nektanebos," *BASP* 22 (1985): 192–93.

9. See my article "Die Zeugung des Sohnes. Bild, Spiel, Erzählung und das Problem des ägyptischen Mythos," in J. Assmann, W. Burkert, and F. Stolz, *Funktionen und Leistungen des Mythos: Drei altorientalische Beispiele*, OBO 48 (Fribourg/Göttingen, 1982), 13–61.

10. W. Spiegelberg, *Der sogenannte Demotische Chronik des Pap. 215 der Bibliothèque Nationale zu Paris nebst den auf der Rückseite stehenden Texten* (Leipzig, 1914); E. Meyer, *Ägyptische Dokumente aus der Perserzeit*, SPAW (1915); and J. Johnson, "The Demotic Chronicle as a Historical Source," *Euchoria* 4 (1971): 1–18, "The Demotic Chronicle as a Statement of a Theory of Kingship," *JSSEA* 13 (1983): 61ff.; and "Is the Demotic Chronicle an Anti-Greek Text?" in *Grammata Demotica*, Festschrift für E. Lüddeckens (Würzburg, 1984), 107–24.

11. W. Spiegelberg, *Demotische Chronik*, 30–32.

12. E. Meyer, *Ägyptische Dokumente aus der Perserzeit*. See also J. G. Griffiths, *The Divine Verdict* (Leiden, 1991), 176–83.

13. IV, 7–8. Spiegelberg, *Demotische Chronik*, 18.

14. III, 20–21. Spiegelberg, *Demotische Chronik*, 17.

15. IV, 9–10. Spiegelberg, *Demotische Chronik*, 18.

16. IV, 10.
17. V, 12.
18. Cf. H. S. Versnel, *Ter Unus. Isis, Dionysos, Hermes—Three Studies in Henotheism* (Leiden, 1990).
19. Ps. Just. cohort. ad Gent. 15 = Orph.fr. 239. Macrobius, Sat. I 18.17, cites the first verse.
20. M. Nilsson, *Grundriß der Griechischen Religionsgeschichte* (Munich, 1974), II, 573–74.
21. II,23–III,4. Spiegelberg, *Demotische Chronik*, 15–16.
22. III, 16.
23. K. T. Zauzich, "Das Lamm des Bokchoris," in *Papyrus Erzherzog Rainer: Festschrift zum 100-jährigen Bestehen der Papyrussammlung der Österreichischen Nationalbibliothek* (Vienna, 1983), 165ff.; id., *LÄ* III, 912–13; Redford, *King-Lists*, 286–87.
24. Her II, 129ff. See G. Möller, "Zu Herodots ägyptischen Geschichten," *ZÄS* 65 (1920), 76–77; C. Zivie-Coche, *Giza au 1er millenaire* (Cairo, 1991), 99. Herodotus' "Mykerinos" ruled in Sais, and his term of office ended immediately prior to Kushite rule.
25. Cf. H. J. Thissen, *Studien zum Raphia-Dekret* (Meisenheim, 1966).
26. Col. II, 5.
27. L. Koenen, "Die Prophezeiungen des Töpfers," *ZPE* 2 (1968): 178–209, and "The Prophecies of a Potter: A Prophecy of World Renewal Becomes an Apocalypse," *XIIth Intern. Congr. of Papyrology* (Toronto, 1970), 249–54; F. Dunand, "L'oracle du potier et la formation de l'apocalyptique en Égypte," in M. Philonenko, ed., *L'Apocalyptique: études d'histoire des religions* 3 (Paris, 1977), 249–54; Redford, *King-Lists*, 284–86.
28. P. Hadot, "Fürstenspiegel," in *Reallexikon für Antike und Christentum*, vol. 8, cols. 555–632.
29. Here I follow R. Meyer's dissertation, *Vom könig- zum gottgeleiten Menschen: Ein Beitrag zur Typologie religiöser Welthaltungen, II. Die ägyptische Tora* (Heidelberg, 1994).
30. E. W. Mühlmann, *Chiliasmus und Nativismus: Studien zur Psychologie, Soziologie und historischer Kasuistik der Umsturzbewegungen* (Berlin, 1961); V. Lanternari, *Movimenti religiosi di libertà e di salvezza dei popoli oppressi* (Rome, 1960); P. Worsley, *The Trumpet Shall Sound: A Study of "Cargo" Cults in Melanesia* (New York, 1968).
31. On the functional equivalence of the king and the sacred animals, see G. Posener, *De la divinité du pharaon* (Paris, 1960), 15–22; D. Keßler, *Die heiligen Tiere und der König* I (Wiesbaden, 1989).
32. Cf. Assmann, *Ma'at*, 24.
33. See L. Koenen, "Die Adaptation ägyptischer Königsideologie am Ptolemäerhof," in E. Van't Dack, P. van Dessel, W. van Gucht, eds., *Egypt and the Hellenistic World* (Louvain, 1983), 143–90.

34. E. Otto, "Das 'Goldene Zeitalter' in einem ägyptischen Text," in *Religions en Égypte hellénistique et romaine,* Colloque de Strasbourg, Bibliothèque des Centres d'Études Supérieures Spécialisées (Paris, 1969), 93–108; J. Assmann, *Ma'at,* 225–26.

35. See above, pp. 362–64.

36. See G. Fowden, *The Egyptian Hermes: A Historical Approach to the Late Pagan Mind* (Cambridge, Eng., 1986), 14.

37. Asclepius 24–26, ed. Nock-Festugière (Collection Budé, 1960), 326–29; Coptic version: Nag Hammadi Codex Vi, 8.65.15–78.43, ed. Krause-Labib (1971), 194–200. See Fowden, *The Egyptian Hermes,* 39–43; J. Assmann, "Königsdogma und Heilserwartung," in *Stein und Zeit,* 287; "Magische Weisheit: Wissensformen im ägyptischen Kosmotheismus," in *Stein und Zeit,* 75; J.-P. Mahé, *Hermès en Haute-Égypte,* vol. 2 (Quebec, 1982), 69–97; Frankfurter, *Elijah,* 188–89. In Coptic, the equivalent to the Latin *inrationabilitas bonorum omnium* is the "absence of good words." The decline of verbal communication and the ascendancy of violence are among the central motifs of Egyptian chaos descriptions.

38. Augustine, *De Civitate Dei,* VIII c.26.

39. *Urk* VI, 14–16.

40. The entire catalogue of sins, of which I have only cited a brief extract here, extends from *Urk* VI, 18,10 to 24,2.

41. The double negation indicates that the end of the judicial court in this land would be a catastrophe.

42. Papyrus Louvre 3129, J, 38–57; Papyrus BM 10252, 11,3–34, ed. Schott (1939), 120–29.

43. See Iamblichus, *De Mysteriis* VI.5: "For the actor threatens that he will either assail the sky, reveal to view the arcana of Isis, expose to public gaze the ineffable symbol of Abydos, to stop the Baris [bark], scatter the limbs of Osiris like Typhon, or do something else of a similar character."

44. Letter of Aristaeus, 139 and 142, after G. Delling, *Die Bewältigung der Diasporasituation durch das hellenistische Judentum* (Berlin, 1987), 9.

45. M. Douglas, *In the Wilderness: The Doctrine of Defilement in the Book of Numbers* (Sheffield, 1993).

46. Herodotus II 41.

47. *Book of the Dead,* chap. 148 (Nu); J. Assmann, *Liturgische Lieder,* 19–20.

48. Lamentations V, 13, ed. Faulkner, "The Lamentations of Isis and Nephthys," in *Mélanges Maspero I, Orient Ancien,* Mem. Inst. Franc. 66 (Cairo, 1935–38), pl. IV.

49. After R. Givéon, *Les Bédouins Shosou des documents égyptiens* (Leiden, 1971), 168–69.

50. Papyrus Salt 825, VII.1.

51. Papyrus Salt 825, VII.5. P. Derchain, *Le Pap. Salt 825: rituel pour la*

conservation de la vie en Égypte I (Brussels, 1965), 168 n. 3 for further references.

52. Corpus Hermeticum XVI, ed. A. J. Festugière and A. D. Nock II, 230; G. Fowden, *Egyptian Hermes,* 37.

53. The term "nationalism" has established itself as a description for various manifestations of Egyptian opposition to the Greeks; cf. E. Drioton, "Le nationalisme au temps des pharaons," in id., *Pages d'égyptologie* (Cairo, 1957); S. K. Eddy, *The King Is Dead* (Lincoln, 1961), chaps. 10–11; A. B. Lloyd, "Nationalist Propaganda in Ptolemaic Egypt," *Historia* 31 (1982), 33–55; J. G. Griffiths, "Egyptian Nationalism in the Edfu Temple Texts," in J. Ruffle, G. Gaballa, K. Kitchen, eds., *Glimpses of Ancient Egypt* (Warminster, 1979), 174–79. In the face of this, Frankfurter, *Elijah in Upper Egypt,* 250ff., recalls Ernst Gellner's criticism of the use of the term "nationalism" in relation to traditional and agrarian societies (*Nations and Nationalism* [Ithaca, 1983], 8–18). Nationalism presupposes a concept of "nation" as a form of collective identity and solidarity embracing the semiologies of an entire society across all borders of locality and estate. In the Greco-Roman Period, such a collective Egyptian identity was particularly conspicuous by its absence.

54. R. L. Litke, *A Reconstruction of the Assyro-Babylonian God Lists An:-Anum, Anu ša Ameli* (Ph.D. dissertation, Yale, 1958). Litke gives only a transliteration, and his dissertation is unpublished.

55. E. Meyer, *Der Papyrusfund von Elephantine* (Leipzig, 1912), 82. Papyrus C 30:13–14; B. Porten, *Archives from Elephantine: The Life of an Ancient Jewish Military Colony* (Berkeley/Los Angeles, 1986). But see G. Burkard, *ZÄS* 121 (1994): 93–105, and 122 (1995): 31–37.

56. C 33, 10–11; Porten, *Archives,* 292–93.

57. Papyrus CPJ 520, after Frankfurter, *Elijah in Upper Egypt,* 189–91.

58. Hecataeus of Abdera, *Aigyptiaka,* apud Diodorus, *Bibl. Hist.* XL, 3.

59. See M. Stern, *Greek and Latin Authors on Jews and Judaism,* 3 vols. (Jerusalem, 1974–1984), 1:20–44. Tacitus also describes the Jewish notion of God as monotheistic and aniconic, see *Historiae,* V, 5.4; Stern, 2:19 and 26.

60. Lysimachos, *Aegyptiaca,* apud Josephus, *Contra Apionem* I, 304–311: Stern, No. 158, 1: 383–86.

61. Stern, 1:309. The Jews are described as "godless and misanthropic" by Apollonius Molon (apud Josephus Flavius, C.A. II, 145, 148, Stern, No. 49, 1:154–55). See also Diodorus, *Bibl. Hist.,* xx-xiv-xxxv,1:3.

62. Stern, No. 164.

63. Chaeremon, *Aegyptiaca Historia,* apud Josephus, C.A.I, 288–92, Stern, No. 178, 1:419–21. On Chaeremon, see P. W. van der Horst, *Chaeremon: Egyptian Priest and Philosopher* (Leiden, 1984), esp. 8–9 and 49–50.

64. Tacitus, *Histories* 5.3–5; Stern, No. 281, 2:17–63.

65. Pompeius Trogus, *Historiae Philippicae,* apud Iustinus, *Hist. Phil.,* libri xxxvi Epitoma, 1:9–3:9, Stern, No. 137, 1:334–42.

66. See C. Ginzburg, *Ecstasies: Deciphering the Witches' Sabbath* (New York, 1991), chap. 1, 33ff.

67. Ibid., chap. 2.

68. H. Schreckenbach, *Die Josephus Flavius Tradition in Antike und Mittelalter* (Leiden, 1972), and *Rezeptionsgeschichtliche und textkritische Untersuchungen zu Josephus Flavius* (Leiden, 1977); Ginzburg, *Ecstasies,* 55 n. 20.

69. Cf. esp. and most recently P. Schäfer, *Judeophobia: Reactions against Jews in the Ancient World* (Cambridge, Mass., 1997).

70. XVII, 19–XVIII, II (abridged); J. Vandier, *Le Papyrus Jumilhac* (Paris, 1961), 129–30.

71. Papyrus BM 10474, X, 19–20.

72. R. O. Faulkner, *The Papyrus Bremner Rhind* (B.M. No. 10188), BiblAeg III (Brussels, 1933), 42–93.

73. Papyrus BM 10188, 22.4.

74. Ibid., 22.6.

75. Ibid., spell 2.

76. Ibid., spell 4.

77. Cf. H. Brunner, "Gefährdungsbewußtsein," in *LÄ* II, 479–83.

78. D. Kurth, *Treffpunkt der Götter: Inschriften aus dem Tempel des Horus von Edfu* (Zurich, 1994), 81.

79. Ibid., 277.

80. Ibid., 175.

81. E.g., Ibid., 124.

82. Ibid., 276–80.

83. Clemens Alex., *Strom.* VI. Cap. IV, 35.1–37; see Fowden, *Egyptian Hermes,* 58–59; see also J. Osing, "La Science sacerdotale," in *Le Décret de Memphis,* Colloque de la Fondation Singer-Polignac, eds. D. Valbelle and J. Leclant (Paris, 2000), 127–140.

84. The Greek title *prophetes* is a rendering of the Egyptian title "servant of god" = high priest, and has nothing to do with the Hebrew concept of "prophet."

85. On the book catalogues, see A. Grimm, "Altägyptische Tempelliteratur: Zur Gliederung und Funktion der Bücherkataloge von Edfu," in *SAK* Beiheft 3 (1988): 168–69); Redford, *King-Lists,* 214ff.

86. B. Stock, "Textual Communities," in *The Implications of Literacy: Written Language and Models of Interpretation in the Eleventh and Twelfth Centuries* (Princeton, 1983), 88–240.

87. Cf. E. P. Sanders, *Jewish and Christian Self-Definition* (Philadelphia, 1980, 1981, 1984).

88. Porphyry discusses Egyptian writing systems in his *Life of Pythagoras,* Clement of Alexandria in book 5 of his *Stromateis.*

89. V. Shklovsky, *Theory of Prose*, trans. B. Sher (Dalkey, 1991), 14.

90. Aleida Assmann, "Im Dickicht der Zeichen: Drei Auswege: Hodegetik, Hermeneutik und Dekonstrution," *Frankfurter Rundschau* 233, 8.10.1991, 26. See also her "Die Sprache der Dinge: Der starre Blick und die wilde Semiose," in H. U. Gumbrecht and K. L. Pfeiffer, eds., *Materialität der Kommunikation* (Frankfurt, 1988), 237–51.

91. On the semantic component of the hieroglyphic writing system, see esp. H. te Velde, "Egyptian Hieroglyphs as Signs, Symbols and Gods," *Visible Religion* IV/V (1985/6): 63–72; cf. H. te Velde, "Egyptian Hieroglyphs as Linguistic Signs and Metalinguistic Informants," *Visible Religion* VI (1988).

92. On the interference between image and script see esp. R. Tefnin, "Discours et iconicité dans l'art égyptien," in *Göttinger Miszellen* 79 (1984): 55–72; and P. Vernus, "L'écriture de l'Égypte ancienne," in *L'Espace et la littérature*, Cahiers Jussier 3 (1977): 60–77; "Des Relations entre textes et interprétations dans l'Égypte pharaonique," in M. A. Christin, ed., *Écritures* II (Paris, 1985), 45–69; and "Les Espaces de l'écrit dans l'Égypte pharaonique," *BSFE* 119 (1990): 35–53.

93. E. Drioton, "Deux Cryptogrammes de Senenmout," *ASAE* 38 (1938): 231–46.

94. A. Assmann, *Die Legitimität der Fiktion: Ein Beitrag zur Geschichte der literarischen Kommunikation*. Theorie und Geschichte der Literatur und der schönen Künste 55 (Munich, 1980).

95. E. Drioton, "Un rébus de l'ancien empire," *MIFAO* 46 = *Mélanges Maspero* I (1935): 697–704.

96. E. Drioton, "Une figuration cryptographique sur une stèle du Moyen Empire," *RdE* 1 (1933): 203–229. A conspicuously large number of language games are found in the tombs of Beni Hasan: see K. Sethe, *ZÄS* 59:62, and E. Drioton, *RdE* 1:205.

97. E. Drioton, "Essai sur la cryptographie privée de la fin de la xviii. dynastie," *RdE* 1 (1933): 1–50.

98. On the Ptolemaic hieroglyphic writing system see E. Winter, "Hieroglyphen," *RAC* 15 (Stuttgart, 1991): 83–103; S. Sauneron, *L'écriture figurative dans les textes d'Esna*, ESNA VIII (Cairo, 1982); F. Daumas, "Du phonème au symbole dans l'écriture hiéroglyphique ptolémaïque," *Le Courrier du CNRS* 29 (1978): 14–21.

99. S. Sauneron, *L'écriture figurative dans les textes d'Esna*, ESNA VIII (Cairo, 1982); D. Kurth, "Die Lautwerte der Hieroglyphen in den Tempelinschriften der griechisch-römischen Zeit. Zur Systematik ihrer Herleitungsprinzipien," *ASAE* 69 (1983): 287–309.

100. Sonnenauge VII, 10. See A. Loprieno, "Der demotische 'Mythos vom Sonnenauge'," in *Mythen und Epen* III, TUAT III.5 (Gütersloh, 1995), 1054.

101. Sonnenauge IX, 10; Loprieno, op. cit., 1057.

102. Iamblichus, *De Mysteriis*, VII.1.
103. See H. Sternberg el-Hotabi, "Die Götterliste des Sanktuars im Hibis-Tempel von El-Chargeh: Überlegungen zur Tradierung und Kodifizierung religiösen und kulttopographischen Gedankenguts," in *Aspekte spätägyptischer Kultur* (Festschrift E. Winter), Aegyptiaca Treverensia 7 (1994), 239–54.
104. Clemens Alex., *Strom.* VI.4, 35–37. Among the "ten hieroglyphic books" is "On the Construction of the Temples."
105. At the same time as the priests intensified the complexity of hieroglyphic script, the knowledge of hieroglyphs declined among the educated literate upper classes. This decline set in much earlier than was previously supposed: see H. Sternberg–el Otabi, "Der Untergang der Hieroglyphenschrift: Schriftverfall und Schrifttod in Ägypten der griechisch-römischen Zeit," *CdE* 69 (1994): 218–48.
106. Sabine Neureither gives a very similar interpretation of Late Period archaism, based on Niklas Luhmann's systems theory. The period to which she refers was not, of course, a period of foreign rule ("Eine neue Interpretation des Archaismus," *SAK* 21 [1994], 221–54).
107. Plutarch, *De Iside et Osiride*, chap. 9 (354C), ed. J. G. Griffiths (University of Wales Press, 1970) 130–1, 283–4. J. G. Hani, *La Religion égyptienne dans la pensée de Plutarque* (Paris, 1976), 244–45.

CONCLUSION
Egypt as Trace, Message, and Memory

1. G. W. Bowersock, *Hellenism in Late Antiquity* (Cambridge, Eng., 1990), 5.
2. But see A. Fodor, "The Origins of the Arabic Legends of the Pyramids," *AOH* 23 (1970): 335–63; D. Frankfurter, *Elijah in Upper Egypt*; see, too, my book *Das kulturelle Gedächtnis*, chap. 4.
3. S. Morenz, *Die Begegnung Europas mit Ägypten*, Sitzungsberichte der Sächsischen Akademie der Wissenschaften zu Leipzig, phil.-hist. Klasse 113 H.5 (Berlin, 1968; new and expanded edition, Munich, 1969).
4. E. Said, *Orientalism* (New York, 1978).
5. V. Lambropoulos, *The Rise of Eurocentrism: An Anatomy of Interpretation* (Princeton, 1993).
6. *Hieroglyphika* of Horapollo Niliacus, written by him in Egyptian and translated into Greek by Philip; first printed in a Latin version in 1505 (Venice), countless further editions since then.
7. On this branch of humanism, see esp. F. E. Manuel, *The Broken Staff: Judaism Through Christian Eyes* (Cambridge, Mass., 1992).
8. See my book *Moses the Egyptian: The Memory of Egypt in Western Monotheism* (Cambridge, Mass., 1997).

9. J. Spencer, *De Legibus Hebraeorum Ritualibus et Earum Rationibus Libri Tres* (Cambridge, Eng., 1685; The Hague, 1686). On Spencer, see esp. F. Schmidt, "Des inepties intolérables: La raison des rites de John Spencer," *Arch. de Sc. soc. des Rel.* 85 (janvier–mars, 1994): 121–36.

10. *The Divine Legation of Moses Demonstrated from the Principles of a Religious Deist, from the Omission of the Doctrine of a Future State of Reward and Punishment in the Jewish Dispensation,* in nine books (London, 1738–41).

11. J. Toland, *Origines Iudaicae* (London, 1789), 118: *Mosem enimvero fuisse Pantheistam, sive, ut cum recentioribus loquar, Spinosistam, incunctanter affirmat in isto loco Strabo.* Toland's book is a commentary on Strabo's report on Moses.

12. I[gnaz] v[on] B[orn] M[eister] v[om] St[uhl], *Die Mysterien der Aegyptier,* Journal für Freymaurer 1 (Vienna, 1784): 17–132.

13. *Die hebräischen Mysterien oder die älteste religiöse Freymaurerey* (Leipzig, 1788; reprinted Neckargemünd, 2001). On Reinhold, cf. G. W. Fuchs, *Karl Leonhard Reinhold—Illuminat und Philosoph* (Frankfurt/Berlin/Berne/New York/Paris/Vienna, 1994). Oddly, the study makes no mention whatever of Reinhold's fascinating book, but it does provide much useful material on the background against which it originated.

14. P. Hadot, *Zur Idee des Naturgeheimnisses: Beim Betrachten des Widmungsblattes in den Humboldtschen "Ideen zu einer Geographie der Pflanzen,"* Abhandlungen der Akademie der Wissenschaften und der Literatur Mainz, geistes- und sozialwissenschaftliche Klasse Abh. 8 (Wiesbaden, 1982).

15. P. A. d'Origny, *L'Égypte ancienne* (Paris, 1762).

16. Beethoven's acquaintance with Schiller's essay dates back to 1825 at the latest, when Matthias Artaria asked him in his conversation notebook: "Have you read Schiller's 'The Legation of Moses'?" See M. Solomon, *Beethoven Essays* (Cambridge, Mass., 1988), 347, n. 24. See also E. Graefe, "Beethoven und die ägyptische Weisheit," *Göttinger Miszellen* 2 (1972): 19–21.

17. See F. A. Manuel, *The Eighteenth Century Confronts the Gods* (Cambridge, Mass., 1959).

18. R. Pococke, *A Description of the East,* 2 vols. (London, 1743/45). F. L. Norden, *Voyage d'Égypte et de Nubie,* 2 vols. (Copenhagen, 1755).

19. *L'Antiquité expliquée et représentée en figures,* 10 vols. (Paris, 1719–1724).

20. Anne Claude Philippe Comte de Caylus, *Recueil d'antiquités égyptiennes, étrusques, grecques et romaines,* 7 vols. (Paris, 1752–1767).

21. See J. S. Curl, *The Egyptian Revival: An Introductory Study of a Recurring Theme in the History of Taste* (London, 1982); N. Pevsner, S. Lang, "The Egyptian Revival," in N. Pevsner, *Studies in Art, Architecture, Design* (New York, 1968), 213–35; F. Werner, *Ägyptenrezeption in der europäischen Architektur des 19. Jahrhunderts* (Weimar, 1994);

D. Syndram, *Ägypten-Faszinationen: Untersuchungen zum Ägyptenbild des europäischen Klassizismus bis 1800* (Frankfurt/Berne/New York/ Paris, 1990).

22. *Description de l'Égypte, ou, Recueil des observations et des recherches qui ont été faites en Égypte pendant l'expédition de l'armée française,* publiée par ordre de Sa Majesté l'empereur Napoléon le Grand (Paris, 1809– 1829).

23. E. Hornung, *Der Eine und die Vielen: Altägyptische Gottesvorstellungen* (Darmstadt, 1971).

CHRONOLOGY

Naqada I	4500–3900 B.C.E.
Naqada II	3900–3500
Naqada III	3500–3300
Dynasty 0	3300–3100

Ni-Hor
Hat-Hor
Iri-Hor
Ka/Sekhen
Hor Narmer
Scorpion

Archaic Period, 3100–2670 B.C.E.

Dynasty I   3100–2820 B.C.E.

Hor Aha
Atoti
Djer
Meretneith
Wadj (Djet)
Den
Anedjib
Semerkhet
Ka'a

Dynasty II   2820–2670 B.C.E.

Hetepsekhemwy

Nebre (Reneb)
Nynetjer
Wenegnebti
Sened
Sekhemib
Seth Peribsen
Neferkare
Neferkasokar
Hudjefa I
Hor-Seth Khasekhem

Old Kingdom, 2670–2150 B.C.E.

Dynasty III   2670–2600 B.C.E.

Sanakht Nebka
Netjerkhet Djoser
Sekhemkhet
Djoser-Teti
Hudjefa II
Khaba
Kahedjet Huni

Dynasty IV   2600–2450 B.C.E.

Snofru
Cheops (Khufu)
Djedefre
Chephren
Bikheris
Mycerinus
Shepseskaf

Dynasty V   2450–2345 B.C.E.

Userkaf
Sahure
Neferirkare
Shepseskare
Neferefre
Neuserre
Menkauhor
Djedkare
Unas (Wenis)

Dynasty VI   2345–2150 B.C.E.

Teti

Userkare
Pepy I Merire
Merenre I
Pepy II Neferkare
Merenre II
Nitocris

First Intermediate Period, 2150–2040 B.C.E.

Dynasty VII   "Anarchy"

Dynasty VIII   2150–2040 B.C.E.
17–25 kings

Dynasty IX–X	**Dynasty XI**	2150–2040 B.C.E.
Herakleopolis	Thebes	
9–15 kings		
Khety		
Khety-Meribre		
Khety-Nebkaure	Prince Antef	
Khety	Mentuhotep I	
Merikare	Antef I	
	Antef II	
	Antef III	

Middle Kingdom, 2040–1650 B.C.E.

Dynasty XI   after the unification (2040):
Mentuhotep II Nebhepetre
Mentuhotep III S'ankhkare
Mentuhotep IV Nebtawyre

Dynasty XII		1994–1781 B.C.E.
	Amenemhet (Ammenemes) I	1994–1964
	Sesostris I	1974–1929
	Amenemhet (Ammenemes) II	1932–1898
	Sesostris II	1900–1881
	Sesostris III	1881–1842
	Amenemhet (Ammenemes) III	1842–1794
	Amenemhet (Ammenemes) IV	1798–1785
	Nefrusobek (queen)	1785–1781

Dynasty XIII
47–62 kings   1781–1650

Second Intermediate Period, 1650–1550 B.C.E.

Dynasty XIV		1710–1650 B.C.E.
Dynasty XV	("Great Hyksos")	1650–1540
	Salitis	
	Sheshi	
	Yaqub-Har	
	Khyan	
	Apophis	
	Khamudi	
Dynasty XVI	("Minor Hyksos")	1650–1550 B.C.E.
Dynasty XVII		1650–1550 B.C.E.
	Theban rulers	
	ending with	
	Seqenenre Ta'a	
	Kamose	

New Kingdom, 1550–1070 B.C.E.

Dynasty XVIII		1550–1295 B.C.E.
	Ahmose	1552–1526
	Amenophis I	1526–1506
	Tuthmosis I	1506–1493
	Tuthmosis II	1493–1479
	Tuthmosis III	1497–1423
	Hatshepsut	1478–1458
	Amenophis II	1425–1401
	Tuthmosis IV	1401–1390
	Amenophis III	1390–1352
	Amenophis IV/Akhenaten	1352–1338
	Smenkhkare	1338–1336
	Tutankhamun	1336–1327
	Ay	1327–1323
	Horemheb	1323–1295

Ramesside Age

Dynasty XIX		1295–1188 B.C.E.
	Ramesses I	1295–1294
	Sethos I	1294–1279
	Ramesses II	1279–1212

Merenptah		1212–1202
Amenmesse		1202–1199
Sethos II		1202–1196
Siptah		1196–1190
Twosre		1196–1188

Dynasty XX		1188–1069 B.C.E.
Sethnakhte		1188–1186
Ramesses III		1186–1154
Ramesses IV		1154–1148
Ramesses V		1148–1144
Ramesses VI		1144–1136
Ramesses VII		1136–1128
Ramesses VIII		1128–1125
Ramesses IX		1125–1107
Ramesses X		1107–1098
Ramesses XI		1098–1069

Third Intermediate Period

Dynasty XXI		1069–945 B.C.E.
Tanis	Thebes	
Ramesses XI	Herihor	1080–1073
Smendes	Pinudjem	1069–1043
Amenemnisu	Masaharta	1043–1039
Psusennes I	Menkheperre	1039–993
Amenemope	Smendes	993–978
Osorkon the Elder	Pinudjem II	978–959
Siamun	Psusennes	959–945
	Psusennes II	

Dynasty XXII		945–715 B.C.E.
Shoshenq I	Iuput	945
Osorkon I	Shoshenq	924
Shoshenq II	Smendes	890
Takelot I	Iuwelot,	
	Harsiese	889
Osorkon II	Nimlot	874
Takelot II	Osorkon	850

Libyan Polyarchy

Dynasty XXII	**Dynasty XXIII**	820–718 B.C.E..
	(in Leontopolis)	

Shoshenq III	Pedubastis I	
	Osorkon III	825
Pimay	Takelot III	773
Shoshenq V	Rudamon,	
	Input II	767

Dynasty XXV	**Dynasty XXIV** (in Sais)	
760–656	730–712	
Kashta		760–747
Piye (Piankhy)		747–716
	Tefnakht	727–718
	Bocchoris	718–712
Shabaka		716–702
Shebitku		702–690

	Dynasty XXVI (in Sais)	
Taharqa		690–664
	Necho I	?–664
Tantamani		664–656

Late Period

Dynasty XXVI (Saite Period)	664–525 B.C.E.
Psammetichus I	664–610
Necho II	610–595
Psammetichus II	595–589
Apries	589–570
Amasis	570–526
Psammetichus III	526–525

Dynasty XXVII (first Persian period)	
Cambyses	525–522 B.C.E.
Darius I	522–486
Xerxes I	486–465
Artaxerxes I	465–424
Darius II	424–405
Artaxerxes II	405–359

Dynasties XXVIII–XXX	
Amtyrtaeus	404–399 B.C.E.
Nepherites I	399–393
Psammuthis	393
Achoris	393–380

Nepherites II	380
Nectanebo I	380–362
Tachos	362–360
Nectanebo II	360–343

Second Persian Period

Artaxerxes III Ochos	343–338 B.C.E.
Arses	338–336
Darius III Codoman	336–332
Khababash	333

Greco-Roman Period, 332 B.C.E.–395 C.E.

KEY TO THE
EGYPTIAN GODS

Apis Sacred bull worshipped at Memphis.

Atum God of preexistence floating in the Nun (the primeval ocean). Atum is a manifestation of the sun-creator-god, and was originally a deity at Heliopolis.

Bastet Oldest and best-known of the feline deities, identified in Memphis with the lion goddess Sekhmet.

Bes A dwarflike tutelary deity of the bed chamber and domestic life, first attested in the Twenty-first Dynasty. His protective power was enhanced by the musical instruments and weapons he was frequently portrayed as brandishing.

Ennead Group of nine deities, the most significant of which was the Heliopolitan Ennead: Re-Atum, Shu, Tefnut, Geb, Nut, Osiris, Isis, Nephthys, Seth.

Geb God of the earth, product of the divine alliance of Shu, the air god, and Tefnut, goddess of fire. Father of Osiris and Seth.

Hemen The town god of Mo'alla.

Hemuset Protective female deities personifying the primal hills created by the goddess Neith and symbolizing the fertility of the soil.

Horakhty A surname appended to the name of the god Re and meaning "Horus of the Horizon."

Isdes An originally independent deity later largely equated with Thoth or portrayed as his messenger. Frequently depicted with a jackal's head.

Isfet The "opposite" of *ma'at*, hence chaos, disorder.

Khnum Ram god of Elephantine.

Khonsu Lunar deity, son of Amun and Mut, forming with them the divine triad worshipped in Thebes.

Min (Menu) God of fertility, symbolizing male sexual potency. Also god of the deserts.

Ma'at Goddess personifying justice, order and truth, or *ma'at*, a concept essential to the ancient Egyptian vision of a balanced, "functioning" universe. One of the central tasks of the king as an agent of the gods was to ensure the maintenance of *ma'at* on earth.

Meskhenet Goddess with the sign of a cow's uterus on her head, the personification of birthplace. Part of the tribunal at the Judgment of the Dead.

Nefertem God equated or associated with the lotus plant and closely connected with the sun god.

Neith Goddess of Sais. Originally perhaps a war deity; later, the patron goddess of the art of weaving and of mummification wrappings; also a goddess of the primeval waters and mother of the sun.

Nephthys Sister of Isis and Osiris; in Plutarch, wife of death; closely associated with funerary ritual.

Nepre (Neper) God personifying the annual growth of grain.

Ogdoad Group of eight deities, the most significant of which was the Hermopolitan Ogdoad: four pairs of male frogs and female snakes symbolizing the primordial forces of chaos preceding creation.

Ptah Chief god of Memphis, patron deity of artisans, later also referred to as a creator god and figuring as one of the three state gods alongside Amun of Thebes and Re of Heliopolis.

Re The sun god. As creator of the world, Re was the most important deity in the ancient Egyptian pantheon.

Sekhat-Hor Goddess in the shape of a cow, associated with the provision of milk and hence of nourishment in general.

Sekhmet Lion goddess, wife of Ptah, responsible for epidemics, plagues, diseases. Physicians were priests of Sekhmet. Related to Bastet, the cat goddess of Bubastis, who was believed to be her mild and gracious counterpart.

Serapeum Underground galleries at Saqqara, where the sacred Apis bulls were buried. Properly speaking, the Serapeum was the name of the Greco-Roman temple dedicated to the syncretic deity Serapis in the Ptolemaic period.

Sia Personification of knowledge in the theology of creation by the word. The seat of Sia is in the heart of the creator god.

Sothis Corresponds to Sirius, the Dog Star. Its heliacal rising was associated by the Egyptians with the inundation of the Nile.

Sutekh Another name for Seth.

Tayt (Tait) Patron deity of clothmaking and weaving.

Thoth God of the moon and hence of the calendar, time computation, mathematics, writing, science, and even the afterlife, since he established the result of the Judgment of the Dead. Thoth was the overseer and protector of the scribes. His two major iconographic forms were the dog-headed baboon and (later) the ibis-headed human.

INDEX

Entries in *italics* refer to illustrations.

ABOUT THE AUTHOR

JAN ASSMANN is a world-renowned expert on the culture of ancient Egypt and the author of several acclaimed books, among them *Moses the Egyptian* and *The Search for God in Ancient Egypt*. Since 1976, Assmann has held a professorship in Egyptology at the University of Heidelberg; he has also taught at eminent institutions worldwide, including Yale, Hebrew University in Jerusalem, and the École Practique des Hautes Études in Paris. In 1998 Assmann was awarded the prestigious German History Prize, the highest national prize in the field of historical research, which is granted only once every three years. His works have been translated into Italian, French, Hungarian, Czech, Turkish, Japanese, and Russian.